American Laughter, American Fury

AMERICAN LAUGHTER, AMERICAN FURY

Humor and the Making of a
White Man's Democracy, 1750–1850

Eran A. Zelnik

Johns Hopkins University Press
Baltimore

2 4 6 8 9 7 5 3 1

Johns Hopkins University Press
2715 North Charles Street
Baltimore, Maryland 21218
www.press.jhu.edu

Library of Congress Cataloging-in-Publication Data

Names: Zelnik, Eran A., 1979– author.
Title: American laughter, American fury : humor and the making of a white
man's democracy, 1750–1850 / Eran A. Zelnik.
Description: Baltimore : Johns Hopkins University Press, 2025. | Includes
bibliographical references and index.
Identifiers: LCCN 2024013771 | ISBN 9781421450605 (hardcover) |
ISBN 9781421450612 (ebook)
Subjects: LCSH: American wit and humor—History and criticism. | National
characteristics, American. | African Americans—History. | United
States—Race relations. | White people—United States—Attitudes.
Classification: LCC PS430 .Z45 2025 | DDC 817.009—dc23/eng/20240607
LC record available at https://lccn.loc.gov/2024013771

A catalog record for this book is available from the British Library.

*Special discounts are available for bulk purchases of this book. For more
information, please contact Special Sales at specialsales@jh.edu.*

In loving memory of my savtas,
Rachel and Miriam,
and my sabas, Otto and Zvi.
May their memory be a blessing.

CONTENTS

American Laughter, American Fury

Introduction

They came dressed for chaos. They came in red, white and blue
face paint and star-spangled superhero outfits, in flag capes
(American, yes, but also Confederate and Trumpian) and flag
jackets and Trump bobble hats. One man came as a patriotic duck;
another as a bald eagle; another as a cross between a knight-errant
and Captain America; another as Abraham Lincoln.

—Vanessa Friedman, "Why Rioters Wear Costumes,"
New York Times, January 7, 2021

The riot at the US Capitol of January 6, 2021, was violent, but the atmosphere
was curiously jubilant. The scene seemed animated by what the scholar of
premodern humor Mikhail Bakhtin would have called "carnivalesque"—a
celebration of a world suspended from everyday life where there are no inhibitions and the id reigns supreme.[1] There were numerous forms of levity
and play enacted that day, but perhaps most commonly, the rioters came as
some version of militiamen. In the minds of many of them, they were restag-
ing the American Revolution, and quite aptly they came in high spirits, for
as this book shows, many of the events leading up to the Revolutionary War,
such as tarring and feathering and the Boston Tea Party, were done in the
spirit of levity and play. They were also reenacting—or cosplaying, since much
of it was masquerade with limited violence—the call to arms at Lexington
and Concord, the moment in American memory when common people rose
up spontaneously to fend off tyranny.[2] In short, armed with Gadsden flags,
the rioters who stormed the Capitol were tapping into a deep vein in American nationalism that defined for them what it means to be freedom-loving

Americans and what it means to be men. There were women present too, but most who took part in the events of the day were men, in particular white men.[3]

Many white men value their freedom, or their intuitive embrace of what it means to them, above all else. This connection is deep and genuine, yet it leads many to intriguing and questionable displays and commitments. In the name of "freedom," guns can appear more valuable than lives, presumably to make ready for yet another moment when common Americans armed with AR-15 rifles, will muster to fend off tyranny. Meanwhile, many white men have railed against prohibitions on their language and particularly their humor. Raising the specter of "political correctness," or more recently "wokeness," many have condemned censorship and other admonitions on language—often associated with offensive racist and sexist vocabulary and comportment—as surefire indicators that the United States is no longer a true land of freedom. Indeed, those white men who perceive themselves to be the truest members of their nation insist on feeling uninhibited and comfortable in their own skin, so much so that as this book documents, many in the past felt curiously comfortable enough to masquerade in the skin of others, especially of Black and Native peoples. Over the centuries, being a white man in America has meant being defiantly uninhibited, even giddy, when enacting one's manhood and nationalism.

American Laughter, American Fury is an attempt to chart the origins of this boisterous American mood, or what Raymond Williams referred to as a structure of feeling, which has become second nature for so many white men.[4] In this regard, it is also an attempt to understand and explain how the Capitol Hill rioters—as well as earlier Americans who wore Indian garb while committing massacres or vigilantes who visited terror on Black Americans while dressed as ghouls or ghosts—conjoined humor and violence so seamlessly.[5] Most of all, though, it is an attempt to account for the "central paradox of American history," as Edmund Morgan famously put it in *American Slavery, American Freedom*: how, contrary to common intuition, violent subjugation and freedom have mutually reinforced each other since the early beginnings of colonialism in North America. As the historian Barbara Fields stressed, in the early years of the country's history, the rise of democracy led to a hardening of oppressive ideologies, especially racial ones. Drawing on this historiographic tradition, my book looks at humor—broadly construed as a giddy spirit of laughter, mirth, and play—to trace how genuine commitments to democracy became wedded to violence and exclusion.[6]

Moreover, this study views humor in American history as a nation-building device. The antiauthoritarian humor of the revolutionary period underscored commitments to a more egalitarian interpretation of the idea of "the people" that Americans developed during those key years. The people, or what scholars of nationalism have come to call the "national community," is one of the definitive ideas of the modern period that Americans made their own. A nation—as opposed to a state or country—is an idea and a fiction, not a set of institutions and laws, though it often complements and reinforces state-building processes, as it did in the early United States. Much work is needed for that fiction to become compelling to the people, for it to bring millions of them together around an intuitive sense that they share a host of commonalities, and in the United States, a "manifest destiny." This was doubly true when the US government was fairly limited in its scope, and therefore its ability to reinforce commitments to the nascent nation, and not long after most Anglo-Americans had previously been proud members of a cohering British national community.[7]

Humor, I argue, was instrumental to the process of American nation building. For instance, when during the revolution Americans enjoyed the upbeat song "Yankee Doodle," they enlisted its raucous energy to proudly celebrate their provincialism, choosing to revel in self-deprecation. Thus, it became their inside joke that also implied that urbane and elitist British types would not be welcome in their novel republican national community. In the United States, the leveling humor of the revolutionary era helped bring together and shape an incipient national community. Such early commitments to antiauthoritarian humor also implied that despite attempts by American elites to cast a more restrictive and hierarchical interpretation of who "the people" were, a key characteristic of this new nation would be an intuitive sense that provincialism and common origins were not problems but rather assets.[8]

Indeed, humor is one of the most important adhesives that creates bonds among people, be it a group of men dressing up as Mohawks to play a defiant joke by turning the Boston Harbor into a teapot at the expense of the East India Company in 1773 or a jubilant crowd enjoying the breakout success of the song "Jim Crow" in the 1830s.[9] In both cases, however, as this humor traveled and captured Americans' imagination, it also forged a nation, facilitating an "imagined community" of humor, to borrow Benedict Anderson's suggestive term.[10] Through the bonds of mirth, it brought together Americans, who were in on the joke. Those who shared in this communion might have been a small group of colonial conspirators—who played a prank on the enemies of liberty by paying them a visit at night dressed as Indians—or members of a nascent nation who came together as they celebrated the boisterous riots of the revolutionary period. This book follows this dynamic as it expanded through humor from small groups of insiders, who often knew each other intimately, to the national community as a whole, with the vast majority of people never having met, let alone having known one another.

Though I initially examined humor to better understand Americans' democratic commitments, the more I considered humor, the more its double-edged nature became clear. Indeed, as with nationalism, and in the service of the nation, humor is also by nature deeply exclusive: it is often targeted at someone, or at least it implies that there is a group of people who are "in on the joke," so to speak, and others who are not. In this vein, humor often contains violent undertones and is seldom innocuous. As I suggest over the last third of the book, this double-edged dynamic became particularly prominent in blackface minstrelsy and Davy Crockett almanacs, two comical popular culture genres that outlined the antebellum national community in negative and positive terms, respectively. Blackness in early American popular culture emerged as an inherently buffoonish and therefore degraded trait whereas whiteness—as captured by the image and cult of Crockett—would become the necessary attribute for freewheeling indigeneity. Thus, humor facilitated both the crucial inclusive and exclusive work central to all national communities.

Humor's double-edged nature, in sum, offers a uniquely insightful lens through which to examine the United States—a paradoxical nation that embodied commitments to freedom and equality as well as to slavery and genocide. Ultimately, for a time in the United States, only white men were fully in on the joke. All other Americans were either not fully party to it or, worse yet, were the butt of the joke. The prevailing humor made it clear that it was not really their nation and that the vast American continent ordained by God for the United States—according to manifest destiny, the nationalist ideology that had cohered by the antebellum period—was not fully their land.

Moreover, in the United States, humor also performed critical work for the national community by deflecting questions arising from the nation's growing commitment to egalitarianism. In other words, Americans' natural attachment to humor and play obfuscated the violent and exclusive dimensions of their national community; they did not have to think of themselves as embodying contradictions and committing reprehensible violence.

Thus, even as Americans grew attached to the opening words of the Constitution, "We the people," and the immortal words of the Declaration of Independence, "all men are created equal," humor helped skirt and naturalize ongoing commitments to racial and gender divides.

The humor discussed in this book is much more than what most of us first imagine when we think of comical exchanges. Rather, it is a structure of feeling that helped to sustain and was also an expression of the prevailing ideology or hegemony. According to Williams, in everyday life and interactions, people often act as a result of deep-seated inclinations developed over a lifetime of social experiences that are often "taken to be private" but are nevertheless part of embodied ideologies. One can therefore plumb broad patterns of humor for "meanings and values as they are actively lived and felt" or "thought as felt and feeling as thought." In early America, humor, broadly construed, was an important component in a newly realized hegemony largely created by and for white men as they simultaneously contested traditional European hierarchies and constructed a polity exclusively for themselves.[11] In this regard, *American Laughter, American Fury* is indebted to the literary scholarship of the first half of the twentieth century that similarly attempted to unearth unique and broad American patterns by examining American humor. Such pioneers as Jenette Tandy, Constance Rourke, and Walter Blair cast humor as one of the most important veins in American folklore and popular culture traditions and helped shed light on the ways that early Americans turned away from European sensibilities and dispositions to cultivate a new culture that was part and parcel of their novel democratic condition. They identified a unique and anti-elitist comfort in what Blair called "horse sense humor" and Tandy dubbed "cracker-box philosophy." Telling tall tales, enjoying ribald songs, and fancying picaresque and self-deprecating misadventures were all part of this comical style that Americans seemed to revel in and cultivate—perhaps more so than one might expect from a culture that also viewed itself as a pioneer society boasting rough and stiff-necked characters. In fact, as these scholars contended, and as I concur in this book, western lore and pioneer and provincial sensibilities were particularly saturated in such mirth and play.[12]

Whereas a century or so ago, studies of American humor tended to be light on critique and intended for Americans to better understand themselves in rather self-affirming ways, my study takes a harder look at such humor and its ability to unpack underlying disturbing narratives. In this vein, rather than an upbeat narrative arc, this book tells a more tragic, or tragicomic, story—one of democratization gone awry. On the one hand, early American humor was an expression of a novel democratic society that at times self-consciously turned away from Europe and propelled commoners to positions of prominence in the new nation. On the other hand, it was deeply committed to the exclusion of all who were not white men from full membership in the national community. Thus, I view the humor of that time as capturing the contradictory and particular settler-colonial nature of American society.

Settler Colonialism

The concept of settler colonialism flows throughout *American Laughter, American Fury*. I use the term *settler colonialism* not merely to account for the violence and genocide visited by the United States and its citizens on Native peoples, but also to serve as a concept with significant power to explain cultural phenomena. As a theoretical body of scholarship, the study of settler colonialism examines how deep structures of othering, displacement, and identity formation shaped the character of settler societies in particular ways. Settler colonial collectives, according to the theorist Lorenzo Veracini, "need to manage in specific ways the triangular relationship involving settlers on the one hand, and indigenous and exogenous Others on the other." In this "inherently dynamic" situation, Veracini asserts, "there are conflicting tendencies operating at the same time on the settler collective: one striving for indigenisation and national autonomy, the other aiming at neo-European replication and the establishment of a 'civilized' pattern of life."[13] As shown in my book, American humor, mirth, and play helped Americans navigate this triangular structure, which pitted them against a metropolitan center in Europe, to the east, and a frontier, then still the domain of Indigenous peoples, to the west. In this vein, it also looks at humor to trace how the center of gravity of the settler colonial collective within this constellation moved over time from east to west across the North American continent.

Examining early US culture as settler colonial expression also helps recast the classic celebratory narrative of the "rise of American democracy" and of the "radicalism of the American revolution," to quote the two most famous studies that unfolded the early history of the United States in self-satisfied terms.[14] It allows one to relate a more accurate historical account of the proverbial "winners" in American history, one that explores what Americans achieved yet also explains, to quote Vladimir Lenin, "who stood to gain" and at what cost to the rest of the people in the country at the time as well as to millions of Americans in the future. Of no less importance, it also permits taking a harder look at the role of white commoners as agents in American history, rather than casting them as deluded simpletons suffering from a "false consciousness" as they have so often been presented.

Morgan famously suggested in *American Slavery, American Freedom* that in early colonial Virginia, a potential cross-racial alliance between the lower classes of the colony found its most explosive expression in Bacon's Rebellion (1675–76). When Virginia elites recognized this impending danger to their rule, however, they enticed Euro-American commoners with the bounties of whiteness and a modicum of economic security, thereby derailing any serious challenge to their hegemony. Ultimately, Morgan explained the transition from indentured servitude to slavery in the wake of the rebellion as the successful execution of such designs. Tellingly, when tackling this dynamic, he turned to the passive voice. Small planters, he asserted, "*were allowed* not only to prosper but also to acquire social, psychological, and political advantages that turned the thrust of exploitation away from them and aligned them with the exploiters." Similarly, he sketched a tripartite social organization of Virginia by the second quarter of the eighteenth century: "a slave labor force isolated from the rest of society by race and racism; a body of large planters, firmly committed to the country, who had become practiced in politics and political maneuvering; and a larger body of small planters who had *been persuaded* that their interests were well served by the leadership of their big neighbors." Indeed, lower-class white men were never full agents in this process; instead, they were always made to adopt racism as they conformed to the hegemonic influence of white elites.[15]

By contrast, this book, whose title evokes Morgan's account, spotlights the power struggle between white commoners and white elites and suggests that both actively participated in the process of forging a culture, a society, and ultimately a polity from which both stood to gain. This approach is not meant to malign unnecessarily, but is rather an effort to better understand how the confluence of social, cultural, and settler colonial structures involving humor resulted in the kinds of cognitive dissonance that I capture by the term *white man's democracy*. One cannot simply deny agency to the majority of white men in attempts to imagine different historical outcomes. This would not lead to the insights necessary for understanding the past either on its own terms or in how it continues to resonate in the present. Looking at humor, in particular when understood as an expression of a triangular settler colonial structure, sheds new light on the challenges posed by the early history of the United States.

In fully grappling with the agency of white men on their own terms, I often withhold judgment on the horrid violence they committed. Descriptions such as "giddy" or "tantalizing," when applied to violence, attempt to establish the genuine attraction white men felt toward violence while combining it with forms of carnivalesque humor. To be clear, nothing about slavery or genocide is funny, yet numerous Americans found it fun and funny to "jump Jim Crow" in the 1830s or to dress up as Indians—the people they aimed to replace—as they prepared for war. That is a paradox one must keep in mind when accounting for the American past. To that end, my morally ambiguous language seeks to capture how these all-too-human historical subjects might have felt giddy, even when considering or committing atrocious violence.

While the sources I use can only offer a glimpse of the ways Americans reveled in their humor, I strive to bring the texts they left or that in some way recorded their thoughts and words as close as possible to the original. Thus, unless explicitly noted otherwise, I have retained all quotes in their original, including italics, misspellings, and dialect, some of which is deeply disturbing. Ultimately, I aim to explain how violence and oppression became palatable or even enticing given the historical conditions—that is, the settler colonial context of white men in a foreign land where they sought to feel indigenous. In part, my (probably far too lofty) hope is that by better understanding the conditions that led people to employ reprehensible violence, we in the present might recognize these conditions in our own societies, and perhaps prevent them from taking hold, including within ourselves.

Similarly, I employ the terms *indigenous* (with a lowercase *i*) and *indigenization* in value-neutral ways when discussing the settler colonial project in North America. This is not to suggest that white settlers became truly indigenous, but rather to indicate how the drive to become, in their own minds, indigenous was an important force in the history of the period. Again, putting oneself, even for a split second, in the shoes of historical subjects, might help to understand what motivated them and how the culture produced by settlers was deeply devoted to these designs. Of course, one must remember that white settlers violently invaded North America, which was then, and still is, home to vibrant and diverse genuine Indigenous (with a capital *I*) peoples and nations. One must also remember that this violence also very much remains a reality to this day. Having survived a genocide, Indigenous Americans continue to resist and thrive in the face of ongoing systemic settler colonial violence.[16]

Humor

The question of humor's inherent nature has posed intriguing questions for theorists for much of known Western history with little agreement ever reached. While numerous theorists have tried to settle the issue through one all-encompassing framework, this study turns to more recent conceptualizations in the field of humor studies that view humor as a multifaceted phenomenon hinging on a wide array of circumstances within which it occurs, what some, including myself, call a humor event. In other words, humor has no single inherent structure, but is deeply contextual, as opposed to, for example, settler colonialism, which Patrick Wolfe has asserted is not an event but a structure.[17] Humor, therefore, is neither intrinsically positive nor negative, but rather rich with the potential for both unsettling power structures as well as reinforcing them. To understand humor more fully, one must construe it as an historic event by fully contextualizing it and identifying the work it has performed for different groups and for societies at large.[18]

Moreover, humor is a slippery and contradictory device that often either challenges or boosts, sometimes at the same time, assumptions that cut to the root of prevailing power structures. Because it toys with taboos and can confound and reinforce social mores, humor harbors weighty potential ramifications for society, yet is notoriously hard to control. Indeed, this study shows how people who wielded humor for a particular purpose often lost control of its meaning and the work it ultimately performed. For example, although British soldiers sang "Yankee Doodle" to disparage American insurgents, it later became the de facto anthem of the American Revolution. Similarly, when Royall Tyler in the 1780s and Seba Smith in the 1830s contrived the figures of Brother Jonathan and Jack Downing as warnings about democratic politics whose vulgar opportunism might harm the nation, the two clownish Yankee figures nevertheless still emerged as affirmations of the common man and of the new nation's novel democratic commitments.[19]

Likewise, because humor can be seductive and induces pleasure, it is often multidirectional in nature; the heady rush it engenders prompts people to search and grasp for new ways to sustain it, or continue its flow, which can send its barbs off in a host of directions, some of them perhaps contradictory. Indeed, much of humor could lend itself to various types of intervention in the prevailing hegemony, and much of humor performs more than one discrete thing. The scholar of humor must, therefore, be constantly aware of such potentialities, and based on the preponderance of the evidence at hand, judge how any particular humor event likely figured in that particular time and place. Even if it did several things, what did it primarily do? In this vein, I contend that much of the 1990s scholarship on early blackface minstrelsy misinterpreted the ultimate work it performed. While such minstrelsy at times contributed to a working-class culture that challenged American elites, when considering the preponderance of the evidence, blackface minstrelsy from its early beginnings was part of a culture that rendered blackness an inherently comical and degraded category. Helping police the borders of the nation during the heyday of slavery and the concurrent rise of a free Black population in the free states, this influential and lasting American genre forged a white man's democracy, or what I at other times call "racial nationalism."[20]

As mentioned above, this study construes humor in ways that are often not intuitive for Americans in the twenty-first century. In fact, I employ it in ways that would have been more familiar to eighteenth- and nineteenth-century Americans, for whom the term *humor* often indicated a general frame of mind. Theirs was a definition still attuned to the word's origins and association with the auspicious balance of "humours," the four liquids—blood, phlegm, choler, and melancholy—once thought to control a person's physical health, nature, and character. In time, the word denoted a certain positive and healthy sensibility that led to laughter, mirth, and sly wit.[21] Though I do not propose that humor is objectively positive, people are attracted to humor as part of their intuitive interest in its sanguine appeal. In this vein, I use a varied vocabulary to refer to this broad construction of humor. Such adjectives as *rambunctious, cheerful, giddy, joyous, raucous, racy,* and *comical*, among others, all capture a general inclination toward what today might be referred to as fun, as opposed to just funny. I also use such nouns as *levity, play, mirth, glee, masquerade,* and *carnivalesque* as well as more intuitive derivatives of the word *humor,* such as *comedy, joke,* or *laughter.* Using this array of words, I hope, helps temper the modern, more restrictive use of *humor* and allows for a more robust understanding of how humor, broadly construed, was an important force in American history.

To parse out the predominant ways in which Americans employed humor, I propose three different modes of cultural production: vernacular, elite, and popular. Vernacular, or folk, cultures pose the hardest questions for historians. From the perspective of historians, they are cultures from "below," seemingly emerging spontaneously from "the folk," and which historians usually associate with premodern processes of culture making. Since folk cultures are largely oral, and the available textual record only offers elusive glimmers of them, historians must resort to some degree of conjecture when attempting to establish their origins and genealogies. Scholars of Western folk humor have often focused on the "carnival" and the carnivalesque, the sensibility associated with it, as the central artery that allowed folk humor to pass from generation to generation through oral transmission. I too focus on carnivalesque humor, but whereas scholars of folk culture often tend to sentimentalize the culture of the carnival as intrinsically liberating, I echo Natalie Zemon Davis's characterization "that the structure of the carnival form can evolve so that it can act both to reinforce order and to suggest alternatives to the existing order."[22] Thus, for example, although carnivalesque humor and play during the revolutionary period challenged elite hegemony, rural white men also turned to carnivalesque practices when they waged war against Native peoples, employing Indian masquerade. Indeed, the American militia experience, I argue in chapter four, became a form of Indian masquerade, writ large, a tool both for carrying out extreme violence and genocide and for delineating the political community—that is, who was and who was not a true member of the nation.[23]

Far more is known about elite cultures, as they were largely associated with written records and often privileged literary forms. These cultures— and the humor associated with them—often operated as a medium of class distinction and therefore as vectors of power. Once again, this is not because of the natural tendency of humor, but has more to do with the power dynamics within Western societies, where elites sought to distinguish "the few" from "the many" through culture. When elite humor achieved this purpose, it could become a vehicle for asserting hierarchies. As shown in chapter two, the Federalists literati in the United States attempted with limited success to employ such humor, what they called "wit," as a means of fending off the leveling implications of the American Revolution.[24]

Whereas vernacular cultures are often associated with the premodern era, the period before the Age of Revolution in the eighteenth century, popular cultures—at least as I deal with them here—are largely a product of the modern era, the nineteenth century and beyond.[25] In general, popular cultures have relied on emerging technologies, especially print culture early on, and a sufficiently literate population to reach larger audiences than either vernacular or elite cultures possibly could. Specifically, I view popular culture in the United States as emerging in conjunction with the heightened nationalism of the 1820s and beyond. In the United States, which as I have argued elsewhere was the first modern nation, popular culture and the humor that became so central to it proved to be one of the most important ways of organizing and forging a national community. This was doubly necessary in the nation's early stages, when state technologies of centralized control were not nearly as robust as in western Europe.[26] Although in the twentieth century popular, or mass, culture would become attuned to the state and to the processes of mass production in an industrialized setting, in the antebellum period, roughly 1820 to 1860, most popular culture was quite tentative and produced by relatively small business operations that pioneered new forms of cultural output, such as comic almanacs, songsters, and blackface minstrel performances.[27]

Organization of This Book

American Laughter, American Fury is divided into three parts, each with its own short introduction. Part one, "Yankees and Gentlemen" (chapters one and two), locates the origins of the American tradition of levity and play in the revolutionary period and the broader culture of riot and revelry that underscored much of the imperial crisis between Great Britain and its North American colonies. It foregrounds the democratic potential of the carnivalesque, revealing how Americans enlisted humor for egalitarian purposes. During the revolutionary period, a growing commitment to a local vein of self-deprecating and leveling humor implied that the intellectual starting points for the new nation would be far more radical than many American patricians had hoped. Part one also fleshes out the way in which other forms of humor that fostered communities through elitist and erudite exclusion fell out of favor. American patricians attempted to cultivate an Augustan culture of wit that would mark themselves—the few fully capable of understanding sophisticated, Latin-laced humor—as the only ones fit to rule. By the War of 1812, however, neoclassical humor had largely disappeared from mainstream American political culture.

Part two, "From Backcountry to Frontier" (chapters three, four, and five), examines the emergence of a unique American frontier vernacular that would in time become central to the American ethos and popular culture and would reframe the territory increasingly associated with the frontier as a carnival-scape fit for freedom-loving American men. It delves into the robust tradition of backcountry carnivalesque misrule, where rural militias challenged the hegemony of Eastern Seaboard elites by enacting vigilante law coupled with humor and masquerade. Locating the myth of the citizen-soldier as the focal point for a new triumphant American nationalism, part two then traces the history of violence against Native peoples during the revolutionary period. As American frontiersmen became members of a democratic republic committed to leveling principles, they also emerged as militiamen ever ready to violently defend the nation from its racialized enemies. What helped wed these commitments, I argue, is the singular mirth and levity of the militiamen, whose way of war—indeed whose way of being American—was a form of Indian play. Part two also follows the development of the nationalist ideology of manifest destiny, suggesting that it represented an American superego, of sorts, that rested over a giddy, if violent, American id associated with Andrew Jackson, the frontier, and the celebrated Hunters of Kentucky.

Part three, "A Tale of Two Clowns" (chapters six and seven), traces the emergence and impact of the two most influential icons of what during the antebellum period would become the first instance of modern popular culture: the black minstrel and the frontier jester. Fueled by a dramatic increase in print publications, in conjunction with the growing reach of popular and racy stage performances, an ever more expansive echo chamber helped consolidate a national popular culture over these years. Standing at the center of this burgeoning popular culture, the two counterpoised jesters served the important function of shaping the American experiment in self-rule as an environment in which only white men could feel comfortable in their own skin. By focusing on nationhood, rather than the traditional topic of class, I argue that blackface minstrelsy was first and foremost a racist genre that rendered the category of blackness so comical as to be completely outside the borders of the polity. In short, it served the period's resurgent racial nationalism far more than it challenged middle-class mores. Thus, the conjoined humor of the white frontier jester and the Black minstrel ultimately cast white manhood as the uninhibited experience of the American landscape, at the expense of Black men, whose bodies they inhabited and whose virility they tapped.

The spirit of full disclosure requires a few comments about the personal and methodological processes behind this book. Though I hope readers will find that this study uses good judgment and demonstrates good faith in its examination of primary sources, as any historical study—whether we concede as much or not—it is also, in part, an attempt to make sense of the present. I started on the path that led me here just after I finished my military service, which I only now recognize was my own unfortunate contribution to settler colonialism in Israel/Palestine. Even as I sought to put much of that behind me and specialize in what I then thought was a very different society half a world away in America, in a curious twist of fate I found that US history seemed eerily familiar in myriad ways. Indeed, I now view myself as somewhat of a specialist in how settler societies look from the inside, as I am a citizen and participant in not one but two of the most iconic settler colonial societies in modern history.

In short, this book became an attempt to make some sense of settler colonialism and the phenomenon of settler nationalism. In doing so, I sought to apply new frameworks, such as settler colonialism and the intersections between race and gender, to older scholarly traditions that I found to be the most insightful when pressing my findings for fitting conclusions. Thus, I drew on the methods of an earlier tradition of American history and American studies scholarship, including the "new cultural history" of the 1970s and 1980s. I found inspiration in the work of John William Ward, Richard Slotkin, and other "symbol and myth" scholars and of such cultural historians as Carroll Smith-Rosenberg and Alexander Saxton. I can only hope that readers will find in my examination the echoes of those valuable scholarly traditions.

In closing, this study has also been guided by my grandparents, all now passed, who as refugees fled Europe for Israel/Palestine and the United States before and during the Holocaust, and in the case of my grandmother Rachel, after having survived it. It is to their memory, may it be a blessing, that I dedicate this book. It is with them in mind that I hope for a truer democracy and seek to expose the cultural methods that support racialization, ethnic cleansing, and genocide. I made the final edits to this book against the backdrop of a genocidal campaign by Israel in Gaza, making these words appear depressingly pertinent.

PART ONE

YANKEES AND GENTLEMEN

According to a dissident news account associated with the Sons of Liberty, the Boston harbor on the evening of September 29, 1768, seemed festive. "Sky rockets" lit the sky, while locals observed aboard the anchored British ships of war "great rejoicing, and that the Yankey Doodle song was the capital piece in their band of music." Two days later, on Saturday, October 1, British troops "marched into the [Boston] Common, with muskets charged, bayonets fixed, colours flying, drums beating and fifes &c. playing, making with the train of artillery upwards of 700 men." The so-called occupation of Boston—a pivotal moment in the narrative Americans tell of their struggle for independence from Britain—had begun. Curiously, as told by American dissidents in the city, the song "Yankee Doodle," struck up by British troops and sailors, provided the arriving forces a merry accompaniment with which to taunt Bostonians.[1]

Once the war started in earnest—after the outbreak of hostilities in the spring of 1775—New Englanders, and later American insurgents more broadly, appropriated the song. Instead of the British reveling in it to mock Yankees, now Americans embraced the tune as their own. In two of the most famous revolutionary-era victories—at Saratoga in October 1777 and at Yorktown in October 1781—it was the Americans who struck up "Yankee Doodle" to deride the British. In fact, John Laurens, the American negotiator, insisted in the Articles of Capitulation at Yorktown that the British troops strike up their "drums beating a British or German march," not an American one. According to reports, it might have been Lafayette himself who signaled for Americans to play "Yankee Doodle" as Cornwallis's troops surrendered at Yorktown in what would become etched in American memory as the moment the Revolutionary War was won.[2]

The curious pendulum swings of the song's significance to Britons in America on both sides of the divide well capture the slippery nature of humor and mirth as well as its prominent role in consolidating the ranks of the pro- and anti-British alliances during the Revolutionary War. Though humor is notoriously hard to control, its capacity to help form strong and compelling bonds of affinity and invest former "brethren" with a sense of "us and them" proved irresistible to Britons engaged in civil war. For denizens of a British world still steeped in premodern notions of community as organic and corporate, crowd actions featuring healthy doses of levity and play became the most salient forms of revolutionary protest that also functioned as community-forging jovial events. Whether the many anecdotes surrounding "Yankee Doodle" were accurate or mere rumor and hearsay that quickly emerged as lore, during the American Revolution "Yankee Doodle" became an important touchstone for raucous energy for both sides as they sought to consolidate their cause by harnessing the bonds of mirth.[3]

For the British, a song that touted Americans as uncouth bumpkins proved alluring as they sought to mock Americans as provincial buffoons. For Americans, embracing the song in self-deprecation channeled its subversive potential, invoking carnival and its capacity for removing inhibitions, destabilizing entrenched authority, and mobilizing mass protests. For both parties, a crowd employing a jaunty tune and comical lyrics—be it in street protests or as part of an organized military force—helped forge community in a struggle, uniting those in on the joke against those whom the joke was on.

Ultimately, the Americans' success at controlling the meaning of "Yankee Doodle," transforming it by the end of the war into their de facto anthem, illuminates the broader dynamics of their struggle. In the context of a culture war complementing a revolutionary struggle that channeled long festering and mutually reinforcing class and provincial versus metropolitan tensions, they proved more apt at wielding mirth and humor for their cause. More importantly, having wired their revolutionary rhetoric—and thus the very makeup of the embattled community they forged—with anti-authoritarian levity, they assented during the war to a democratizing logic that became impossible to restrain once the revolution ended. The elite gentlemen who led the revolutionary struggle would thus need to come to terms with the triumph of the commoners who in time made the new republic their own. It was often commoners' comfort with leveling and egalitarian language and humor—uninhibited by the hierarchies of the Old World—that marked them as true citizens of the young republic.

Chapters one and two follow the tug of war between gentlemen and commoners during the revolutionary period and into the early national period.

The late eighteenth century was a time of flux, when premodern societies, still localized in nature and steeped in older formulas of community cohesion and discipline, grew exposed to print culture, the novel construct of "the people," and the revolutionary notion that the future could be fundamentally different from the present and the past. As traditional tensions between elites and common folk and expressions of them in vernacular culture and tropes converged with revolutionary ferment, an egalitarian and antiauthoritarian impulse that had always been part of premodern carnivalesque culture acquired a new, more forward-looking meaning. Indeed, the humor of the revolutionary period, chapter one argues, not only helped unite the patriot camp, but also insinuated a novel mode of self-rule that challenged entrenched hierarchies and empowered people of common origins. As chapter two shows, although the British, and later Anglophile American elites, attempted to employ humor and play to stifle these trends, by the early nineteenth century they felt like strangers in their own country. The discursive terrain had largely shifted, and it was in no small part a result of a new regime of humor.

CHAPTER ONE

The Joyous Multitude

Humor and the Premodern Crowd
in the Revolutionary Era

On Thursday, August 14, 1765, a market day, Bostonians woke to an effigy of Andrew Oliver, the appointed stamp officer for Massachusetts, hanging in Hanover Square from a large elm tree, soon to be christened the Liberty Tree. The carefully choreographed scene was strewn with puns and comical references. Hanging "near by" the effigy "was a Boot [a play on Lord Bute, a former British prime minister] with a little devil peeping out and thrusting the stamp officer with an horrid fork." The soles of the effigy's shoes were painted green, a reference to sitting prime minister, George Gre[e]nville, and a note attached to it featured the couplet "How glorious is it to see; a stamp officer hang on a tree."[1] The whole scene was interactive as well.

Farmers who came to market that day participated in the charade by having the effigy stamp their goods as they passed by, poking at the Stamp Act (1765), recently passed by the British Parliament to tax various forms of stamped paper across the North American colonies. Much to the delight of one account, the effigy "hung to the view of the joyous multitude, the whole day." Another chronicler wrote of the "vast number of spectators" who "were immediately inspired with a spirit of enthusiasm . . . that scarce any could attend to the task of day labour." The day continued into the night as leaders in the crowd cut the effigy down, "layd him out & carried in triumph amidst the acclamations of many thousands who were gathered together on that occasion." The joyous multitude then made its way to what they thought was "the stamp office lately erected on Olivers dock" and used "all the wood this building afforded" to burn the effigy on top of Fort Hill. Fittingly, the night ended with an attack on Andrew Oliver's house, which stood nearby.[2]

Hindsight reveals the events of that day to be the first in a series of jubilant and rowdy colonial protests marking the rising tensions between the North American British colonies and the British metropole, the imperial crisis for the British Empire that would erupt a decade later in the Revolutionary War. The day's events also demonstrated that the "joyous multitude" played a central role in the events that comprised the American Revolution. As a host of subsequent crowd actions in this vein demonstrated, such events facilitated the formation of an anti-British coalition by fomenting and harnessing bonds of mirth. As Bostonians and visitors from nearby towns entered the carnival-scape of the city on August 14, they reveled in the joke played on the so-called enemies of liberty. By the same token, those the joke was on, first and foremost Andrew Oliver but also other representatives of British authority, felt far less comfortable, and likely even terror, given the violent undertone of the events and their symbolism. Indeed, they knew that when it came to the crowd and laughter started, fury might quickly follow.

As the anecdote in the introduction to part 1, featuring the British playing "Yankee Doodle" suggests, levity and play were not limited to colonial dissidents. Pro-British factions in the colonies as well as British troops also relied on the bonds of humor and had their own set of merry practices, rallying their own multitude against uncouth Americans and their provincial ways. They harnessed levity and participated in what amounted to a culture war that complemented an increasingly militant struggle between the provinces and the metropole. As Britons in North America struggled to forge a sense of us versus them in what was just as much a civil war as a revolutionary war, they took to what embattled communities had always done: they employed humor, one of the most effective devices for consolidating communities privy to a joke against those made the butts of the joke.

Featuring potent forms of levity and play pregnant with potential to both challenge and affirm the social fabric, carnivalesque humor offered competing factions in colonial North America rich traditions to harness in their efforts to shore up support for their respective causes. In this tug of war, the rebel colonists prevailed, because the carnivalesque better suited their more radical and ultimately revolutionary cause. For anti-British, patriot elites, who during the revolution sought to hold on to a more conservative version of republicanism, there would be a price to pay. As these joyous outbursts increasingly challenged the nature of authority itself, elites on both sides quickly learned to their chagrin that humor and joyous multitudes, once rallied, could not be easily controlled. Both British authorities as well as the elite leaders of the patriot coalition could not fully contain the leveling, indeed uninhibited, logic of the premodern carnival that infused and helped sustain revolutionary ardor and rhetoric in the American colonies.

In this vein, this chapter traces the origins of a leveling, antiauthoritarian and often jubilant frame of mind that would in time become a mainstay of the social fabric of the United States—at least insofar as it concerned the citizenry of white men. An examination of the crowd in colonial cities and the vernacular practices and traditions employed in challenging British administrators and local elites suggests that antiauthoritarian practices of carnivalesque misrule fused vigilante violence, levity, and play with a growing sense of American identity. As humor—often expressed as uninhibited mirth—facilitated the process of forging a community of Americans who identified as provincial and self-consciously rustic and crude, they came to view their one-time fellow Britons as "others," who bore the markers of a corrupt and effeminate European heritage. In turn, the American community forged through such rowdy and playful practices would prove intractable to any attempts to impose on it a more austere and less egalitarian version of republican ideology. Thus, one may well consider such emerging sensibilities from below as contributing to a distinct democratic and vernacular tradition that emerged from the crucible of revolution and civil war.

From Pope Day to Colonial Unrest

Rowdy and violent, yet at times surprisingly organized and carefully orchestrated, events such as those on August 14, 1765, in Boston have intrigued scholars and persuaded them of the need to view such moments as suggested by the historian Pauline Maier—as "extra-institutional in character more often than . . . anti-institutional."[3] Indeed, premodern Britons accepted the crowd itself as an institution with an established role in regulating the affairs of the community. Scholars see this as part of a subtle balance of power that underscores the concept of a "corporation" in a stratified society that views itself as organic and sustained by tradition. According to corporate assumptions on the origins and rituals that bind people, a community shares a common heritage traceable to a mutual social compact in which all members understand their very different duties to and expectations of their fellow community members, high, low, and middling. Failing to abide by these expectations can lead to regulatory communal actions, or regulations, in which the community as a whole, or portions of it, come together and assume the task of imposing community standards. While the crowds in colonial America did not reserve such practices solely for actions against elites, they proved to be an ongoing, poignant reminder to premodern English (after 1707, British) patricians that hegemony over the plebs had its limits.[4]

New Left historians who traced the migration of numerous British and European vernacular traditions to American shores found that as Americans applied vernacular practices to new circumstances and challenges, they borrowed significantly from old and often surprising traditions and, in the process of adaptation, adjusted their outlook and the application of these practices. Thus, much of the familiar forms of protest from the revolutionary era—from tarring and feathering to liberty pole–raising, to home attacks, and more—were cultural artifacts that exhibited both "retention" and "innovation."[5] Behind almost every such case one finds the joyous multitude navigating the shifting and contested terrain of the patrician–plebeian divide. The focal points for premodern vernacular culture were communal festivities. By the eighteenth century, the onset of market forces and the diminishing hold of institutionalized religion over the lives of the lower classes undermined corporate convictions, but festive days became more commonplace in the British Isles and in the North American British colonies. In fact, precisely because premodern power structures associated with corporate ideals increasingly gave way to modern ones, vernacular culture and the crowd as bulwarks of lower-class power proved as volatile and testy as ever.[6]

In the colonies, these dynamics were perhaps most evident in the festive tradition of Pope Day, a local colonial variant on the British festive tradition of Guy Fawkes Day, celebrated on November 5. Peter Oliver—whose brother Andrew became the first well-known victim of Boston crowds as the butt of their joke in August, 1765 on Hanover Square—ruefully noted about the tradition, "The first book that *New England* children are taught to read . . . depicted the pope, stuck around with darts," referring to the image appearing on the title page. "The sight & memory of this," he explained, "creates and keeps up an aversion to popery."[7] Indeed, the festivities of Pope Day channeled an emerging tradition in England and in the colonies, especially within Puritan circles, of celebrating the failed Catholic causes, often called the Jacobite rebellions, of the pretender kings James and Charles Stewart in 1715, 1719, and 1745. In England Guy Fawkes Day or Gunpowder Day was built on the anti-Catholic tradition that reveled in the failure in 1605 of Guy Fawkes and other Catholic conspirators to kill King James I. Severing the connection with the cause of James I, for whom Puritans harbored little love, the commemoration in New England instead emerged as Pope Day, or Pope's Day, and came into its own during the early decades of the eighteenth century.[8]

Much like Guy Fawkes Day in England, Pope Day in the American colonies drew on the rich tradition of the premodern festive days of carnival. Originally a reference to the celebrations before lent known as Carnival, for scholars of premodern Europe the word has come to encompass premodern notions of festive times more broadly, in which the "better sort" treated their social inferiors to excessive amounts of food and drink complemented by raucous jubilee, masquerades, parades, and role reversals. Though authorities sought to restrain and control such festivities, during carnival, laughter, argued the literary theorist Mikhail Bakhtin, was "directed at all and everyone, including the carnival's participants. The entire world [was] seen in its droll aspect, in its gay relativity." Designated by the community as a festive time, the mundane paused, the whole community immersed itself in spectacle. It was "the people's second life, organized on the basis of laughter." Carnivalesque practices, then, allowed members of the community to embrace the joyous mood that the masses derived from the suspension of hierarchies and inhibitions.[9]

Such vernacular traditions testify to the uneasy tensions that undergird the fiction of an organic corporate community. Even though everyday life revolved around clear distinctions between the various ranks of British society—low, middle, and high—when the crowd gathered, latent tensions could bubble up. The expectation of elites that the "meaner sort" defer to their "betters," which usually dominated daily encounters, might suddenly be ignored when the crowd realized its strength in numbers. Furthermore, the ideological fog that usually hid the conceits of "the few" from "the many" appeared to evaporate during days of carnival, in which burlesque and role reversal were the rule. In fact, festive days were often known as celebrations of antiauthoritarian "misrule." "Carnival," in Bakhtin's words, "celebrated temporary liberation from the prevailing truth and from established order." It "was a reversal of hierarchic levels," in which "the jester was proclaimed king." Indeed, since carnivalesque laughter "overcomes fear, for it knows no inhibitions, no limitations," festivities were moments pregnant with the potential for social change, when celebrants could turn to communal memories of more flush and egalitarian times that lay in the mythic past. During the revolutionary period, they increasingly hinted at new possibilities altogether. In a British world divided during the seventeenth and eighteenth centuries into the landed and merchant gentry, on the one hand, and the lower and middling ranks, on the other, the crowd was a constant reminder that polite gentlemen could not always get their way, especially when faced with raucous multitudes. Not surprisingly then, for lower-class Britons, vernacular culture traditions such as Pope Day often merged, literally or symbolically, with the institution of the crowd.[10]

First emerging in Boston and New England, Pope Day had spread to the rest of the colonies in full carnivalesque form by the mid-eighteenth century. The centerpiece of the event, observed one member of Boston's elite, was the "foolish custom of carrying about [effigies of] the pope & the devil . . . thro' the streets of town" while the community made fun of them and any other prominent enemies of the Protestants.[11] Perched on a platform and carried around the town, all the figures were presented as grotesque and comical, and the pope was usually covered with tar and feathers; boys dressed like little popes and smeared with tar and feathers circled the platform while using strings to make the effigies gesture comically. The crowd, making its way by the best homes, demanded money to buy the "pope" a drink, lest they do damage to the dwelling. Furthermore, Boston developed a tradition of competing processions—one in the North End and the other in the South End—that usually battled violently to capture the other's effigy throughout the night. The festivities culminated with a large bonfire, as the town's more unruly sectors burned the effigies in often violent and drunken revelry. Though such celebrations supposedly mocked the devil and his Catholic minions, under the auspices of misrule, the town seemed ironically captive to the devil's influence.[12]

Although the very existence of such unruly folk traditions—which authorities sought to curb, control, or eliminate—testified to a simmering counterhegemony from below, community leaders nevertheless often exerted varying degrees of control over such events. For instance, much of what happened on August 14, 1765, was planned and orchestrated by a faction of leading Bostonians who opposed the Stamp Act. Indeed, such vernacular and potentially subversive traditions could also prove opportune for certain factions within the community's elite to tap into the power of the crowd and wield it to their own ends. It was a tricky game that could quickly backfire, but when it worked, it proved quite effective. The members of the Sons of Liberty, the emergent, loose organization that led many of the colonial protests in the wake of the Stamp Act crisis of 1765, usually belonged to longstanding political factions in local politics; its leadership consisted of elites and the upper echelons of the middling folk, such as prominent artisans and ship captains.[13]

Nevertheless, as the revolution itself would reveal, and as one contemporary author put it, "mobs once raised, soon become ungovernable." As much as dissident elites sought to curb the excesses of the insurgency, the lower ranks of society also laid claim to colonial protests and later to the revolution itself. Another contemporary observed that although for a time "the gentry will deceive the people," they will also eventually "forfeit a share of their confidence," and before too long, "the mob [will] begin to think." When that happens, "fairwell aristocracy." In short, when Pope Day began, elites hoped for the best, but had to brace for the worst. The day after the festivities, newspapers tended to laud the public as demonstrating "great decency and decorum" or decry the "scandal and infamy" of the "Protestant mob," depending on how well elites managed to assert control over events.[14]

Peter Oliver suggested in his history of the American Revolution that the tenor of the street protests that ignited the revolutionary ferment were in effect variations on Pope Day rituals.[15] Later historians of the period concurred, casting the urban unrest from 1765 to 1775 as largely grafted onto the tradition of festive days, especially Pope Day, when even typically mild-mannered community members might partake in what one scholar called "licensed regression."[16] Indeed, a few months after the events of August 14, 1765, Pope Day itself became an opportunity to protest the British government across the colonies and would continue to serve as an anti-British celebration for the next few years. After the Stamp Act took effect—on November 1, 1765, four days before Pope Day—many of the protests throughout the colonies that day borrowed heavily from Pope Day traditions, and Pope Day itself became an extension of the November 1 protests.[17] This tradition of converging anti-British protest with Pope Day continued into the early years of the Revolutionary War. In 1775, for instance, a loyalist stranded in Alexandria, Virginia, witnessed an anti-British Pope Day celebration there. Previously in his journal writing, "New Englanders by their canting, whining, insinuating tricks have persuaded the rest of the colonies that the government is going to make absolute slaves of them," he later blamed Pope Day in Virginia on the hated Yankees: "New England masters of vessels that lie here . . . had the pope, Lord North, Barnard, Hutchinson, and the devil burnt in effigy after carting them through the town with drums and Fifes."[18]

Festive days, suspending everyday life and featuring jovial anti-British protests, became popular over the decade following passage of the Stamp Act (1765), emerging as the centerpiece of colonial unrest before outright hostilities broke out in 1775. Alongside Pope Day, the commemoration of the events of August 14 as well as the celebration of the repeal of the Stamp Act, on March 18, 1766, often endured as days of merriment and protest, in Boston and elsewhere. For instance, March 18, 1768, in Boston saw the first street protest against the Townshend Acts (1767), a series of laws that levied taxes on imports and enforced new regulations on the colonies. Combining the commemoration of the repeal of the Stamp Act and St. Patrick's Day, two effigies of customs officials Charles Paxton and John Williams were hung from the Liberty Tree. In addition, people drumming and firing guns, and crowds gathering around the tree and overnight around the homes of Paxton and Williams, marked the day as festive, though terrifying to the two magistrates.[19]

Meanwhile, in New York City, one festive day designed to celebrate authority and loyalty to Britain morphed into something far more subversive. On June 4, 1766, two weeks after learning of the repeal of the Stamp Act, the city's elites sought to pander to the crowd by celebrating the repeal together with the king's birthday, organizing formal festivities that included the raising of a flagpole and plying the crowd with food and drink. New Yorkers managed, however, to transform the event into the festive inauguration of what would be their first Liberty Pole. Probably the result of subversive messaging by some of the event's planners, as one onlooker perceptively noted, the flagstaff bore the wording "George [King George III], Pitt [William Pitt], and Liberty," purportedly celebrating the king, but the "word Pitt the most distinguished." The elder William Pitt was seen as the force behind the Stamp Act's repeal. The staff thus in fact celebrated repeal, and according to the prevailing symbolism of the period, constituted an affront to British authorities.[20] For New Yorkers, the pole quickly became a symbol of their anti-government sympathies and for British troops stationed in New York a symbol of colonial disloyalty to the king. In the following months and years, it evolved into New York's version of Boston's Liberty Tree.

Poles and Trees

American dissidents designated specific spaces for festive events. Both the Liberty Tree in Boston and the Liberty Pole in New York as well as their offshoots throughout the colonies evoked the European tradition of the maypole and the town center or marketplace as the loci for most communal affairs, including festive days. During court days, market days, holidays, and, most of all, festive days such as Pope Day or May Day, the premodern town assumed a carnivalesque aura that emanated from the center of town. During May Day celebrations, a maypole erected in the center of town symbolized fecundity and fertility. Dating back to pre-Christian celebrations of the coming of summer and the harvest, May 1 was also a day of dancing round the maypole and sexual intercourse between young men and women. Indeed, the maypole's phallic imagery and its association with fertility, with the help of excessive consumption of food and drink, imbued it with carnal possibilities and licentiousness. Such festivities also bestowed upon the participants a giddy, subversive edge, encouraging them to entertain thoughts and actions that might otherwise lie outside the realm of the normative and thinkable.[21]

May Days and maypoles were probably quite common in colonial America, especially in the mid-Atlantic colonies, but less so in New England, where Puritan authorities clamped down on the custom. By the revolutionary era, May Day in Philadelphia had become associated with a burlesque society, the Sons of St. Tammany, which made a mythic Native American sachem (chief) into a patron saint of the town and then celebrated him while garbed in Indian costumes on May 1.[22] One also finds a reference to the maypole in association with the New York Liberty Pole in one of the earliest dated "Yankee Doodle" stanzas, written to celebrate the rehoisting of the Liberty Pole in New York in 1770:

> Let every body laugh and sing
> And be a very gay soul
> For we have got another Post
> As big as any MAY POLE.

Another stanza in the same version mocks Lord Butte:

> In *London* I've a *name-sake* got: As sharp as any Razor
> He'd make Lord BUTE befoul himself
> And quiver like *Belshazer.*[23]

For the formative decade from 1765 to 1776, Alfred Young has counted thirteen trees and fifty-five poles christened with the modifier "liberty" in the colonies, most of them in the mid-Atlantic and New England colonies. They functioned as centers of unrest, misrule, and organized action, and consequently also as focal points for tensions and skirmishes between pro and anti-British forces and between plebs and patricians.[24]

For premodern elites, symbol and spectacle were paramount for maintaining authority. In a society in which the lower ranks of society were far more accustomed to oral and performative communication than the written word, controlling symbolism proved essential for upholding authority writ large as well as for maintaining the crucial fiction that some people stood elevated above others by virtue of their birth. Decision-makers in Britain and magistrates in the colonies, therefore, often responded with urgency to symbolic affronts. By the same token, when unruly colonists employed symbolism, they knew full well that it was not mere play and that play itself was seldom innocuous.[25]

The symbolism of British authority proved even more compelling to the Boston crowd when conjoined with the festive aura of a tree, hallowed through spectacle, as communal witticism: a "liberty tree." The tree would make the shaming ritual of forcing Andrew Oliver to resign his office as stamp commissioner in December 1765 a poignant reminder of the power of a boisterous crowd, not to mention an entertaining and festive spectacle for all assembled. Though Oliver had tendered his resignation on August 15, the day following the attack on his house and his likeness in effigy, reports circulated several months later that his commission as stamp distributor had nevertheless arrived from England. Now the Sons of Liberty, to demonstrate their command of the situation and appease the Boston crowd, insisted that Oliver resign in public under the Liberty Tree. Oliver, one of the highest-ranking members of Boston's merchant elite, tried to maintain his dignity by submitting his resignation elsewhere, but the insistent crowd of thousands gathered outside his house had its way, and Oliver resigned under the Liberty Tree and then rebuked the Stamp Act to a round of cheers.[26]

After a symbol became etched in the public consciousness, both sides attempted to plumb its symbolic potential, all the better if they could find ways to imbue it with merriment and spectacle. The effort to suffuse symbol with mirth led Bostonians to again tap the trope of the Liberty Tree when they declared the shoemaker Ebenezer Mackintosh "Captain General of the Liberty Tree," for having directed much of the crowd activity in Boston during the Stamp Act riots. As Young noted, the designation "burlesqued the full title of the royal governor," even as the royal governor, Francis Bernard, and others of his milieu stood aghast at the power that a low-ranking shoemaker exerted over the Boston crowd.[27]

In New York, where British troops had interacted daily with residents prior to the "occupation of Boston" in 1768, the Liberty Pole became a symbolic site of conflict between the two sides. Just two months after British troops raised the British flag in 1766 in celebration of the king's birthday and repeal of the Stamp Act, as noted above, they removed the pole. In response, New Yorkers assembled the next day to confront troops stationed nearby and then proceeded to hoist it again, dubbing it their "liberty pole."[28] Months later, on March 18, 1767, New York's Sons of Liberty employed the Liberty Pole's symbolism to anchor their celebration of the first anniversary of the repeal of the Stamp Act. As one of the celebrants noted, "such manifestations of victory were becoming exceedingly unpleasant to the king's officers, and the soldiers could not endure the sight of processions to commemorate their monarch's defeat." Thus, a day after the celebration "they assembled in the night, and cut down the obnoxious symbol." As before, the Sons of Liberty raised the pole again the following day, and for the next few days it remained the scene of confrontations. British troops tried to dismantle it even as New Yorkers maintained a guard around it at night to ensure its safety.[29] Similarly, three years later, in January 1770, more violent protests and skirmishes erupted over the pole. At one point, British soldiers blew it up only to see it hoisted again by the ever more resentful New York crowd.[30]

"New Fashion Dress"

Tarring and feathering, the most famous form of protest of the revolutionary era, seems to have first occurred in Virginia in 1766. Once it arrived in New England in 1768 as an elaborate, and violent, joke played on the "enemies of liberty," local crowds seemed to take to it with particular glee. Tarring and feathering stands as a classic example of retention and innovation being combined in colonial vernacular culture. The act of applying sticky tar and then feathers as punishment had by the mid-eighteenth century appeared across the Atlantic world (all of the regions brought together by European expansion around the Atlantic, including Africa and South America), including in Pope Day celebrations, while the festive shaming ritual that followed, parading the offender through town as a crowd loudly hurled abuse, borrowed both from Pope Day processions and from boisterous communal punishments called skimmingtons, rough music, or charivari. Whereas communities usually carried out skimmingtons against transgressors of sexual or marital mores, colonial crowds applied tarring and feathering to people deemed enemies of liberty.[31]

Tarring and feathering as a communal shaming ritual involved significant, if measured, violence against the body of the alleged offender. The practice almost never killed the victim, because the pine tar was usually not hot enough to cause mortal wounds. Since the tar was usually applied on the skin, however, any attempt to remove it could severely damage it; sometimes the ordeal could leave the targeted individual on the verge of death. In an early tarring and feathering incident in Providence, Rhode Island, for example, one account reported that after they "stripped [the victim] naked, covered him from head to foot with turpentine and feathers," they also "bound him by the feet, threw dirt in his face, and repeatedly beat him with their fists and sticks, then threw him down on the pavement" and "cut his face." After "an hour and a half" of that, he "was near expiring, and now lies dangerously ill."[32]

Combining physical and symbolic affronts, tarring and feathering was also an elaborate form of street theater that, on the one hand, instilled a sense of community among its participants and, on the other, shamed their enemies. Reporting one of the earliest tarring and featherings in Salem, Massachusetts, in the summer of 1768, the local paper noted that after the victim was tarred and feathered, he was "exalted to a seat in front of a cart, and in this manner, led into the main street." "[The] scene drew together within a few minutes several hundred people, who proceeded with huzzas and loud acclamations through the town."[33] Reports from Boston on May 18, 1770, had it that a "mob of upwards a thousand people" apprehended "a tidesman of the customs, who had seized a small coasting vessel." He was then "stripped, and carted about the town for three or four hours, besmeared with tar and then covered with feathers."[34] In Charleston, South Carolina, in 1775, the victim was given "a decent tarring and feathering, for some insolent speech he made." Then, in the manner of Pope Day processions, "There [was] hardly a street through which he was not paraded; nor a Tory house, where they did not halt." In front of one of the Tory houses, they made the man drink grog and toast "damnation" to the home's owner.[35]

In one of the earliest comprehensive accounts of the revolution, William Gordon observed that tarring and feathering "took so with the lower class of people" that after its initial applications, "it was not confined to informers." Attempting to account for the spectacle's popularity with the masses, Gordon explained that it gave the victims a "ridiculous appearance, and laid them under a difficulty to clear themselves of the dress imposed upon them."[36] If making fun of and doing violence to an effigy gave a rise to the crowd, giving a flesh-and-blood person the appearance of a chicken raised the stakes, bonding the crowd with an even more giddy rush of antiauthoritarian adrenalin. In a letter to the *Boston Gazette,* one onlooker "Own[ed] I could not help laughing very heartily the other evening when the informer was carted by my house, tarr'd and feather'd so compleatly."[37] After a tarring and feathering in Charleston, South Carolina, a member of the local Council of Safety testified that the "people were in such humour," and another jested that the victim "had a new suit of clothes yesterday, without the assistance of a single taylor."[38]

Indeed, newspapers could not stop themselves from sharing in the fun. One report quipped that a Charleston crowd "furnished" two offenders "with a suit of cloathing, of the true American manufacture,"[39] while an account from New London, Connecticut, described the locals as giving "one Captain Davies . . . the new fashioned dress tar and feathers."[40] Even in a very pithy and sympathetic (to the victim) account, future Revolutionary War general Joseph Spencer wrote Connecticut governor, Jonathan Trumbull, that their mutual acquaintance Dr. Beebe received a "new fashion dress of tar and feathers."[41]

In short, tarring and feathering became for many a singular American joke played on the enemies of liberty. The colonists' sympathizers in England agreed, distributing a set of prints reveling in this new American custom. One of them elaborated on the joke, suggesting that tarring and feathering was a "new method of macaroni making" (figure 1.1), referring to contemporary satirical renditions of ostentatious, Frenchified, and effeminate gentlemen who wore elaborate wigs.[42]

Though some higher-ranking opponents of Britain's taxation policy expressed support and even planned and organized violent crowd actions like tarring and feathering, others otherwise generally supportive of the cause expressed far more ambiguity over what elites usually portrayed as "mob" violence. As Gouverneur Morris, future New York delegate to the Continental Congress, famously put it, even some patriots feared they might end up "under the domination of a riotous mob."[43] John Rowe, a prominent leader of Boston's opposition to the Townshend duties recorded in a diary entry the unrestrained raucous behavior of the "mob" on October 29, 1769: "[They] got hold of one George Greyer, an informer who they stript naked & painted him

A New Method of MACARONY MAKING, as practifed at BOSTON.

Figure 1.1. "A New Method of Macaroni Making, as Practised at Boston," probably 1774. A British pro-American broadside endorsing the American practice of tarring and feathering. Foppish men who wore elaborate wigs were called macaroni. The tea kettle probably references the Boston Tea Party, which took place on December 16, 1773. The number 45 on one man's hat refers to John Wilkes, the radical journalist and politician who was hailed in the American colonies and elsewhere as a champion of liberty after being persecuted for criticizing the British government in the forty-fifth edition (1763) of his satirical newspaper *North Briton*. Library of Congress, https://www.loc.gov/item/2004673300/.

all over with tar & then covered him with Feathers & put him in a Cart & carried him thro' all the main streets of town huzzahing &c." Rowe added, uneasily, "This matter occasioned much terror &c in some fearful People among the inhabitants," also noting that he had been part of the posse that attempted to calm the crowd. Perhaps not incidentally, in his next diary entry he noted in contrast, with some relief, that on Pope Day, just a few days after the rowdy affair, "The people have behaved very well." [44]

Crowds usually reserved such "hilarity" for the enemies of liberty, but it was also clearly a joke that only the "lower sort" could feel truly at ease with. To be sure, many higher-ranking members of the community sought to manage and harness the potential of the raucous crowd, reveling in an ebullient moment. Yet, others, including at times the "orchestrators" of such events, understood that they were never fully "in" on the hilarity, and worse yet, at some point might become the butt of the crowd's humor. In short, unlike the masses, members of the elite rarely found the actions of the joyous multitude truly funny.

Making Tea in the Boston Harbor

As far as formative, watershed events in US history go, it would be hard to find one invested over the years with more humor than the so-called Boston Tea Party. In fact, that name for the event came into widespread use more than half a century after it occurred. It emerged as yet another pun in a long line of puns devised to merrily portray the suggestive moment when on December 16, 1773, Boston dissidents destroyed more than 90,000 pounds of East India Company tea by hurling it into the Boston harbor. [45]

By the end of 1773, Bostonians had developed a vibrant tradition and reputation for leading the opposition to the British government through rowdy crowd actions. Trying to live up to expectations, the Boston Sons of Liberty felt that their only course of action to protest the tax on tea and the East India Company's monopoly was to destroy the tea in the harbor and defy the British government. As before, they turned to crowd action, or at least the cover of it. Despite the hand wringing of some elites some of the time, they could hardly turn on the unruly crowd and instead had to resort to asserting as much control as they dared and could over it. Once the crowd became the dominant agent of colonial opposition to adverse British policies, there was no turning back. Unsurprisingly, plenty of levity made its way into the event, both at the time and in the way it is remembered.

The destruction of the tea was one of the best planned and executed crowd actions of the revolutionary period, especially from the perspective of the elites. By all accounts, the dozens of men who boarded the ships and threw the tea into the harbor were disciplined, careful not to injure anyone or destroy cargo aboard the ships other than the tea. The men, masked to avoid identification, enjoyed a buffer created by a large crowd of sympathetic on-lookers. They worked quickly and efficiently, and when the event was over, observed strict secrecy. Their discipline and the sense of gravity on the part of the planners brings into further relief the levity its organizers and chroniclers nevertheless injected into the affair.[46]

The most notable form of mirth incorporated into the action that evening was, of course, the decision of the perpetrators to assume the guise of Indians. As most accounts report, after the town meeting voted that it had exhausted all efforts to address the situation formally, a loud yell, which many identified as an Indian war whoop, announced the transition from an orderly and formal body of the people to the carnivalesque, extra-institutional realm of the joyous multitude. "I heard an hideous yelling in the street at the s. west corner of the Meeting house," reported one onlooker, "some imitating the powaws of Indians and others the whistle of a boatswain, which was answered by some few in the house."[47] Another local testified that, subsequently, "two or three hundred persons, in dress and appearance like Indians . . . hastened to the wharf, where the tea ships lay."[48] A third corroborated this, writing, "whether they were [Indians] or not, to a transient observer they appear'd as such, being cloath'd in blankets with the heads muffled, and copper color'd countenances, being each arm'd with a hatchet or axe, and pair pistols, nor was their dialect different from what I conceive these geniusses to speak, as their jargon was unintelligible to all but themselves."[49]

From the perspective of those who carried out the act, such humor and levity appeared to complement the sense of excitement and help offset the unease felt before a potentially dangerous action, where the stakes were clearly high. One of the perpetrators, George Hewes, remembered that he "dressed . . . in the costume of an Indian," "equipped with a small hatchet," which in jest he and his "associates denominated a tomahawk."[50] Another recalled, "We surely resembled devils from the bottomless pit rather than men," and though "we stirred briskly in the business from the moment we left our dressing-room," he added, "we were merry, in an undertone, at the idea of making so large a cup of tea for the fishes." Similarly, other accounts attested that upon heading to the wharf, one of the men quipped enthusiastically, "Boston harbor a tea-pot to-night!"[51]

Though many of the men dressed in hastily made disguises, and some only blackened their faces, the ruse spread quickly that the affair was undertaken by "Indians," specifically by Mohawks, perhaps the most well-known nation of the Haudenosaunee (Iroquois) Confederacy in what is today Upstate New York (figure 1.2). At what point that became part of the plan is hard to tell. It appears, however, that the theme evolved from an earlier threat in New York papers that was published three days before the event in the *Boston Post-Boy*. The piece was an anonymous warning to New Yorkers not to offload tea in New York City's harbor, lest "our nation" pay them "an unwelcome visit." It was signed "THE MOHAWKS."[52] Observers and chroniclers were quick to pick up on the joke and elaborate on it. In a letter to the colonial agent in London, Benjamin Franklin, written the day following the destruction of the tea, the Boston clergyman Samuel Cooper wryly called it "a remarkable instance of order and justice among savages," and the patriot poet and playwright Mercy Otis Warren waxed poetically about the "champions of the Tuscararan race," a reference to the Tuscarora, another member nation of the Haudenosaunee Confederacy.[53] Even a British account promoted the joke,

Figure 1.2. "The Boston Tea Party. Destruction of the Tea in Boston Harbor, December 16, 1773," by John Andrew, *Ballou's Pictorial Drawing-Room Companion* 11, no. 4 (July 16, 1856): 56–57. The colonists' use of Indian masquerade became part of American mythology. Reproduced courtesy of the Yale University Art Gallery.

noting that Samuel Adams, assumed by most contemporaries to lead the Sons of Liberty, "seems to be acquainted, and speaks without an interpreter [with the] Mohawk Indians."[54]

As a form of protest and a burlesque performance, the Boston Tea Party constituted a social and cultural meeting point between patricians and plebeians. As an action, it exhibited the full hierarchy of the town at work and the machinations of deference in full swing. Elites who were the public face of the Boston Sons of Liberty, including such men as Samuel Adams, John Hancock, and Josiah Quincy, had given orders to carry out the affair, while remaining conspicuously behind in the meeting hall. Thus, they could not be held responsible as less notable men of the upper echelons of the middling classes led the crews—consisting mostly of young tradesmen, journeymen, and apprentices—who destroyed the tea on the ship. Regardless, it was, all told, a brazen protest that defiantly destroyed property of a company commissioned by the British government. It was an expression of order and of disorder; an expression of elite control but under the cover of, and with the support of, Boston's infamous joyous multitude. Fortunately for the elites, the crowd this time around remained disciplined, never deviating from the script issued from above.[55]

The method of action as well as the performance of it exhibited the capacity of elite and vernacular cultures to converge, itself an act of broader political significance that suggests a tacit compact between the few and the many. The comical mode in which Bostonians cast the events drew both from elite traditions of eighteenth-century Augustan-age, neoclassical humor as well as the vernacular and carnivalesque traditions of masked and anonymous crowd protests. When contemporary writers made clever puns that required erudition and assumed witty, often Latin, pen names, they drew from the tradition of Augustan-era wits and essayists, such as Joseph Addison and Richard Steele, who sought to combine wise counsel in the British republican, or what historians call whig, tradition with whimsical salvos of wit.[56] While this form of humor took on some of the gravest issues of the day, it also enlivened its message with comical references that attested to the level of erudition and sophistication of the commentator. Thus, even as such writers espoused forward- thinking republican ideas, they also engaged in an elitist scheme designed to ensure that only upstanding, college-educated gentlemen of good breeding could fully partake in the levity. By the same token, it also envisioned a republic of letters in which men of good wit and erudition naturally distinguished themselves as the better sort.[57]

Though Augustan humor tended toward elitism, it was never exclusively so. Following in the tradition of Shakespeare, not to mention Rabelais and Cervantes, such eighteenth-century British authors as Henry Fielding and Jonathan Swift often incorporated vernacular comical conceits and even scatological humor into their writings. Augustan witticisms often appeared in even tamer form in the colonies, where few elites would have counted as true gentry in the British Isles, and where many who thought of themselves as gentlemen came from the free yeomanry and the artisan class. For instance, Benjamin Franklin's Silence Dogood letters and *Poor Richard's Almanac* watered down the elitist tendencies of such comical schemes as mocking pseudonyms and knowing, tongue-and-cheek references with homespun, common sense wit that appealed to a broad section of American colonists.[58]

Between 1765 and 1775, the years of the imperial crisis between the colonies and Britain, American dissidents assumed witty pen names and identities as well as other forms of word play in their protests in print and in street theater. Though most evident in many of the more satirical anti-government pamphlets and newspaper articles of the period, such humor was also abundant in the puns and witticisms accompanying crowd protests, such as hanging boots in reference to Lord Bute and dressing up as Mohawk "savages." Likewise, when weeks before the Boston Tea Party the families that the East India Company tapped to sell its tea in Boston received a threatening letter urging them to meet the Boston crowd "on Wednesday next" by the Liberty Tree, it was signed in a combination of terror and jest by none other than Oliver Cromwell, the standard-bearer of Puritan republicanism.[59] Around the same time, an author making a series of threats in Boston papers took the pen name Joyce Junior—a knowing reference to one of Cromwell's more storied followers—and claimed to hold the fabricated position of chairman of the Committee for Tarring and Feathering.[60] Cromwell, a symbol of tyranny and disorder in the minds of most British elites in the eighteenth century, had by then become a patron of the opposition to the British government in New England, where many, especially middling folk, still held him in high esteem.[61] This too demonstrated the convergence of a vernacular strain of popular reverence for Cromwell and the more genteel formulas associated with wit.

In most crowd actions of the revolutionary period, such wit intersected with and amplified vibrant vernacular practices of communal public theater. In the case of the Boston Tea Party, the mode of action resembled a growing rural colonial tradition of vigilantes who challenged the authority of elites by terrorizing them while clad in Indian garb. Much like other folkways, this too was an adaptation of vigilante traditions from rural Britain, often associated with woods, in which poachers in disguise as black-faced social bandits would lay claim to hunting territories reserved for elites. When this European tradition of costumed banditry challenging elite hegemony emerged in North America, however, the woods evoked fearful images of skulking Indians, who supposedly roamed the woods with impunity. The result was that rural vigilantes, often "Indian fighters," dressed up in Native American garb and appropriated their warpaint customs.[62]

For the New England crowd, rowdy masquerades also served as tacit affronts to Puritan authorities, who held carnival traditions and misrule as ungodly and suggestive of the work of the devil. The Puritans could only stomach Pope Day because of its decidedly anti-Catholic spirit. The joyous multitude pressed its challenge to Puritan tradition even further by taking to Indian dress given that the Puritan imagination viewed markers of Native American culture, especially song and dance traditions, as the devil's influence. Indeed, the very nature of the carnival plumbed an alternative universe of taboos and reveled in a world turned topsy-turvy. As early as 1627, Thomas Morton, who led Merry Mount, the aptly named non-Calvinist rogue settlement just north of Plymouth, had already rendered the link between carnivalesque practices and Indian dancing quite real in the minds of Puritan authorities. William Bradford, governor of Plymouth, noted that year, "Morton became the lord of misrule" and even "set up a May-pole, drinking and dancing aboute it, inviting the Indean women, for their consorts, dancing and frisking together . . . and worse practices."[63] Thus, when adopting Indian play, the so-called Mohawks who raided Boston harbor also enlisted a long-simmering communal id at once enamored with and terrified of the "savage devils" of America.

In this vein, the Boston Tea Party not only captured the emerging nature of the patriots' compact as an uneasy cross-class alliance but also as a uniquely settler colonial struggle in which settlers in search of identity in a new continent sought to cut themselves off from the fountain of their culture across the Atlantic.[64] They did so through such settler colonial customs as forming the Sons of St. Tammany, a genteel fraternity that adopted Indian play and burlesqued a mythical Native American sachem, and turning the Boston harbor into a teapot while clad in Indian attire in one of the most daring challenges to the British Empire to date. Thus, the mirth surrounding the so-called tea party attests quite adequately to the nature of the nascent republican society that would soon declare its independence from Great Britain. Such antiauthoritarian humor and play helped unite them in struggle for the "common cause," and it would also prove central to the sensibilities at the heart of the fledgling republic.

The "Royal Mob"

As the anecdote of the British playing "Yankee Doodle" while docked in the Boston harbor suggests, British troops and loyalists also employed mirth and even carnivalesque humor to shore up support for their cause. During the revolutionary period, "Yankee Doodle," a lively tune often complemented with jaunty lyrics, itself became contested terrain between the insurgent American and British camps, as each sought to energize its followers through its carnivalesque appeal. Although the song's origins are murky, and it appears that both sides reveled in the tune, the earliest known records of the song's use—from the garrisoning of Boston from 1768 to 1770 and from 1774 to 1776—suggest that before 1775 the British more successfully employed the tune to the great consternation of New England Yankees.[65]

The three earliest reports of "Yankee Doodle" being played come from the same patriot news outlet, the *Journal of the Times*. Chronicling the presence of British troops in Boston after their arrival in the summer of 1768, the news outlet cast them as an oppressive occupying force and wove "Yankee Doodle" references into a broad agenda to generate hostility toward the British government and sympathy for Boston's Sons of Liberty across the colonies. The last of the "Yankee Doodle" accounts appears particularly suggestive, asserting that on July 24, 1769, local authorities in Boston encountered John Bernard, son of the governor of Massachusetts, as he participated in illegal "entertainment given by a band of music" on the Sabbath. The wardens chastised his behavior, and as a group of British soldiers passed, they urged Bernard, seemingly intent on walking away, to join them for his own protection. Then, according to the report, "The officer of the guard, in a sneering manner, called upon the musicians to play the Yankee Doodle tune." In conclusion, the story claimed that such use of the tune "completed the conquest of the military and afforded them a temporary triumph."[66] Taken together, the three accounts indicate that readers understood the deprecating application of "Yankee Doodle" by the British and that the *Journal of the Times* writers employed these depictions of the song's use to incite their readership and to portray British troops as disrespectful to the locals.

Furthermore, the last account is also part of a long series of recurrent complaints in the *Journal of the Times* of British troops disturbing the Sabbath, by law in New England a day devoted to prayer and rest. During the Sabbath, stressed the influential Puritan theologian Jonathan Edwards, "We ought carefully to watch over our own hearts, and to avoid all sinful thoughts. We ought to maintain such a reverence for the sabbath, as to have a peculiar dread of sin."[67] Indeed, for Puritan authorities, the Lord's day was in many ways the antithesis of the debauched festive days, such as Pope Day, influenced by the devil. In November 1768, just a few weeks after the arrival of British troops, the *Journal of Times* complained in three different Sunday entries, "The minds of serious people at public worship were greatly disturbed with drums beatings and fifes playing, unheard of before in this land." To them, having the army parade on Sunday was clearly "eradicating the sentiments of morality and religion." Although the playing seemed to have stopped for a few months after the selectmen of Boston urged Colonel John Pomeroy to halt the practice, by the summer of 1769 complaints of music on the Sabbath appeared once more in the *Journal*'s pages.[68]

When British troops returned in force to Boston in 1774 in the wake of the Tea Party, they took to offending the local populace once again. Less than a month before the Battles of Lexington and Concord, fought on April 19, 1775, one account related that on a Thursday, "a day of fasting and prayer; in the forenoon of the day when service began, a number of officers, and soldiers of the 4th, or king's own, regiment, brought two markee tents, and pitched them within 20 feet of the meeting house, at West Boston; then sent for three drums, and two fifes, and kept them beating, and playing, Yankee Doodle, all service time, so that the congregation could scarce hear the minister."[69] A week earlier and even more damning, some soldiers had tarred and feathered Thomas Ditson, a "countryman" visiting Boston from Billerica, who according to his testimony, quite innocuously tried to purchase a gun from them. They paraded him around town, including by the Liberty Tree, and according to the Whig press, "to add to the insult," the "royal mob" played "Yankee Doodle." In fact, according to a later report the song "had become their favorite tune ever since that notable exploit . . . of tarring and feathering a poor countryman in Boston."[70] Thus, the weeks leading up to the outbreak of war, a period when striking up "Yankee Doodle" was especially popular with British soldiers, were rife with tension over the perceived humiliation by debased British troops. Not only had the British appropriated "Yankee Doodle" to deprecate the colonists, they had appropriated tarring and feathering as well.

Furthermore, as tensions rose in Boston and British troops returned to the city in large numbers, British officers cultivated a variety of ways to insult the local populace and its leaders. These included enacting mock congresses and burlesquing the republican process that New Englanders, and American settlers, more broadly carried out as part of the transition to "home rule." On the day in March 1775 when locals published a recently delivered oration by Doctor Warren marking the fifth anniversary of the Boston Massacre, "a vast number of officers assembled in King Street" to mock the commemoration of the day British soldiers shot indiscriminately into a Boston crowd, killing five. They chose "a moderator and seven out of their number to represent the selectmen," who then together went to the "coffee house balcony." There they joined a "fellow apparrell'd in a black gown with rusty grey wigs and fox tail hanging to it . . . who deliver'd an oration from the balcony to a crowd of a few else beside gaping officers." As one aggrieved Bostonian described the oration, "It contain'd the most scurrilous abuse upon the characters of the principal patriots here, wholly made up of the most vile, profane, blackguard language as ever was express'd." A few weeks later, some officers, according to the same indignant Bostonian, enacted a burlesque "procession . . . from the coffee house to the cockloft in the town house," in a "silly parade" that "consisted of a president with a borrow'd scarlet cloak and perriwig, with a wand in one hand and a book in the other, follow'd by six others, alike apparell'd, who stil'd [styled] themselves the selectmen, together with about thirty others in uniforms walking two and two." To the further outrage of Bostonians, officers in Boston published and enacted a few plays that mocked local leaders and the character and manners of New Englanders. From the perspective of the increasingly besieged troops in Boston—who, no doubt had heard of the massive resources and energy devoted by the colonists to organizing and preparing the adjoining countryside for an insurrection— such theater provided much needed comic relief and helped foster a sense of cohesion in the face of the hostile population surrounding them.[71]

Tensions between British troops and colonists were nothing new and had their origins in encounters between British soldiers and American colonists in the early and mid-eighteenth- century wars: the War of Jenkins' Ear immediately followed by King George's War (together 1739–48) and the Seven Years' War (1754–63). Many colonists had answered the call of empire and joined the ranks of the British armed forces, encountering, often for the first time, their British brethren and the British army's disciplinary regimen. As one historian noted, such encounters with poorly treated British regulars, who suffered under severe British army discipline, left in the colonists' minds "no doubt that they were the moral superiors of the redcoats." Civilians, especially in bustling port cities such as Boston, also first engaged with the British military during impressment efforts that became more common as the wars for empire dragged on. Indeed, the largest Boston riot before the Stamp Act erupted after an impressment sweep there in 1747.[72]

By the same token, British regulars as well as their officers harbored little love for the colonists and viewed them as a provincial set of inferior Britons. The officers viewed American troops as intractable and disorderly colonial subjects. Thus, for instance, even though the Yankee troops proved crucial to the Louisbourg campaign of 1745, after Charles Knowles assumed command of Louisbourg he dismissed them from duty, disparaging "these New England folk" as "lazy," "obstinate," "licentious," and "undisciplined."[73] A decade later, during the campaign for Canada, Brigadier General James Wolfe complained, "Americans are in general the dirtiest most contemptible cowardly dogs that you can conceive."[74] Although the British regulars and officers were often at odds, they could all agree on their hatred for the colonists, especially the haughty New England "Yankees," who considered themselves superior. Thus, regular British troops, who cherished a sense of community and camaraderie within their regiments, increasingly also cultivated an identity as truer Britons vis-à-vis provincials, knowing well that the colonists viewed them with disdain.[75] The song "Yankee Doodle" was a direct result of these tensions.

From 1740 to 1760, as the colonists and the troops reified the contentious identities of "American" and "British," the droll ditty emerged as a discursive battleground between them.[76] Thus it was no surprise that when British troops arrived in Boston in 1768, they announced their arrival with "Yankee Doodle" and that the locals found such usage abrasive. It also suggests that parading up and down the Boston Common on the Sabbath, time and again, while playing fifes and drums, was never innocuous, but part of an ongoing joke played on pious and proud New Englanders. As noted above, as late as March 1775, the British appeared more successful in tapping the song's carnivalesque potential to slight the Americans, but the Battles of Lexington and Concord a month later would prove decisive for the Americans in laying claim to "Yankee Doodle." The patriotic effusions that swept the North

American colonies in the wake of the victory at Concord and on the road back to Boston, followed by the siege of Boston, prompted the rhetorical subversion of the song. It was now the New Englanders who took command of the tune's jovial energy and with joyous self-deprecation unabashedly celebrated their identity as Yankees.

In the poem *M'Fingal* (1775), one of the most popular satires of the period, even John Trumbull—a conservative Connecticut wit who would later help write the antidemocratic satire *The Anarchiad* (1786–87) in response to the Massachusetts uprising known as Shays's Rebellion—revealed his appreciation for the success of the self-deprecating ditty. In capturing the travails of "Yankee Doodle," *M'Fingal* contributed to the heady climate in the wake of the patriots' early successes in Massachusetts. At a townhall meeting where a loyalist, M'fingal, and a patriot, Honorious, present their case, M'fingal inadvertently discredits his own side by depicting the British as falsely claiming "Yankee Doodle" for themselves:

> So tho' our war few triumphs brings,
> We gain'd great fame in other things.
> Did not our troops show much discerning,
> And skill your various arts in learning?
> Outwent they not each native Noodle
> By far in playing Yankee-doodle;
> Which, as 'twas your New-England tune,
> 'Twas marvelous they took so soon?
> And ere the year was fully thro',
> Did not they learn to foot it too,
> And such a dance as ne'er was known[77]

Subsequently, Trumbull used M'Fingal's oration to strike a more personal note against "Col'nel Nesbitt," the British officer who weeks before the Battles of Lexington and Concord had led the tarring and feathering of the poor Billerica man, Thomas Ditson, through the streets of Boston. Appearing in the verse right after recounting how the British pirated "Yankee Doodle" from New Englanders, the Colonel Nesbitt anecdote also lambasts the British habit of emulating American vernacular practices, in this case, tarring and feathering:

> Did they not lay their heads together,
> And gain your art to tar and feather,

When Col'nel Nesbitt thro' the town,
In triumph bore the country-clown?[78]

Such was the nature of rhetorical and symbolic sparring between the emerging camps in a struggle for usable cultural resources in what amounted to a civil war. Each side constructed combative identities by incorporating barbed flourishes of humor that quickly became elaborate and ongoing inside jokes that only Britons in America could fully appreciate and understand.[79]

Even before war broke out in earnest in the spring and summer of 1775, numerous humorous and satirical essays, poems, ballads, plays, farces, mock letters and news reports, comical imprints and illustrations, street theater, and other productions appeared in the colonies and the British Isles. They ran the gamut from high-brow Hudibrastic verse to raunchy "Yankee Doodle" ditties and from sophisticated multilayered satire to slapstick and ribald humor. By the outbreak of hostilities, authors, playwrights, and artists on both sides engaged in a culture war employing a host of tropes, symbols, and personalities, real and imaginary, as comical weapons against their enemies. Together, they produced a contested vocabulary, fully familiar to the other side, as they dug their heels in and sought to rally their respective bases as well as fight for the hearts and minds of anyone who remained neutral. While recent work by Robert Parkinson has done much to show that the famous John Adams remark that "the revolution was in the minds of the people and this was affected from 1760 to 1775" was an exaggeration, surely American patriots had by 1775 crafted an incipient language of liberty that allowed them to feel a sense of shared destiny throughout the North American colonies. Humor helped forge the language and, perhaps more importantly, the antiauthoritarian sensibilities that allowed many Americans to imagine themselves as part of a forward looking and egalitarian "common cause."[80]

Humor and the Common Cause

Culture wars between American insurgents and their loyalist foes would continue doing the Revolutionary War (1775–1783), as Americans fought and died to realize their emerging national feelings. Indeed, overt hostilities turned what during the years of the imperial crisis had largely been a combination of rambunctious rioting and limited violence into a revolutionary and civil war. As Trumbell's *M'Fingal* demonstrates, although "Yankee Doodle" was originally a feature of the crowds, like other forms of vernacular culture from the period, it reverberated farther and wider and ultimately became central to the so-called common cause. With the help of print and the cultural brokers who wrote for and controlled the presses, "Yankee Doodle" and other crowd-forged humor—like so much other material traced by Parkinson in *The Common Cause*—continued to follow wherever American soldiers went and wherever patriot print culture reached. This was the point where the dialectical interaction between vernacular and elite cultures ushered in a nascent national culture. Thus, patriots of various stripes wove the humor and mirth of the revolutionary era into the ideological fabric of the emerging American community.[81]

As both sides in the conflict groped for the most poignant insults to hurl at their enemies, they found tropes associated with manhood particularly appealing, or—if they were the target of these attacks on their virility—infuriating. In fact, "Yankee Doodle" and tarring and feathering were both direct attacks on manhood. *Yankee* was originally a derogatory epithet conferred on New Englanders as provincial, country bumpkins, an application of the trope of the boorish "country clown" to New Englanders, while the term *doodle* was associated with failed manhood, as in the rooster's cock-a-doodle-do cant. Not incidentally, when crowds tarred and feathered their victims, they too rendered them roosters, a trope of comical, ostentatious, and abortive attempts at gentility in British imagination. .[82]

As it turned out, broad structures in the British world involving the intersection of manhood and class gave the upper hand in masculinity contests to the Americans. The British settlers in North American, more willing to embrace misrule and more comfortable with its subversive implications for their rebellion, also inflected the contest over manhood with revolutionary, antiauthoritarian impulses. The dynamics of this are perhaps best illustrated by the events, accounts, and cultural output surrounding the British general John Burgoyne, who arrived in Boston in 1775 with reinforcements during the patriots' almost year-long siege of the city. In him, the patriots found an ideal villain to spar with and around which to construct narratives. Burgoyne, aptly known as "Gentleman Johnny," was a rising man of fashion in British government circles who captured the outward-facing predicament of genteel manhood with his refined manners, endless ambition, and flamboyant airs. Even as he attempted to mark himself as a member of the gentry through refinement and politeness, Burgoyne found it increasingly difficult to maintain a firm grip on his manhood—at least as far as the Americans were concerned. The narrative of his affairs during the war demonstrates the vulnerability of genteel manhood and the context in which more simple and less refined Americans successfully harnessed the vocabulary of manhood to the common cause.[83]

For patriots, Burgoyne quickly became the quintessential effeminate and urbane specimen of English genteel culture, equipped with all the polish and refined trappings of London high society. In "A Voyage to Boston" a poem written in 1775 during the patriots' encirclement, Philip Morin Freneau casts Burgoyne and the colonial militiamen outside Boston as antithetical. Freneau especially mocks Brugoyne's pompous letter exchange with the American general Charles Lee conducted through the press:

> Hard by Burgoyne, his ample chair supplies,
> And seem'd to meditate in studious guise,
> As if again to grant the world to see,
> Long, dull, dry letters writ to Gen'ral Lee,
> Huge scrawls of words, thro' endless circuits drawn
> Unmeaning as the errand he's upon[84]

In a later version of the poem, Freneau adds the lines below, casting Burgoyne as an effeminate *fop*—a term associated at the time with the performative airs of corrupt, Frenchified gentlemen who had lost all touch with republican virtue:

> Is he to conquer—he subdue our land?—
> This buckram hero, with his lady's hand?
> By Cesars to be vanquish'd is a curse
> But by a scribbling fop—by heaven, is worse![85]

By contrast, Freneau in another poem lavished all the manly qualities he could marshal on the American soldier, juxtaposing British effeminacy and foppery with American virility. Here, too, he invoked the trope of the fop as a foil:

> Just in the center of the camp arose
> An elm whose shade invited to repose,
> Thither I rov'd, and at the cool retreat,
> A brave, tho' rough cast soldier chanc'd to meet;
> No fop in arms, no feather on his head,
> No glittering toys the manly warrior had,
> His auburne face the least employ'd his care,
> He left it to the females to be fair;

And thought the men whom shining trifles sway,
But pageant soldiers for a sun shine day.[86]

Later that year during the siege but before returning to England for the winter, Burgoyne wrote a farce titled the "Boston Blockade." In the only short excerpt that remains of the play, he introduces one of the characters, "Doodle"—who appears to be a local Bostonian betrayed by his patriot brethren—with the following ditty:

Ye tarbarrell'd lawgivers, yankified prigs,
Who are tyrants in custom, yet call yourselves Whigs;
In return for the favours you've lavish'd on me,
May I see you all hang'd upon *Liberty Tree*.
Mean time take example, decease from attack,
In war and in love we alike are betrayed,
And alike are the laughter of BOSTON BLOCKADE.[87]

The farce was performed in Boston on January 8, 1776, as part of an ongoing effort to provide diversions for British troops and as an affront to Puritans in the city who opposed the loyalist cause and viewed theater going as sinful. As the fragment and other accounts of the work suggest, Burgoyne sought to mock the rebels as crude and hypocritical.

While it is impossible to know the full extent of the assault waged by Burgoyne without his completed text, the piece proved sufficient to induce one lettered Patriot to in response write *The Blockheads: Or the Affrighted Officers* (1776).[88] Written after British forces evacuated Boston in 1776, the play satirizes the plight of the British troops and loyalists in Boston during the last days of the siege. The plot focuses primarily on two male characters, "Lord Dapper," a foppish representation of Lord Percy, another British commander stationed in Boston—Burgoyne had by then returned to England—and "Simple," a deceived common man who laments his choice to support the loyalists. The plot revolves around the plight of Simple, who suffers under the yoke of the women in his life—his deceitful wife and daughter, who for their own personal gain have persuaded Simple to join the Tory cause. Lord Dapper, the prototypical fop and rake, outdoes the two women's chicanery, seducing Simple's daughter and offering her and her mother the false hope of a refined aristocratic lifestyle. The audience soon learns that Dapper, of course, had no such intentions. Simple abandons his ties with his wife and daughter and seeks to atone for his failings.[89]

The play on the one hand illustrates the prevailing wartime sentiment in the colonies toward genteel culture—equated with corrupt and effete British decadence—and on the other depicts common provincial culture, associated with virtuous and manly colonial society.[90] In one of the arguments between Simple and his wife, he laments the loss of his farm, and she responds as follows:

> Now forsooth you are going upon your old whining scheme—because you see I am acquainted with the *gentry*, you begin on these canting topics—you are afraid I shall ask you for a silk gown, or a new cap; that I shall want to see the plays, &c . . . You may depend upon it, I shall begin to want these things, and shall expect no hesitation or denial. Do not think I am to lead my life like a mope, as when we were *rusty farmers*—we are now *gentle-folks*, and shall expect to do like gentle-folks . . . Come my dear, rouse yourself, don't think about your fat farm, let it go, it is all *dirty stuff*, only fit for *yankees*.[91]

To be a provincial hard-working Yankee, clearly, had become a rallying cry. As with so many other cultural products of the day, "Yankee Doodle"—with its celebration of new England simpletons and its appropriation after Lexington and Concord—made its way into the play. Toward the end of the piece, while British soldiers poke fun at their pitiful retreat from Boston, a reference to the British decision to abandon Boston in the spring of 1776 and regroup around New York, one of them remarks, "Ha ha ha—yankee doodle forever—I wish *Lord North* was here, to see his brave troops in their present plight, running away with their *breeches down*—who can help laughing at what a *tom fool's* errand we have been sent upon." Later in the same scene, another soldier comments, "*Burgoyne* could not have contrived a prettier *satyr*."[92]

By 1777 Burgoyne had made a name for himself throughout the colonies, as local papers jeered the flamboyant general everywhere he went. For instance, the *Pennsylvania Packet* listed a series of remarkable events from the previous year, among them that "General Burgoyne came over to America to coax the Gentlemen and to dance the Ladies into submission to the British Parliament."[93] Some accounts had it that Burgoyne had boasted before the king prior to leaving for his 1777 expedition in Canada that he could easily march through the colonies with five thousand soldiers. Thus, it was the stuff of satire when on October 17, 1777, Burgoyne surrendered at Saratoga after a miserable campaign, and his vanquished troops marched in defeat to the tune "Yankee Doodle"—played by Americans.[94] The Reverend Wheeler Case captured the spirit of the day in "The First Chapter of the Lamentations of General Burgoyne," a poem he wrote in the battle's wake:

> Yes, is this little spot of ground,
> Enclos'd by *Yankees* all around.
> With this five thousand—yes with ten,
> And these *Great Britain's* chosen men.

Case concluded the poem by referencing "Yankee Doodle":

> As they begin to march, as soon
> The conquerors all agree
> To sound the "Yankee Doodle" tune
> Upon the highest key[95]

Indeed, the revolution had become an American satire in which Yankees and other colonists emerged as simple, yet manly specimens, while the British played the role of the corrupt, effeminate villains.

By the same token, however, American gentlemen too would face a more formidable challenge after the revolution's conclusion, having to contend with a similar predicament and ultimately failing to uphold traditional British class divisions and mores in the United States. Here again, "Yankee Doodle" is instructive. During the revolution, the most popular sequence of stanzas, known as the Visit to Camp sequence, depicted a young New England country bumpkin visiting an army camp and encountering for the first time the supposedly great "wonders" of army life, such as cannons, drums, bayonets, and so on. While the song had fun with the provincial Yankee who knew nothing of the world and its machinations, when Americans sang it, they also reveled unapologetically in his fresh and sincere perspective, untainted by metropolitan corruption. In this vein, in the same sequence, the Yankee narrator encounters General Washington and his retinue. While the American bumpkin is awed by Washington's grandeur, the stanza also offers a dose of criticism for the haughty airs of colonial elites who sought to control and rein in the colonial upheaval:

> And there was captain Washington
> And gentlefolks around him,
> They say he's grown so tarnal proud,
> He will not ride without 'em.[96]

For all of Washington's attempts to pioneer a usable version of gentility suited for the new republic, he still had to share the stage with an American yokel who did not hesitate to mock his prideful airs.[97]

In the classic *Ideological Origins of the American Revolution* (1967), Bernard Bailyn proposed that the great heritage of the revolutionary era was a "contagion of liberty," which would in time sweep the new republic.[98] In other words, during the revolution, American rebels cultivated a new revolutionary and forward gazing variant of republicanism that hinged on unwavering commitments to freedom and equality. Associated with the revolution and the common cause, these convictions would continue to animate the thinking and even the mythology behind the new nation Americans forged. The success of tarring and feathering, effigy burnings, mock burials, and the emergence of "Yankee Doodle" as the de facto anthem of the American Revolution suggests that infectious mirth, or a contagion of laughter, helped drive the percolation and success of revolutionary language and ideals.

CHAPTER TWO

The Witty Few

Augustan Humor and the Politics of Exclusion

The elites of the early national period boasted a remarkable cast of revered leaders, the so-called founders—John Adams, Thomas Jefferson, Alexander Hamilton, and James Madison, to name a few—who set the tone for the political culture of the period. Their cohort is less well known for its ostentatious and reactionary literary scene and its decadent poets, but, among them, jolly cliques of flamboyant gentlemen cultivated high wit and indulged in hedonistic escapades in conjunction with serious debates over the future of the republic. In the early United States, groups of young literati founded like-minded coteries that celebrated sophisticated literary pranks, neoclassical verse, and a conservative view of contemporary politics. The members of these cliques saw themselves as the witty few who stood poised to fend off Edmund Burke's "swinish multitude," especially as the French Revolution appeared to spiral out of control in the 1790s. During the period between the end of the Revolutionary War (1774–83) and the War of 1812 (1812–15), their literary efforts emerged as a telling feature of the culture wars waged over the nature of the nascent United States. Comic literary pieces, an important part of the Federalists' cultural output of the day, defined an exclusive community of wit and humor that competed with and sought to curb the leveling logic of the revolutionary crowds and self-deprecating traditions that celebrated rustic provincialism.[1] This chapter traces the rise and fall of this tradition of Federalist humor as an influential presence in the public sphere of the early United States.

The first such group to attain national fame was the Hartford Wits, a group of Yale graduates brought together by literary bonds during the American Revolution and in its wake. Following their lead, several other groups sharing similar backgrounds and Federalist politics emerged predominantly around colleges and in the larger seaboard towns, but sometimes even in small rural towns, such as Walpole, New Hampshire. While some of the wits contributed a smattering of forgettable poems to local newspapers, others became lively voices offering an alternative vision of the young republic vis-à-vis the one propagated by American commoners and their allies in the Democratic-Republican Party, then emerging in opposition to the governing Federalist Party. Once the Democratic-Republicans came to power in 1801, these literary circles emerged as nodes of partisan dissent and a counterculture of sorts to the prevailing national currents.

Among these groups was the secretive Anchor Club in 1790s Philadelphia, to which William Cliffton, William Cobbett, and John Ward Fenno belonged. In Boston, the first such literary circle was the 1790s milieu of Thomas Paine (of Boston), J. S. J Gardiner, and Josiah Quincy III, followed later by the circle of literati that formed the Anthology Club in 1804 and included an older Gardiner as well as Joseph Smith Buckminster and William Smith Shaw. Two more circles emerged around the enigmatic Joseph Dennie, one in Walpole, after he moved there in 1795, attracting the participation of Royall Tyler and Thomas Green Fessenden, and the other in Philadelphia, where in 1801 he formed the Tuesday Club together with the likes of Charles Jared Ingersoll, Thomas Boylston Adams, and a young Nicholas Biddle. In New York, a tight-knit group of young wits formed the Lads of Kilkenny, which included the brothers William and Washington Irving, James Kirke Paulding, and Gulian Verplanck.[2] Goaded on by a conservative audience thirsty for literary buoyancy, they sought to produce, in the words of the Federalist luminary Fisher Ames, "satire and wit that would flash like the electrical fire" as it once did in Augustan-era England.[3]

If the trajectory of the political, street, and print cultures of the revolutionary era captured the increasingly antiauthoritarian commitments of emboldened American commoners, the cultural output of these Anglophile literati served as a rejoinder in the form of an elitist backlash, an attempt to reclaim American culture, society, and ultimately, of course, American politics. Whereas revolutionary humor, especially when embodied by the culture of the "joyous multitude," tended toward the many, the high-brow humor of the witty few challenged that vision, furnishing American elites with a refined and erudite alternative to the crude mediocrity of the masses. This elitist brand of humor featured flashy attempts at sophisticated wit that required more than a bit of learning to unpack. Contemporary wits infused them with explicit as well as implicit calls for the few to retake what was rightfully theirs from the forces of democracy and upward social mobility. As one contemporary cautioned in the verbose language the would-be Augustan wits made their own, "In a country, where splendour of mental embellishment can be totally eclipsed by the daub of a house, the varnish of a carriage, or the polish of buttons; where the stupid cant of a gilded dunce has charms more enamouring, than all the melody of an Orphean lyre, false and shallow notions will easily become public and influential." In other words, the stakes were high. If the few failed to fend off the forces of "mobocracy," the United States would become a land dominated by crude nouveau-riche "nabobs," doomed to languish in abject mediocrity.[4]

Indeed, as jolly, carefree, and insincere as the wits often sought to appear, a nervous, and even morbid, anxiety pervaded their satirical texts. Though wits in Augustan England typically felt most at home decrying the social mores around them, in America the situation seemed particularly dire. As the 1790s gave way to the 1800s, many increasingly suspected that in America, as Fenno, the Federalist editor of the *Gazette of the United States*, conceded, "Genius is a lowly, wild and neglected shrub, shooting up apparently by fantastic accident, amidst the confines of a dreary, desolate waste." Fenno elaborated in the same foreboding tone, "When an universal irruption of Gothicism upon any country, hath overpowered and decomposed all the energies and nobler faculties of the mind, as it seemeth here to have done, the case is hopeless; no morning dawn need be again looked for, but in the eventual purgation of the earth and the renovation of nature."[5] In 1803, some two years after President John Adams lost reelection to Thomas Jefferson, the defeated incumbent's son Thomas Boylston Adams lamented in no less stark terms, "Egyptian darkness was not more visible, than that which reigns over the future destinies of America."[6]

The literati's shrill condescension notwithstanding, such observations were not entirely wrong. Indeed, by the War of 1812, Augustan wit would largely disappear from American public life, beating a retreat to the private parlors and drawing rooms of East Coast brahmins. From that point on, the United States would become a nation where upwardly mobile social climbers could wield just as much if not more power than the descendants of patrician families. It would also become a country never shy about championing crude personalities and yokels as national icons. Regardless, the efforts of these often tiresome and blustering wits, even though they failed, remain worth noting.

Acknowledging cultural forms that the new nation pushed aside allows for a more accurate accounting of the shape and texture of the popular culture that would emerge in the United States by the antebellum period. Furthermore, examining alternative profiles of the kinds of cultural work humor performed permits fuller consideration of humor's fungible nature and potential. It also reveals that the honing and propagating of certain types of humor were neither inevitable nor simple. Rather, an array of Americans from many walks of life was required to innovate and participate in the production and dissemination of the patterns of humor and broader popular culture that would underscore the eventual course of republican self-rule in the United States.

"What Is This Wit, Which Must Our Cares Employ?"

In the early eighteenth century, the high point of the "age of wit" according to one scholar, Alexander Pope posed the question, "What is this wit, which must our cares employ."[7] The answers Pope offered up in the rest of "An Essay on Criticism" (1711) were witty, but like much else about wit, confusing and ambiguous. Britons revered wit, even as they hotly debated what exactly it was, how it worked, and its uses and abuses. In social gatherings and across the pages of numerous contemporary publications, some of the most revered literati in British history, including the likes of Joseph Addison, Alexander Pope, and Jonathan Swift, became famous for their wit and for their self-conscious appraisals of its nature and significance.[8] In this regard, assessments of wit appeared quite similar to some of the famous treatises from the period on republican society and its predicaments.

Both wit and British republican, or whig, ideology wallowed in similar contradictions and tensions, and the stakes for resolving and navigating them seemed to many greater than ever before. British whig discourse centered debates on how to best realize the public good, and for many contemporaries, wit was one of the most critical tools for achieving that goal.[9] Although at times synonymous with humor, wit was both less and more. It often implied oral or written gestures that produced mirth of a certain variety and imbued with a distinct intellectual rigor that required erudition and good judgment.

Thus, wit, for its champions, was much more than humor; it was a means of getting at the truth, of producing virtue and for attaining the common good. Furthermore, in the British world, wit emerged as a useful tool during a period that saw an emerging contest between state power and the republican ideal of a free commonwealth that championed a robust public sphere and the rights of the people vis-à-vis the monarch. As proponents of criticism, wits often found themselves negotiating and challenging the power of the state and its attempts to assert control over the public realm. In this context, wit offered intellectuals and critics of the state a veneer of humor that painted them innocuous, gay hedonists. Thus, clubs and coteries could hide behind wit even as they used it to challenge authority.[10]

As with many ideological formulations, perhaps the most explosive and tricky subject for the interwoven discourses of wit and republicanism was the question of power: who should hold power over whom and by what means? This was doubly true in the period following the civil wars and revolutions of the seventeenth-century British Empire that resulted in foundational transformations in its economy, society, and polity—the very matrices of power. The answers each of the discourses attempted to provide came with complementary forms of cognitive dissonance littered with contradictions, evasions, and ambiguities. For the emerging ruling gentry class that more-or-less cohered in Britain around the Glorious Revolution of 1688, which established the power of Parliament over monarchy, one of their most challenging tasks was reconciling the republican search for virtue and the common good with their class interests. Furthermore, since many of these same elites had recently wrested power from the monarch by invoking such constructs as the sovereignty of the people, natural rights, and liberty, they tended to take these ideas quite seriously. After all, they could hardly renege on them now that they held power.[11]

The gentry resolved the tension between their class interests and liberal commitments by contending that a republican society was highly volatile and that only certain conditions could produce a citizenry and leadership capable of upholding a political structure without legally entrenched hierarchies and a powerful monarch. These conditions of course essentially mirrored the circumstances of their class: the leaders of the republic should be wealthy, to maintain their financial independence, and thus the capacity for true selflessness; they should also be educated men of merit, to capably navigate society around the many pitfalls intrinsic to any regime, let alone a vulnerable republican one. Together these ideas morphed into the concept of a "natural aristocracy," as opposed to an inherited one, although in reality, the landed elites continued to exert vast and disproportionate power through inheritance. Wit was one of the most salient markers of this natural aristocracy. In this vein, the famous wits of the era were the most sagacious cultural brokers of the period, helping to uncover deceit and hypocrisy and lead society away from ruin by applying their genius for the betterment of society.[12]

One reason the intellectual gymnastics of a natural aristocracy proved successful was that they also enlisted support for the new social order from the emerging middling classes, who saw in the ideal of merit, implied by a natural aristocracy, a path for social mobility.[13] Meanwhile, the success of some men of "wit and genius" from middling backgrounds, such as Benjamin Franklin and Samuel Johnson, stood out as examples of the unparalleled promise of British society, proving that whig ideas uplifted deserving men for the benefit of all. Not surprisingly, both Franklin's autobiography and James Boswell's celebrated biography of Johnson became two of the most iconic books of the late eighteenth century and beyond.

Thus, many young would-be American patricians, especially those armed with a college education, saw wit as the best way to introduce their arrival as a new generation of accomplished elites. After all, in the colonies, where few could boast of aristocratic lineage let alone an aristocratic title, a college education was one of the most prestigious markers of gentility. Surely, it entitled graduates to expect to acquire positions of privilege and power in the new nation. Since few in the United States had wealth enough to lead the idealized life of genteel leisure that would truly mark them as gentlemen, they had to undertake the more humdrum calling of serving as ministers, doctors, or lawyers. These, many suspected, were hardly occupations befitting a true, ruling gentry. Moreover, whereas humor's capacity for noncommittal ambiguity helped protect wits in Britain from state repression, wit lost some of its multifaceted nuance in America, where there was less need to temper criticism of the state and where most elites felt that the revolution had gotten out of hand. In postrevolutionary America, therefore, neoclassical Augustan wit would become more unequivocally elitist in orientation and part of a broader cultural program to curb what youths of the patrician class deemed as the forces of mobocracy.

As an alternative scheme for sorting the wheat from the chaff, young literate Americans turned to witty effusions. They did so within the broader conceptualization of a republic of letters, an idea cultivated by British literati in Augustan-era England that imagined educated men of letters plumbing the long-hallowed tradition of learning and literature stretching back to antiquity.[14] Indeed, this was not an individualized effort, as many of the wits preferred to collaborate and partake in a community of letters and wit that transcended time and space; they therefore often published pseudonymously or collaboratively. Even more so than in Britain, where wits were just as often associated with the emerging middle classes and their interests vis-à-vis the aristocracy, theirs was a class-oriented effort of self-styled elites. By fostering a public sphere drawing from the greatest tomes of knowledge and by producing new knowledge, the literati envisioned an elite class ready to provide vital guidance to any society truly invested in the public good. Their vision for the republic was a Platonic one, and in their enlightened republic, Americans would appreciate a class of men of "learning and genius"—men who bore the stamp of wit—as best equipped to meet the challenges that loomed around every corner.

In the nascent republic, witty effusions converged with the ebullient new nationalist orientation of the revolutionary period. As Linda Kerber astutely noted, during the early national period, "Americans frequently used literary and oratorical accomplishment as an index of national greatness." Aspiring to an American Augustan age to rival Augustan Rome and England, those bred on whig teachings yearned for a cadre of literary giants in the mold of Rome's Virgil, Horace, and Ovid and England's Pope, Addison, Swift, and Johnson).[15] As the exuberant era of revolution and ratification merged with the euphoria of youth, many college graduates and other aspiring men of letters thought "Why not me?," or as circles of eager young men convened in giddy mirth, "Why not us?"

The Hartford Wits

Some of the earliest nationalist literary efforts during the revolutionary period were by young college graduates trying their hand at the epic poetry genre they had revered in college.[16] Many took a stab at it, but the Hartford Wits did so with more urgency and diligence than anyone else. Indeed, two members of the group, Timothy Dwight and Joel Barlow, would pursue epic poetry far beyond their college years, writing ambitious neoclassical verse. Dwight in *The Conquest of Canaan* (1784) and *Greenfield Hill* (1794) and Barlow in *The Vision of Columbus* (1787) and *Columbiad* (1807), all full-length poems, attempted to give Americans the epic verse that in their minds was needed to signal the United States' arrival on the world stage "among the powers of the earth."[17] Hard as they tried, however, epic poetry of their grave and ostentatious variety never quite succeeded. The reviews were tepid and sales few.[18]

Meanwhile, during the revolution a different form of epic poetry—satirical, mock-epic verse—proved more successful with American audiences. Dwight's college friend and collaborator John Trumbull proved particularly nimble at this genre and tone. Trumbull wrote numerous pieces of short satirical verse, but his most famous and successful efforts were relatively long mock-heroic poems in the mode of the famous satires by Samuel Butler, Alexander Pope, and Charles Churchill. The first by Trumbull was *The Progress of Dulness* (1772), followed a few years later by *M'fingal* (1776; completed version, 1782). While *The Progress of Dulness* offered a critique of education in the colonies and lacked explicit national or revolutionary themes, *M'fingal* became one of the most successful patriot pieces from the revolution, with new print editions issued for many years thereafter.[19]

Trumbull's success with mock-epic poetry, together with growing pressure within conservative circles to lash out against what even the anti-Federalist Elbridge Gerry called an "excess of democracy" during the 1780s, inspired the piece often referred to as *The Anarchiad* (1786–87), the Hartford Wits' most famous collaborative effort.[20] Unlike the quite polished *M'Fingal*, however, *The Anarchiad* was a somewhat disjointed collaborative series of twelve installments appearing in local newspapers under the title "American Antiquities" over the course of about a year. Applying a combination of satirical prose and verse toward conservative, antidemocratic political ends, the first installments appeared in 1786, during the early stage of Shays' Rebellion, the rural insurrection that challenged Massachusetts' establishment, and the last installments against the backdrop of the Constitutional Convention in the summer of 1787. Together the pieces denounced the anarchy, as the authors saw it, fomented by Shays' rebels and probably constituted the most deliberate and notable literary intervention in the debates that led to the Constitutional Convention and its centralized government agenda. In sum, it was the first important piece of Federalist literature.[21]

More so than *The Anarchiad*'s conservative content, its collaborative and elaborate ruse marked the emergence of circles of jolly wits brought together through shared mirth to play out their Augustan fantasies. The work's central conceit is the alleged "recent discovery" in the Ohio Valley "of a great number of papers, manuscripts &c., whose preservation through such a long lapse of years . . . must be deemed marvelous." "Among these relics of antiquity," the fictional antiquarian author finds "an epic poem, complete" and

titled *The Anarchiad*, on the subject of the "restoration of chaos and sub-
stantial night in twenty-four books."[22] For most of the series, the fictional
author entertains his readers by sharing excerpts of the epic poem he has
discovered as well as his own commentary and analysis about it. Though
the contextualizing prose of the piece usually maintains the ruse that it is
ancient and written by pre-Columbian, Native American poets, the poem's
"excerpts" quickly shed any pretense by explicitly invoking contemporary
themes. Thus, as mock-epic poetry written from a Federalist perspective, it
broaches such issues as Shays' Rebellion, opposition to paper money, and the
underlying notion that democracy begets anarchy.

The men who became identified with the Hartford Wits had been in touch
with each other prior to *The Anarchiad*, but it was the collaborative effort of
Trumbull, Joel Barlow, Lemuel Hopkins, and David Humphreys on the
mock-epic that first prompted American audiences to view them as a group of
American wits, first as the Wicked Wits and later as the Hartford Wits or
Connecticut Wits. Associated with them through literary, friendship, and
regional ties, Timothy Dwight—by then the accomplished author of the *Conquest of Canaan*—joined the mix. A later generation of young, Connecticut-
based wits carried on the tradition under the guidance of Hopkins, who issued
his pointed satirical thrusts through the 1790s, at which time Richard Alsop,
Theodore Dwight, and Elihu Hubbard Smith also became Hartford Wits.[23]
Now Americans, too, could boast of a group of wits in the Augustan tradition
of the British Scriblerus Club and the *Spectator* magazine. England had John
Arbuthnot, Pope, and Swift, who together collaborated on the satirical *Memoirs of Martinus Scriblerus*, and it could boast of Addison and Steele, who created the persona of the Spectator for their magazine bearing the same name,
and America now had Barlow, Dwight, Humphreys, and Trumbull.

Much like Addison, Steele, and the Scriblerians and numerous other coteries who cultivated their witty camaraderie around fictive personas and
inside jokes, American men of letters reveled in *The Anarchiad* as a literary
prank. It drew elation, first from the wits themselves, but also from all those
who could participate in the broader real and imagined communities of
the republic of letters. Of course, to fit in, one also had to enjoy the conservative content of the piece. Indeed, reports suggested that *The Anarchiad* was
passed around as gentlemen debated these very topics in convention halls
during the drafting and ratification of the Constitution.[24]

The fun did not stop there. Alongside satirical jabs at a host of well-known
local, national, and international foes, other references and asides were added

to *The Anarchiad* to stoke the mirth of the learned reader. The first installment sets the tone by satirizing Philadelphia's Philosophical Society, presenting its alleged new finding as part of a host of "wonderful inexhaustible
materials" discovered in recent years by the "society of critics and antiquar-
ians" to which the author purports to belong. The author remarks, "One of
our worthy associates has favored the public with a minute and accurate
description of [a] monstrous new-invented animal [a possible reference to
Jefferson, who had recently published *Notes on the State of Virginia* (1785)] . . .
Another has regaled his readers with a most notable catfish," and a "third
has brought them acquainted with a hermit who surpasses all other her-
mits in longevity." A bit later in the same piece—after presenting the discovery of *The Anarchiad*, which the author calls a work of the "first rank in
merit amongst the productions of human genius"—he notes, "In a future
essay, I shall attempt to prove that Homer, Virgil, and Milton, have borrowed many of their capital beauties from it."

Of course, the excerpts from the piece were written by none other than the
Wits themselves, in vying to elevate American literature to the status of Augustan Rome and Britain. In a further comical twist, after presenting the first
excerpt, parts of which ring similar to Alexander Pope's mock-epic *The Dunciad* (1728), the author remarks with a wink, "The critical reader will probably have already observed, that the celebrated English poet, Mr. Pope, has
proven himself a noted plagiarist, by copying the preceding ideas, end even
couplets almost entire, into his famous poem called 'The Dunciad.'"[25] Indeed,
as American writers bent on meeting an impossible bar set by European
literati, the Wits were more than happy to have a bit of fun at their own
expense, so long as they came across as clever and erudite. The more readers understood the various layers of their references, the more the wits drew
the reader into their community of gay wit—unless of course, they were its
target, in which case the idea was to cast them as outsiders to the republic
of letters and its jolly and erudite community.

Anti-Jacobin Verse

Shays' Rebellion inspired *The Anarchiad*, but the French Revolution and its
reverberations in the United States during the 1790s lent even more fodder
and urgency to the Federalist literati, whose Augustan mock poetry served
as the preferred vehicle for witty attacks. While some of their works maintained the kind of artistic detachment that Augustan wits revered and tried
to maintain, other pieces proved far more shrill and personal, hardly consti-

tuting a serious artistic effort. Regarding the former, the young Philadel-phia wit William Cliffton—hailed by some as the "American Dryden"—versified with more flair than most, usually employing mock-epic poetry to attack democracy in broad strokes, rather than the more vulgar practice of personal attack. Moreover, when he did round on specific individuals, they were for the most part notable figures clearly worthy of criticism, according to conservative standards, such as Thomas Paine, author of some of the most radical treatises of the day, and the opportunist French diplomat Tallyrand, and often only through suggestive references. At other times, he attacked groups as stock characters, such as Irish immigrants and French philosophes, but seldom specific persons by name. In one typical salvo, from "Rhapsody of the Times," Cliffton invokes Paine's *Age of Reason* (1795), rather than the author himself, and cautions in suggestive language against "bold reformers" who "make appear"

> That rapine, sacrilege, and treason,
> Do constitute the Age of Reason . . .
> 'Tis they who strive to patch and press
> Democracy in freedom's dress,
> To lead the multitude astray
> They clothe her out in colours gay . . .
> But lo beneath her placid mien
> The fiend licentiousness is seen:
> See frantic horror at her side,
> Her hands with guiltless blood bedy'd[26]

Cliffton ends the segment by exclaiming that ultimately in a democracy, even "the noblest man becomes a brute."[27]

Similarly in another satirical poem, *Chimeriad*, Cliffton mock-celebrates the witch Chimeria, a metaphor for French philosophy, without naming spe-cific figures. Turning to symbolism, he blames enlightened philosophy for ushering in a desolate landscape in France and potentially in the United States, "where never cheerful sound composed the soul" and "blind faction burrows in her secret hole."[28] He continues,

> Curst is the spot, upon famish'd ground,
> No flower is seen, not one loan leaf is found,
> But scragged rocks with human sculls between,
> Swell the wild horrors of the bloody scene."[29]

Cliffton insinuates in vivid poetry that the United States is becoming such a wretched, democratic place.

As with *Chimeriad* and following on the heels of *The Anarchiad*—itself inspired by the *The Rolliad* (1784–85) and Pope's *The Dunciad* (1728)—the Federalists tended to use the alleged voice of their enemies against them, the central conceit of the mock-heroic form. To stamp such pieces as part of the Augustan tradition of mock-epics, they often turned to the "-iad" titular ending, which in the case of *The Anarchiad*, for instance, purports to celebrate anarchy. Thus, they gave the literary world an unending parade of other such titles—among them *The Democratiad, The Jacobiniad, The Milkiad, The Porcupiniad*, and *The Spunkiad*. Meanwhile, *The Baeviad* and *The Maeviad*, by the British author William Gifford, were two pieces particularly favored by Federalists. Certainly, some of the mock-epics were only marginally partisan, and one piece, *The Porcupiniad*, was a retaliatory Republican attack on the Federalist editor William Cobbett. Nevertheless, many more satires in verse were Federalist literary efforts condemning the French Revolution and its allies in the United States, including J. S. J. Gardiner's *The Jacobiniad* (1795), Lemuel Hopkins's *The Democratiad* (1795), and Cliffton's *Chimeriad*.³⁰

Unlike Cliffton's relatively artistically removed and tame pieces, *The Democratiad* and Gardiner's *The Jacobiniad* are more common for the period: quite shrill, if disguised as erudite, personal attacks on the authors' most hated republican enemies. Of the two, *The Jacobiniad* is the more elaborate and closest to its model, *The Anarchiad*. The piece, an uneven assemblage of poetry and prose, appeared as ten installments in the *Federal Orerry*, the Boston newspaper edited at the time by Gardiner's fellow wit Paine. Like its inspiration, it also combines excerpts and commentary on an alleged epic poem, *The Jacobiniad*, which "relates the rise of Jacobinism; its progress; its present situation in Europe and America; and describes the principal supporters of it in both countries."³¹ Though an attempt was made to keep up the ruse of an epic poem celebrating the French Revolution, the title itself—a reference to the Jacobin clubs that helped orchestrate the rebellion—easily betrays the tone and agenda from the outset. By then the label "Jacobin" had become a Federalist rallying cry, a stand-in for what they saw as the horrors of the revolution—the chimera of democracy, mobocracy, and anarchy. More specifically, Gardiner took aim at the Democratic societies, the clubs emerging across the country that drew inspiration from the French Revolution and the Jacobin clubs. In fact, much of the piece is an attack on local members of the Massachusetts Constitutional Society, Boston's version of these Democratic societies.[32]

Pulling few punches, attack pieces like *The Jacobiniad* also show that during the 1790s, blatant elitism came quite naturally to some young conservative writers. Not only did Gardiner make every attempt to demonstrate his erudition through numerous references to a host of classical works and by interspersing Latin in his texts—as was the norm with such pieces—he also explicitly attacked specific members of the local Democratic society as uneducated and of inferior status. Though Augustan etiquette held personal attacks to be a vulgarity beneath true wits and required veiled attempts to assert one's intellectual superiority, many American contemporaries like Gardiner could hardly suppress their rage and anxiety. For example, in one installment of the series, he makes fun of his relatively uneducated antagonists in the Massachusetts Constitutional Society by creating a fake, error-strewn "copy of a compact to be signed by every candidate, previous to his admission into the constitutional society (alias jacobin club) at Boston." The spelling mistakes are on a level even conspicuous for late eighteenth-century standards. After hearing of the rage his attacks had generated, Gardiner noted in the next installment that since the *"gentlemen* (we humbly beg pardon if we have miscalled them)" of the constitutional society "are neither pleased with [our] poem itself nor with our remarks on it," they "appointed a committee, to write an answer to the *Jacobiniad.*" With unrestrained condescension, he claims that the committee "consisted of *seven* persons, containing *every* member of the club, who could *read* and *write,* (the secretary included)." In another cheap shot, Gardiner notes that when discussing what form of verse to use for the piece, one member of the committee who "consulted a poetical acquaintance," suggests "Mr. POPE, as a writer of approved excellence." However, "At the sound of POPE, they were extremely alarmed; and having never heard of the poet of that name, immediately concluded that their brother meant the *Pope of Rome.*" The men of the society, he insinuates, were so lowly that they had never heard of Alexander Pope, the greatest British wit in recent memory. Similarly, in an earlier installment, he also resorts to ridicule in asserting that "the former president of the *jacobin* club, was a *cobbler,*" and while "well qualified . . . for *mending shoes,* we cannot think him equally qualified for *mending laws,* of giving a new *sole* to a constitution."[33]

Wit in Periodical Essays

As many of the hybrid pieces of poetry and prose demonstrate, it was often more the prose adjoining *The Anarchiad* or *The Jacobiniad* that proved successful at delivering light-hearted and mirth-inducing moments. Indeed, American authors often employed humor-inflected, jolly prose more deftly than poetry, which is inherently more difficult to control or structure. Many writers sought to tap the vibrant Augustan tradition of witty periodical essays in the mold of the pseudonymous essays of Joseph Addison and Richard Steele, Samuel Johnson, and John Hawkesworth, to name a few. Around the turn of the nineteenth century, other models of comedic prose also appealed to American authors, including comedy of manners and the picaresque, but periodical essays stood out in popularity.

Once more following Augustan precedents, American authors attempted to enliven their prose with layers of wit and literary ploys. The suggestive pseudonym was the most basic ruse that almost all of them, including "serious" essay writers, adopted. The selection of a pseudonym involved contriving a fictive authorial persona as an alter ego. Thus, Steele wrote as Isaac Bickerstaff and together with Addison as the Spectator, while Johnson assumed the personas of Rambler and the Idler and, together with Hawkesworth and others, the Adventurer. Likewise, in the early United States, Joseph Dennie assumed the guises of the Farrago, the Lay Preacher, and Oliver Oldschool. J. S. J. Gardiner used the Restorator. Timothy Dwight occasionally wrote as Farmer Johnson; William Biglow as Charley Chatterbox; William Cobbett as Peter Porcupine; Thomas Green Fessenden as Thomas Spunkey; Judith Sargent Murray as the Gleaner; Washington Irving as Jonathan Oldstyle. The idea was to construct a character with whom readers would grow familiar and whose essays they looked forward to, and even relied on, for entertainment as well as moral improvement.[34]

Confirming the notion that these essays were part alter ego, the genre of the lively periodical essay was often of two minds, vacillating between the moral and the whimsical. The ideal was to strike a careful witty balance that ultimately delivered a clear moral thrust when taken as a whole.[35] Typically, however, most young men bent on irreverent, giddy salvos of wit found themselves gravitating toward the whimsical, while the moral components of their essay became an afterthought. Both the impulses and the stakes involved are well captured by the career of Dennie, the most famous essayist in the United States in the 1790s and considered by some the "American Addison."

Living in Charlestown, near Boston, during the first half of the 1790s, Dennie struck a carefree, and sometimes even hedonist, tone under the guise of the Farrago, publishing a series of essays in a few local newspapers. Invoking the work of the essayists Addison and Steele, who wrote with "suavity" and "sprightliness," and Johnson and Hawkesworth, who demonstrated a "sublime morality," Dennie professed his intention to provide moral guidance, but often disingenuously, and ultimately proved far more attached to whimsical and verbose digressions in the manner of his favorite author, Laurence Sterne. Thus, he often resorted to a steady dose of witticisms, such as confessing his intent, in his first Farrago essay, to "fix volatility, and rouse indolence, neither too abstruse for the young, too prolix for the busy nor too grave for the fair." While at times striking an ostensibly graver tone, he upends the effect by subsequently expressing a preposterous effort to convey "more useful knowledge to mankind than all the ponderous tomes of Aristotle." Likewise, the Farrago advises both "indolence" and "mental improvement," admitting that essays are both a "waste" and an "improvement" of time. Indeed, the Farrago consistently rebukes—and then champions—his own hedonism and idleness, at one point weaving the two seemingly contradictory perspectives by formulating an ideal of "strenuous indolence" as a prerequisite for literary genius.[36]

Other American essayists followed Dennie's lead, often invoking him and his well-known jolly indolence in a knowing manner, as was customary in such essays. Of course, Dennie himself had merely taken up themes introduced by Oliver Goldsmith, Johnson, and Sterne under such carefree names as the Idler or Rambler or the more droll-sounding Tristram Shandy, respectively. In the first issue of *Salmagundi: Or, the Whim-Whams and Opinions of Launcelot Longstaff, Esq. and Others* (1807)—the pet project of the brothers Washington and William Irving and James Kirke Paulding—the fictional editor Launcelot Langstaff, who delivers his essays while lounging in his "elbow chair," echoes the more-than-a-decade-old first essay of Dennie's Farrago, on the sprightly and even hedonistic intent of the publication. "If in the course of this work, we edify and instruct, and amuse the public; so much the better for the public," asserts Langstaff. He also promises, however, "If we moralize, it shall be but seldom; and on all occasions we shall be more solicitous to make our readers laugh than cry; for we are laughing philosophers, and clearly of the opinion, that wisdom, true wisdom, is a plump, jolly dame, who sits in her arm-chair, laughs right merrily at the farce of life and takes the world as it goes."[37] Though Farrago's persona was not quite suited to the tastes of New Englanders in the 1790s, *Salmagundi*'s jolly wit became a hit with New York literati during its one-year run.[38]

Meanwhile, in the second half of the 1790s, Dennie assumed a more successful literary persona, the Lay Preacher, demonstrating the advantages of striking a more moral tone, especially in New England, where Dennie lived until moving to Philadelphia in 1800. Though the witty prose of the Farrago essays best fit Dennie's inclination and talent, by 1795 he had dropped the character after realizing that such unabashed genteel wit did not comport with his New England readership. As he wrote to his mother in 1797, scolding himself and his region and country, "To imagine that a refined and classical style of writing will be encouraged here is absurd." Therefore, he searched for a different voice more palatable to his audience. Accordingly, he assumed the Lay Preacher persona, whose "sermons" advocate traditional values packaged with Republican gravitas. Dennie explained his design in the above letter to his mother: "I thought I would attempt to be useful, by exhibiting truths in a plain dress to the common people."[39] Published as the opening contribution in each edition of the *Farmer's Weekly Museum*, the newspaper Dennie began editing in 1796 in Walpole, New Hampshire, the Lay Preacher essays demonstrate a significant degree of restraint in both form and content.

Dennie limited his use of levity and wit and almost exclusively referenced biblical texts, rather than Augustan or classical writings. Following the well-established and respectable genre of the sermon, the Lay Preacher essays begin with a biblical quote that he subsequently explicates by extracting a moral imperative for his news-reading "congregation." Since the newspaper was avowedly Federalist, and Dennie himself did not hide his partisanship, the Lay Preacher would often weave disdain for the spirit of democracy and praise for the Federalist government into his sermons. These, however remained generally tame, as one might expect from a reserved and responsible figure. The Lay Preacher made Dennie the most famous American essayist of the day and helped propel the *Farmer's Weekly Museum* to national success. Thus, a small country paper and its editor, based in New Hampshire, emerged as a formative Federalist voice during the second half of the 1790s.[40]

Dennie's presence in New Hampshire, coupled with his newspaper editorship, made the Upper Connecticut River Valley an unlikely center for American literati. As with the Lower Connecticut River Valley and the presence of the Hartford Wits, it emerged as a center of jolly, literary collaboration. Furthermore, this group of wits ratcheted up the conceit of periodical essay writing by creating a fictive community of witty essayists who contributed to the local newspaper, each contriving their own fictional characters. In this vein, Fessenden, attending nearby Dartmouth at the time, assumed the pseudonym of Simon Spunkey, Isaac Story was Peter Quince, and John Curtis Chamberlain wrote as the Hermit. Most notably, Royall Tyler—author of the play *The Contrast* (1787) and the picaresque novel *The Algerine Captive* (1797), who had recently moved to nearby Brattleboro, Vermont—collaborated with Dennie on "The Shop of Masseurs Colon and Spondee," a recurring section of the paper that often featured acerbic attacks against the rising spirit of democracy. [41]

For most would-be wits, the combination of real and fictive communities—with the help of pet periodicals—best delivered on their Augustan fantasies to forge a community of friendship, wit, and genius in the likeness of the bonds between Addison and Steele or Pope and Swift. Although numerous circles of wits attempted to embody this model, those created through the publications edited by Dennie, the *Farmer's Weekly Museum* and later the *Port Folio*, and even more so by Washington Irving, *Salmagundi*, probably best lived up to Augustan formulas of wit.

Ambivalent Yankees, Ambivalent Nationalists

Boston's literary scene in the 1790s demonstrated the diversity of Federalism even in Congregationalist-dominated New England. Leading the way were three of the period's most colorful conservative young men of letters: Joseph Dennie (before he moved to Walpole in 1795), J. S. J. Gardiner, and Thomas Paine (who would change his name to Robert Treat Paine Jr. in 1800 to distinguish himself from the "odious" radical Thomas Paine). Unlike the Hartford Wits, who were largely traditional New England Congregationalists—Timothy Dwight would eventually become a leading authority in Congregationalism—the members of this group rebelled against Congregational hegemony while at the same time maintaining a socially conservative outlook. As a leader of the Episcopal Church in New England, Gardiner embodied an alternative to Congregationalism. Dennie, who preferred Episcopalianism himself, detested Puritans as the "Jewish and canting and cheating descendants of those men, who during the reign of *Stuart fled away* from the claims of the creditor, from the tythes of the church, from their allegiance to their sovereign and from their duty to their God." Meanwhile, Paine, a notorious man of fashion and supporter of the theater, was the bane of Boston Puritans and is said to have referred to that "vandal spirit of puritanism." Furthermore, both Gardiner and Paine campaigned in favor of opening a theater in Boston in the face of Puritan opposition and proved themselves to be avid theater goers once it opened. Paine even wrote and performed the prologue with which the theater was inaugurated in February 1794. He would also marry, much to the disgust of Boston's Puritans, including his own father, the actress Eliza Baker.[42]

Around the turn of the century, these three wits—Paine still in his twenties and Dennie and Gardiner straddling thirty—captured the peculiar combination of flamboyant young men of conservative sensibilities. Iconoclastic and irreverent toward local authorities, they were also old souls. Paine at one point lamented the "decay of manners" in America, stressing that there was "as wide a difference between the old school and the new, as there was between the polished ease of the reign of Augustus and the rude turbulence of the epoch of the Gracchi."[43] Dennie, in a touch of self-conscious levity, chose Oliver Oldschool as his pseudonym at the age of thirty-two.

Indeed, even as some men of letters were forward, or westward, looking, waxing in epic poetry that followed George Berkeley's famous mantra, "Westward the course of empire takes its way," many young Federalists gazed eastward and backward in time toward Britain's Augustan period. While the Hartford Wits drew influence from Berkeley and rehearsed similar themes, others—and at times the Hartford Wits as well—wistfully hoped to curb the increasingly progressive elements underscoring the American experiment, especially once they suspected that the republic taking shape before their eyes would have no place for true genius and wit. Such reactionary sympathies were bound to complicate the Federalist version of US nationalism, especially after Thomas Jefferson's election as president in 1800.

The Federalists had for the most part controlled the politics of the 1790s and lost in 1800 to the Democratic-Republicans by a slim margin. As the 1790s had progressed, they were ill equipped to tackle the growing dissent with equanimity, and disaffected voices gained momentum; many leading gentlemen felt they had lost their grip on American society. Worse yet, they experienced an increasing sense of alienation from the democratic, and to them boorish, convictions that seemed to be seeping into the very foundation of American culture. In sum, for men of letters who had long nurtured imagined and real literary bonds with British counterparts and the British-

Augustan tradition, the imagined community of the young republic they perceived seemed less and less compelling. When a few months before the 1800 election it appeared that the Democratic-Republicans were gaining momentum, one young Federalist attempted to reassure himself, writing, "I do not believe that the Most High will permit a howling atheist to sit at the head of this nation." When a few weeks later the same New England pastor got wind of an erroneous wishful rumor that Jefferson had died, he confided in his diary, "It is to be hoped that it is true."[44] In time, even for some of the most avid nationalists, such morbid thoughts prompted questions about the national project altogether. Just a few years into Jefferson's presidency, even the indefatigable Federalist leader Fisher Ames succumbed "to the apathy that benumbs my friends . . . I will try opium with the rest of them." He concluded fatalistically, "Our country is too big for union, too sordid for patriotism, too democratic for liberty."[45]

Every nationalism harbors tensions and numerous forms of sectional impulses. While at times sectionalism can reside quite comfortably under the imagined construct of a nation and even reinforce the idea of it, at other times allegiances can be seriously tested. As historians of early US nationalism have shown, Federalism for the most part constituted a certain version of nationalism that reinforced both a New England identity as well as the idea of the nation as an indivisible union in the mind of its denizens.[46] It is also clear, however, that certain stress points led some Federalists to dabble not only with radical sectionalism, but also with genuine anti-nationalist sympathies, leading them to develop a counter-culture somewhat at odds with broader American sentiments.[47] While historians often focus on New-England sectionalism with good cause, the notion of the republic of letters, and of wit, was another form of allegiance that tested Federalists. If men of letters in early America viewed themselves part of a transhistorical and transnational community of learning, it stood in potential conflict with the imagined community of the United States and in solidarity with Britain.

One option was to do as the renegade Hartford Wit Joel Barlow did: jump ship to the Democratic-Republicans and endorse a more Franklinian version of wit and republicanism that held higher hopes for commoners to achieve true virtue.[48] Meanwhile, others, like the brothers Timothy and Theodore Dwight, held fast both to New England identity and to nationalism, envisioning New England mores and traditions as the guiding force for the nation. They did so all the way through the infamous Hartford Convention (1814–15), which the Federalists had organized in opposition to the War of 1812 but in the end marginalized them politically for their alleged treason.[49] While extreme, Dennie's case lies at the other end of the spectrum, offering broader insights into conservative Federalists, who at times surely entertained similar ambivalent feelings toward the young American republic.

Dennie was an eccentric character who felt out of place in the United States. By the end of the 1790s, and certainly early 1800s, he, like some other "high Federalists," demonstrated a growing allergy to all things American and a tendency to embrace all things English. Despite his continued efforts to establish a community of refined and lettered men in the United States, he increasingly bemoaned his missed opportunities at greater literary success, blaming American culture and society for limiting him. As one of the leading wits and Federalist editors of his day, he could hardly afford to reveal his true feelings, although one could sometimes glimpse them between the lines of his published materials. Far more explicit, some of his private correspondences, especially with his mother, reveal striking confessions.

In 1797, during Dennie's peak of success as editor of the *Farmer's Weekly Museum*, he complained to his mother, "In my editorial capacity, I am obliged to the nauseous task of flattering republicans; but at bottom, I am a malcontent, and consider it a serious evil to have been born among the Indians & Yankees of New England." A few years later, in 1800, in a letter to his parents, he noted wistfully, "Had the *Revolution* not happened; had I continued a subject to the king, had I been fortunately born in *England* . . . my fame would have been enhanced . . . But in this *Republic*, this region . . . what can men of liberality and letters expect but such polar icy treatment, as I have experienced." By contrast, later in the same letter he commends the English character, as opposed to that of the Americans, as "the most honest, the most generous, the most frank and liberal," and further proclaimed, "Foul is that day in our calendar, and bitterly are those *patriotic*, selfish and Indian traitors to be cursed who instigated the wretched populace to declare the 4th day of July 1776, a day of independence."[50]

Few Federalists evinced deep dislike for the United States publicly or privately, but Dennie and others made their ambivalence known in nuanced ways. One peculiar, albeit quite common way was to lash out against the sense that the American creed had become obsessed with the prosaic world of business and money making. This was in fact a typical talking point leveled at Americans by foreign visitors, but also one taken up quite avidly by ambivalent nationalists.[51] As noted, Dennie, for one, employed several different witty fictive personas over the years who advised both "indolence" and "mental improvement." Even as the tame Lay Preacher, he artfully starts one "sermon" by betraying his own indolence in sharing his supposed struggle to write that very sermon—about indolence. Too much business activity and too much social mobility could undermine the kind of organic, pastoral, and traditional society that Dennie envisioned when assuming the persona of the Lay Preacher. "Daring and impudent as it may appear in this leveling age, to avow respect for birth or talents," he laments in one of his many Burkean moments, "I shall not . . . say a word to the prejudice of the ancient and honourable families . . . but shall wish them a quiet repose on their ancient foundations, and that neither a Frenchman nor a Virginian should abridge their immunities, nor disturb their possession." "Restlessness," the Lay Preacher sermonizes, "is ever a capital defect in character . . . 'Then where, my dear countrymen are you going,' and why do you wander?"[52]

The authors of *Salmagundi* employed similar devices that made them all the rage with Federalist audiences during its short, 1807 run. In the hands of brothers William and Washington Irving and James Kirke Paulding, the magazine was the closest publication the United States had to Britain's revered *Spectator*, after which it was modeled, including its set of fictive personas. Striking a leisurely and detached tone, its writers ensured the public from the outset "that so soon as we get tired of reading our own works, we shall discontinue them without the least remorse; whatever the public may think of it." This they did, after issuing twenty irregular numbers in a noncommittal fashion. In a similar vein, when writing for *Salmagundi*, both Paulding and the Irvings, above all else, did not want it to appear as if they had any financial interest in their literary pet project. That would be much too vulgar—and American. As they put it in the introductory note to the reader in the first issue, "We beg the public particularly to understand, that we solicit no patronage. We are determined, on the contrary, that patronage shall be entirely on our side. We have nothing to do with the pecuniary concerns of the paper; its success will yield us neither pride nor profit—nor will its failure occasion to us either loss or mortification."[53] In addition, the three authors did not want to appear to have so vulgar an interest in the project themselves and therefore relinquished the rights to *Salmagundi* to their publisher, David Longworth, even though they were not particularly wealthy. They would come to regret it when the publisher cashed in on the popular publication in later years, printing and selling several collected editions of the beloved work.[54]

The Problem of Benjamin Franklin

The opposition of wits to the increasingly democratic and prosaic creed of Americans inevitably led them to confront the legacy of Benjamin Franklin, one of the most famous Americans and certainly the most famous wit in his day. Franklin's position as the preeminent American wit came across clearly in jestbooks from the period. With consumers increasingly interested in American themes, printers attempted to Americanize British jestbooks instead of simply reprinting or importing English collections. One of the simpler ways to do so was to insert into the corpus of jests and anecdotes an array of stories about famous local figures. Since Franklin was not only one of the most famous Americans, but also America's wit, many such anecdotes unsurprisingly featured him, creating a growing corpus of Franklin tall tales and anecdotes. Much as the Yankee clown joined the ranks of the Irishman or Yorkshireman in many a comical anecdote, Franklin joined the ranks of Samuel Johnson, Alexander Pope, and Jonathan Swift as one of the leading wits. Indeed, in such titles as *Funny Stories: Or, the American Jester* (1795), *The American Jest-Book, Containing a Curious Variety of Jests, Anecdotes, Bon-Mots and Stories* (1796), and many more, one finds Franklin outwitting his interlocutors amid the growth of his legend, which spread through his autobiography and other writings. Franklin emerged not only as the most popular and familiar American in his lifetime, but his legend would continue to grow in the United States and abroad after his death, in 1790. The French even credited a Franklinism for "Ça Ira," the song most associated with the early stages of the French Revolution. Reportedly when Franklin's French friends asked him about the American Revolution, he responded, "Ah, ca-ira" (Oh, it will be fine).

Thus, as haughty American wits railed against social mobility and commercialism, they also lashed out by proxy at the most conspicuous symbol of the new American creed, Franklin, whose famous Poor Richard persona affected a more down-to-earth take on wit. Indeed, here one gets a better sense of how different forms of wit or humor conjured different kinds of communities. While Franklin's Poor Richard made him popular with a broad American audience that took pleasure in an emerging American nexus of home-spun and self-deprecating, if edifying, humor, Federalist wits presented themselves as an exclusive community of erudite men in their style and themes.

Despite Franklin's mythic status, including being one of the few "men of genius" Americans could take pride in, some literati nonetheless aimed their sallies of wit at Franklin, their towering competitor. As might be expected, Dennie was more aggressive than most. For instance, in one of his many essays on indolence, he conjures a tongue-in-cheek image of the "modern Sluggard," who had only demonstrated vivacity "when he threw Dr. Franklin's works into the fire, for saying that 'Time was money.'" More explicitly, he says of Franklin in another essay, "The economicks and the proverbs of this writer have been over rated," and "His system of frugality is such as every prudent old gentleman draws up for the use of young Hopeful, when bound to sea or to college."[55]

William Cobbett—the firebrand Federalist editor who had by then become entangled in a personal feud with Benjamin Franklin Bache, editor of the Democratic-Republican *Aurora* and Benjamin Franklin's grandson—attacked the elder Franklin as "a whore-master, a hypocrite and an infidel" and as a "treacherous and malicious old Zanga," among many other rebukes. Less scathingly, but still critical, another Federalist essayist, the Remarker, observes, "The literary character of the doctor has no claim to admiration." Franklin "may have few faults," yet "he displays no striking beauties."[56] Meanwhile, others proved more subtle in their attacks on Franklin, among them the authors of *The Anarchiad*, who merely mocked the American Philosophical Society, the institution founded by Franklin for the pursuit of knowledge and the sciences. As Gordon Wood noted, upon Franklin's death, Federalists kept surprisingly quiet, especially when compared to the many eulogies he received in France and the national effusions upon the death of George Washington a decade later.[57]

Above all else, Dennie and other conservative wits seemed to intuitively recognize Franklin's most significant mythic legacy for the new republic— securing an ideological commitment to social mobility through the myth of the self-made man. Several decades before Alexis de Tocqueville, Dennie, Washington Irving, and others demonstrated considerable prescience in recognizing the historical irony of the political debates of the 1790s. Although Hamiltonian Federalism championed commerce and industry, the competing Franklinian-Jeffersonian version of republicanism—for all its obsession with agriculture and its aversion to a nebulous idea of commerce—probably complemented the rise of modern market capitalism even more than its Federalist competition. By subscribing to libertarian principles that severed the traditional ligaments of institutionalized hierarchies and deference that bound Americans to one another, this rising American ideology released individualistic entrepreneurial energies that strengthened the market's grip over the nation's economy. Indeed, many wits' fascination with indolence was a means to wrestle with the symbolism of the revolution and its heritage, which, as they correctly perceived, increasingly hinged on the creed of social mobility and enterprise.[58] While the alternative vision for the republic they promoted usually remained vague on many accounts, it proved consistent in its homage to tradition, status, and (non-Franklinian) wit.

American Fops

Many Federalist literati demonstrated through their personal style a consistent attraction to deportment and sensibilities that would appear anathema to radical interpretations of republicanism, upward mobility, and vibrant market forces. It was no coincidence that at times they sounded and appeared almost like caricatures. Take, for example, a story about Robert Treat Paine Jr. as relayed by one of his friends: Paine suspected that some of the people at a dinner party, "treated him with disrespect," so he "monopolized the table, by commencing a dissertation upon Juvenal and his satires, with some pointed applications to the persons and characters of those whom he wished to punish." Once the "obnoxious individuals" left the table "neither pleased nor edified," Paine "exclaimed with an air of triumph, 'I have made these great men so sensible of their littleness, that they cannot endure it.'" As this story and others like it suggest, by the mid-1790s Paine had achieved notoriety as an erudite and flamboyant man of fashion. Indeed, testified the same friend, "no beau was ever a greater favorite in the beau monde!"[59]

Stories about Joseph Dennie often struck similar tones. Rumors spread of his participation in what contemporaries called gay circles, groups brought together by wit and merry living, as well as his eccentric and patronizing comportment. Several years after the wit's death, Royall Tyler recalled, "Dennie was a gentleman of a refined taste and a fastidious sensibility, which attached him, not merely to the elegant in literature, but the elegant in manners, and which made him turn with equal disgust from a bald writer and a vulgar speaker." Likewise, many tales of Dennie and Paine's compatriot J. S. J. Gardiner made him out to be an ostentatious elitist. In Gardiner's case, some of his detractors painted a picture of dissipation even more dire. One critic accused Gardiner, an Episcopalian minister at the time, of shirking his duties to his parishioners to instead "bellow out applauses at the theatre" and "show his dexterity and spirit at the card table." Meanwhile, other critics drew Gardiner as a rake, who enjoyed "female circles in the gay world."[60] Paine, however, more than Gardiner, best embodied the prototype of the dissipated poet—dying young, impoverished, and dejected, probably of complications related to his alcoholism. Dennie, too, died the same year, 1811, with a similar aura of crestfallen genius and dissipation about him.[61]

In the context of the cultural tug of war over the character of the United States, the whimsical form and often outrageous content employed by wits, both in their literary and real-life personas, held significant symbolic potential, conjuring the familiar trope of the fop. Purposefully assuming the comportment and sensibilities that patriots had once employed to cast British culture as corrupt and effete, Dennie, Gardiner, Paine, and others feigned levity in discussing weighty questions, thereby undermining the gravity with which contemporary republican ideologues addressed the country's future. Though the fop—also the coxcomb, beau, or dandy—as a literary trope rarely matched the complex and multifaceted variety of personas and characteristics of actual historical subjects, Dennie, Gardiner, and Paine probably came as close as any American of their day to embodying it. For them, the personal was political; their comportment itself constituted a contribution to the culture war over the nature of the young republic. For most other literati who followed their lead, such pioneering specimens of British-style foppery stood as archetypes who opened avenues to playing the fop when they sought to assume a condescending whimsical demeanor in real-life interactions, but perhaps more importantly in their literary efforts.[62]

Many of the literati tended to cultivate their foppish dissipation among homosocial circles of male friends who celebrated wit and debauchery. One prototype for these fraternities of wit and merriment were the literary and theater clubs that emerged at colleges and initiated young would-be wits into the wild world of literary extravagance accompanied by heavy drinking and loose living. Such clubs had been around since the colonial period, but they seemed to grow more raucous and profligate after the revolution. Among them, Harvard's Porcellian Club, also known as the Pig Club, achieved the most notoriety as a debauched and aristocratic hothouse of young literati making good on the club's motto, "While we live let's live," which they of course recited in Latin, *Dum vivamus, vivamus*. Paine was one of the founders of the Porcellian Club, in 1791, while Tyler and Dennie participated in earlier versions of Harvard's rowdy literary scene.[63]

After graduating from Harvard, Dennie continued to enjoy cultivating similar coteries, becoming a central figure in gay circles in Boston and Walpole as well as Philadelphia, where he began editing the literary magazine *The Port Folio*, while convening the rowdy Tuesday Club for like-minded wits. Thus, even though Dennie was more outrageous in his demeanor and more reactionary in his politics than most, he put his stamp on the culture of the period, with his eccentric, magnetic persona influencing a number of young men of letters who rallied around his intellectual and personal style. On an impressive short list of famous literati who considered Dennie a mentor or a close friend are Tyler and Gardiner along with Thomas Boylston Adams, John Curtis Chamberlain, Thomas Green Fessenden, Charles Jared Ingersoll, Jeremiah Mason, Josiah Quincy III, Elihu Hubbard Smith, and Roger Vose.[64]

Dennie also loomed as one of the muses who inspired James Kirke Paulding and the young Washington Irving in 1807 to pursue *Salmagundi,* the most audacious Augustan magazine in the United States.[65] Indeed, even Dennie's literary magazine—despite lamenting that "in America, the solemn the sedate, the humdrum appear to be the reigning vogue"—conceded that "a few brilliant exceptions present themselves . . . That amusing work, the *Salmagundi* of New York, was remarkable for spritely sallies of wit."[66] Much like the relationship between Walpole's literary club and the *Farmer's Weekly Museum,* or the Tuesday Club and the *Port Folio, Salmagundi* reflected the cheerful social life Irving and Paulding cultivated in New York City. The two bachelors were part of a group of local young, boisterous, and erudite men that Irving liked to call the Lads of Kilkenny, who in Irving's words engaged in "riotous, roaring, rattle-brained orgies at Dyde's" and "feverish enjoyments of Madeira and champagne." At one point the two, with the help of Washington's older brother William, decided to complement their social life with a comical publication to contribute to the whimsical and raucous spirit they so cherished.[67] That publication, *Salmagundi,* made Washington Irving famous, but it was his next work, *A History of New York,* that marked him as the preeminent wit in the United States in his day and a transitional figure in American literature. It would also mark the end of an era.

The Last Hurrah

Washington Irving's *A History of New York from the Beginning of the World to the End of the Dutch Dynasty, by Diedrich Knickerbocker* (1809) was probably the most successfully conceptualized and executed local effort at wit from the period. Fittingly perhaps, it turned out to be something of a swan song for the project of introducing Augustan humor to America. In the years to come, humor would take a very different direction. As one might expect, *A History of New York* was also one of the most mischievous literary pranks of the period. It appeared after several carefully placed newspaper ads related to the unknown whereabouts of "a small elderly gentleman, dressed in an old black coat and a cocked hat, by the name of *Knickerbocker*," who there was reason to believe "is not entirely in his right mind." The ads ultimately revealed that a hotel owner by the name of Seth Handaside had found in Knickerbocker's deserted room "a very curious kind of written book," which he planned to publish to offset the man's unpaid "bill for boarding and lodging."[68]

The tone Irving struck drew most from the mad rambling prose of François Rabelais and Laurence Sterne. Irving crafted a fantastic Dutch New York in an attempt to imagine an alternative-origins story and perhaps sketch a way forward for Americans that drew on both the Old World and the New World—fully embracing conservative European inclinations even while subverting and Americanizing them. Employing the character of a mysterious and comical Dutch historian, Knickerbocker, Irving wrote a unique pseudo-history that blended real historical research he had conducted in the New York Historical Society with whimsical half-mad wit. The reader, of course, could not tell where facts ended and fiction began.[69]

Irving opens the text with a giddy ramble through "the history of the world" and then divides the narrative into three parts conforming to the administrations of three fictional Dutch governors of New Netherlands loosely based on three real historical figures. Irving cast the first administration as a lost golden age under the leadership of Wouter Van Twiller, also known, according to Knickerbocker, as "Walter the doubter," because "he always conceived every subject on so comprehensive a scale, that he had not room in his head, to turn it over and examine both sides of it, so that he always remained in doubt."[70] During those heady days, "every respectable citizen ate when he was not hungry, drank when he was not thirsty, and went regularly to bed, when the sun set . . . all which being agreeable to the doctrines of Malthus tended so remarkably to the population of the settlement."[71]

By contrast, Irving crafts the second administration—under Wilhelmus Kieft, known as "William the Testy"—as a Swiftian satire of Jeffersonian America. As a caricature of Jefferson, Kieft possesses a tempestuous nature and upon any perceived insult issues strong proclamations of rebuke. He would ultimately do little more than rave, however. At most, he might order an ineffective embargo, a reference to the one Jefferson imposed in 1807 in the wake of the *Chesapeake* affair, the most infamous of numerous British raids and assaults on the US Merchant Marine. Furthermore, "under the administration of Kieft the disposition of the inhabitants of New Amsterdam experience an essential change, so that they became very meddlesome and factious." In a barely veiled antidemocratic tirade, Irving notes, "the mob, since called the sovereign people, like Balaam's ass, began to grow more enlightened than its rider, and exhibited a strange desire of governing itself." Thus, once-contented people, who lived in tranquility, had now grown certain that they "were a very unhappy deluded, and consequently, ruined people!" Ultimately havoc comes to rule the land, which ushers in a world turned mad in which "cobblers abandoned their stalls and hastened hither to give lessons in political economy—blacksmiths left their handicraft and suffered their own fires to go out, while they blew the bellows and stirred up the fire of faction; and even taylors, though but the shreds and patches, the ninth parts of humanity, neglected their own measures, to attend to the measures of government."[72] This, suggests Irving, is what happens once the excesses of democracy set into a place.

Although the third part of *A History of New York* unfolds at the end of the period of Dutch rule, which is coupled with the arrival of the Dutch enemy, the English, the Yankees of New England stand out as the ultimate villain of this chapter in the annals of New York, as they do in Irving's work more generally. In *A History of New York*, already during Kieft's rule, "the name Yankee became as terrible among our good ancestors, as was that of Gaul among the ancient Romans."[73] During this third epoch, which reads like a mock heroic, even the mythical leader of the colony, Peter Stuyvesant (as Irving casts him, at least), cannot stop the encroachment of the Yankees. "Scarcely a month passed but what the little Dutch settlements on the frontiers were alarmed by the sudden appearance of an invading army from Connecticut." Unfortunately, wherever these Yankees went, they "would in a little while completely dislodge the unfortunate Nederlanders . . . For it is notorious that wherever these shrewd men of the east get a footing, the honest dutchmen do gradually disappear, retiring slowly like the Indians before the whites; being totally discomfited by the talking, chaffering, swamping, bargaining disposition of their new neighbors."[74]

Like many other wits from the period, Irving appeared to despise the upwardly mobile, mercantile creed that he witnessed in Jeffersonian America. He, too, expressed a fascination with indolence and hedonism, and though he considered Jefferson's administration complicit in this sad trend, he saw the Yankees as the real driving engine behind this enterprising impetus. Thus, in *A History of New York* and later in his short stories, the Dutch were usually plump, lazy, and mild, and the Yankees lank, industrious, and severe. Indeed, his sympathy for most things Dutch, albeit often as figments of his imagination, served as an alternate to what he perceived as the chokehold New England traditions and origin stories had on the young republic.[75]

A tragicomedy, *A History of New York* was the last hurrah of Augustan wit in America. Despite its spellbinding creativity and energy, it was ultimately a failure as a nationalist text, an agenda most ambitious literary efforts from this period shared in one way or another. While quite a feat in its examination of an alternative past, in both form and content it did not offer enough Americans the material they needed or wanted for national myth-making going forward. It did, however, hold enough engrossing substance to endow the city of New York with mythic qualities that persist to this day.[76] It represented something of a dead end for Irving, too, as he would write very little in the next decade and leave the United States for a long stay in England. He would also eventually develop a new, more modern voice. Indeed, by the end of the War of 1812, there was not enough rarified air left in the United States to support Augustan literary projects. When Irving returned to writing, it was with a greater sense of acceptance toward the new American cultural climate, as "Rip Van Winkle" (1819) illustrates. When the lazy but sympathetic Van Winkle wakes from his magically induced twenty-year daze to learn of the revolution he had slept through, rather than maintain old ties with "his former cronies," he "preferred making friends among the rising generation, with whom he soon grew into great favor."[77] This new blend of romantic levity proved more suited for the modern sensibilities of Americans.

Other wits disappeared from the public scene in one way or another or, like Irving, forged ahead by embracing a new style of literature and nationalism. Dennie and Paine died before the War of 1812, while other New Englanders receded from public life or recalibrated their worldviews in one way or another. Meanwhile, Paulding, Ingersoll, and eventually even Washington Irving embraced the invigorated nationalism that swept the nation with the War of 1812.[78]

PART TWO

FROM BACKCOUNTRY
TO FRONTIER

As the collective memory of the American Revolution morphed into national myth, several key events and themes became what the historian Pierre Nora calls sites of memory (*lieux de mémoire*)—"moments of history torn away from the movement of history, then returned . . . like shells on the shore when the sea of living memory has receded." According to Nora, such moments are a residual form of collective memory still accessible to moderns "stranded in the present."[1] When Americans recall the revolution, they visit such realms of memory as the Boston Tea Party and tarring and feathering; the legend of the hardened Continental Army led by Gen. George Washington, usually along with the winter at Valley Forge; or the vaunted leadership of the Continental Congress, hallowed in memory as the body that drafted and issued the Declaration of Independence. Another long-celebrated realm of memory probably did even more to help forge a nation that embraced revolutionary sentiments and dispositions: the myth of the rural American militia and its singular virility crafted around the legend of the minutemen.[2]

More than any other historical events of the last 250 years, the Battles of Lexington and Concord have functioned to link in memory and legend the revolution and the elevated position occupied by hardy common (white) men in the national community. Conjuring images of rural farmers who answered the call to arms as minutemen, the battles on April 19, 1775, remind Americans that their unique homegrown prowess and determination miraculously repelled an armed invasion by a far larger and better-trained force sent by haughty authorities in the British metropole to crush freedom-loving provincials. Such a fiction proved especially apt for those forces in American society that wished to unsettle the entrenched hierarchies of the Old World and create a new more egalitarian republican society. In time, the rowdy, rough-and-tumble backwoods militia became one of the most usable and compelling metaphors for the nation.[3] Furthermore, it was part of a broader commitment to transforming the American environment into a carnival-scape in which American settlers could feel themselves native to the land—and nation—that they now inhabited.

Part one of *American Laughter, American Fury* looked at humor to capture the back and forth between the urban crowd and genteel Americans during the revolutionary and early national periods. Examining a broader timespan, roughly 1750 to 1835, part two highlights the Janus-faced character of carnivalesque mirth and play during that time. Indeed, it uncovers the nature of early American history as a tragic story of democratization gone awry. On the one hand, chapter three shows that a uniquely American tradition of levity and play was part and parcel of emergent and enduring democratic convictions that helped challenge traditional hierarchies and propelled common, white men to positions of prominence in the young republic. On the other hand, as chapter four illustrates, this mirth-infused structure of feeling, which so often found its expression in the myth of the frontier militia, emanated from the settler colonial project of indigenization that occurred in a bloody war of dispossession and annihilation, as frontier folk well knew, not on a blank slate, as myth would have it. Though Americans have fond memories of the militias known as minutemen rising up to defend the land from British tyranny, this militant tradition originated as a force designed to defend against the Indigenous peoples of North America, and later to purge the continent of them, and to protect settlers from slave rebellions. Uniting democratic commitments with racialization, the institution of the militia became a key agent in the process of indigenization that conversely relied on the practice of whites assuming Native identities even while waging a genocidal war against the very same Native peoples.

This does not mean that the process of democratization should be taken lightly. Rather, as chapter three shows, it was a genuine process with deep vernacular origins. One must, however, account for how it became wedded to genocide and a racialized war against Native peoples. Together then, chapter three, with its emphasis on democratic traditions, and chapter four, which highlights the darker genocidal aspect of this story, help explain the deeply contradictory nature of the American experiment in self-rule. Chapter five moves the discussion of these rural traditions into the antebellum period, examining the process through which antiauthoritarian practices that enlisted mirth and play helped underscore the white-washed republican ideology of manifest destiny. So, as the title to part two suggests, the West, once viewed as an unruly backcountry, had become a promising—indeed, carnivalesque—frontier by the first decades of the nineteenth century. In the process, westering settlers transformed themselves from liabilities into champions of a new westward-gazing nation. Every step of the way, white male settlers enlisted levity and play to help reinvent themselves and their nation.

CHAPTER THREE

Laughter in the Wilderness

Transgression and Mirth in Rural America

Though myth has it that the Massachusetts minutemen emerged spontaneously from their farms to repel a British invasion at Lexington and Concord, in truth they had been preparing for the moment for almost a year. Indeed, the counterassault waged by select, well-trained members of the Massachusetts militia on April 19, 1775, can be traced to the revolt that had begun in earnest in the summer of 1774 after word of the so-called Coercive Acts, passed by the British Parliament in retaliation for the Boston Tea Party, reached the colonies.[1] That summer, the center of the colonists' nascent insurrectionary movement shifted geographically as the "joyous multitude," the unruly crowds in coast cities that had ignited the imperial crisis with the Stamp Act riots of 1765, passed the baton to the yeomanry of rural Massachusetts. By the summer of 1774, it was no longer a "Boston rabble" taking local affairs into their own hands, noted Thomas Gage, commander of the British forces in America, "but the freeholders and farmers of the country" who set about removing and abusing anyone suspected of loyalty to the British.[2] As one petitioner summed up the situation in rural Massachusetts during that year, many of the most prominent men of the colony "have been deprived of their liberty, abused in their persons and suffered such barbarous cruelties, insults, and indignities, besides the loss of their property, at the hand of lawless mobs and riots as would have been disgraceful even for savages to have committed."[3]

This, however, was not the typical course or goal of most rural rebellions during this period. Indeed, the revolt in rural Massachusetts, which directly bled into the broader revolutionary struggle, was part of a broader pattern of premodern insurrections in the colonies and early United States that saw its peak in the decades following the Seven Years' War (1754–63). In many of the colonies, and later the states, rural settlers mounted militant challenges to eastern metropolitan centers of power, employing similar tactics of transgression through levity and play. Though responding to distinct grievances and circumstances, these localities shared a number of patterns. As with the Massachusetts revolt of 1774–75, some of the other uprisings broke out largely in response to the conduct and policies of administrators and officeholders in England or in coastal urban centers. These include the rebellions by the Black Boys (1765–69) and Paxton Boys (1763) in Pennsylvania, the North Carolina Regulators (1765–71), and the more well known Shays' Rebellion (1786–87) in Massachusetts and the Whiskey Rebellion (1794) in western Pennsylvania.[4] Rural violence also erupted over land disputes between various claimants, starting with the New Jersey land riots (1740s–1750s), followed by the anti-renters and Green Mountain Boys of New York (1760s and beyond), the Wyoming controversy (1760s–1790s), and the Liberty Men of Maine (1760s–1810s).[5] While most of the militant movements cast themselves, with varying degrees of merit, as part of the broader revolutionary struggle, historians rightly regard them as phenomena unto themselves belonging to the broader category of rural, premodern regulation and rebellion. Occurring during the transition to the modern era, these regulations drew on European and later colonial premodern traditions, even as some of them became enmeshed in the revolutionary struggles that signaled a new forward-looking consciousness.[6]

In recent decades, social historians have cast these militant challenges to Eastern Seaboard elites as driving some of the more radical interpretations of the revolutionary generation. Such narratives, however, usually relayed these revolts in tragic terms, as fleeting alternatives for a moment portending revolutionary and radical possibilities before the elites managed to quell them, along with much of the radicalism that animated them. According to this interpretation, sometimes considered a neo-progressive view, elite gentlemen dulled the radical edge of the American Revolution, forcing a

conservative vision of republicanism down the throats of American commoners that would never fundamentally restructure American society.[7]

As historians who champion the trajectory of early US history as a process
of ongoing democratization note, however, a different, more sanguine picture
emerges when one puts aside the immediate outcomes of many of these rural revolts and takes a broader view of the post-revolutionary period. By the
early nineteenth century, the United States had become something far closer
to the egalitarian place these rural rebels envisioned for the country. If Americans had once abided by traditional European class hierarchies, they by
then had turned to a new creed that championed the idea of the self-made
man and social mobility. Thus, for instance, by 1801 a new more populist
party took power, the Democratic-Republicans, and by the 1830s, traditional,
entrenched British divisions between gentlemen and commoners had largely
dissipated. According to this uplifting narrative, by then most Americans had
come to embrace the word *democracy*, and states removed most property
qualifications for voting, resulting in almost full white-male suffrage. The onset of capitalism and the increasing hold of market forces on the economy
might not have been the vision that rural rebels entertained, but these developments, at least in part, stemmed from the leveling logic unleashed by
American commoners and their sensibilities and dispositions.[8]

Most accounts of democratization in American society in this period re-
volve around the emergent party system, but the focus here is on the culture
fostered by rebellious rural Americans, often still viewed by many social historians as the purported losers of the revolutionary period. Democratization
and neo-progressive historians largely tally the back and forth between elites
and commoners, but focusing on the settler colonial dimension of early American history offers a synthesis of the democratization and neo-progressive
narrative arcs. Though these rural movement fostered radical challenges to
the powers that be, they at the same time cultivated aggressive exclusionary
practices. The key is that both antiauthoritarian impulses and violent repression were expressions of the same structure of feeling.

For Raymond Williams, the structure of feeling concept helps trace how
certain generations or classes with similar accumulated lived experiences internalize them, producing broad cultural and intellectual patterns. Thus, it
is an interpretation of intellectual history and ideology that accounts for
"meanings and values as they are actively lived and felt," such as "impulse,
restraint, and tone." In the early United States, a homegrown structure of

feeling animated by levity and play fused antiauthoritarian camaraderie with violence against racial enemies and made them appear to be natural extensions of each other. Thus, it naturalized the borders of a novel egalitarian political community, limiting the process of democratization to white men.[9] Indeed, rather than a story of democratization, this account tells the story of democratization for some.

This chapter foregrounds a narrative of democratization gone awry by relating the democratization part: rural revolts helped foreground an antiauthoritarian and egalitarian structure of feeling that many if not most white Americans, especially white men, came to embrace as a touchstone of their national character by the 1830s. These uprisings, or more accurately the structure of feeling that they fostered and spread, would help ensure the United States' evolution into a nation devoted to leveling principles. Indeed, they would become one of the most enduring facets of the American mythology—the United States as a nation of commoners. The Massachusetts revolt of 1774–75 and memories of it were a critical linchpin in this regard, marking the early and auspicious beginning of the process that saw localized and rural structures of feeling transition into broad cultural patterns vital to how the national community understood itself. Thus, early Americans cultivated a distinct settler colonial variation on premodern rural commitments to vigilantism and misrule that enlisted mirth and play to challenge entrenched hierarchies.

Origins of Rural Misrule

As with the crowds that gathered to challenge authorities in urban areas of colonial America, the anti-authoritarian actions of rural vigilantes also drew on European traditions. In rural Restoration England (1660–88), a renewed zeal by the British aristocracy to limit hunting to themselves—reinforced by a new generation of "nabobs" who coveted the prized privileges of their recently acquired higher status—elevated poaching as a particularly symbolic form of illegal action. Challenging the hegemony of the landed aristocracy and their laws, those no longer allowed to legally hunt often viewed the illegal practice of poaching as a necessary, extralegal regulatory activity to sustain communal assumptions regarding traditional rights. Britons of the period regarded their communities, both on the small scale of a village and on the broader scale of the kingdom, as corporations, which was quite different from modern interpretations of the term. To them, it meant that all members of the community must by tradition adhere to clear rights, privileges, and responsibilities determined by their rank and position in society as agreed to in a mythic past. Violating revered communal commitments at times would elicit violent actions by aggrieved members of the community animated by a sense of moral clarity emanating from the perception that their attempt to recover their traditional rights was fully justified.

Thus, after Parliament passed the Black Act (1723)—which mandated the death penalty for certain types of poaching and prohibited people from blackening their face to conceal their identity—many condemned poaching laws as the height of arbitrary tyranny by an overbearing aristocracy, and poachers emerged as quasi-mythic vigilante heroes. Indeed, the Black Act was in response to a high point in organized poaching by gangs known as the Blacks, so-called for their practice of blackening their faces. Tapping carnivalesque energies and assisted by the liberating effects of alcohol, these self-styled vigilantes in blackface scampered off to terrorize gamekeepers and hunt illegally. Although their grievances were deeply local and specific in nature, evidence exists that in their flights of fancy they envisioned themselves part of a long tradition of what Eric Hobsbawm called social bandits, whose activities stretch back to mythic communal memories, most notably the legend of Robin Hood and his band of merry men.[10] To the extent that their acts were a form of rural rebellion, however, as with the myth of Robin Hood's band of merry men, they were not modern revolutionaries, but of the mold of earlier notions of revolution that sought to restore an imagined primordial social order. Thus, they could fancy themselves the true guardians of English freedoms and traditions dating back to before the Norman Conquest. Like their legendary forerunners, they engaged in anti-elitist pranks to ensure the cohesion of their besieged communities.[11]

In the American colonies, the tradition of the Blacks, challenging elite hegemony in tame English forests, encountered the wilderness of the American woods. Rather than bands of merry men, "skulking Indians" supposedly roamed the woods of North America with impunity. Since so many rural Americans had vivid memories of Native American raids, it proved particularly liberating and euphoric for the settlers to stage burlesques of "Indian raids" against hated coastal elites or their representatives in the backcountry. Thus, even if the memories of violent raids were not the stuff of humor, such actions often employed levity and play, probably even more so than in Britain, among a community that had long cohered in response to Indian attacks. As with the "Mohawks" of the Boston Tea Party, it was also a markedly settler colonial practice by which settlers declared themselves the natives of the American woods; it emerged as a process that facilitated their transformation into the "true" heirs to the land, thereby aiming to usurp and replace the Native peoples who inhabited the woodland regions east of the Mississippi River.[12] The revolutionary spirit that swept the colonies during the 1760s and beyond infused regional resistance to British policies and eastern elites with more ambitious egalitarian projects as it converged with a nascent nationalism that lent the term *revolution* a new, forward-gazing meaning. One can discern an antiauthoritarian, provincial, and leveling creed—largely forged from vernacular impulses and traditions—emerging from this crucible.

For settlers of backcountry New England, the White Pine Acts (1691, 1711, 1722) were akin to the poaching laws, which restricted England's rural inhabitants, and the Navigation Acts (passed in 1651 and regularly modified), which regulated shipping and trade to and from the colonies and aggrieved New England's mariners and merchants. British administrators had sought to monopolize the large white pine trees which they prized as sturdy masts for the empire's expanding navy starting with the Massachusetts Charter of 1691 and later followed up by legislation in the colonies and in Parliament. For many rural New Englanders, who viewed access to the bounty of the woods as their prerogative and had come to rely on white pines, such laws were an unacceptable impingement on their corporate rights. Not surprisingly, at a time when rural English gangs raided and harassed gamekeepers, and as New England traders and seafarers nurtured the grievances that would erupt in the Stamp Act riots of 1765, rural New Englanders developed a parallel tradition of opposition to enforcers of the White Pine Acts. Before the passage of the Coercive Acts (1774), one nineteenth-century historian of New Hampshire declared, "The pine tree law . . . was more oppressive and offensive to the citizens of New Hampshire than all the above acts [the Sugar Act, Stamp Act, and Townshend Acts] combined, and contributed more to unite the yeomanry in hostility to the British government."[13]

Matters first came to a head in Exeter, New Hampshire, in 1734. By then David Dunbar, surveyor of the woods, had concluded that the region around Exeter was a hotbed of lumbering activity churning out hundreds of thousands of board-feet of planking made from illegally logged white pines. He, therefore, sent some of his men to confiscate the lumber. When local lumber workers—"a class of men . . . not easily intimidated with high words," as one of the earliest New Hampshire historians put it—got wind of the presence of the surveyor's agents in town, "a number of persons, disguised like Indians, attacked them . . . whilst others cut the rigging and sails of the boat" they planned to use to haul the confiscated wood. According to one of the victims, the attackers "beat" and "dragged" him, and "then with a clubb did knock him down upon the ground giving him several blows with w'ch was in great danger of his life having rec'd several wounds, & lost a great deal of blood." Dunbar returned to Exeter with a larger contingent of hired men and proceeded to destroy one of the sawmills. In short order, the locals, led by Nicholas Gillman, a militia officer and a mill owner, organized a posse and attacked Dunbar and his men, once again driving them from town. Because of Gillman's close ties with Jonathan Belcher, the governor of Massachusetts, Dunbar failed to bring any of the culprits to justice.[14]

For the next forty years or so, surveyors of the woods and their agents struggled to enforce the law, while opposition to the White Pine Acts continued. This cat-and-mouse game led to occasional flare-ups, and on at least two occasions resulted in large-scale incidents that resembled the Exeter "riot" of 1734. In 1765 in Hampshire County, Massachusetts, a local posse terrorized two hapless deputies of the surveyor of the woods who had been tracking illegal timber operations in the region.[15] More famously, in Weare, New Hampshire, in April 1772, a year and a half before Bostonians masqueraded as Mohawks to spoil tea belonging to the East India Company, a sheriff and a deputy attempting to serve arrest warrants for violation of the acts met with a night attack at an inn by "more than twenty men" who "rushed in, faced blacked, switches in their hands." The attackers proceeded to cross "out the account against them of all logs cut, drawn and forfeited" on the sheriff's "bare back" and "made him wish he had never heard of pine trees fit for masting the Royal Navy." Finally, "with jeers, jokes and shouts ringing in their ears," the two men were sent reeling out of town on "their horses, with ears cropped, manes and tails cut and sheared." One can only imagine the hearty laughs shared locally in the wake of the event and for many years to come, as the story circulated and emerged as local mythology. Slightly more than a hundred years after the event, one local historian, exaggeratedly claimed, "The only reason why . . . the 'Boston Tea Party' [is] better known than our Pine Tree Riot is because [it has] had better historians."[16]

A somewhat separate tradition of rural opposition to major landowners paralleled many of the actions employed by opponents of the White Pine Acts, especially the practice of night raids by belligerent, black-faced assailants. About a year after the 1734 Exeter raid on the surveyors, a similar nighttime assault occurred in Hopewell, New Jersey, in July 1735. According to the two victims, Duncan Ogullian and John Collier, "divers persons unknown, to the number of twelve or more, being all disguised, having their faces besmear'd with blacking, and armed with clubs, and sticks in their hands, did in an insolent, violent, and riotous manner, break into and enter" their houses "and did assault, beat, and wound" the two men. "Cursing, swearing, and threatening in a most outrageous manner, that they would kill and murder" Daniel Coxe, who they blamed for selling the land to the two men. They also expressed "defiance of all law and government."[17] For the next century or so, similar nocturnal raids and other forms of militant opposition to a diverse set of land claims would erupt in various parts of the colonies and later the states. Those perpetrators, too, would see themselves as aggrieved provincials seeking to defend their rights, and many would likewise take to Native American burlesque, fostering camaraderie through mirth and play, that also alienated their opposition as outsiders to the American wilderness.[18]

There is little indication that assailants self-consciously employed blackface as Indian play during the land disputes in New Jersey, but in other such actions, including in the Wyoming Valley and in Maine, raiders quite explicitly masqueraded as Indians. In fact, these rural insurgents were occasionally called "white Indians."[19] Ultimately, whether instigated by opposition to coastal and metropolitan policies or in response to land disputes, a unique rural tradition of transgression through mirth had formed in America by the last third of the eighteenth century. In most of these movements, Indian play in the form of carnivalesque humor became part of the conceit communities employed to affirm their struggle and bonds. Thus, an idiosyncratic settler colonial variation on traditional forms of misrule took shape in rural America.[20] Two distinct pre-revolutionary rural insurrections suggest some of the texture of these movements, and how they employed levity, play, and terror to cultivate provincial solidarity in opposition to metropolitan elites and their agents.

The Black Boys

Perhaps more than any other rural rebellion, the one involving James Smith and the Black Boys of rural Pennsylvania captured the settler colonial nature of the revolts. In their case, not only did rural settlers take to Indian burlesque, but their ultimate goal was to deny Native peoples in the region supplies promised to them under an emerging peace between the British Empire and local Native nations in the wake of a broad Indigenous uprising, Pontiac's Rebellion (1763–64). Thus, the irony was two-fold: settlers who had disinherited Native peoples appropriated Indian customs, in this case, as part of a broader campaign against those very Native peoples, with whom they were still in a bloody and ongoing conflict.

James Smith was a typical product of these trying years. He had spent much of the Seven Years' War in captivity by the Caughnawagas, a Catholic subgroup of the Haudenosaunee, and upon his release applied his knowledge of "Indian ways" as a scout for the British during Pontiac's Rebellion. After Smith settled in the Conococheague Valley, a frontier region in Pennsylvania due west of the Susquehanna River, locals in the region organized a ranger company for defense against Native raiders and gave Smith the captaincy. When early in 1765 Smith and his men learned that a convoy of "Indian goods," provided by the British, was headed toward Fort Pitt, they became convinced that the colonial government had abrogated its responsibility to the settler population of the region. "To supply them [the Indians] now," James Smith wrote years later to account for his actions "would be a kind of murder, and would be illegal trading at the expense of the blood and treasure of the frontier."[21] Thus, as he recalled, "I collected ten of my old warriors that I had formerly disciplined in the Indian way, went off privately, after night, and encamped in the woods. The next day, as usual we blacked and painted, and waylaid them near Sidelong Hill." When the convoy arrived, Smith instructed his men to keep up a "constant, slow fire, upon them from front to rear" and then ordered the victims to "take [their] private property, and immediately retire." Smith's men successfully scared off the convoy's personnel, who fled unharmed to nearby Fort Loudon. Subsequently, on the evening of March 6, 1765, Lieutenant Charles Grant, commander of the Highlander troops stationed at Fort Loudon, dispatched a sergeant and twelve men to retrieve what was left of the cargo and to arrest any of the culprits they might find. After a long arduous night that included several engagements with local "country men" the detachment returned to Fort Loudon the next day with several prisoners and "a few horse loads of rum," which was all they could salvage.[22]

Smith's band was not about to leave their men captive, so on March 9, 1765, as Lt. Grant observed, "a body of armed men appear[ed] before this fort." During the verbal exchange, Smith threatened to attack any soldiers escorting the prisoners to the Carlisle jail, as Grant said he had planned to do. For the next two days, the local rangers-cum-vigilantes held Fort Loudon under siege. It appears that Smith's men took prisoners of their own at this time and eventually exchanged them for their own men.[23]

Thus, the Black Boys, as they became known for blackening their faces in the Indian manner, imposed a pseudo-legal regime on the west bank of the Susquehanna. At one point, General Thomas Gage even proclaimed in a letter that the region seems "to be in an actual state of rebellion," as Black Boys, almost with impunity, monitored, and, when thought necessary, disposed of goods they suspected were intended for Ohio Valley nations. About one month after the initial raid, William Johnson, the Northern Department's superintendent for Indian affairs, reported that very few of the goods that made their way from Philadelphia arrived safely at Fort Pitt.[24]

Brazen acts designed to insult British authorities and make them feel vulnerable would continue unabated in the region for the rest of 1765 and many years after that. In this vein, on May 28 a group of five men led by Smith managed to apprehend and detain Lt. Grant about a mile from Fort Loudon, declaring him the "kings prisoner." The Black Boys demanded the eight rifles Grant had confiscated from the prisoners taken more than two months prior. They released him several days later, but only after Grant, who saw no other way out of the situation, gave them a £40 bond as security and promised to deliver their arms. Several months later, Smith and the Black Boys again laid siege to Fort Loudon and finally retrieved their rifles. After the second siege of the fort, the Black Boys finally got rid of Grant and his forces. After a relief force came to their aid, they evacuated Fort Loudon and headed to Fort Pitt.[25] Four years later, Smith again turned to his trusted rangers when British authorities imprisoned some Black Boys for raiding Indian goods at Fort Bedford. He wrote, "I collected eighteen of my old black-boys that I had seen tried in Indian war." Smith then claimed that with the assistance of his band of vigilantes he took over Fort Bedford in 1769, releasing the prisoners. With the benefit of hindsight, he also made the case that Fort Bedford "was the first British fort in America, that was taken by what they called American rebels."[26]

The Green Mountain Boys

Perhaps the most successful rural insurrection of the period laid the groundwork for the creation of the state of Vermont. Although the colony of New York claimed the region of the Green Mountains—between the Connecticut River and Lake Champlain—by the 1760s it had been mostly settled by New

Englanders, thanks to cheap and controversial New Hampshire land grants, making it contested terrain between absentee New York landowners supported by their colony and Yankee settlers. Between 1770 and the outbreak of the revolution in 1775, local settlers led by Ethan Allen organized the Green Mountain Boys militia and forcibly repelled attempts by the hated "Yorkers" to clear the Yankees from the land.[27] Into the Anglo-American tradition of corporate regulation, they injected mirth and masquerade, combining it with limited and regulated violence that stopped short of mortal harm.

The insurgency in the region began in earnest over the summer of 1770, after several settlers chased surveyors off their land, and New York officials declared them rioters. Although the first attempt to arrest one of the so-called rioters proved successful, local settlers violently thwarted all further attempts to serve "processes" (writs) against the rebellious Yankees. Thus, during the second attempt, in December, after apprehending the settler Moses Robinson, "the constable who had the charge of serving these processes" was assaulted by a "great number of persons settlers thereabouts under the grants of New Hampshire having their faces blacked, and otherwise being disguised." They "rescued from him Moses Robinson," and after the constable and his men attempted to arrest Robinson again, they "rescued assaulted him again in the highway." When the constable in "His Majesty's name commanded them to disperse and surrender up his prisoner, telling them they were acting against law," the settlers "damned the laws of New York, and said they had better laws of their own, and finally obliged the said constable and his assistants to fly for their lives."[28]

Over the next few years, New York agents repeatedly attempted to stake a claim in the contested region only to be foiled by "disguised and disfigured" Green Mountain Boys.[29] Reports suggest that the incidents were accompanied with heady doses of carnivalesque revelry. In one case, for example, the Green Mountain Boys intimidated Samuel Gardiner who tried to settle in the region under New York claims. Refusing to recognize the legitimacy of any New York grants, as Gardiner later reported, "Rioters came to" his house "to the Number of One Hundred, some of whom disfigured with Black; others with Wigs and Horse Tails and Women's Caps, and other Disguises" to intimidate him.[30] In another incident, a group of the boys led by Robert Cockrun fell upon a surveying party. They "rudely seized" the surveyor and "his party as prisoners, and conducted them to their tribunal, as if they had really been the malefactors. After deliberating upon their fate, it was resolved to chastise them severely." While most of the party "were beat with clubs unmercifully . . . , the deputy surveyor they showed a little more lenity, and he received only three blows from Cockrun; who boasted of his exploits, and that he was a son of Robin Hood, and would follow his mode of life; a sentiment which his party received with great applause!"[31] In the colonies, reenactments of skulking Indians, merry bands of legendary forest men, and carnivalesque misrule drew from the same pool of id, over time resulting in a distinct pattern associated with rural settlers.

In a telling moment of the nascent insurgency, in the summer of 1772, the Green Mountain Boys demonstrated their conviction in the face of what they thought would be a large-scale invasion by British troops led by the governor of New York. An insurrection in the Hudson River Valley had recently been quashed by British troops, and the new governor, William Tryon, had overseen the large mobilization that crushed the North Carolina Regulators a year earlier in the Battle of Alamance (May 1771). When word reached the contested grants that Tryon was leading a large convoy of troops up the river, the Green Mountain Boys were certain the intelligence was sound. As Ira Allen, Ethan Allen's younger brother, remembered, the plan was to send marksmen, who would "station themselves at a certain place in a wood near the road that the enemy were to march; the Governor was to be pointed out, and the expert marksmen were to fire, one by one at him, until he fell from his horse, then to give an Indian *whoop* and raise their ambuscade."[32] As it turned out, the British troops were actually headed to relieve the garrisons at Oswego, Niagara, and Detroit, but the Green Mountain Boys' faith that their plan could have succeeded portended things to come.

Like the Massachusetts uprising of 1774–75, the militant land dispute between New England settlers and New York elites demonstrated how during the revolutionary era, limited regulation, largely careful to stop short of inflicting death, could quickly turn into a militant independence movement. This was also part of a growing sense by many rural settlers that in the American forests their ways of "bush fighting"—as one of their leaders, Remember Baker, asserted—could prevail over European troops, who had little knowledge of Indian ways of war.[33] After all, as natives of the Green Mountains, and like the Indigenous peoples of America, they knew how to fight in the American woods better than the effeminate, city-bred Europeans.

Profanity and Misrule

Plumbing the Anglo traditions of carnivalesque misrule, rural rebels turned to transgressive acts and utterances—such as profanity, scatological humor, and macabre theatrical enactments—to instill terror in the minds of their enemies. As in the case of subcultures that cultivated insular transgressive traditions, such as pirates and highwaymen and poaching gangs like the Blacks, this use of levity and play also fostered a sense of an embattled community, even as and, indeed, because it instilled terror in their targeted enemies. The humor of misrule, after all, draws its potency from mirth derived from transgressing society's mores and is best honed and experienced by a community of "insiders" who take pleasure in a joke being played on terror-stricken "outsiders."

At a time when the spoken word was taken at face value, and held in far higher regard than today's textually overstimulated sensibilities can fathom, the illicit vocabulary of curses and profane language carried an almost magical aura. As many of the curses involved profanities, invoking God or the devil in some fashion, a word like *damn* or a disparaging reference to God literally conveyed the potentially terrible consequence of eternal life in hell. So great was the power of such language, often referred to as blasphemy, that it was largely illegal in the colonies and in the early United States.[34] Thus, for rural rebels—who knew well that coastal elites as well as metropolitan Britons viewed them as a crude, lower class of humanity, little better than Native Americans—using illicit language was doubly seductive. It packed two jokes into one; not only did they know that such language terrified their victims, they also knew that when spoken by raiders, especially when clad in Indian garb, it further convinced their targets that they might expect terrible and unholy treatment inflicted by the hands of "savages" themselves. Therefore, nighttime raiders who invoked eternal damnation while masquerading as Indians, who many regarded as instruments of the devil anyway, represented an immense divide between those in on the joke and those whom the joke was on. On the one side, a tight-knit group of accomplices cohered around transgressing boundaries and the culture of misrule, and on the other side, the terror-stricken became the laughingstock of insider communities as reports of their misfortune circulated.

The Green Mountain Boys, led by the likes of Ethan Allen, the deist (or maybe atheist and heretic), and Remember Baker, known for notorious, profanity-laced speech, proved particularly adept at building cohesion through transgressive language and theater. The woes of Alexander McNaughton, who settled under New York grants in the region claimed by the Yankee insurgents, were quite typical. Noticing "nine men who call themselves New Hampshire Men . . . all having fire arms & attempting to demolish his house," McNaughton "came & earnestly desired them to stop where-upon one surnamed Allen, another Baker," and a few others "said that they would burn it for that morning they had resolved to offer burnt sacrifice to the gods of the world in burning the logs of that house." Threatening Mc-Naughton with clubs, they entreated, "Go your way now & complain to that damned scoundrel your governor. God damn your governour, laws, king, council & assembly. That said Allen & Baker repeated said horrible curses." When McNaughton "reproved them for" their language, "Allen said G—d damn your soul . . . and further said that if ever any constable attempted to arrest them they would kill them."[35]

Another attack, about two years later, illustrates the theater of misrule the Green Mountain Boys sought to enact. This time the victim was Benjamin Spencer, a justice of the peace and a resident in the township of Durham, where he and others had settled under the hated New York titles. On the night of November 20, 1773, after "breaking into his house . . . with an ax Remember Baker and Ethan Allen rushed into the room" while Spencer's "family were in bed." Then "Ethan Allen with some curses ordered [Spencer] to rise and go with them and told [him] that he had been a damned old offender and the township of Durham a hornets nest in their way." While Spencer was held captive, Benjamin Hough, a fellow area resident, demanded of Allen "to know the causes or reasons of their conduct" toward Spencer. In response "Allen used many curses and imprecations on the people of the province of New York by the name of *Yorkers*, and said the day of judgment was come when every man should be judged according to his works, with much other language of that kind." Allen also told him "that if they ever had come to Durham again they would lay all Durham in ashes and leave every person in it a corpse." To make matters worse, it was all proclaimed on the Sabbath!

After a few days of subjecting Spencer to "frequent threats, and many insults by the most opprobrious language," the Green Mountain Boys enacted some of their favored theatrics. In mockery and contempt of New York laws, they "erected what they called a *Judgement Seat*," while "Ethan Allen and Seth Warner, Remember Baker and Robert Cockran took their seats as judges." Having listed all of Spencer's purported transgressions, they decided to burn his house down in front of him, which they subsequently did to the backdrop of "great shouting of joy and much noise and tumult" and threatened him "not to act as a magistrate or do any thing against their interest on pain of the severest punishment." As a parting shot, Allen and Baker "damned

the government, said they valued not the government nor even the kingdom . . . & that they had force and power sufficient to protect themselves
against either."[36]

Although the Green Mountain Boys, no doubt inspired by the iconoclastic
religious ideas of Ethan Allen, took to such language with particular zeal,
one can find versions of it being used in other rural rebellions of the period. In
fact, the Black Boys took things a step further by publishing their transgressive mirth in a broadside they distributed within the territory they sub-
jected to their extralegal regime in western Pennsylvania. An advertisement
posted by the Black Boys near Fort Loudon in March 1765 in preparation for
vigilante activity announced that those who chose to join the movement and
congregated at the local tavern would "fill their belly's with liquor and your
mouth with swearing" and then go on to participate in "any outrage we have
a mind to do." Identifying their meeting spot as "Hell's town," the advertisement concluded, "God bless our brave loyal volunteers, and success to our
Hells town."[37] The text captures how a combination of levity, play, and transgression helped mold a community into an antiauthoritarian stance against
metropolitan elites, in this case against the British Empire itself.

Rural Carnival-scapes

The language and nature of the broadside advertising the escapades of the
Black Boys provide a useful window into the broader dynamics at play in
many of the rural rebellions. As with urban carnivalesque riots, the community of accomplices taking part in rural insurrections also sought to suspend space and time, to usher people into a different reality with distinct
rules that only groups of insiders fully understood. They attempted this by
transforming the landscape itself into a carnival-scape, where events transpired according to a new logic of transgressive mirth. To achieve such a
novel ontological state, the community had to exert a modicum of control
over transpiring events, but more importantly, project a sense of complete
mastery over the landscape to the community privy to the scheme as well as to
outsiders who were not. Although well-planned and carefully choreographed
actions stood at the heart of such carnivalesque regimes, the community of
accomplices also sought to support such specific actions with a discourse
of mirth, play, and insider humor that people passing through would encounter. In this new landscape, members of the community felt themselves to be
the only true natives of their region. By contrast, strangers or outsiders to
this carnivalesque if terrifying environment experienced the terrain itself as

treacherous, which reinforced the delight community members took in it. One can find echoes of such dynamics in many of the rural rebellions, but from the available evidence, the masters of this approach were the so-called whiskey rebels, who hated and militantly resisted the tax that Treasury Secretary Alexander Hamilton proposed, and Congress passed, on distilled spirits in 1791.

The backcountry revolt in western Pennsylvania started in earnest on July 16–17, 1794, when skirmishes erupted between local settlers, many of them members of the local Washington County militia, and tax collector John Neville and his subordinates, resulting in several deaths. In the immediate aftermath of events, notices penned under the somewhat playful pseudonym Tom the Tinker began to appear in various places. John Reed, a local distiller who had refused to cooperate in resisting the tax on spirits— that is, whose name was "entered on the excise docket, contrary to the will and good pleasure of his fellow citizens"—was one of the first to receive such a notice, on July 19. Noting that "a certain John Reed . . . came not forth to assist" in the attack on John Neville's house, the letter stressed, "I, Tom the Tinker, will not suffer any certain class or set of men to be excluded the service of this my district, when notified to attend on any expedition carried on in order to obstruct the execution of the excise law, and obtain the repeal thereof."[38] Like messages of this kind in other rebellions, the purpose behind the notice was to employ the specter of an elusive and fear-inducing, if clownish, foe to terrorize into submission any locals who betrayed the cause. Injecting levity into such threats sent signals to local insiders as well as to outsiders that helped the ringleaders galvanize opposition by inducing reluctant community members to join the in-crowd or remain uncertain of their safety.

Hugh Henry Brackenridge, a prominent community member in Pittsburgh with a front row seat to events in western Pennsylvania in the climactic summer of 1794, described the scene during those heady days, before 13,000 soldiers under the command of Alexander Hamilton arrived and spoiled the merriment. His view of the lay of the land emphasized that local men organized an uprising using the signature frontier combination of carnivalesque jubilation and terror. In his telling, settlers erected liberty poles over the countryside, exercised vigilante justice against various members of the community, pillaged and burned property, and paraded a flag of six stripes, representing the six Pennsylvania and Virginia counties the rebels hoped to unite against Eastern Seaboard authority. Brackenridge noted the appearance of Tom the Tinker along with his reign of terror and mirth and explained the origin and nature of the name:

> A term had come into popular use before this time to designate the opposition to the excise law; it was that of Tom the Tinker. It was not given, as the appellation Whig originally was, as a term of reproach by adversaries, but assumed by the people who were active in some of the masked riots which took place at an early period. A certain John Holcroft was thought to have made the first application of it. It was at this time of the masked attack on a certain William Cochran, who rendered himself obnoxious by an entry still [whiskey distillery], according to the law. His still was cut to pieces; and this was humorously called mending his still; and the menders of course must be tinkers; and the name, collectively, became Tom the Tinker. Advertisements were now put up on trees on the highways, or on other conspicuous places, under the signature of Tom the Tinker, threatening individuals or admonishing or commanding them in measures with regard to the excise law . . . It was not now, "Are you Whig or Tory?" But, "Are you a Tom the Tinker's man?"[39]

Though many in western Pennsylvania seemed to cherish the comic spirit of Tom the Tinker, Brackenridge did not appear to appreciate the humor. A humorist himself, he knew well that the tone imparted by Tom the Tinker carried an aggressive undertone—with suspect gentlemen associated with the eastern establishment like him as its target. Even if Brackenridge understood the joke, he could not remain certain that he was deemed "in on it." He tried to appear supportive of the uprising to save his own skin, but feared that Tom the Tinker would uncover his ruse. Thus, when he happened to encounter John Holcroft, who he suspected of posting such messages around the countryside, Brackenridge felt acute fear for his well-being: "Heavens! thought I, is this Tom the Tinker? Is he to get his sons to help murder me, that he is taking me to his own house?"[40] Clearly, Breckenridge felt the palpable terror that the Tom the Tinker accomplices meant for him and others to feel. By contrast, one can only imagine the adrenaline rush experienced by those who wrote the Tom the Tinker messages and communicated with each other in this knowing fashion.

A similar pattern emerged in Maine, where the rural revolt burned slowly over decades, allowing locals time to hone their unique blend of mirth, play, and terror. In much need of maintaining group solidarity in the face of large proprietors who sought to capitalize on their land claims, the Liberty Men of

Maine adopted the patterns of a rural insurgency transforming the landscape itself into a carnival-scape where they were the masters. "After 1800," the historian Alan Taylor explains, "the settlers imaginatively elaborated the mock-Indian identity that they originally adopted simply to disguise their identities as a shield from criminal prosecution. They gradually began to call themselves White Indians rather than Liberty Men."[41] By embracing Indian visages, they sought to both terrify their enemies and render themselves natives to the region. Taking to mock Native American raids and war practices, they incorporated Indian customs, complete with painting their faces and adorning themselves to fashion the "horrid visages" of "savages" and even created a pidgin language that mimicked their impressions of Native American speech and helped hide their identities. Furthermore, they claimed to follow the lead of a local "Indian king," and they distributed threatening notices in the vein of Tom the Tinker, warning locals that "every Indian that is absent and dont come into a leigance with the rest will be Lookt upon as an einimy to the Cause of Justice and a traitor to our Indian king and a destroyer of our Indian rights and privilidges."[42] Thus, a struggle between gentlemen land proprietors and common folk became a settler colonial crucible that helped transform settlers into indigenous Americans—at least in their own minds—who felt certain of their unique claim to revel in the carnivalesque landscape they inhabited.

Forged in opposition to metropolitan condescension and inhabited by bands of like-minded merry men whose common origins and jovial camaraderie served as staples, the frontier landscape was also uniquely egalitarian. Some of the leaders of rural rebellions, among them Ethan Allen, couched their ideas in republican rhetoric and participated in the radical republicanism of the revolutionary Atlantic that would emerge as a new self-described democratic creed by the turn of the nineteenth century.[43] Most rural settlers, however, never fully articulated their leveling commitments. Instead, it became second nature to view common folk like themselves as equals, and Eastern Seaboard elites as foreign to their ways, and to attach to this outlook a jovial demeanor that challenged elite claims to superiority. It helped them cast urbane easterners as oppressors and themselves, rural hardy Americans, as the truer heirs to the revolutionary tradition. This structure of feeling was also an idiosyncratic American and settler colonial adaptation that blended older corporate communal assumptions and dispositions with the settler colonial condition of provincial colonists, who sought to declare themselves true natives vis-à-vis their metropolitan adversaries.

Mirth, Memory, and Nation

Traditions of misrule that enlisted carnivalesque play to challenge authority had been commonplace in premodern Europe for centuries. The difference in the American case is that although they began on the margins of the social hierarchy and daily life and achieved limited success during the eighteenth century, by the early decades of the nineteenth century the sensibilities and dispositions, the structure of feeling, as it were, that unruly Americans had cultivated on the margins would increasingly emerge as mainstream. With them, the leveling and antiauthoritarian logic that these sensibilities implicated became national staples. Indeed, rather than a counterweight to elite and middle-class hegemony, as they were and would largely remain in nineteenth-century Europe, in the early United States they would in time insinuate themselves into the very heart of an American popular culture.

Fortunately for rural Americans, there was no better way to start this transition from a rural counterculture to a national popular culture than the events of April 19, 1775, when hostilities erupted between British regulars and American insurgents. As stories circulated among the colonies about the events of the day, when Massachusetts minutemen repelled a British military column intent on seizing arms stored in the town of Concord, and by day's end had laid siege to the city of Boston, two distinct sensibilities reigned supreme. First, was the righteous indignation at the purported heinous behavior of British Regulars on the Lexington green and elsewhere that day, perhaps best captured by the all-caps headline for Ezekiel Russell's broadside—"BLOODY BUTCHERY, BY THE BRITISH TROOPS"—accompanied by two rows of coffins above it, one for each of the Americans killed.[44] The second was an outpouring of giddy euphoria over the American victory. "I confess I am pleased with my countrymen," one typical report exalted, "but if the sweet hope of liberty will not induce a free-born American to fight, what will?" Another proud American hailed it a "circumstance that highly spirits us, when we consider that with all their vaunts of infinite superiority, our militia, suddenly assembled, without plan or leader, and at no time equal to them in numbers, could force them to retreat with confusion and loss."[45]

Yet, in the immediate aftermath, perhaps the most widespread elated account of the events of that day focused on the song "Yankee Doodle." Rumor had it that to antagonize the locals, the British reinforcements led by Lord Percy struck up "Yankee Doodle" as they made their way through the New

England countryside, certain that they were simply marching to support a triumphant British column returning from Concord. A dialogue between two New Englanders in a comedy by a Philadelphia Whig, John Leacock, captures the colonists' sentiments. When observing the British column, the two stock Yankees report a "kind of brutish music, growling something like our favourite tune Yankee Doodle . . . seeming vastly pleased . . . with their mimickry." A while later, however, one conveys to the other, "Did you not hear how their mirth was turn'd into mourning?"[46] Indeed, as the story went, later that day it was the New Englanders who played "Yankee Doodle" to the hasty retreat of British regulars. According to a particularly widespread anecdote, the retreating British troops were all too aware of the irony: "Upon their return to Boston, one asked his brother officer how he liked the tune now . . . 'damn them, returned he, they made us dance it till we were tired.' Since which Yankee Doodle sounds less sweet to their [British] ears."[47]

John Trumbull adeptly captured the popular anecdote in the opening to his mock-heroic *M'Fingal*, which appeared to much acclaim later that year:

> When Yankies skill'd in martial rule,
> First put the British troops to school;
> Instructed them in warlike trade,
> And new manoevres of parade;
> The true war dance of Yankee-reels,
> And val'rous exercise of heels;
> Made them give up, like saints complete,
> The arm of flesh and trust the feet,
> And work, like Christians undissembling,
> Salvation out, by fear and trembling;
> Taught Percy fashionable races,
> And modern modes of Chevy-chaces.[48]

The latter reference is to the "Ballad of Chevy Chase," a British favorite that also featured Percy's namesake, the Earl of Northumberland, who went on a hunting expedition only to meet his death at the hands of Scottish forces. It is also a reference to a story from April 19 that circulated so widely that even William Gordon included it in his history of the revolution a decade later. Gordon explained that on Percy's way to reinforce Smith's forces, "a smart boy observing" the regulars "playing by, way of contempt, *Yankee Doodle* . . . made himself extremely merry with the circumstance, jumping and laughing, so as to attract the notice of his lordship." When Percy asked "at what he was laughing so heartily," the boy "answered, 'To think how you will dance by and by to *Chevy Chase*,'" thus supposedly anticipating the hasty retreat of the British forces only hours later. Thus "Yankee Doodle" became the American, or as Trumbull had it, the "modern mode" of "Chevy Chase."[49]

Indeed, the Battles of Lexington and Concord were also the moment when New Englanders—and the colonists more broadly in celebration of the minutemen's success—recaptured the prized tune. As they made the British soldiers "dance" their way back to Boston to "Yankee Doodle," at least in contemporary imagination, if not in reality, they helped shape the legend of the merry, if virile, rural American yeomen into a fledgling national myth. They also helped cast the American environment as a setting for carnivalesque acts of American homegrown virility. Thus, Mercy Otis Warren rehearsed a familiar refrain in her history of the American Revolution, written in the years immediately after the war but published decades later, in 1805:

> Not dismayed or daunted, this small body of yeomanry, armed in the cause of
> justice, and struggling for every thing they held dear, maintained their stand
> until the British troops, though far superior in numbers, and in all the advan-
> tages of military skill, discipline, and equipment, gave ground and retreated,
> without half executing the purpose designed, by this forced march to
> Concord . . . For, notwithstanding their superiority in every respect, several
> regiments of the best troops in the royal army, were seen, to the surprise and
> joy of every lover of his country, flying before the raw, inexperienced peas-
> antry, who had ran hastily together in defense of their lives and liberties.[50]

By the time the likes of Ralph Waldo Emerson and Henry Wadsworth Long-fellow respectively waxed poetic about "the shot heard round the world" and how Yankee "farmers gave them [British Regulars] ball for ball," the Battles of Lexington and Concord and the myth of the hardy yeomen-soldier was hallowed national ground.[51]

An American Clown

The above account of how Americans recovered the song "Yankee Doodle" during the events of April 19, 1775, did not itself become American mythology, but by the end of the war it had emerged as the de facto anthem of the revolution and would continue to figure prominently in the American imagination. Moreover, the character of the Yankee associated with the song would come to embody the American character. This too was a joke, as the Yankee character was a buffoonish provincial, an Americanized variation on the European country clown—a self-deprecating joke that nevertheless helped bound a nation around their common origins. Thus, following the reverberations surrounding the imagery of the Yankee clown in the fledgling popular culture of the early United States provides a sense of how rural antiauthoritarian sensibilities and political commitments increasingly found their way into the national consensus.

In premodern Europe and its offshoots, the trope of the jester or clown alluded to a low-ranking member of society who was literally everyone's laughingstock. At the same time, however, clowns and jesters were allowed to mock almost anyone, even as they often made fun of themselves. In fact, clowns engaged in a battle of wits with their interlocutors, with the final tally ultimately hinging on power and group dynamics. At court, rulers of course held the most power and could usually influence the humor of the jester to affirm that power, but a clever court clown could negotiate situations to potentially render everyone, including a king or a queen, the butt of a joke. "The pleasures and dangers of laughter," one scholar of jester humor noted shrewdly, "are also the pleasures and dangers of power."[52] In fact, this is what made clowns so appealing: they created situations rife with tension and release—the stuff of humor. They were creatures of both subversion and discipline, focal points for both hegemony and counter-hegemony.

In seventeenth- and eighteenth-century Britain—an era marked by the transition to republicanism, rise of market forces, and rural-to-urban migration—the "country clown" emerged as a particularly potent comical device and the most prevalent jester trope. At times, the monikers "country man" and "country clown" were practically interchangeable. Appearing in jestbooks, theater, literature, and song, the country clown induced mirth by plumbing a cluster of anxieties, tensions, and power struggles that developed around the symbolism of city and country.[53] Clowns were never fully stable stereotypes by their very nature and often morphed into or appeared alongside other stock characters. In this vein, the fate of the country clown became entwined with another clown, the urban fop, as humor thrived on pitting crude and boisterous yokels alongside overly refined and haughty city gentlemen.

Songs and jests—including the version of "Yankee Doodle" familiar to most Americans today—found mirth in the comical gait of the country clown assuming the airs of a fop. Arriving in town and adopting ostentatious airs in an attempt to blend in, Yankee Doodle famously "put a feather in his hat and called it macaroni." In this vein, he ineptly tries to mimic foppish city gentlemen who wore outrageous wigs that were commonly mocked at the time as "macaroni." Thus he emerged as a particular comical version of the city dandy—that is, a Yankee Doodle Dandy.[54] While British elites traditionally employed such clownish tropes to deprecate the lower classes and mock unworthy attempts at social mobility, in America the Yankee became a national hero, and lower-class men working their way up the economic ladder would come to symbolize America. Thus, when American elites sought to appropriate such tropes for their purposes, they often unwittingly played into the hands of their lower-class opponents. Indeed, with the decline of Old World status structures, the common people's humor—or their interpretation of humor—tended to win out, elevating an uppity rural clown as the embodiment of the American way. In short, the song "Yankee Doodle" and the Yankee character were Trojan horses embraced during the revolution by Americans of all walks of life. Only later would it become obvious how rural Americans and their humor penetrated and came to occupy a central position in the American imagination and national commitments. Few if any cultural artifacts from the immediate post–Revolutionary War period captured the social tensions of the day and demonstrated how they played out in this novel republican landscape better than *The Contrast*, the comedy of manners by Royall Tyler, and the story behind it.

In March 1787, after a winter campaign against Shays' Rebellion, the rural insurrection in western Massachusetts, the Massachusetts Council dispatched Major Royall Tyler, aide-de-camp to General Benjamin Lincoln, to New York City to seek cooperation in tracking down renegade rebels. A few days earlier, Tyler had returned to Boston after pursuing the rebel leader Daniel Shays into Vermont, but officials there—many of them former Green Mountain Boys—pled ignorance of his whereabouts. He had better luck in New York City, where he arrived on March 12, obtaining the cooperation of New York's state government. More famously, however, during the first weeks of his stay in the city, Tyler wrote *The Contrast*, the first American play to enjoy commercial success at home. Debuting at the John Street Theatre on April 16, 1787, the play notably featured two Yankee protagonists: an American officer, Colonel Manly, and his servant, Jonathan—both of whom, like Tyler, had arrived in New York in the wake of the campaign against Shays' rebels.[55]

By pairing the quixotic duo of a grave officer and a clownish, rank-and-file soldier, both recent participants in quelling the Massachusetts insurrection, Tyler comically captured the political and cultural conflicts of the tense period between the outbreak of Shays' Rebellion in the summer of 1786 and ratification of the Constitution in 1789. Indeed, at one point in the play Tyler implies that the two Yankees of very different stripes also entertain oppositional social and political sympathies. When asked if he had taken "part with the insurgents," Jonathan intimates in his usual droll manner that he "did think the sturgeons were right."[56] The colonel, however, corrects his servant's misdirection, declaring it a "burning shame for the true blue Bunker Hill sons of liberty . . . to have any hand in kicking up a cursed dust against a government which we had, every mother's son of us, a hand in making." Jonathan, heeding his superior, follows Manly, acting as his servant in the campaign against the rebels.[57]

After the end of the war for independence in 1783, Americans turned their attentions to determining how revolutionary their nation would be—to what degree their republican form of government would veer from the British formula that had until then organized their political and social lives. Fearing anarchy, Massachusetts elites sought to establish their leadership with a new state constitution ratified in 1780 that gave them outsized influence and empowered them to levy high taxes to repay war debt, some of which would go to them as creditors of the state. For their part, rebels felt betrayed by an austere version of republicanism and taxes that burdened them even more than at the height of British taxation policies and viewed these economic policies as self-serving and corrupt. Thus, emotions ran high during Shays' Rebellion—and, as the play itself demonstrated, not only on the side of the rebels. After rural Massachusetts farmers violently shut down many of the country courts, eastern patricians organized to curb the rural insurrection. As most histories of the period have it, this violent eruption in the summer and fall of 1786, subsequently curbed during a winter campaign in early 1787, galvanized the movement for a new founding contract, which culminated in the Constitutional Convention in the summer of 1787.

Tyler, who took part in the winter campaign, wrote *The Contrast* in spring 1787 as a moral tale and contribution to the debates and conflicts surrounding the nature of self-rule in the new republic. Surprisingly, given the elitist disposition of his service in the late campaign, Tyler gave Americans the first celebrated stage representation of an Americanized version of the European country clown, the Yankee, now embodied in Brother Jonathan. Although Tyler tried to represent rural Yankees somewhat ambiguously, as clownish and inept and therefore unfit for republican politics, the revolution tied his hands, ultimately resulting in the rather favorable image Americans increasingly cultivated of their own homegrown rustic clown. In Europe the country clown offered elites an effective tool for belittling rural people of common stock, but in post-revolutionary America, the discursive landscape proved trickier to navigate given that the struggle between commoners and gentleman had turned a crucial corner. Having harnessed the joyous multitude as part of the struggle against the British, and having embraced leveling language that appeased revolutionary crowds and provincial inhabitants of frontier and rural regions, elites found it far harder to restrain the leveling logic and commitments that had been so central to the colonial revolt. They did, however, try.

In many respects a product of British literary tradition, *The Contrast* sought at face value to instruct Americans on how to construct a usable version of gentility. In this vein, the main villain in the play, as in many other comedies of manners from the period, is a rakish, effeminate fop. Hence the contrast: whereas Colonel Manly inspires virtue and republicanism, the play's leading antagonist, Billy Dimple, represents a warning against the excessive and corrupt airs of gentility, that could undermine the vigor of the young republic as it had Britain. While Manly is patriotic, Dimple is an Anglophile rake and fop; Manly is honest and frugal, Dimple the consummate conniving profligate; Manly cultivates virtue, Dimple cultivates appearances and deceit. Further, as both contend for the hand of the virtuous Maria, Manly wants to marry her, deeming her a paragon of feminine virtue, while Dimple courts two additional women behind Maria's back. As a morality tale, *The Contrast* attempts to provide audiences with positive and negative examples of gentility.

During the cultural struggles that ensued between rural Americans and more urban and refined elites over the nature of the American body politic, young gentlemen sought to contrive a formula of elite manhood reconciling revolutionary language with republican ideology. They tried to walk a fine line to avoid accusations of genteel corruption, effeminacy, and refined airs— the traits associated with the British gentleman during the revolution—but at the same time to maintain the natural superiority of well-born Americans over common-born folk. As they encountered rural Americans in real life, and perhaps even more often in their imagination, they sought to firmly plant an adapted version of the British gentleman in American soil. During the latter part of the eighteenth century, it was above all else the trope of the "man of feeling" and "sensibility" that stood out as the best formulation combining manhood and gentility to adequately contend with the challenges of the day.[58] In Colonel Manly, the upright hero of *The Contrast*, Tyler seeks to shore up American virtue, sensibility, and manliness of the highest order. He clearly modeled Manly after the image of the American officer cultivated by George Washington, whom Manly directly identifies as his inspiration and role model.[59]

The play's structuring of contrasts, however, ultimately frustrates clear-cut advocacy of the contemporary ideal of gentility. The second comic foil for Colonel Manly is the Yankee Jonathan, a crude bumpkin and Americanized version of the British country clown. Here's the rub with that: although the juxtaposition of Manly and Dimple serves as the play's main axis, the pairing of Manly and Jonathan spoke to American audiences the most. *The Contrast* introduced the character of the Yankee clown to American theater in the form of Jonathan and demonstrated the traction of the local bumpkin character with American audiences, foreshadowing the later success of the popular American genre of Yankee theater that came into its own in the 1820s. In fact, theatergoers primarily went to see the boisterous portrayal of the Yankee by the famous comedic actor Thomas Wignell, not the tiresome and sober Colonel Manly. In Wignell, esteemed by one contemporary critic as the "Atlas of the American theatre," Tyler found the perfect actor to secure the play's comic action and success, and Wignell delivered, perhaps all too well.[60] Tyler exerted only limited control over his most famous literary flair, Jonathan.

Like the eponymous Yankee Doodle, Jonathan manifests many of the traits of the British country clown and its offshoots adapted to the American context. Indeed, one memorable scene—Tyler winks at the crowd by having Jonathan attend the very same New York theater—suggests that Jonathan is based on the clownish Irishman Darby from *The Poor Soldier*, the comedy Jonathan supposedly watched, written by John O'Keeffe. Unsurprisingly, especially for a play written by a New Englander, the Yankee looms as the obvious model for an Americanized Darby. Much like his European "cousin," Jonathan knows nothing of urban polite culture, mispronounces basic terms, is uncouth with women, fails at basic logical deductions, and lacks strong self-will. Furthermore, like most other theatrical country clowns, Jonathan actually has little to do with the main thrust of the plot, primarily providing comic relief and embellishment. Like many clowns before him, though he committed gaffes and behaved improperly, Jonathan proved charming as a comical figure, grabbing the attention of the audience and its affection. Indeed, although certain aspects of Jonathan's character are negative or even repulsive, as a prototypical rustic buffoon and the anchor of the play's whimsical nature, Jonathan tallies more positive responses than negative ones.[61]

More disturbing perhaps from Tyler's perspective, Jonathan overshadows his master, Manly. Although Tyler might have viewed his play as a morality tale and Manly as the unquestionable hero, his medium of choice, comedy, undermines his convictions vis-à-vis the questions he poses. It turns out, the play not only paints Dimple as foppish, as one would expect, but it also burlesques the grave and severe Manly. How else would a staid, humorless man of feeling seem in a comical context? How would a theater-going New York crowd view a character whose Puritanism and virtuous republicanism would have prevented him from stepping inside a theater, let alone taking in a comedy of manners? Had Tyler written a tragedy, perhaps modeled after Addison's *Cato*, one of George Washington's favorite plays, he could have asserted more control over the moral tone of the play. Instead, as during the revolution, humor proved hard to control. In fact, Manly and his ilk could never have been part of the play's comic element. They were never in on the joke.[62]

Moreover, Jonathan proved harder to control than a British country clown because in post-revolutionary America, the Yankee occupied a more central position than his British relations had in Europe. Thus, in *The Poor Soldier*, Darby proves quite likable despite his many flaws, but in *The Contrast*, Jonathan emerges as the most memorable and beloved character. Darby only carves out a niche as a mainstay in the production's comical action, but Jonathan mounts a more serious challenge to Manly's dominance. Much like Yankee Doodle competing with General Washington in memories of the war, the clownish Jonathan subverts Colonel Manly's gravity, fundamentally challenging his moral hegemony.

To associate Jonathan with the recent developments in Yankee tradition, Tyler wove certain stylistic elements into the portrait of his clown, including his name, Jonathan, the prototypical Yankee moniker at the time, and his recognizable Yankee dialect, derived from many of the famous "Yankee Doodle" versions. In this fashion, Jonathan spoke of his family in a comically familiar way as "father" or "mother" (rather than "my father" or "my mother"), used quaint idioms, like "thick as mustard," and entertained those he met with surprising applications of the word "nation" and "tarnation."[63] At one point, Jonathan of course bursts into a rendition of "Yankee Doodle," comically apologizing for only being able to "sing but a hundred and ninety verses" of the famous tune.[64]

On a substantive level, Tyler also introduces differences in character that afford Jonathan a more heroic stature than traditional British bumpkins could hope to boast. For instance, *The Contrast* celebrates Jonathan as something of a role model, albeit a comical one. For Americans already given to self-deprecating mirth, this was hardly a setback. This stature comes across particularly well in the scenes pairing Jonathan with his primary antagonist, Jessamy, Dimple's servant. Though Tyler primarily juxtaposes Manly and Dimple as the most glaring contrast, from which the play takes its name, it also contrasts everything American with everything English. Thus, as part of his scheme of contrasts, the duo of Jonathan and Manly embody American honesty and manliness, respectively, versus the Anglophile duo, Dimple and Jessamy, who together exemplify duplicity and corruption. Therefore, as the antithesis of the conniving Jessamy, Jonathan is cast in a positive light.

Indeed, Tyler insinuates Jonathan's superiority over his European lower-class counterparts, whether a buffoonish Irishman or a clumsy Yorkshireman. In the aforementioned theater scene, when Jonathan knowingly references his likeness to Darby (also played by Wignell) from *The Poor Soldier*, mentioning his affinity to him, he adds, "There was one thing I didn't like in that Mr. Darby; and that was, he was afraid of some of them 'ere shooting irons . . . Now, I'm a true born Yankee American son of liberty, and I never was afraid of a gun yet in all my life." Thus, Tyler explicitly admits that rural New Englanders commonly known as Yankees, the heroes of Lexington and Concord and of Bunker Hill, possessed true manly qualities. Indeed, Jonathan never misses an opportunity to associate himself with the heroics of the revolution. Furthermore, in the final scene, Jonathan intercedes in a sword duel, declaring that he "feels chock-full of fight" and that he would like to "shew him Yankee boys play," clearly a reference to the heroics of Lexington and Concord and Bunker Hill.[65] Thus, in *The Contrast*, the Yankee, though portrayed with some ambiguity, and vulgar though he may be, emerges as a hero.

Because refined gentlemen were associated with urbane effeminacy and foppery, Jonathan might have appeared more manly than Colonel Manly himself. Not unlike "Yankee Doodle," although *The Contrast* ostensibly focuses on the struggle between British and American cultural alignment and identity, it serves just as well as a textual repository that offers incisive insight into the conflicts between commoners and elites. Further, like "Yankee Doodle," the confluence of themes—the British-American and plebeian–

patrician divides—problematized the position taken by those who became associated with the specter of British corruption: Eastern Seaboard elites. Indeed, if the song "Yankee Doodle" and Yankee stock characters were uniquely American jokes, rural Americans could increasingly feel themselves part of the nation more so than genteel Americans. In this regard, the Yankee was Tom the Tinker on a national scale.[66]

The Yankee in the Early Nineteenth Century

Despite attempts by educated elites such as Royall Tyler to employ the trope of the Yankee to disparage rural Americans, the bumpkins would ultimately turn the joke on its head in the early United States. Mirroring the demise of the Federalists and the political rise of the Democratic-Republicans, by the early decades of the nineteenth century, the country clown, especially in his Yankee persona, offered Americans an adaptable and effective national icon. Yankee stock characters regularly appeared on the American stage, and by the 1820s Yankee theater, revolving around celebrated performances of Yankees by specialist actors, would become popular across the United States. According to scholars of the American stage, it eventually developed into a full-fledged American theatrical genre that would see its heyday in the antebellum decades, 1830–1850, on both sides of the Atlantic. By that time, depictions of Yankees were usually both comical and ambiguous, though on the whole more positive than negative.[67] Also by then, another iconic clown—the frontier jester in the form of Davy Crockett and his ilk—would overshadow the Yankee as an even more effective and promising bumpkin for the cultural work of a country not only reconciled to provincialism, but also championing independent and virile western frontiersmen.[68]

For the purposes here, one last literary character of national acclaim provides a fitting send-off for the Yankee: Jack Downing, the brainchild of the New England satirist Seba Smith. In Portland, Main, during the early 1830s, the so-called age of Jackson, Smith published fictional letters from Jack Downing, a backwoods Maine yokel, sharing his adventures in the "metropolitan," Portland, with his relatives back home in the country. In his early letters, full of Yankee jargon, Jack typically focuses on his impressions of democratic politics. "Another thing I've been waiting for," Downing wrote to his uncle about a deadlock in the Maine legislature, "was to tell you who was governor. But, O dear, I cant find out half so much about it now, here in this great city of Portland . . . as I could six months ago among the bear traps and log houses in our town, way back in the woods."[69]

Enjoying ever more success and popularity, Smith sought in 1831 to use Downing's letters to satirize Jacksonian politics by having the Maine bumpkin arrive in Washington at the actual time of the upheaval in Andrew Jackson's administration over the Eaton affair. Thus Downing, the crude commoner, stumbles into the political drama that erupted when the Washington gentry shunned the lower-class Margaret Eaton, wife of the secretary of war. Having heard that four of Jackson's secretaries had resigned, Downing writes, "I think it's the duty of all true republicans . . . to take hold and help the president along in these trying difficulties . . . What a shame 'twas that them are secretaries should all clear out, and leave the poor old general to do all the work alone."[70] He then proceeds to Washington, and although Downing does not receive a position as secretary as he had hoped, Jackson awards him a captain's commission with personal orders on the president's behalf. The story of the uncouth Yankee social climber who commits numerous gaffes ensued in this manner, on and on, to the great delight of Americans. Indeed, the Downing letters proved so successful that by 1834 Smith and Davy Crockett, by then a legendary frontiersman, colluded to publish a supposed correspondence between Downing and Crockett, feeding a national audience hungry for ever more droll provincial utterances by the two. Smith also successfully released multi-edition collections of Downing's letters that included illustrations.[71]

A Maine native from a simple background who attained a college education, Smith as an adult was socially and geographically well positioned to create a Yankee character in a piece of political comedy. He was both partial to the folk traditions of Maine, in New England called Down East, as well as critical of and anxious about US society. Smith perceived the United States as having turned into a place where common, uneducated country clowns could climb the social ladder to hold real positions of political power. As with Tyler's comedy, Smith's satire expressed an unease with the coming of democracy, but also reflected an attempt to provide constructive criticism to promote a sounder republican culture. Yet again, however, American audiences ended up embracing Jack Downing, as they did Tyler's Jonathan, not as a cautionary tale, but—in the self-deprecating yet comforting tandem central to the appeal of Yankee lore—as the true embodiment of the American way. Ironically, Smith was not fully in on his own joke.[72]

Although some Americans, primarily those in opposition to Jackson, registered the ambiguities Smith intended to convey, the majority did not think of them in quite the same critical terms that Smith did. Over the 1830s, a

Figure 3.1. "Yours til Deth, Major Jack Downing," from Seba Smith, *Letters of Major Jack Downing of the Downingville Militia* (New York, 1866). Depictions of the character Jack Downing would influence the stock image of Uncle Sam. Library of Congress, https://www.loc.gov/item/43033786/.

critical mass of Americans came to genuinely relish their common origins. Perhaps most telling is that according to some reports, Jackson himself took a liking to the *Jack Downing Letters*. Thus, in the figure of Jack Downing, who became Andrew Jackson's right-hand man, the Yankee clown had firmly established himself as a lasting feature in the political community of the United States. By then, democracy too had spread to almost all white men, regardless of class status. The leveling promise of the revolutionary era, at least in this important regard had been fulfilled. Common American men had become, not only full members of the polity as voting citizens, but had also emerged as full-fledged national icons. Indeed, with time, the depiction of Jack Downing in the illustrations accompanying the collected editions of *Jack Downing Letters* became the personification of the United States in the figure of Uncle Sam (figure 3.1). Thus, in the people's court, the jester became the celebrated face of the nation.[73]

CHAPTER FOUR

The Laughter and the Fury

Terror and Masquerade on the American Frontier

On April 19, 1775, during the Battles of Lexington and Concord—or more accurately, during the fighting on the road back to Boston later that day—the Massachusetts militia carried out irregular "bush-fighting," continually attacking the retreating British column from behind cover, largely avoiding a pitched battle. As both sides declared, it was primarily this American way of war, or what settlers sometimes called the "skulking way of war," that won the day. "The rebels never made one gallant or manly attempt at us," railed one British officer. "[They] fought like savages of the country." The British viewed such warfare as cowardly and uncivilized, the way Indians and barbarians supposedly fought. For Americans, however, this form of "irregular" warfare was a marker of their unique virility, particularly in their own "wilderness." Those "few irregulars" taking to the "Yankee way of bush fighting" laid waste to "chosen men," enthused one typical American response in a letter.[1] The unique American environment and traditions, many American settlers believed, or very much wanted to believe, made every man both a capable citizen and a soldier. The Battles of Lexington and Concord as well as the subsequent fighting at the Battle of Bunker Hill (June 1775) appeared to prove them correct.

As a euphoric martial spirit swept the colonies after Lexington and Concord, many Americans showed surprising faith in their militias, especially given that they were about to wage war against the most formidable military power of the day.[2] One Philadelphian, not yet sure how he felt about American independence, wrote a friend days after news of Lexington and Concord arrived: "The parliament seem determined to force us into an acknowledgment of their supremacy, I dread the worst, for I am sure they never can do it, from the number of inhabitants, and the very situation of this country; besides our rifle men, who are used to shooting in the woods, will never come to an open engagement; they are very expert at the Indian manner of fighting." In the summer of 1775, a Virginian conceded to a friend in London, "Though British officers may be better qualified for carrying on a regular war, . . . the nature of the country will render their superior skill useless . . . The Americans think they could easily vanquish them in the woods of America . . . [where] they will shew them buckskin play."[3] The American militias, as an extension of American society, could outperform a stodgy European regular army, especially in the American woods. After all, they had honed their prowess at arms and acumen in that environment through almost two centuries of bloody struggle with the wild "savages" of North America. They even boasted typical Indian buckskin dress to show for it.

Indeed, in America, the militia was the center of a military tradition that deviated markedly from European warfare and was largely modeled after settlers' (often skewed) conceptions of Native American warfare. Although settler militias inflicted real deadly violence on the British during the Revolutionary War, they developed and usually reserved this form of brutal and irregular warfare when making war on Indians. Outside the period of outright hostilities, both white militias and mobs applied limited violence that usually stopped short of death when engaging the "enemies of liberty." In contrast, most of the fighting in America had developed and would continue to occur as part of the endemic wars between settlers and Native peoples or mixed forces of both. "For the first 200 years of [US] military heritage," the military historian John Grenier wrote, "Americans depended on arts of war that contemporary professional soldiers supposedly abhorred: razing and destroying enemy villages and fields; killing enemy women and children; raiding settlements for captives; intimidating and brutalizing enemy noncombatants; and assassinating enemy leaders." Ironically, although Europeans in America became convinced that guerrilla warfare, which they called the "skulking way of war," was innate to Indians' supposedly savage condition, they sought to enlist Native peoples in their wars and developed a militia tradition of ranger companies that specialized in skulking, supposedly as well as any Indian.[4]

American settlers, convinced of their mastery of the Indian way of bush-fighting, embraced this new way of war as their own and as a marker of their virility, but there were important distinctions. Whereas Native forces usually sought to inflict violence over a relatively short campaign, as part of their logistical calculations and goals, European settlers in America introduced the settler colonial logic of elimination: extended, scorched-earth campaigns that sought to extirpate their foes. Native warfare employed caution and the element of surprise, to inflict damage while suffering as few casualties as possible to great effect—often translated into what today is called guerrilla warfare. Europeans mimicked such tactics, but also combined them with their logistical capacity to support longer campaigns and extirpative goals.[5] Indeed, as the theorist Patrick Wolfe famously asserted, since British settlers came "to stay" and displace the Native population in North America, they ultimately waged a genocidal campaign of extermination. The "logic of elimination" behind the goals of the British and later American settlers made genocidal violence an ongoing feature of North American settler colonialism.[6]

American militias, part of the infrastructure that carried out one of the most extensive ethnic-cleansing projects known, were also bands of "merry men" who came together to drink and frolic, away from their wives and children. One common refrain was that militiamen did little more than drink and boast; in fact, one of the most time-honored traditions associated with militia musters was to retire to the tavern as soon as possible.[7] Timothy Pickering, who attempted to reform Massachusetts militia traditions, found the militiamen's habit of firing in good fun at whomever they pleased particularly appalling. "It had been the custom in Salem," Pickering wrote, "from my earliest remembrance, and of fifty or perhaps a hundred years before to fire at the officers, under the senseless notion of doing them honor . . . and it gave them a singular satisfaction to make women the objects of their dangerous diversion. Nor did strangers escape the hazard and inconvenience of their inhuman inhospitable sport."[8] Indeed, for many participants, the militia was much of the time a largely social affair, where much mirth was to be had. Such levity and play animated the militiamen who organized as the Green Mountain Boys, the Black Boys, the White Indians of Maine, and many more. Levity and play—eerily combined with anxiety, terror, and deadly violence—would also infuse the identity and practices of some of the same militiamen when they wore buckskins and painted their faces to carry out ruthless warfare against Native peoples.

This chapter examines the darker currents that animated the antiauthoritarian masquerade adopted by rural Americans during the second half of the eighteenth century, especially when they organized as militias. As a key way for white men to transform themselves through shared masquerade into "true" natives and to claim "their" land, militias had both lasting leveling and violent implications for the nation. As the militia tradition played out during anti-colonial as well as settler colonial wars, it constituted—on the ground and perhaps even more so in the American imagination—a national form of Indian play, writ large, through which Americans became "natives," even as they violently decimated Native peoples or drove them away. Militias were a powerful metaphor for the new nation that brought together a giddy and leveling belief in the common man—as citizen and fighter—and their embrace of Indian warfare and visages induced the heady notion that they were true products of the American environment. Thus, each militia represented a microcosm of the new nation, a way for men to understand their place in the nation and to help render such an abstract idea as a nation real and compelling in their minds. Since militias viewed themselves as bands of virile men protecting white women from racial others, it was also clear that only white men could join the fun—and the nation.

The militias' Indian masquerade proved capable of uniting democratic convictions with brutality and violence of a completely different magnitude than militia or mob violence against the "enemies of liberty," examined in previous chapters; it was the kind of horrific violence that white settlers largely reserved for racial others.[9] By rendering such violence palatable and even enticing, humor helped naturalize both the genocidal violence endemic to North American settler colonialism as well as naturalize white settlers to the American landscape. Thus, the militia emerged as an important crucible in which a peculiar combination of mirth and violence forged a nation of "indigenous" white men, who would claim the American continent as the perfect landscape for enacting their merry and often violent escapades.

The Militia

The idea of the militia has a long history in English and European thought and emerged as a particularly generative metaphor for the community of citizens in republican thought. Most whig thinkers cherished the vision of the militia and of the citizen-soldier, often invoking the memory of the Roman republic, which according to myth had thrived when it relied on independent citizen soldiers, but declined after coming to rely on large, standing armies. In British republican thought, this concept of the citizen-soldier was often associated with the free yeomanry, who were to be entrusted with militia service, as opposed to suspect standing armies. In the North American colonies, where radical whig thought reached a particularly high pitch in the years leading up to the Revolutionary War, virtually all the leading figures of the revolution, the so-called founders, also expressed reverence for the idea of the militia and suspicion of standing armies. Their regard for it grew even more so after British troops garrisoned, or in the view of American settlers "occupied," colonial towns.[10]

The ideal of the "citizen-soldier" was largely maintained in Britain by radical whig theorists suspicious of standing armies. By the eighteenth century, Britain had come to rely on standing armies, with only a small segment of the population participating in the militia as a last line of defense in case of invasion and was rarely mobilized. In colonial North America, by contrast, the militia was both an idea and a necessity of life, required to defend settlers from Native and European enemies as well as from the slaves the economy had come to rely on. Thus, the republican ideal of the yeoman citizen-soldier also contended with the realities that shaped the institution of the militia over decades and centuries of intermittent war. Established by local laws across the colonies, with the exception of Pennsylvania, as a potential army to heed the call to arms at any given moment, militias served in wars against Native enemies to some degree. When large scale wars broke out, however, they usually had to be reorganized and reassembled, as the everyday militia structure was not sufficiently effective. Thus for many, the local militia muster they attended (or skipped altogether) served more as a social gathering that also reinforced communal hierarchies. Nevertheless, large-scale conscriptions of provincial units were made more wieldy by militia laws requiring all members to own their own arms, if they could afford it, and providing members with basic training and familiarity with warfare. Such organization also made it all too easy for Americans to believe that these men, by virtue of their militia experience, were capable of daring military feats.[11]

The militia in colonial America became over the years "less an army per se," as one historian put it, and more "an all-purpose military infrastructure" employed in a variety of ways.[12] It served as a home guard to protect the community as the last line of defense, as a pool of recruits when settlers fielded provincial armies (usually with separate command structures), and as the basis for special volunteer units, such as the minutemen, the snowshoe men, and various other ranger companies. During the Seven Years' War (1754–63)—which informed the memory of American colonists fighting the Revolutionary War—the most important divisions emerged not between standing armies and militias, but between regulars and provincial regiments; the latter were regular troops who relied to some degree on the militia structure and ways. Nevertheless, in the minds of the Americans, the distinction between standing armies and militias remained as important as ever. Indeed, it was even more important as a symbolic node of their tensions and later struggle with the mother country and its institutions.[13] Moreover, although the militia often furnished regular provincial regiments, Americans took pride in and paid more attention to their so-called ranger units, viewed as embodying American virility and militia tradition.

Indeed, ranger companies or riflemen units emerged in the American imagination as an adaptation of the traditional British notion of a yeomen's militia, which according to whig doctrine was superior to any standing army. Such virile and virtuous men, republican theory taught, and Roman history supposedly demonstrated, could easily defeat an army of corrupt mercenaries. Since many colonists felt increasingly inclined to view hardy American provincials as more virile and virtuous than British army regulars of inferior Old World stock, it was not too big a leap to perceive rangers as modern-day Robin Hoods, independent yeomen who emerged from the forests when called to defend the citizenry of the land. In this vein, in the immediate aftermath of the militias' success at Lexington and Concord, when New England militiamen arrived in New York to help with its defenses, one local observer exclaimed, "They have not that sprightly and foppish appearance of regular forces when nicely powdered; however they are hardy, can endure fatigue, and have made themselves masters of the essential parts of military skill." Waxing poetic about the Battle of Bunker Hill, a young H. H. Brackenridge concurred, extolling his common countrymen "a people brave, who never yet, of luxury, or soft delights, effeminate, and false, have tasted."[14] Thus, rangers or riflemen—as opposed to regular fighters armed with muskets and bayonets—emerged as a potent symbol of American manhood. Over the midcentury war years, and even more so after Lexington and Concord, Americans came to believe that they were the hardy indigenous men of America, true specimens of their natural habitat. The masquerade associated with these units, wearing Indian garb and practicing the skulking way of war, suggests that mirth played a role in facilitating their sense of transformation from colonists to natives. Indeed, Americans came to endow the image of militia companies, especially when organized as ranger or riflemen units, with a certain lighthearted levity, somewhat lax discipline, and fraternal democratic camaraderie. Thus, for instance, they increasingly refused to be assigned commanders from above, insisting instead on choosing their own command structures, signaling themselves the furthest thing from British regulars and their ilk. In fact, the militia spirit proved to be a problem for American military leaders, including George Washington and Andrew Jackson, as they struggled to field well-disciplined and professional armies. They knew full well the limits of the militia, but also had to contend with the hold the idea of the militia had over the people's imagination.[15]

The Ranger Tradition

Two separate ranger, or ranging, traditions emerged independently in the colonies during the last quarter of the eighteenth century. In New England, Benjamin Church organized the first ranger company during King Philip's War (1675–76). It consisted of 60 colonists and 140 Native allies, and its mission was to carry out search and destroy operations against the Wampanoags and Narragansets. In this way, some colonists learned the skulking way of war from their Native allies and began the vaunted American tradition of Euro-Americans supposedly fighting like Indians. Similarly, in Virginia, ranger units first appeared at the time of the Susquehannock War (1676), during which Virginians sought to develop a highly mobile fighting force uniquely designed to defend the colony from Native attacks. Such units, with orders to "range" between frontier settlements for their protection, would with time become a mainstay in the southern colonies. They would also form the backbone of the Virginia, Kentucky, and Tennessee traditions of the Indian fighter, who were sometimes called "long knives." Such traditions in many of the colonies were reinforced by bounties on scalps, which as Grenier noted, created self-appointed or semi-formal ranger forces akin to the privateering tradition on the seas, with state-sponsored incentives prompting men to specialize in Indian fighting. Thus, not only did many Indian fighters take to Native ways, as they understood them, to fight Native peoples, many also came to appropriate the Native American tradition, as they understood it, of bringing back scalps from raids as evidence of their accomplishments.[16]

During the first half of the eighteenth century, almost all North American British colonies, save Quaker-influenced Pennsylvania, experimented with and came to rely to some degree on Native forms of warfare, employing

Native allies, ranger units, or both. By midcentury, the term *rangers* had become familiar to most Americans given the decades of ongoing wars against various French, Spanish, and Native alliances. During these years, the success and celebrity of Gorham's Rangers during King George's War (1745–48) and Father La Loutre's War (1749–55), and, even more so, Rogers' Rangers during the Seven Years' War, firmly established this tradition as a point of pride for Americans.[17] A letter from a Colonel Blanchard published in local newspapers captured contemporary convictions. In it, Blanchard praised Major Robert Rogers, for "the signal honour you have acquired by your martial attempts and success, in defense of your country." "The enterprising youths from our frontiers, who have and are joining you for the ranging service," he proclaimed, "are not the gleanings, but the first fruits of North-America." Thus, in the decades leading up to Lexington and Concord, Americans developed an attachment to self-affirming notions of their militias and ranger units that would lead them to quickly construct the events of April 19, 1775, as myth.[18]

By the same token, it was also quite clear to American colonists that Native allies, and enemies, were a force to be reckoned with. In the Seven Years' War, early defeats at the hands of French and Native warriors employing irregular warfare to great effect reinforced such convictions. "However insignificant the remains of the Indian Natives might appear to shallow politicians," observed one writer in the wake of such defeats and Indian terror, "every man must now be convinced that they are the most important allies, and the most formidable enemies . . . Three or four hundred Delawares and Shawanese have kept three populous provinces [Maryland, Virginia, and Pennsylvania] in play, ravaged and depopulated whole counties, butchered and captivated hundreds of families, and spread terror and desolation wherever they went, and that almost with impunity."[19]

Indeed, though it would take time for British administrators and military commanders to fully recognize the utility of rangers and Native allies—even after the shame of General Edward Braddock's defeat by French and Native forces at the Battle of the Monongahela (1755)—Americans had by then committed to irregular warfare. Benjamin Franklin's portrayal of events leading up to the battle, somewhat suspect for being written with hindsight, was nevertheless telling. According to Franklin's autobiography, he warned General Braddock before the campaign to beware of "ambuscades of Indians, who, by constant practice, are dexterous in laying and executing them." Braddock infamously replied, "These savages may, indeed, be a formidable enemy to your raw American militia, but upon the king's regular and disciplined troops, sir, it is impossible they should make any impression."[20] Regardless of the accuracy of Franklin's representation of events, the warning intimated that the Americans appreciated guerrilla warfare, considering either local rangers or Native allies as crucial for any successful campaign. In nearby New Jersey, Franklin's son, Governor William Franklin, echoed such convictions in a speech to the colony's assembly. "By acting on the Defensive only, you give them [the Indians] almost every Advantage they could desire," he warned:

> But if we were to send parties of rangers into their country, to cut off the communication between their several places of residence, surprise them in their hunting and fishing, destroy their corn fields, bring off their women and children, and burn their habitations, we should, in a little time be able to oblige them to accept whatever terms we might think proper to dictate. In short, if we would fight them in their own way, we should find that an Indian war would soon be stripped of all its terrors.[21]

Thus, before the British even considered modifying their tactics, when violence erupted up and down the colonies in the mid-1750s, every colony (including Pennsylvania) had recruited ranger units. As a result, a growing number of frontier settlers became comfortable with fighting "Indian style," creating a large pool of fighters with some degree of familiarity with ranger tactics and practices. By the end of the decade, and certainly by the time of Pontiac's Rebellion (1763–64), both British and local administrators and commanders could rely on the significant body of knowledge accumulated by locals familiar with guerilla warfare. Indeed, many of the leading minutemen at Lexington and Concord were veterans of the Seven Years' War, lending their military acumen to their skulking attacks on the British column retreating to Boston. Demonstrating such convictions, just months before Lexington and Concord, one Massachusetts militia commander urged his troops to keep their spirits high as war with the British seemed imminent, reminding them that given "all the battles [we] had gained for his Majesty, in the last war" it was quite clear that "the Regulars must have been ruined but for [us]."[22]

Ultimately, Braddock's devastating defeat in 1755 even led smug British generals to admit that their forces would need Native allies and ranger companies to win the war against combined French and Native forces. Thus, even outside the ongoing local use of ranger companies, the British started recruiting regular, American-manned regiments to specialize in irregular warfare. The two most famous regiments were Henry Bouquet's 60th Royal American Regiment and Thomas Gage's 80th Light Infantry, both of which relied on ranger tactics, methods, and training. Bouquet and Gage also sought to provision their troops with equipment better fitting for navigating woodlands terrain, such as lighter gear, shorter muskets, and Indian dress. Though the high command denied Bouquet's request that his regiment be clad in a Native style, a few years later Gage's 80th would be known for their brown leather coats (ditching the traditional red coats) and shortened muskets.[23] Gage, an experienced British officer, distrusted Americans, so he enlisted only British officers and sergeants yet recruited Americans as the rank and file. In fact, the irregular nature of these regiments, it appears, ensured that the Americans, who much preferred the ranger service, would be easier to come by. After Gage finished raising his regiment, General Jeffrey Amherst informed Field Marshall John Ligonier in a snide, bemused tone, "Brig. Gage's light infantry who wanted a great many men are compleated, the Yankees love dearly a brown coat."[24] Thus, uniforms, in this case brown coats that looked like woodsmen garb, became potent identity touchstones. Similarly, when George Washington requested provisions for his Virginia Regiment, he remarked, "Were I left to pursue my own inclinations I woud not only cause the men to adopt the Indian dress but officers also, and set the example myself." Of course, for the most part, regular and even provincial troops were encumbered by British military protocol. Meanwhile ranger units emerged as local heroes who dressed, painted their faces, and fought like Indians.[25]

After the Seven Years' War, even leading British officers who often denounced American troops at times conceded that hardy American frontiersmen were necessary for their campaigns. Bouquet, for instance, did not hold back on praise during Pontiac's Rebellion, confiding in Colonel Adam Stephen, then living on the Virginia frontier, "But I have so great an opinion of the courage and experience of the inhabitants of your frontiers, that I would think myself certain of success could I be joined by three or four hundred of them under proper officers of their own choice." Indeed, Bouquet was in such need of American rangers that he was willing to put up with their antics, such as insisting on choosing their own commanders.

Though Bouquet's words were to some degree flattery necessary to oil the machinery of war—days later he would rebuke Pennsylvania frontiersmen with equal zeal—it was also clear that as much as most British commanders hated to admit it, they relied heavily on frontier rangers, and valued their contributions enough to put up with their lax discipline and irreverent ways.[26]

Likewise, as much as elites living on the Eastern Seaboard enjoyed ridiculing backcountry bumpkins, they at times also drew inspiration and faith, tinged with a sense of virility, from their mastery of arms. During the tense standoff in Massachusetts in the fall of 1774 that would months later erupt into hostilities, for example, one Bostonian took inspiration from a local tall tale about a "countryman" who bragged about his shooting skills in front of a regiment of British regulars after the soldiers had all failed to hit a target. Vowing that he could hit it "ten times running," the countryman hit it three times in a row, while "the officers as well as the soldiers *star'd*, and tho't the devil was in the man. *Why*, says the countryman, I'll tel you *naow*. I have got a *boy* at home that will toss up an apple and shoot out all the seeds as its coming down."[27] Thus, city gentlemen, many of whom complained endlessly about uncouth backwoodsmen, found themselves leaning on provincial prowess to assuage their fears of war with the British.

Such latent dispositions to favorably view provincialism meant that following the early successes in Massachusetts in the spring and summer of 1775, American faith in their virility and military prowess was at an all-time high. Once organized into militias for the Revolutionary War effort, they often adopted some form of Indian garb as their official uniforms, as one observer noted in delight: "Every man has a hunting shirt, which is the uniform of each company—almost all have a cockade & buckskin tale in their hats, to represent that they are hardy resolute, & invincible Natives of the woods of America."[28] Some observers reveled in the manhood of these purported specimens of the backwoods. Another report painted a particularly attractive scene of a company of Virginian veterans of Dunmore's War on the way to join the forces organizing under General Washington at Cambridge, Massachusetts: "They bear in their bodies visible marks of their prowess, and show scars and wounds which would do honor to Homer's Iliad . . . These men have been bred in the woods to hardship and dangers from their infancy. They appear as if they were entirely unacquainted with, had never felt the passion of fear. With their rifles in their hands, they assume a kind of omnipotence over their enemies."[29] "At night," after demonstrating uncanny shooting skills, they enacted a tantalizing Indian masquerade:

> A great fire was kindled around a pole painted in the court house square, where the company, with the captain at their head, all naked to the waist, and painted like savages . . . indulged a vast concourse of people with a perfect exhibition of a war-dance, and all the maneuvers of Indians, holding council, going to war, circumventing their enemies by defiles, ambuscades, attacking, scalping, &c. It is said by those who are judges, that no representation could possibly come nearer to the original.[30]

Indeed, Virginians seemed to take to such dress and revolutionary fervor with more verve then most. "The people all over America are determined to die or be free," explained one Virginian, who also depicted how the local militia expressed such pathos in their uniquely American garb: "The general uniforms are made of brown Osnaburghs, something like a shirt, double caped over the shoulder, in imitation of the Indian, and on the breast, in capital letters, is the motto, Liberty or Death."[31]

Yet, such euphoria was also a contrivance, long nurtured by Americans to alleviate deep-seated anxieties. During the revolutionary period, American settlers internalized poignant apprehensions over their situation as Euro-Americans about to sever their cultural lifeline to their mother country in Europe, all the while continuing to engage an indigenous enemy in the "new world." Americans performed fantastic intellectual acrobatics to negotiate the triangular, settler colonial crucible that on the one hand pitted them against their cultural metropolis, which claimed vast superiority and cast them as little better than savages, and on the other the original inhabitants of the land, who could outperform them in the North American woods, to which they had a truer claim. In a further ironic twist, the two peoples they were most anxious about and wished to outdo—the British and most Native nations in the region—became allies, joining forces to curb American settlers. For them there was no other way, but to insist that they were more qualified than their British kin to form a just and civilized republican, even democratic, society, and at the same time to declare themselves better than Indians in their own way of war. In doing so, American settlers pioneered a host of practices, along with conflicting convictions and talking points, and forced them to abide together under the same cognitive canopy, contradictions be damned.[32] Such strained ideological and cultural production proved all the more urgent for male settlers, given that for many it involved an ongoing struggle to maintain their hold on a particularly valuable form of cultural cache—their manhood.

The Gender Frontier

In recent years, historians have come to understand the underpinnings of cultural encounters along the lines of what Kathleen Brown has called a gender frontier: "the site of creative and destructive processes resulting from the confrontations of culturally-specific manhoods and womanhoods."[33] One of the most curious findings by this scholarship is that Native peoples and frontier settlers had much in common, even in the realm of gender, where earlier scholarship had emphasized differences. Paradoxically, however, similarities all too often seemed to make the differences between them all the more explosive. For instance, while genteel European elites often cast Indian manhood as vastly different from European manhood—usually interpreting Indian men's refusal to practice agricultural labor as indolent and oppressive toward women—white frontiersmen could find much more in common with Natives. In fact, genteel elites were all too eager to pounce on such similarities, stressing that frontiersmen were little better than the indigenous peoples of America. One British gentleman who toured the Ohio Valley observed, "The backwoodsmen . . . are very similar in their habits and manners to the aborigines, only perhaps more prodigal and more careless of life. They depend more on hunting than on agriculture, and of course are exposed to all the varieties of climate in the open air. Their cabins are not better than Indian wigwams."[34] To be sure, white settlers understood little of the significance Natives attributed to gender divisions, let alone the balance-centered cosmology in which they existed. Likewise, Natives did not observe or fully understand European patriarchal notions of gender hierarchy before the law and God. Yet there was much overlap. In times of peace, for instance, men of both cultures demonstrated their manhood by skillfully providing for their social circle. For both groups, hunting and woodcraft skills proved central in asserting manhood and commanding the respect of their social circles.[35]

Likewise, in times of war, increasing numbers of Natives and settlers in the region tended to view warfare as an ever more important realm of manly performance. In their minds, courageous and successful warfare, along with poise in the face of danger, and above all outperforming, indeed "outmanning," the enemy exceeded all other manly accomplishments. By the same token, failure induced derision and association with effeminacy. John Bricknell, a settler who spent the early 1790s being held captive by Ohio Valley

Delaware, stressed, "If a man proved cowardly the finger of scorn is soon pointed at him, and he hears 'Squaw!' pronounced." Similarly, the missionary Charles Post reported that when the threat of violence loomed over the Delaware, a Delaware chief proclaimed, *We are now men, and not so easily frightened.*" In this vein, too, Daniel Boone, Samuel Brady, George Rogers Clark, and Samuel Kenton—whose alleged exploits became frontier mythology and made them the heroes of white men on the Ohio Valley frontier—were all celebrated for their ability to fight bravely, facing down danger with equanimity, and even mirth, better than any Indian.[36]

Thus, as violence engulfed the colonies during the second half of the eighteenth century, militant bands of men on both sides prevailed over other forces in their societies that had traditionally balanced the interests of warriors. Though women did not necessarily constitute a peaceful force in either society, their agendas often challenged men's dominance. Consequently, the mutually reinforcing cycle of hyper-masculinization that swept the borderlands undermined women's power in their respective societies. Euro-American frontiersmen, who enjoyed the privileges of patriarchy in law and custom, became even more powerful rulers of their domestic domains. The frontiersmen's ability to assert more control over their dependents was enhanced by the distance of elites—who during the early modern period had come to champion politeness toward women and had instituted self-control as a manly virtue—and militant insistence on men as protectors and fighters. One gentleman who visited the house of a rough Ohio Valley frontiersman related what might have been a common dinner scene: "supper being announced by the mistress of the cabin, we made a hearty meal on her brown bread and milk, while she attended her self-important lord with all due humility." He then added that it was a "custom which I observed to be very common in the remote parts of the United States, of the wife not sitting down to table until the husband and the strangers have finished their meal."[37]

Furthermore, once the economic realities of the post-revolutionary era undermined the fictions projected on the frontier by men who sought to secure their economic, and therefore social and political, independence, women and other dependents all too often bore an even greater share of the burdens. For instance, in Kentucky immediately after the revolution, tight-knit combinations of local and Eastern Seaboard elites quickly monopolized much of the land, rendering most other Kentuckians landless tenants or even itinerant workers, a far cry from the independent heads of households they had hoped to become in the land of opportunity that the frontier supposedly embodied. A culture insistent on the myth of the self-made independent male homesteader, coupled with challenging economic realities requiring all family members' participation to sustain the household, led to an even more vigorous assault on women and other dependents. "The social forces that rendered men's work visible and relegated female labor to the shadows," writes historian Honor Sachs, "were particularly potent in the celebrated lore of early western households."[38]

Parallel dynamics were at play in many Native societies. Although scholars do not fully agree on the extent of gender parity or hierarchy in Native American cultures east of the Mississippi, and despite considerable differences among different Native peoples, historians largely agree that women in European societies suffered more systemic and far-reaching subjugation than Native women. As with Euro-American frontier culture, however, it appears that during the periods in which war swept "Indian country," power in Native societies tilted toward warriors, militant men who largely asserted their manhood through the practice of war. This was partly the result of the cosmological belief that war, and woods generally, were the realm of men, while women in most Native societies in the region drew their cultural and social capital from their agricultural work and authority over domestic affairs. Thus, the wars in which settler forces targeted fields, crops, and Native villages often severed women from their traditional sources of power. By the same token, as Native peoples grew more dependent on European goods and fought over access to markets, reliance on warriors and hunters rose.[39]

One must also examine the history of intertribal tensions to fully plumb the particular context in which Native men asserted their manhood in areas ravaged by mid-century wars, primarily the St. Lawrence River Valley, western Pennsylvania, and the Ohio River Valley. Native men from nations that felt stifled by a century of Haudenosaunee (Iroquois) Confederacy hegemony, in particular, Shawnee and Delaware men, acted to assert their manhood with renewed zeal. As the power of the Haudenosaunee ebbed toward mid-century, backing their claims to domination over the Ohio Valley region primarily with words and treaties rather than war parties, many Delaware and Shawnee leaders resolved to declare their independence from the confederacy in a show of manhood. In this context, the gendered tropes used by both sides to characterize their relationships with each other took on new meaning. The Delaware and Haudenosaunee acknowledged a past understanding between them, which assigned the confederacy the role of men and the Delaware the role of women in their relationship. With changing circumstances, each side sought to tap and reinterpret these analogies and metaphors to best serve their shifting interests.[40]

The Delaware preferred to interpret these tropes as symbolizing a pact between them that promised symbiosis rather than subjugation, which echoed their belief in the ideal of balance between men and women. Since men were expected to protect the interests of women in intertribal affairs, the failure of the Haudenosaunee to protect Delaware interests implied that the members of the confederacy had betrayed their commitment as men. By contrast, and perhaps influenced by European notions of gender, the Haudenosaunee asserted that the understanding between them implied effeminacy and thus subjugation of the Delaware. Delaware (and Shawnee) men bristled in response to such impositions and ongoing Haudenosaunee claims to dominance over them. In this context, the remark by the Delaware chief that *"we are now men* and not easily frightened" alludes to a newly realized sense of Delaware independence and manliness.[41]

This manly self-assertion informed the actions of Natives who made war against frontier colonial settlements when the Seven Years' War erupted with force in the region. When, in May 1757, the governor of Pennsylvania asked Haudenosaunee leaders why their dependent nations—that is, allies and conquered nations—had refused to submit to the league's authority since the beginning of the war, Haudenosaunee representatives quoted a message they had lately received from the Delaware and Shawnee: "We are men and are determined not to be ruled any longer by you as women; and we are determined to cut off all the English, except those that make an escape from us in ships. So say no more to us on that head lest we cut off your private parts and make women of you as you have done of us."[42] Indeed, the outburst of violence that began in 1755 was not only a response to European aggression, but also a gesture targeted at the Haudenosaunee, who over these years undermined the interests of other Native peoples in the region in their efforts to keep themselves afloat. In the 1744 Treaty of Lancaster, and even more infamously in the 1768 Treaty of Fort Stanwix, the Haudenosaunee neglected those who they deemed their dependents, ceding lands to the British and opening the way for new settlement in western Pennsylvania and the Ohio Valley. Thus, the Delaware, Shawnee, and other nations of the region, by asserting their manhood, signaled their refusal to play by the rules determined by the Haudenosaunee-British axis of treaties known as the Covenant Chain. Such exchanges permeated frontier discourse and exacerbated an already heightened self-conscious struggle over manhood.[43]

Well aware of Natives' embrace of gendered tropes, particularly in mocking fashion, Euro-American settlers reinvigorated their own attempts to assert manhood vis-à-vis Indigenous peoples. Humor operated as a tool of social control in many Native societies, and former captives told of their experiences as the butt of Natives' taunts, often intended to inculcate them to their customs. For instance, James Smith, later leader of the Black Boys, recalled that early on during his captivity, he had mistakenly helped women working in the cornfields; when other Native men got world of this, they reproved and mocked him, insisting that he "must not hoe corn like a squaw."[44] Indeed, one area of Native American humor that settlers seemed familiar with, or at least thought they understood, was their use of gendered taunts—often aimed at white men. In this vein, the ranger Robert Rogers, the most famous Indian fighter of his generation, presented his understanding of gendered taunts by Natives in *Ponteach*, a play he wrote about Pontiac's Rebellion. In a scene involving Pontiac's two sons—Phillip, the more militant of the two, and Chekitan, the more peaceful one—Phillip reproved his brother: "Thou always wast a coward, and hated war, and lov'st to loll on the soft lap of peace. Thou art a very woman in thy heart." Similarly, John Long, a trader who lived in the vicinity of and at times among Native peoples, reported "some Americans shooting at a loon . . . several times without success. An Indian standing by, laughed at them and told them they were old women." Like many other contemporary observers, Long, who as a European man was predisposed to pay close attention to such language, repeated impressions of gendered Native language throughout his account. Clearly, Long, Rogers, and others registered such gendered vocabulary and at least in part misinterpreted them as scathing insults, which they would have been for European men steeped in a culture of honor and manhood that required males to treat challenges to their manhood with the utmost gravity.[45]

Expecting Native mockery, a pamphlet published at the start of the Seven Years' War, years of French aggression and British defeats warned that French initiative and vigor had had a resounding influence on the Native nations of the region. Noting that even their Haudenosaunee allies have lately asserted, "The French behave like Men, the English like Women," the pamphlet's author concluded that if things continue in this manner, the Indians "will look upon the English as dastardly cowards; upon the French as brave men." Around the same time, another dour writer observed, "The miscarriages in all our enterprises have rendered us a reproach and to the last degree contemptible in the eyes of our savage Indian, and much more inhuman

French enemies." Further, "Those of the Indians that call themselves our friends despise us, and in their march through our inhabited country . . . insult and annoy us."[46] For American frontiersman, whose hypermasculine culture deemed such accusations intolerable, mockery was a tough pill to swallow. The enduring predicament for the colonists was that although they could boast of superiority in numbers and a supportive imperial apparatus, Native men better negotiated the frontier environment.[47]

In fact, frontiersmen, who perceived most Native men as the more skillful and intimidating fighters, ultimately desired to "out-Indian" the Indians; they yearned to skulk like Indians. Since the symbolism of the woods proved powerful in the white frontier imagination, the association of Indian manhood with skillful woodcraft and woodland warfare, the skulking way of war, loomed large in their minds. As the woods and Natives conjured real fear, white frontiersmen entertained fantasies of inhabiting both the woods and Indian bodies.[48]

Such anxiety coupled with envy served as proxies of tensions between similarity and difference. Despite significant commonalities, Natives and Euro-Americans—though internally divided along various axes—held deep convictions regarding the fundamental differences that set them apart and that would prove central to their identities. As settler and Native groups came closer and more familiar to one another, notions of difference usually hardened around strong racial animosities that superseded differences within their respective kaleidoscopic societies. To be sure, challenges to simple notions of distinction arose, and with time some people identified with both white and Indian racial constructs, but the need to keep cultural, and ultimately racial, distinctions alive evolved as a defining feature of frontier culture. Although this proved truer for the settlers, to some degree it increasingly applied to Natives, who realized that American settler society had no place for them and that their very survival depended on stopping colonial expansion as a united race.[49]

The story of James Smith, held captive in the Ohio Valley by the Caughnawagas from 1755 to 1759 and upon his return led a local ranger company, illustrates the ways in which settler-Native tensions took shape on the ground. In organizing his company, Smith sought as subalterns "two active young men . . . who had also been long in captivity with the Indians." He then dressed his company "uniformly in the Indian manner, with breech clouts, leggins, mockesons and green shrouds. In place of hats [they] wore red handkerchiefs, and painted [their] faces red and black like Indian warriors." He emphasized that he taught his company the "Indian discipline . . . , which would answer the purpose much better than British," even as he led them to fight Indians. A couple of years later, Smith would lead the same ranger company, reorganized as the Black Boys, to undermine peace negotiations between the British and the Ohio Valley and Great Lakes confederacy of Native nations. After returning from captivity, Smith made clear where his sympathies lay—with his white brethren, even though he had lived for several years with the "savages" and presumably appeared as something of an Indian himself when he first returned to white society. Of note, Smith had mostly good things to say in his memoirs about his treatment in captivity, perhaps because he published them some four decades after his return from captivity, that is, at a time when he would have felt secure in his status as a white man.[50]

Daniel Boone and Simon Girty

Even the celebrated Daniel Boone faced charges of disloyalty to his race after returning from Indian captivity. To his great consternation, the accusation followed him, haunting him for years. Thus, his first act to prove his loyalty after he returned to Boonesborough was to lead a band of settlers "who assumed the disguise of savages" in a raid against an Indian village. Moreover, he designed the narratives he told of his life in part to also assuage doubts. Curiously, the success of his narratives, which over time became the definitive account of the early frontier, stemmed from the ambiguous racial identity underlining the narrative: Boone was a white man who could live with Indians—in fact, he could do anything an Indian could do but better—yet he chose white civilization over Indian savagery. The narrative surely excited white male anxieties only to relieve them, but the need to identify evidence of white superiority indicated that such anxieties were never far from frontiersmen's minds.[51]

As it turned out, such conflicting combinations of anxiety, tense racial animosities, and Indian play were rich soil for cultural production, including the myth of the white American frontiersman. In time, the caricature of him would overshadow all other American mythological creations, except perhaps the terrain that he inhabited and became one with—that is, the West itself. In this respect, literary scholars typically point as a watershed event to the publication of John Filson's "Adventures of Daniel Boone" (1784), featuring his interviews with Boone, which he appended to a Kentucky booster pamphlet (figure 4.1). In the short fanciful text, Filson delivers what Americans yearned for most—an American settler at one with the woods. As a legendary hunter

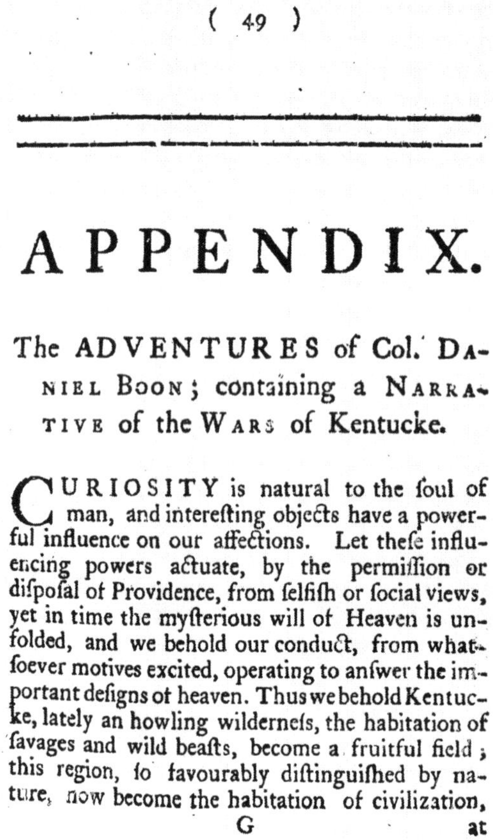

(49)

APPENDIX.

The AD VEN TUR E S of Col. DA-
NIEL BOON; containing a NARRA-
TIVE of the WARS of Kentucke.

CURIOSITY is natural to the foul of
man, and interefting objects have a powerful influence on our affections. Let thefe influencing powers actuate, by the permiffion or
difpofal of Providence, from felfifh or focial views,
yet in time the myfterious will of Heaven is unfolded, and we behold our conduct, from what-
foever motives excited, operating to anfwer the important defigns of heaven. Thus we behold Kentucke, lately an howling wildernefs, the habitation of
favages and wild beafts, become a fruitful field ;
this region, fo favourably diftinguifhed by nature, now become the habitation of civilization,
G   at

Figure 4.1. Title page of the appendix from John Filson, *The Discovery, Settlement and Present State of Kentucke and an Essay towards the Topography, and Natural History of That Important Country: To Which Is Added, an Appendix, Containing, The Adventures of Col. Daniel Boon, One of the First Settlers* (Wilmington, DE, 1784). Filson added a biography of Daniel Boone, the intriguing frontiersman he encountered in Kentucky, as an appendix to a booster pamphlet encouraging settlement there. This short biography launched the legend of Daniel Boone and the western frontier. Early American Imprints, ser. 1, Evans. Courtesy of the American Antiquarian Society, accessed through Readex.

and fighter, Boone embodied the growing similarities between white and Native cultures, yet he was also the champion of white Americans in their racial
wars against Native peoples.[52]

   As told by Filson and remembered by his growing reading audience,
Boone's myth relies heavily on his performance as a true specimen of man-

hood. Perhaps the most memorable portion of the narrative concerns the capture of three young women, including Boone's daughter Jemima, by Shawnee and Cherokee raiders and their subsequent rescue by Boone and his men in heroic pursuit. While Boone's son is killed a bit earlier in the narrative, and other men die over time, the story of the abduction of young white girls by Indians proved far more alarming for readers, who naturally gravitated to it, especially since the story quickly comes to a satisfying resolution in the girls' rescue. Thus, these episodes embody one of the most elemental nodes of frontier myth: Boone and his men protect the ultimate symbols of civilization, white women, from marauding racial others. Few images in American history have cast a longer shadow than young white women abducted by supposed racial predators, and few if any feats of manhood could outdo the rescue of white women from Indian captivity. Indeed, despite little evidence that Natives peoples actually inflicted violence on white female captives, the specter of savage violence against women, including rape, would continue to animate the white imagination. Inscribed in white Americans' minds, the recent memory of Jane McCrae, a white women who became a mortal victim of Indian violence during the Revolutionary War and whose myth remained a touchpoint for racial anxieties throughout the conflict and for decades after, surely informed impressions of the story of Boone and Jemima. In fact, this well-known Boone story was the inspiration behind *The Last of the Mohicans* (1826), James Fenimore Cooper's widely popular novel, in which the hero, Natty Bumppo, repeatedly saves white women from Indian violence and captivity. This was no accident. American nationalism to a significant degree revolved around such symbolism.[53]

Another highpoint of adventure and suspense in Boone's story arrives in his travails during several months spent in Indian captivity in early 1778. Here, too, the resolution is swift, satisfying, and laden with highly suggestive symbolism, for even in captivity, Filson stresses Boone's capacity to do as he chooses, almost with impunity, manipulating his circumstances as he sees fit. Thus, he transforms what might have been, and for a time was, a damning experience into an uplifting tall tale. At first, Boone happily lives as an adoptee with a prominent family, attempting to gain the Natives' trust. While in captivity, he demonstrates his superior skills as a marksman when he chooses, often preferring "not to exceed many of them in shooting; for no people are more envious than they in this sport." As Boone navigates the tense circumstances of these competitions, he observes with bemused condescension "the greatest expressions of joy when they exceeded me."[54] Here at long last is a white man, who appears no less indigenous to the American environment than the Natives themselves. Indeed, he was so comfortable with his manly superiority that he felt little need to demonstrate it before his rivals! Boone ultimately escapes effortlessly when he deems it most advantageous—that is, in time to alert his people of the Indians' planned attack on Boonesborough.

One must remember, however, that when Boone related the story to Filson, he was still reeling from his compromised status as a recently escaped former captive whom some felt might have been far too comfortable among the Natives. On the frontier, a fine line separated hero from villain. The story of Simon Girty—"the most hated man on the early American frontier," as the subtitle of his biography aptly put it—offers a glimpse of what Daniel Boone and James Smith avoided. Captured in 1756 on the frontier of western Pennsylvania less than a year after James Smith suffered a similar fate, Girty lived for about five years as a Seneca, until they returned him to the British in 1761. In the following years, Girty, whose fluency in numerous Native languages proved highly useful for the British Indian Department, worked as a valued interpreter and intermediary. During Lord Dunmore's War (1774), pitting the colony of Virginia against several Ohio Valley nations, and the early years of the American Revolution, he served as a ranger for the colonists.[55]

In 1778 Girty defected to the British, and alongside two other known "renegades," Alexander McKee and Matthew Elliot, served as a British Indian agent in the Ohio Valley for the duration of the war and after it. The full picture behind his life-changing decision remains unclear, but it appears that a host of grievances informed his decision, including a failed promise of promotion and disillusionment with settlers' treatment of Native peoples, epitomized by the murder of the two Indian leaders, Cornstalk and White Eyes, under a flag of truce. In any event, Simon Girty quickly became the scourge of the frontier, as his real and imagined exploits as the mastermind behind numerous Indian attacks on the frontier became infamous. Even more than Elliot and McKee, Girty's name became synonymous with the worst form of treason a white man could commit—against one's own fraternity of fellow white men.[56]

One heinous event in particular, the torture and burning of Colonel William Crawford, became associated with Girty's infamy for decades. In the spring of 1782, several hundred western Pennsylvania militiamen under Crawford's command embarked on an expedition deep into the Ohio Valley to attack several Wyandot towns. The expedition quickly went awry, and after a short battle, the settler forces scattered, and several of them were taken into captivity, including Col. Crawford and Dr. Knight, a surgeon accompanying the expedition. Despite attempts by British agents, including Girty, to prevent Crawford's execution, his captors determined to torture and burn him because they believed that he had led the expedition two months earlier that committed the nearby Gnadenhutten Massacre of 97 unarmed, Christianized Indians. This was not far from the truth. Many of the militiamen from Washington County, Pennsylvania, who committed the massacre had also participated in Crawford's expedition, including Colonel David Williamson, commander of the earlier expedition who incidentally also served as Crawford's second in command on the Wyandot expedition and managed to escape capture.[57]

There is much conflicting evidence over Girty's conduct during Crawford's torture and execution, but it indeed appears that both Girty and Elliot were there and had attempted to prevent it. Nonetheless, the rumor quickly spread throughout the frontier that Girty had stood by during the execution and even took joy as a spectator. More than any other testimony, that by Dr. Knight, who managed to escape just prior to his own planned execution, made Girty into the greatest villain on the frontier. According to Knight, "in the midst" of "extreme tortures," Crawford "called to Simon Girty and begged him to shoot him; but Girty making no answer he called him again. Girty then by way of derision, told the colonel he had no gun, at the same time turning about to an Indian who was behind him, laughed heartily, and by all his gestures seemed delighted at the horrid scene." Girty, after learning of his reputation among settler society and of the $1,000 bounty the U.S. government placed on his head, became even more committed to the British and Native American alliance against the fledgling republic. About a decade later, in 1791, he would play a major role in St. Clair's Defeat, the greatest military loss inflicted on the US army by Native forces.[58]

Daniel Boone, James Smith, and Simon Girty, as expert frontiersmen who lived for a time in Indian captivity, theoretically embodied possible alternatives to racial violence in the second half of the eighteenth century. In the Ohio Valley, however, the hyper-masculine and hyper-racialized frontier left little space for ambiguity and complex identities. Go-betweens familiar with both Native American and European cultures and languages had long proved invaluable in making peace treaties and to some degree would continue to be, but viable avenues for cultural brokers became increasingly fewer for settlers while those for Indian fighters grew. After Boone and Smith returned from captivity, the decision to demonstrate their unwavering loyalty to their race must have been quite simple. They were ultimately rewarded with acclaim. After all, here were two white men who could have lived as Indians if they wanted, but they chose the supposed superiority of white civilization. What better evidence that the future of the continent was tied to white manhood? Their preference for white civilization appeared all the more important in light of the many white captives who found that they preferred the "savage" life of Natives to the "civilized" ways of whites.[59]

Terror, Race, and Masquerade

Although American settlers had a skewed and limited understanding of Native warfare and violence, they understood quite well the part that Native warriors often sought to emphasize most—terror. Historians have found a similar dynamic in the wake of each new wave of settler invasion in numerous different regions and periods. Despite attempts to find ways to mutually occupy the same territories, once Native warriors realized that settler society was bent on their destruction, they often turned to terror to defend their homelands as best they could given their limited numbers. It appears that Native peoples had long employed psychological tactics in their military engagements, but the form of terror that involved night raids by painted warriors howling as they inflicted large-scale death as well as the terror of mangled bodies and ostentatious destruction appears to reflect the enormous challenge and festering anger posed by the racial, violent, and unyielding character of settler colonial invasion and expansion. Nothing induced more fear in colonial frontier settlements, Natives soon learned, than the specter of painted Indian warriors descending upon them from the woods.[60]

Bred on Christian fears of the devil and his minions lurking in the figurative and literal darkness of the woods, Euro-American settlers seemed particularly predisposed to internalize the terror of Native warriors. In a sermon delivered to provincial troops during the early days of the Seven Years' War, one Albany preacher sought to prepare the men for their first encounter: "The scene of war is a horrid scene . . . Painted savages, cruel barbarians, deformed and disfigured as devils incarnate, stark naked like infernal serpents, lie skulking and stalking about, thirsting after blood; now hovering hither and thither, as vultures and harpies of prey; then rush in, yelling and screaming, as hell-hounds destroying human kind."[61] Indeed, many pastors like this one helped inflame Christian rage in the colonies against the "heathen savages" of the woods. A rising tide of holy rage certainly armed colonial troops with a zealous hatred for Natives, but it also played into Indian terror. Although terror failed to ultimately stop the encroachment of Euro-American colonists on their lands, it helped Native nations project more fear than their numbers warranted, slowing down, and at times even reversing for a short while, the settler colonial enterprise.

Despite denouncing guerilla warfare and terror as savage, Euro-Americans in the colonial period displayed a double standard in regard to irregular warfare; they adopted the very same, supposedly "Indian," tactics themselves. Moreover, realizing their relative disadvantage, the European settlers often relied on Native allies to fight for them or with them and teach them how to make war in the American woods. On the one hand, they sought to use such derisive terms as *stalking* or *skulking* and *savage* to cast terror and guerrilla warfare not only as products of a lower civilization, but also as unmanly and cowardly behavior, but on the other hand, they envied Native peoples for their ability to better execute such forms of war more effectively.[62] Consequently, and despite their best efforts to control the very terms that informed notions of manhood, the colonists implicitly conceded preeminence over the gendered terrain of the frontier to Native men.

Despite conceding the terms of manhood to Native warriors, the settlers could hardly admit that they were lesser men than the "savages." Indeed, figures like Boone were tools for convincing themselves that they were just as savvy in frontier warfare as Native warriors. Thus, the settlers increasingly infused consciousness of their shared white identity with an incipient local patriotism that they tied to the virility of frontiersmen and their superior stock. This conflation of whiteness and colonial frontier identity derived much symbolism from the ability of frontiersmen acting as rangers to fight Native peoples successfully—at least some of the time. Reporting from Carlisle, Pennsylvania, in 1763, one letter writer proudly listed all the military successes of local frontiersmen against Native peoples. Reports he cited from Virginia seemed sanguine as well: "It is certain they have had on that frontier [Virginia] frequent alarms, and several skirmishes with the Indians, in which the white people always beat the enemy." He concluded, "And it is worth remarking that since this War broke out, there has not been one engagement in which the Indians got the better of our people, on any part of the frontier, that I can recollect."[63]

Through self-assuring praises of the above kind, Americans increasingly celebrated rangers for their effectiveness at negotiating and fighting in the frontier environment, but perhaps even more so for fulfilling settler colonial fantasies of inhabiting Native bodies and the woods in which they presumably prowled. As settlers pursued a slow and violent war of attrition, conjuring images of virile Indian-clad white men inflicting terror on Indians—or better yet, enlisting as rangers and attempting to enact such fantasies—helped allay the anxieties of frontier life. Regardless of the rangers' actual efficacy, frontier inhabitants scrutinized the outcomes of frontier engagements in the hope of identifying signs of their racial and regional superiority. Moreover, by the Revolutionary War, it had become clear to many Americans that Indian-style "bushfighting" was the greatest advantage Americans had over British regulars.

Of all the famous figures of the Revolutionary War, Daniel Morgan emerged as the embodiment of the ranger tradition, his name becoming synonymous with the valor of the Virginia riflemen and their supposed superiority vis-à-vis British Regulars. Riflemen units represented the definitively American fighters, having innovatively dropped the musket and bayonet in favor of the more accurate rifle. As ranger forces, they dressed and fought in the Indian style and used American-made hunting rifles.[64] Like Smith, Boone, and Girty, Morgan was a product of the mid-century Ohio Valley borderlands wars, having first witnessed combat while serving as a wagoner during Braddock's defeat in 1755. During the next decade, he made a name for himself as a ranger and an Indian fighter. In Lord Dunmore's War, he raised a company and gained a reputation as an able commander and one of the most adept Virginians at bushfighting. Thus, when the Revolutionary War erupted, and Virginia had to raise two riflemen companies, Morgan was the obvious choice to lead one of them.

Morgan famously equipped his riflemen with hunting shirts and caps bearing the motto "Liberty or Death." Several reports during the many campaigns that Morgan and his men participated in, mentioned his predilection for Indian dress.[65] For the 1776 New Jersey campaign, General Washington, apparently aware of Morgan's reputation, thought him and his men ideal for an Indian masquerade, although it was never carried out. According to the plan, Morgan was to "dress a company or two of true woods men in the right Indian style and then make the attack accompanied with screaming and yelling as the Indians do." Washington hoped that "it would have very good consequences especially if as little as possible was said, or known of the matter before hand."[66]

Once Washington noticed Morgan's growing reputation, he seemed quite enamored with sending his favorite Indian fighter to meet fire with fire. Thus, after the New Jersey campaign, Washington dispatched Morgan in the summer of 1777 to help in the northern campaign, where the British had enlisted the support of Indians allies. "The people in the Northern Army seem so intimidated by the Indians that I have determined to send up Colo. Morgans corps of rifle men who will fight them in their own way," Washington informed General Israel Putnam. A few days later, in a letter to Major General Horatio Gates, he intimated his "apprehension of the Indian mode of fighting," consequently he had "dispatch'd Colo. Morgan with his corps of riflemen to your assistance." "This corps I have great dependance on," Washington declared, "& have no doubt but they will be exceedingly usefull to you, as a check given to the savages & keeping them within proper bounds . . . & animate your other troops from a sense of their being more on an equality with the enemy."[67] Figuring prominently in such key moments as the New York campaign of 1777, including the celebrated Battle of Saratoga, and the southern campaign of 1780–81, including the famous Battle of Cowpens, Morgan and his men helped reinforce the myth of the able frontier warrior who could show the British and even Indian enemies "buckskin play." It was also quite clear that fighting Indian style and wearing Indian dress had become second nature for the most celebrated Indian fighters. Perhaps more importantly, for an emerging nation and even for Washington, such a reputation stood as a badge of honor and virility.

In short, then, Indian-clad and -painted rangers ironically became the shock troops of the cultural and material project of white settler colonialism. Indeed, the peculiar regimen of terror combined with carnivalesque enactments of Indian disguise not only proved central to the project of ethnic cleansing, it also catered to the psychological needs of frontier culture: it helped construct the subjectivity of white men anxious to transform themselves into the indigenous inhabitants. Evidence suggests that wearing war paint in the Indian manner proved particularly transformative for American men on the frontier. The famed Indian fighter George Rogers Clark recalled in his memoir that during the Revolutionary War, his troops had lost their morale deep in Indian country. Before a river crossing, they "ran from one another bewailing their situation." After a minute of thought, "[I] took some water in my hand, poured on powder, blacked my face, gave the war hoop, and marched into the water without saying a word." Consequently, "the party gased and fell in after another without saying a word like a flock of sheep."[68] For similar reasons, the commander of the Western Department during the revolution, Colonel Daniel Brodhead, seemed eager to deploy his rangers painted like Indians. He also made a point of conjuring virile images of his painted warriors in his superiors' imagination. "Captain Brady, with twenty white men and a young Delaware chief, all well painted, . . . set out towards the Seneca country," he informed Governor Joseph Reed of Pennsylvania in a letter. The next day he sent General Washington a similar letter emphasizing again that Brady and his twenty men were "all well painted." About two months later, in a letter to General James Sullivan, he assured his superior that although "the Indians sometimes take a scalp from us . . . my light parties which I dress & paint like Indians have retaliated in several instances." It is no wonder that within a year, Brodhead had urged Governor Reed to help him acquire more war paint. "I have often applied to the Honble. Board of War for some paint," he complained, "but, have received none, it is essentially necessary for my parties, and I shall be much obliged if Your Excellency will be pleased to order some."[69]

Of course, before Europeans appropriated it, painting one's face in preparation for battle had long been a crucial practice for Native warriors. As the Haudenosaunee representative at one point intimated in a treaty, Native warriors knew well that painting their faces made them "seem terrible and put a dread upon our enemies."[70] It was clearly, however, much more than just a terror tactic. Alongside singing war songs, fasting, and reenacting memories of past battles, it helped motivate Native warriors for battle. Scholars of rituals theorize that such customs often hinge on creating a place suspended from reality, what Victor Turner called "liminality." It appears that disguise in particular facilitates the suspension of previously held beliefs and allows for the assumption of changed states of consciousness. While the full significance of Indian war preparations might never be fully revealed, what is known suggests that wearing war paint not only armed warriors with a strong sense of conviction, linked them to their traditions, and tapped the forces in their cosmology that might prove crucial in battle, it also transformed their mental state . Ultimately, it facilitated the quantum leap necessary for people to overcome perhaps the most primordial fear intrinsic to any human subjectivity—that of death.[71]

White rangers coopted this custom in part for preparing psychologically for battle, but they also harnessed it for their particular needs—constructing a subjectivity attuned to the needs of "anxious patriarchs" in a vulnerable setting.[72] White frontiersmen suspected that Indian men—part of the very texture of the menacing natural environment—outperformed them in the American woods. Thus, as a psychological defense mechanism, donning Indian disguise challenged such deep-seated apprehensions by plumbing a carnivalesque spirit pregnant with the potential for madness—for a world turned topsy-turvy. In such a world, white men wearing Indian attire became part of the American environment; they became indigenous. The liminal ontology created by the carnival—the space suspended between realities and that Victor Turner and Mikhail Bakhtin have recognized as rife with creative possibilities—helped conjure an alternative universe in which they could equal and perhaps outman the Indians in their own game on their own turf.[73]

Whiteness loomed larger over white frontiersmen's subjectivity than manhood, class, regional allegiances, and any other facet of their identity. In this regard, playing Indian proved critical. Ironically, underneath the Indian dress and war paint, white men developed an acute awareness of their whiteness in the American woods.[74] For white settlers, wearing a disguise proved volatile, blurring racial distinctions only to reify those distinctions with an amplified racial vengeance, quite literally as the stories of Smith, Boone, and Girty demonstrate. Ultimately, white men celebrated their whiteness in disguise through an unequivocal and violent racial stance in the face of the racial ambiguity of the frontier, where Native peoples and settlers increasingly acted and dressed like each other. Though such logic exposed itself fully when white rangers committed massacres, even mere fantasies of massacres could serve a similar purpose.

Backwoods Indian play, with its slippage into brutal terror, also demonstrated that while the carnivalesque lent itself to subversion and liberation, it also tapped a corporate tradition of regulatory practices that imposed discipline through violence, both within and without the community. Though Bakhtin regarded the carnivalesque as intrinsically subversive and liberating, anthropologists have found evidence that community jubilations, depending on the specific context, can impose and perpetuate severe and violent discipline just as well. As with humor more generally, it was in fact a moment of opportunity, both for liberation and subjugation, for the creating, and disciplining, of communities.[75] In short, when merry groups of common white men, who insisted on choosing their own officers and who abhorred genteel condescension, organized as rangers and entered the woods, they fused the leveling spirit of democracy with genocide.

Take for instance the case of the militia from Washington County, Pennsylvania, that committed the Gnadenhutten Massacre in March 1782. Living in the eastern part of the Ohio Valley close to western Pennsylvania, the Christianized Natives at the Moravian mission at Gnadenhutten had tried to maintain neutrality throughout the revolution; they barely held on, as both sides in the war harbored deep suspicions about their loyalties. When rumors spread of the Moravians providing hospitality to an Indian raiding party, the nearby Washington County militia quickly organized to "investigate" the allegations. After three days of cool deliberation, they took a vote in the corporate egalitarian tradition of white frontiersmen and decided to murder the Moravians literally like cattle. They herded the ninety-seven men, women, and children they could find into the mission's cabins and slaughtered them systematically as one would livestock.[76]

Perhaps not incidentally, Washington County would also be at the center of the Whiskey Rebellion a decade later, in the summer of 1794. As Secretary of the Treasury Alexander Hamilton noted at the time, the county "uniformly distinguished its resistance by a more excessive spirit than has appeared in the other counties." If the militia "be ordered out in support of civic authorities," admitted Hamilton, "very few could be gotten that were not of the party of rioters."[77] Hamilton also reported that the Mingo Creek Society, Washington County's Democratic society, had become the center of treasonous events. Indeed, H. H. Brackenridge would later regard the Mingo Creek Society as the "cradle of the insurrection."[78] Brackenridge also took particular notice of the Washington County militia as they crossed the Monongahela River on their way to the large gathering of locals on Braddock's Field on August 1, 1794, that marked the highpoint of the insurrection: "They were dressed in what we call hunting shirts, many of them with handkerchiefs upon their heads. It is in this dress they equip themselves against the Indians." That same day, Brackenridge also observed, "Fifteen men had painted themselves black, as the warriors among the Indians do when they go to war." This group went off in pursuit "of one who they considered an accomplice of John Neville, the excise man." In this light, it might not be too much of a stretch to speculate that the Washington County militia also masqueraded as Indians when they descended upon and massacred the inhabitants of Gnadenhutten twelve years earlier. They had animated both anti-authoritarian misrule and genocidal violence against Native peoples with whimsy and Indian play. In the process they conjoined democratic principles with violent exclusion into a structure of feeling that rendered what should have been contradictory into a seamless and edifying whole.[79]

The People, the Nation, and the Militia

Both the Declaration of Independence and the Constitution of the United States invoke the notion of "the people," whose sovereignty, Edmund Morgan quipped, might be a "more fictional fiction than the divine right of kings." During the revolutionary period in the United States and the broader Atlantic world, leading thinkers and politicians conceived new ideas about the most central political principles, in the process forging the concept of the people as perhaps the most powerful construct of the age. For an idea to be meaningful and compelling, however, it must be imaginable, and while a king is easy to imagine, pointed out Morgan, a people is not.[80] To make an abstraction such as the people real and compelling, it had to be conjured in some way—for instance, attached to symbols, such as a flag or an anthem; imagined through the joint consumption of newspapers and other sources of information; associated with institutions; celebrated in song and parades; understood as lines on a map and physical borders; and conflated with marshal experiences, both real and imagined, such as service in the army or in a militia. All these processes were in full swing in the United States during its formative first post-independence decades, and still are, for that matter.[81]

Scholars have not yet fully appreciated the role of the militia—or the spirit of mirth that often infused the institution of the militia—in reality and perhaps even more importantly as an idea. As noted, since the immediate aftermath of the Battles of Lexington and Concord, Americans have employed the myth of the minutemen to understand and define themselves. In the wake of the battles, they held on to the notion of the militia as one of the basic metaphors of the nation. Especially for those who participated in militia companies, it offered a compelling lens through which to imagine themselves part of a nation. For those who might not have had such an experience, the myth could serve the same purpose just as well. Today, for many staunch gun-rights advocates, the Second Amendment—establishing "the right of the people to keep and bear arms" as part of a "well regulated militia"—offers a suggestive touchstone for associating themselves with the powerful mythology of the militia and therefore the nation. Indeed, the militia seems to have served as an extremely powerful tool for white men to negotiate the fiction of the nation and their position in it as defenders of hearth and home. The idea became so ingrained that many have yet to let go of it more than a century after the Militia Act of 1903 authorized the National Guard to assume the role of the militias.[82]

For Americans, the militia was also a merry affair, where men came together to fraternize and play with guns, all the while conducting a masquerade designed to negotiate anxieties over their manly competencies in the American woods. A device for transforming themselves and their environment, the hardy but merry militia was an adaptation on the carnivalesque for the purposes of war. Thus, as militia companies assumed Indian visages, deftly negotiating the American environment as well as or better than any Indian, they became as indigenous as the Natives, or so they very much wanted to believe. It is this same conflation of ideas and their expression in an intuitive sense of morality, impulse, and comportment, this structure of feeling, that still leads many Americans to grab their guns and go play in the wilderness. It is this notion that also inspires some of them to form independent and informal militia companies, dress up as soldiers, play war games, and imagine themselves preparing to heed the call to arms when the need again arises, as some thought it recently had, resulting in the events of January 6, 2021. Even in the case of the solo bombing attack by Timothy McVeigh on the FBI building in Oklahoma City, it was no coincidence that he chose to act on April 19, 1995, the 220th anniversary of the Battles of Lexington and Concord. It was his rejoinder to the shot heard around the world.[83]

At the same time, the idea of the militia as a metaphor for the nation also offered Americans something else no less attractive: a way to imagine the idea of the people as exclusive. One strength of the idea of the people is that as much as it is compelling, it is also flexible. Indeed, the idea of the people is flexible enough to render it, if done deftly, as both exclusive and inclusive at the same time. The idea of the militia fit perfectly within this scheme: it was a metaphor for the nation that brought together members of the community in a fraternal bond, but as a militant metaphor it also suggests an enemy from whom the community must defend itself. In the United States, a fraternity of white men perceived themselves as defending white women from racial others, so the nation was easily imagined as a community of white men whose participation in the militia entitled them to participate in the nation as equals. The rest, it was "self-evident," were not active members of the nation, as in the case of women, or in the case of non-whites, outside the bounds of the nation altogether.[84]

While in theory the idea of the people appears manageable, in reality it is far more complicated. It was easy to invoke the people in abstract in the Declaration of Independence and the Constitution, but when it came to legislating who constituted the people in more precise terms, decisions had to be made. What they decided sheds some light on the ways the founders understood their political and national community. The first mention of the racial designation "white" in the law books, for instance, was the Naturalization

Act (1790), passed by the 1st Congress. When legislators had to decide who the people would be in this formative instance, they enshrined the category of whiteness.[85] It is just as telling that the same category, in the form of "white male citizen," appeared two years later in the law books with the first Uniform Militia Act (1792). In it, Congress stipulated that "every free able-bodied white male citizen of the respective states, resident therein, who is or shall be of the age of eighteen years, and under the age of forty five years . . . shall severally and respectively be enrolled in the militia."[86] It is also telling that legislators passed this law just a short while after General Arthur St. Clair's stunning defeat in November 1791 by a Native American coalition in the Northwest Territory, still regarded as one of the most humiliating losses in US history. Fearing that Native American successes in recent battles would inspire further attempts by raiders to descend on frontier settlements, American legislators passed an act to empower local communities to organize militias in self-defense as they saw fit. Thus, American law books, until 1862, when during the Civil War they were changed to allow Black men to join, also conjured the notion of white men defending their homesteads and families from howling "savages."

CHAPTER FIVE

Alligator-Horses

The Frontier Jester and the Origins of Manifest Destiny

The decades surrounding the turn of the nineteenth century were a golden age for travel accounts. They became one of the most popular genres in the English-reading Atlantic world, offering a seemingly unending variety of truthful, quasi-truthful, as well as wholly fictional accounts. Some of the latter relied on firsthand knowledge of the countries portrayed, although some authors, for a host of reasons and agendas, wrote their accounts based on a passing familiarity or even constructed them from whole cloth. Curiosity about the new republican experiment in the United States emerged as a central current of this widely varied genre. Thus, during the first half century or so after the founding of the new American republic, a stream of observers reported their impressions of its early effort at self-rule, culminating with the so-called travel war of the 1830s following the publication of *Domestic Manners of the Americans* (1832), Frances Trollope's scathing rebuke of the United States.[1]

Although the accounts from the period most familiar to readers today—those by the French commentators Crèvecœur and Tocqueville—were relatively sympathetic, numerous other contemporary accounts, especially by British travelers such as Trollope, were far more hostile.[2] Embittered by the Revolutionary War and the rising tide of revolutionary radicalism in France and elsewhere, British observers scrutinized the land for hopeful signs of the republic's impending demise. Not surprisingly, they found fault with every-thing, from America's natural environment to the political and social makeup of the country to the character and manners of its inhabitants. In a fictional travelogue conceived as a counterpoint to negative British ac-counts, James Fenimore Cooper went so far as to wonder whether the British government itself had employed "itinerant circulators of calumny, who journeyed, or pretended to journey through our states, in order to dis-cover and to expose the nakedness of the land."[3]

As Cooper's response suggests, it did not take much to rankle the Ameri-cans, who during the decades immediately before and after the War of 1812 (1812–15) issued vigorous retorts to negative accounts of the young republic. In the sanguine rejoinder *Letters from the South by a Northern Man* (1817), James Kirke Paulding expressed contempt toward "the false malicious views of this country, given by so many British writers and travelers." Voicing the strongly held feelings of many Americans, he wrote, "My country is my mis-tress; I can see her faults, but I will not stand quiet and hear her run down by strangers."[4] Unsurprisingly, given the American knack for aggressively defending their country, even Tocqueville exhibited frustration with the Americans' "troublesome" and "garrulous" patriotism. "It wearies even those who are disposed to respect it," he said in his famous treatise, *Democracy in America* (1840).[5]

Americans as well as interested observers in Britain and elsewhere in Europe understood accounts of the United States and American responses as salvos in the broad cultural struggle with Britain that erupted in outright war in 1812. Since they were written primarily by metropolitan elites, examining such accounts provides a window into the ebbs and flows of genteel and re-publican apprehensions over America. This was a new, postcolonial chapter in the long-running Anglo-American culture wars between province and metropole.[6] Thus, couching such texts in the broader cultural output of the period allows one to examine how Americans found relief for their anxieties. Fueled by democratic energies and confidence from below, American elites during the "era of 1812" seemed to regain faith in the idea of the west and its rustic and provincial settlers, increasingly championing them as virile frontiersmen rather than troublesome and unruly backwoodsmen. Thus, cultural production by nationalist literati of the period played a key role in constructing and disseminating a new popular culture that underscored an emergent faith in the settlers of the western country—the general term at the time for all the lands to the west of the more settled, inhabited regions.

These nationalist writings formed the foundation of the new westering nationalism captured by John O'Sullivan's 1845 turn of phrase "manifest destiny." American frontiersmen cultivated a hyper-masculine, democratic camaraderie of freeborn militiamen in the rural west by harnessing the mirth evoked by the carnivalesque practice of Indian play and other giddy acts of terror or violence against those they deemed to be the enemies of liberty. Their practices and convictions were still quite localized before the War of 1812 and usually frowned upon by eastern elites. Once the irreverent and egalitarian "white Indians" of the frontier aligned with republican cultural brokers, however, they together constructed a novel popular culture and propelled it to a hallowed position in American mythology. Tapping the vitality emanating from the west, a rising generation of nationalist authors and editors would alleviate a nation's festering anxieties about the fate of the republic and help bridge looming sectional divides. While at times white American men turned to sober republican pride later captured by the phrase "manifest destiny," at other moments they took to carnivalesque, tall-tale bluster that conveyed an unbridled American masculinity. This uniquely American structure of feelings relied on newly productive tensions between rustic western sensibilities and an emergent middle-class republican ideology. To borrow from Sigmund Freud, in the antebellum United States a democratic communal id—embodied by the frontier jester Davy Crockett—stirred uneasily, but buoyantly, beneath a republican super ego suggesting providential design set upon a world stage.

Early Negative Accounts

Anglo-Americans began settling west of the Alleghenies in the early 1760s, at the end of the Seven Years' War, once Britain gained control of the region. Until the 1790s, most of these early settlers inhabited the region south of the Ohio River in what would become Kentucky and Tennessee. After the Treaty of Greenville (1795), between the United States and the Native confederacy in the northwest, opened large swaths of land for settlement north of the Ohio River and the region became less dangerous, what had been a trickle of settlers turned into a torrent. Many eastern elites thought the onslaught of migrants moving westward spelled danger for the character of the young republic. The seaboard establishment in the colonies and later the young republic had long harbored anxieties about the western country. They were all aware of European theories predicting doom for American culture and society and questioning the viability of large republics. In the early 1790s, the

French Revolution appeared poised to rip the fabric holding societies together in Europe, while across the Atlantic, the so-called Whiskey Rebellion (1794) and numerous filibustering debacles, including Aaron Burr's infamous attempt to "liberate" New Spain during 1806–7, raised fears over republican self-rule to new heights. The spread of the young nation westward, many suspected, could seriously endanger the fledgling union.

As western lands became the most valuable commodity in the young nation, and as Americans migrated west beyond the reach of traditional and more entrenched power structures on the East Coast, the fragile republican society seemed at times on the brink of anarchy. How could this new society, so bent on profits and already on the move, find the moral compass necessary to steer clear of the pitfalls endemic to republican forms of government? Few affairs seemed to capture this predicament as well as the Yazoo land fraud, an attempt by a group of powerful land companies to obtain Georgia's (questionable) claim to the Yazoo region, some 35,000,000 acres of land in much of what is today Alabama and Mississippi. To obtain the title, the companies bribed Georgia legislators to sell them the title to the vast territory for a trifling $500,000. By the time the public outcry forced Georgia's legislature to repeal the transaction, many third parties across the country had bought claims to Yazoo lands. Between 1795, when the scandal became public, and 1814, when Congress passed legislation to settle the land claims, "Yazoo" became, as one historian put it, "a watchword for scandal and greed." Fittingly, one opinion piece from 1805 likened the Yazoo scandal to a disease that "extends from one end of the continent to the other . . . [Y]ou may trace this disease thro' every city, town, and village of consequence on the continent."[7]

During the quarter century following the ratification of the Constitution (1789), a period of intense political conflict, questions about the country's direction often became proxies for partisan disputes. It was no surprise, therefore, that one of the main points of contention was the Louisiana Purchase (1803), which when approved by Thomas Jefferson's administration doubled the United States' western holdings and conjured troubling images of millions of unruly and crude settlers out west compromising the Union. New England Federalist authors, in particular, warned genteel readers about the nature of the settlements and the character of the settlers south of the Ohio River in the new states of Kentucky and Tennessee. They feared that western expansion—especially in those regions more to the south, primarily fed by migrants from Virginia and North Carolina—would extend both the influence of southern ideas and customs and Democratic-Republican politics.

Visiting the region in 1803, one prominent New Englander reported through his travel account that all the rumors he had heard of the "back settlers" are true. "The abundance of wild game allures them to be huntsmen," he wrote. Thus, they "neglect the cultivation of the land" and "acquire rough and savage manners." "Sloth and independence are prominent traits in their character."[8] Whether "foresters or pioneer," noted the conservative icon Timothy Dwight in his own travel account, "[they] manage their own concerns worse than any other men," and further, they have the audacity to think "they could manage those of the nation far better than the agents, to whom they are committed by the public."[9] Meanwhile, Fisher Ames, one of the most esteemed Federalist politicians of the day, proclaimed with typical condescending flair that a "republican form" of organization is better suited for otters than for the band of "savages and adventurers, whose pure morals are expected to sustain and glorify the republic."[10] Federalist elites in the northeast, feeling like an embattled minority in a society slipping from their grasp, cultivated an emboldened Anglophilia, echoing traditional European talking points about the degradation of culture and society in America.[11]

As postcolonial tensions built toward a tense economic and military standoff between Britain and the United States, British and at times even sympathetic French travelers reinforced and often outdid Federalists in their pejorative accounts of the westward lands, especially the regions south of the Ohio River. Thomas Ashe, notorious for the anti-American *Travels in America* (1808), excoriated "the Virginean, Kentuckeyan, Tennessee, and Carolean states," where "the whole labor of citizens is to storm, to give loose to the worst of passions." Isaac Weld Jr., another condescending British traveler, proclaimed, "of all the uncouth human beings I met with in America, these people from the western country were the most so," adding that when stopped by some of them on the road, it was hard to distinguish them from a "highwayman that was going to demand my purse."[12] Even a more sympathetic French traveler agreed with this view when describing frontiersmen as the "very worst set of men in all America, and perhaps the whole universe. The sentiments and even the very idea of honesty and humanity are unknown to them."[13]

To add insult to injury, British and other European commentators were just as quick to disparage what they viewed as the vulgar commercial habits of most Americans. One especially acerbic author, claimed that the visitor to America is immediately "beset by a swarm of speculators of a superior order; if he will bank, one can recommend him to a capital house—another to a good speculation in land-lottery—land-jobbing—building a town—or a bridge." Others, meanwhile, might offer a "share in manufacture of weavers' shuttles—a patent for improved fish-hooks, or cutting spike nails—or buy up unpaid-for British goods at 20 per cent. under prime cost."[14] Indeed, to many conservative observers within and without the United States, the country's leveling spirit seemed to have inspired every low-born, crude bumpkin to devise brash schemes for personal economic improvement.

While Federalist authors to varying degrees tended to agree with these negative accounts, a young generation of gentlemen chose to disengage from the Federalist Party during this period. Embracing Jeffersonian Republicanism, they took upon themselves the mantle of American nationalism as they rose to defend the republic. In the years before the War of 1812, as British warships assaulted American vessels and impressed American citizens into its navy, it became harder for many young gentlemen bred on Federalists principles to strike a balance between Anglophile Federalism and American nationalism. The ensuing war, which Federalists opposed, and its resolution left Federalism out of the mainstream altogether, except perhaps in New England. This was certainly the case for many of the emerging literary figures of the period, such as James Fenimore Cooper, James Kirke Paulding, and Samuel Woodworth, as well as John Quincy Adams, who as a young Federalist senator crossed the aisle to the Republican side when voting in support of the Louisiana Purchase. Later, as an ambassador representing President James Madison's Democratic-Republican administration, Adams became one of the few prominent New Englanders who approved of the war.[15]

The writer and politician Charles Jared Ingersoll was another young recruit to the nationalist, anti-British cause. Although he had at one point considered the notorious arch-Federalist writer and editor Joseph Dennie his mentor, perceived British rebukes to American honor led Ingersoll to find his nationalist voice. Given the nature of contemporary literary assaults on the United States, it was only logical for Ingersoll to defend the republic with a travel account of his own, albeit a fictional one. Ostensibly a collection of letters written by an Irish Jesuit traveling to the United States, *Inchiquin: The Jesuit's Letters* (1810) sought, as Ingersoll proclaims in a letter to President Madison, to "put the country in good humor with itself, by endeavoring to expose the prejudices that prevent its proper estimation."[16] The work opens with a set of cautionary letters about America that Inchiquin had received from his European friends, a foil to which later, more favorable letters would respond. "The American Federation, I suppose, cannot maintain itself much longer," opines one European correspondent. Another of Inchiquin's relations instructed, "endeavour to penetrate, if possible, the spirit and policy of that unaccountable union of disjointed sovereignties, which seems so often to hang on the brink of a rupture." Familiar with European talking points, Ingersoll has the Jesuit's European friends save their most caustic commentary for the commercial spirit of Americans: "As commerce is their national bond of union, is not knavery their predominant national characteristic? That trade, which seems to be their sole pursuit, unless undisciplined, within due bounds, will lead from base submission to bloody hostilities and inevitable destruction." "Absorbed in trade and re-publicanism," warns another, "[they] seem to know and desire no distinction, but such as are to be earned with the sweat of their brows."[17]

Ingersoll, betraying many of his own misgivings about the republic, then moves on to mollify his countrymen's apprehensions, as well as his own, through positive depictions of the United States. His response in the remainder of the piece is a Madisonian defense of the United States that casts commerce and western expansion as assets rather than hindrances to the well-being of the nation. "The lien of this 'mighty continental nation,'" proclaims Inchiquin in one of his letters, "is commercial liberty: not mere political liberty, but positive freedom; geographical absolution from all but the slightest restraints." This "brave spirit" pervades the "whole republic," he asserts, "binding it together by an influence, not less powerful, because its current is propelled by an animating contrariety." At one point he even foreshadows the language and vision of manifest destiny: "The American people dispersed over an immense territory, abounding in all the means of commercial greatness, to whom an opportunity was presented at an early period of adapting their government to their circumstances, followed the manifest order of nature." Several decades later, in the wake of the Second Great Awakening, God would replace nature as the organizing principle for the nation's so-called manifest destiny.[18]

Despite the effusive rhetoric, however, Ingersoll, like many others of his generation, remained uncertain of the nation's future. Such apprehensions seep from time to time into the text, including in Inchiquin's later, favorable letters. Not surprisingly for a patrician gentleman from Philadelphia, Ingersoll seemed particularly anxious about the character of the westerners. The rural people of America, he pronounces, "are more prone to intoxication, litigation, gambling and turbulence, than the inhabitants of cities." Ingersoll then states that the failed filibuster "attempt by [Aaron] Burr," which rattled the country, had "been perpetrated not by means of town mobs, but frontier settlers, or what are known here by the denomination of backwoodsmen." At the same time however, Ingersoll was no less uncertain about his own milieu of eastern elites. Born after the revolution and raised on the myth of the Spirit of '76, he casts "the American revolution as a period when the American character shone forth with considerable distinction." He expresses concern, however, that "the same nation, in part the same men, after thirty years of peace and prosperity, are supposed to have lost the energy of patriotism they then displayed . . . can the time be so soon arrived for the tide of American declension?"[19]

Indeed, for all the hand wringing about the character of western backwoodsmen, many American gentlemen were perhaps more anxious about their own role as the leaders of the nation. It would be a tall task living up to the fabled Spirit of '76 and the legend of George Washington, whose recent hagiographic biographies had just been published to wide acclaim. A fictitious American-written travel account released the same year as *Inchiquin* summed up the mood of the period. This time, a "Chinese traveler" lionizes the United States "as the only kind of government in which human nature is not insulted, despised, oppressed and degraded," but also expresses grave doubts that "it may not last."[20] Indeed, how could it survive when Americans— eastern elites more so than others—seemed obsessed with commerce, banking, and land speculation? Thus, on the eve of the War of 1812, John Quincy Adams, the son of a legendary founder, likely felt the pressure mounting on his generation more keenly than most. He, too, expressed doubts about the republican experiment, in a letter to his mother, Abigail Adams: "Instead of a nation, coextensive with the North American continent, destined by God and nature to be the most populous and most powerful people ever combined under one social compact, we shall have an endless multitude of little insignificant clans and tribes at eternal war with one another." Almost as troubling, the United States might find itself as "the sport and fable of European masters and oppressors."[21]

Regeneration through Violence

With doubts festering about the republic, and the Union itself seemingly insecure, Americans went in search of the same revolutionary ardor that had filled their parents' generation with feelings of self-confidence and unity. After years of suffering insults at the hands of the former mother country, and yearning for new nationalist heights, a younger generation of Americans declared war on Britain. That is, they set out on a quest for what Richard Slotkin called "regeneration through violence." In a Fourth of July oration in 1812, as the United States prepared for war, Ingersoll captured the jingoistic spirit of the day, combined with republican visions of citizen soldiers: "The whole population of a free empire, scattered over an immense range of territory, springing from the ease and enjoyments of profound relaxation, to grasp the rusted sword, and brighten it in the blood of their aggressors—their phalanxes filled with voluntary levies, studded here and there with a relic of the revolution, like well known stars in firmament, to guide and reflect its general brilliance." The historian Steven Watts explained, "For many citizens, the British confrontation appeared as an immense blank slate on which they wrote their hopes and fears."[22]

Gentlemen in the new states to the west no less so than eastern literati and politicians felt the same way. Indeed, support for the war relied on an east-west alliance of young gentlemen eager to prove themselves to the nation and prove their nation to the world. Eastern men of letters concentrated in the mid-Atlantic cities of New York, Philadelphia, and Baltimore, who for years provided the bulk of the cultural work of national reinvigoration, found natural allies among the inhabitants of the western country whom they were otherwise somewhat uneasy about.

Their most important ally in this regard and probably the greatest booster the western country would ever know was Andrew Jackson. In 1807 Jackson had been forty years old. He felt his personal affairs, as well as those of his nation, to be out of sorts. Over the preceding few years, Jackson had gained notoriety for killing a man in a duel and had associated himself with Burr's failed filibuster against New Spain. Furthermore, although he had held various civil appointments, from regional prosecutor to US senator, he put his energies not toward the good of the Union, but into enhancing his social and economic position in Tennessee. In 1802 he changed course by turning to a military career, securing the rank of general of the Tennessee militia. On July 4, 1805, now a military man ready to sacrifice for his people, he openly declared the rising ambitions of westerners in a toast: "The rising greatness of the West—may it never be impeded by the jealousy of the East." Indeed, rather than stew in jealousy, eastern men of letters would reverse course on their frontier brethren, devising a way for their fellow easterners to live vicariously through westerners and the wild, invigorating, and carnivalesque place they made the west out to be.[23]

The War of 1812 was, therefore, exactly what a new crop of unproven westerners and eastern leaders needed to prove their generation's mettle. "The people of this portion of the union," declared Jackson in an 1809 address to the people of Nashville, "are assembled here to-day to give vent to their feelings, and pledge their lives and fortunes in defense of their own and the nation's rights . . . we are deeply impressed with the truth & importance of the maxim—united we stand—divided we perish."[24] Thus, in late 1811, when clashes with the northern Ohio Valley Native nations began in earnest, Jackson quickly appealed to General William Henry Harrison, tasked with bringing a new wave of Native resistance to heel: "Should the aid of part of my division, be necessary . . . I will with pleasure march with five hundred or one thousand brave Tennesseeans. The blood of our murdered countrymen must be revenged—That banditti, ought to be swept from the face of the earth."[25]

Harrison declined the offer, but Jackson finally got his opportunity when a civil war broke out between rival Creek factions shortly after the War of 1812 had gotten underway. Thrusting themselves into the imagined breach, Jackson and other western leaders rode the wave of militarism sweeping the country, seizing the opportunity to conquer much of the southwest, broadening the War of 1812 into a war for expansion. From the position of conqueror, Jackson not only made the vanquished Creeks, but the American-allied Creeks and other friendly Native nations as well cede vast portions of their land for white settlement.

Thus, for westerners, Jackson was not only the hero of the Battle of New Orleans (1815), but the "liberator" of vast tracts of lucrative land, including the very heart of what would become the Deep South. These war treaties directly opened much of what would soon be Alabama to white settlement. The War of 1812 also directly led to the First Seminole War (1816–18) and the land cessions and removals of the 1820s and 1830s, much of them carried out by Jackson in his capacity as general and later as president (1829–37). Taken together Jackson's efforts in his various capacities following the War of 1812 secured the future states of Mississippi and Florida along with portions of Georgia, Kentucky, North Carolina, and Tennessee. Moreover, by defeating both Native American confederacies and, in the Battle of New Orleans, Great Britain—the empire whose machinations supposedly animated "Indian savagery"—Jackson and his men released the south from the grip of fear itself. Of no less importance for the course of US history, these military campaigns and ethnic cleansing policies also secured the future expansion of slavery into what would soon become the cotton belt.[26]

Above all else, the Battle of New Orleans, fought early in 1815, propelled Jackson, the frontiersmen, and the western country itself to mythical heights. The War of 1812, on its face at least, did not lend itself to greater confidence in the American republic, or the American militia system, but westerners and Americans more broadly yearned for such faith so thoroughly that they found ways to convince themselves, as they had after Lexington and Concord, that common American citizens, organized as militias, had gloriously vanquished the best professional army in the world—for the second time. It was fortunate for them, in this regard, that the last major battle of the war, at New Orleans, was by far the greatest American military victory of the war and that significant numbers of Kentucky and Tennessee militia under the command of an emergent iconic figure were at hand to participate. Though the battle was fought after the United States and Britain had signed the Treaty of Ghent (1814), it is hard to overestimate its significance for American morale and as myth-making material. In the months and years following the victory, Americans were hard at work rewriting the events of the Battle of New Orleans and the War of 1812. Although in reality a diverse coalition of forces—including regulars, local citizens, Creoles, free Blacks, and even pirates, in addition to the lauded western militia—had repelled the British invasion of Louisiana, in the American imagination, the narrative unfolded as the triumph of the American spirit, of patriotic western militiamen and their immortal leader, General Jackson. Much like the generation of '76, common Americans led by a heroic general answered the call to arms when the country needed them most. Whereas the War of Independence made the myth of Washington and the minutemen, the War of 1812 made the myth of Andrew "Old Hickory" Jackson and western militiamen, later consecrated in song as "The Hunters of Kentucky."[27]

Consequently, in the wake of the Battle of New Orleans, a similar euphoria overtook the nation as it had forty years earlier after Lexington and Concord and Bunker Hill. This time, however, westerners emerged with a sense of purpose; it was their time to step into the limelight. Jackson, of course, met with great personal honors everywhere he went, but he also became a vehicle for westerners to celebrate themselves. In a broadside printed to encourage militiamen to salute Jackson on his way back from New Orleans to Tennessee, Natchez militia officers asserted, "The gratitude of free-men is the high-minded soldiers' richest reward," and declared Jackson one "who so justly merits this reward as the gallant saviour of the western world." Continuing to pat both Jackson and themselves on the back, they declared, "It is the brave alone who know how to appreciate the services as well as the feelings of the brave."[28]

Similarly, western papers were quick to pronounce the glory of their region front and center. "The Battle of Orleans consummates the military glory of the western country, already high in the scale of honorable renown," exclaimed one Lexington newspaper when word of the victory reached the city. The paper made particular mention of the state's militiamen, who despite having arrived late and unarmed to the scene of battle somehow emerged as the greatest heroes of the whole affair: "History will scarcely authenticate the mighty deed, effected by citizens who left their homes late in November, reached the scene of action in boats on the 4th of January, and four days after destroyed and captured more than a hundred of the enemy for one of their own men."[29]

Thus, the last battle of the War of 1812 became for the generation of 1812 what the first battles of the American Revolution, at Lexington and Concord, had been for the revolutionary generation and beyond—an expedient fiction that helped Americans tell the story they wanted to hear. According to these tall tales, the virility of America's climes made the people into the greatest citizen-soldiers the world had seen since the glory days of the Roman republic. This held not only for westerners, but the rest of the nation as well—with the exception of pockets of New England—who took to extolling the western country, its militia, and Jackson with almost equal zeal, insinuating that their new heroes reflected on the American character more broadly. Here was the beginning of the realization that rather than a liability, the western areas could serve as a place teeming with potential for the nation. One of the earliest opinion pieces in eastern papers on news of the victory at New Orleans argued, "[Jackson] has proved to the enemy that there are, in every part of America, men who in defense of their firesides are determined and able to repel the most numerous and disciplined hosts of an invading foe." When a resolution thanking "General Jackson and the troops under his command for their gallantry in defense of New Orleans" reached the House of Representatives, George Troup, a young war hawk representing Georgia, declared it "defective," since "it [did] not record the prominent fact which more than any other contribute[d] to the brilliancy of General Jackson's triumph—the fact that the triumph was the triumph of militia over regular troops." In his motion to amend the resolution Troup rehearsed the myth of the minutemen, almost word for word, extolling the image of the "yeomanry of the country marching to the defense of the city of Orleans leaving their wives and children and firesides at a moment's warning . . . I came, I saw, I conquered, says the American husbandman." Thus, in one fell swoop, the nation set in motion the project of once more invigorating the myth of the American yeoman.[30]

Alligator-Horses

Much like the mythic characters of the frontier, from Daniel Boone to Buffalo Bill, the idea of the frontier itself was an elusive synthesis of truth and legend that is often impossible to disentangle. For the purposes here, it is less important to know the truth about life in the western country than to know how ideas about the region changed over time. Once more, travel accounts and their reverberations in popular culture offer valuable insight. Positive impressions of the western country and westerners swelled during the revolution but by the turn of the nineteenth century had ebbed, as most travel accounts of rural western settlements were not generous in their descriptions of the settlers' character. As noted above, even travelers who penned a more nuanced or even favorable account of the United States usually viewed areas to the west, and especially to the southwest, as a breeding ground for despicable patterns of behavior, including hard drinking and violence.

The germs of such an impression can be found in travel accounts from the late colonial and revolutionary eras in which especially rural southerners come off as far more ominous than mere country bumpkins or crass Yankees. While travelers mocked rural New Englanders for their droll language and such quaint practices as bundling, rural southern men emerged from period accounts as violent drunkards who reveled in fighting over the slightest affront. One early account from a genteel traveler who toured the rural southern colonies before the revolution reported that Virginians "act like tygers and bears . . . biting one anothers lips and noses off, and gowging one another." A few years later, an English officer during the revolution described such supposedly ritualistic violence as "this most barbarous custom, which a savage would blush at being accused of" that "is peculiar to the lower-class people in the rural south."[31]

Meanwhile, as tensions rose once more between Britain and the United States, British travelers of the era drew on and reinforced such earlier accounts, painting a dire picture of the southwestern country. Thus, one account related around the turn of the century that in the rural south, "it is by no means uncommon to meet with those who have lost an eye in a combat, and there are men who pride themselves upon the dexterity with which they can scoop one out. This is called *gouging*." Thomas Ashe explained how such events transpired: "Yesterday two fellows drinking in a public house, the conversation turned on the merit of their horses." After a long affair replete with gambling over horse racing and heavy drinking, "two individuals, a Virginian . . . and a Kentuckian [engaged in] rough and tumble," a form of fighting in which none are to "hinder either combatant from tearing or rending the other on the ground." Ashe reported that such events "were common, frequently two or three times a week," especially "on the left-hand side [Kentucky and Virginia side]" of the Ohio River. "Many small inns on the Virginia and Kentucky shore, were held . . . by persons of infamous character" and were places where "there were always persons at no loss for a subject of quarrel." Even the far more moderated Fortescue Cuming related a similar tale. Explaining that the "backwoodsmen . . . are very similar in their habits and manners to the aborigines, only perhaps more prodigal and more careless of life," he told of their "frequent meetings for the purpose of gambling, fighting, and drinking." "They fight for the most trifling provocations . . . kicking, scratching, biting, gouging . . . and doing their utmost to kill each other." Together such accounts suggested that the rural south and the new states inhabited by rural southerners, Kentucky and Tennessee, had cultivated a deeply ingrained tradition of fighting, known there as gouging, in which the ultimate goal was to seriously maim one's foe, as in, for instance, gouging his eye out.[32]

During the second decade of the nineteenth century, however, especially following the victory at the Battle of New Orleans, there was a decisive change of tone, particularly among American travelers, in accounts of frontiersmen and their purported violent ways. One way to assess this transition is through the trajectory of the idiom that stuck to American frontiersmen over this decade: "half horse, half alligator" or "alligator-horses." It appears that the earliest published account using this phrase or similar ones was in *The Magic Lantern*, a satirical play performed in the United States that mocks the leading figures in Burr's infamous filibuster. An excerpt published in local newspapers included a reference to a monster "'half Horse, half alligator,' mounted on the stump of a tree, with a barrel of whiskey before him." The creature appears to be a trope for a western frontiersman, in this case, portrayed quite negatively.[33] In *A History of New York*, Washington Irving, an avid theater goer, picked up on the trope, noting that the "back-wood-men of Kentucky are styled half man, half horse and half alligator, by the settlers on the Mississippi, and held accordingly in great respect and abhorrence."[34]

A more oft-quoted reference of this type flowed from the pen of an American traveler whose intervention in the trans-Atlantic war of words attempted, as he notes in the preface, to correct the "mistakes, misrepresentations and fictions" contained in Thomas Ashe's notoriously pejorative account. Christian Schultz toured western country in 1807 and 1808 and in an otherwise favorable account, comes off as condescending, yet amused, by the violent and foul-mouthed altercation he witnessed. Walking "down to the Levee" in Natchez, Schultz overhears some "very warm words," describing a dispute between two Mississippi boatmen over a *"Choctaw lady"*: "Although I might fill half a dozen pages with the curious slang made use of on this occasion, yet I prefer selecting a few of the most brilliant expressions by way of sample. One said 'I am a man; I am a horse; I am a team. I can whip any man *in all Kentucky*, by G—d.' The other replied, 'I am an alligator; half man, half horse; can whip any *on the Mississippi* by G—d.'" Relating a few more such exchanges, Shultz testifies that, finally, "They went like two bulls, and continued for half an hour, when the alligator was fairly vanquished by the horse." Although noting with some journalistic delight the unique vernacular of the "natives" of the western region, who incidentally were fighting over a Native American woman, Shultz maintains a condescending and detached air toward the whole affair. Many future accounts of origins of the term *alligator-horse*, or some derivative of it, would cite Schultz as its source.[35]

Whether these specific representations of western jargon actually originated in the western country itself, they rang true for contemporary readers. Moreover, although one can probably assume that accounts about the region were often exaggerated, they rang true for many westerners, who did not shy away from such accusations, acknowledging it as gritty violence that animated the western spirit. Indeed, although both Irving and Schultz seem a bit ambivalent about the people they came across—reporting on crude westerners more as a curious regional phenomenon than American traits to take pride in—westerners by and large seemed to revel in such extravagant accounts of themselves. For example, as early as 1813, the *Kentucky Almanac* featured the above passage from Schultz's travels as part of its collection of entertaining and local patriotic anecdotes. Like "Yankee Doodle," it fit well into the self-deprecating provincial tradition in American vernacular culture that sought to defuse the sting of metropolitan mockery and cultivate a self-edifying image as hardy, manly, and defiantly provincial Americans.[36]

In the western country, such language also lent itself to the decades-long tradition of casting frontiersmen as hyper-manly and indigenous to the wild environment of the region. It was a means of offsetting anxiety vis-à-vis the real natives—the Native peoples of trans-Appalachian America who still retained the ability to strike terror in the hearts of westerners.[37] In this vein, vivid, extravagant, and humorous depictions of westerners aligned with the tradition of "Indian play," as westerners nurtured an aura of self-assured and even giddy poise in the face of danger and violence. This form of western pride was more pronounced among settlers in Kentucky and Tennessee than other areas in the region. The men of Tennessee and Kentucky, many of whom migrated from Virginia and North Carolina, thought of themselves as more rugged, more manly, and more able than frontiersmen of other regions. This tradition dates back to the early days of encounters between frontier Virginians and Natives of the Haudenosaunee Confederacy in the first half of the eighteenth century. The Haudenosaunee called Virginians "Long Knives," probably after the long swords they carried, and over the years Virginian men embraced this moniker to cultivate their self-image as the hardiest frontiersmen. In fact, due to the Haudenosaunee name for them, Virginians liked to think that the Indians regarded them with more respect than they did northern frontier settlers.[38]

The male citizens of Kentucky and Tennessee, in a display of their militant ferocity as well as their republican commitments to a polity of free-born men, took to militias with more enthusiasm than anyone else in the Union during the War of 1812, especially in its early stages.[39] Indeed, both elites and commoners in the west seemed to instinctively reach for language underlining the crucial links between participation in a militia, male citizenship, and republicanism. For gentlemen groomed on republicanism, this proved central to casting the western country as the cradle of freeborn virtue. For frontiersmen bred on an egalitarian, antiauthoritarian, and hyper-manly camaraderie of free men, this language proved self-serving in identifying them with the idea of "the nation" and elevating them to the same level that formerly only gentlemen had inhabited. Thus, when the United States declared war on Britain in the summer of 1812, nationalist militarism swept Kentucky and Tennessee like nowhere else in the country. Over the next years, westerners engaged in a concentrated effort to demonstrate to the nation and to themselves their virile character as citizen-warriors; for them the war became a boosterism campaign of sorts.[40]

To prove their point, westerners had to uphold the valor of their state militias and reconfirm American faith in the militia as a central republican and American institution. General Jackson reflected as much in an address to militiamen under his command when he learned of the government's decision to rely on state militias for the coming war:

> Citizens! Your goverment has at last yielded to the impulse of the nation. Your impatience is no longer restrained. The hour of national vengeance is now at hand. The eternal enemies of American prosperity are again to be taught to respect your rights, after having been compelled to feel, once more, the power of your arms.
>
> *War is on the point of breaking out between the United States and the king of Great Britain! and the martial hosts of America are summoned to the tented fields!*
>
> Citizens! an honourable confidence in your courage and your patriotism has been displayed by the general goverment. To raise a force for the protection of your rights she has not deemed it necessary to recur to the common mode of filling the ranks of an army.
>
> No drafts or compulsory levies are now to be made.[41]

By invoking the notion of a citizen-soldier as most fitting for the war effort, Jackson paid tribute to the hallowed republican, American (as in Lexington and Concord), and western traditions of the militia as the cornerstone of communal vitality. In truth, Jackson knew well that the militia under his command was ill-prepared to tackle the military challenges of the day, and before the war and even more so during the war, thought poorly of the militia system that had been instituted. He could hardly afford to betray such sentiments, however, or deny the compelling ring such sanguine faith in the state's militia offered contemporaries.[42]

It took a few years for the mythology of the Battle of New Orleans and the War of 1812 to cohere. As Americans searched for tropes and idioms to celebrate the virility of western militia men, however, the boisterous, rough-and-tumble notion of the alligator-horse proved compelling. Thus, several months after the victory in New Orleans, one popular comical poem used the emerging genre of Black dialect lyrics to feature the battle from the perspective of a runaway slave who joined the British cause. At one point in the poem the narrator notes that the "backwood Yankee," who rebuffed the British invasion called himself "one half horse, half an alligator!"[43] Of course, during the war and in its immediate aftermath, not all Americans received the "correct" script on the War of 1812. Some celebrated naval heroes, while others seemed more interested in the pirates who rallied to defend New Orleans. Within several years, however, Americans had weeded out the less palatable aspects of the story of the battle. In so doing, they rendered memory of it western, and American, mythology.

This process of myth making culminated with the popular ditty "The Hunters of Kentucky" (ca. 1818/19). Written by Samuel Woodworth, this song, more than any other popular cultural product, forged early links between raucous and carnivalesque performances of manhood and the western country to create the new fountainhead of virility for the nation. "The Hunters of Kentucky" saw much success both in print and in live performances across the country before eventually being harnessed to Andrew Jackson's 1828 presidential campaign. In broadsides, it sometimes appeared fittingly alongside the image of a ferocious half horse, half alligator beast (figure 5.1). The trope of the alligator-horse is evoked, respectively, in the first and fourth stanzas of the song:

> We are a hardy, free-born race,
> Each man to fear a stranger;
> Whate'er the game we join in chase,
> Despoiling time and danger
> And if a daring foe annoys,
> Whate'er his strength and forces,
> We'll show him that Kentucky boys
> Are alligator horses,
>
> A bank was rais'd to hide our breasts,
> Not that we thought of dying,
> But that we always like to rest,
> Unless the game is flying.
> Behind it stood our little force,
> None wished it to be greater,
> For ev'ry man was half a horse,
> And half an alligator.[44]

John William Ward ably told the story of the song's early success some seventy years ago, but the digitization of newspaper and print materials allows it to now be told with even more clarity.[45] After the song's lyrics appeared

Hunters of Kentucky, or Half
HORSE AND HÂLF ALLIGATOR.

YE gentlemen and ladies fair,
 Who grace this famous city,
Just listen if you've time to spare,
 While I rehearse a ditty;
And for the opportunity
 Conceive yourselves quite lucky,
For 'tis not often that you see
 A hunter from Kentucky.
Oh Kentucky, the hunters of Kentucky!
Oh Kentucky, the hunters of Kentucky!

We are a hardy, free-born race,
 Each man to fear a stranger;
Whate'er the game we join in chase,
 Despoiling time and danger
And if a daring foe annoys,
 Whate'er his strength and forces,
We'll show him that Kentucky boys
 Are alligator horses.
                Oh Kentucky, &c.

I s'pose you've read it in the prints,
 How Packenham attempted
To make old Hickory Jackson wince,
 But soon his scheme repented;
For we, with rifles ready cock'd,
 Thought such occasion lucky,
And soon around the gen'ral flock'd
 The hunters of Kentucky.
                Oh Kentucky, &c.

You've heard, I s'pose how New-Orleans
 Is fam'd for wealth and beauty,
There's girls of ev'ry hue it seems,
 From snowy white to sooty.
So Packenham he made his brags,
 If he in fight was lucky,
He'd have their girls and cotton bags,
 In spite of old Kentucky.
    565   Oh Kentucky, &c.

But Jackson he was wide awake,
 And was not scar'd at trifles,
For well he knew what aim we take
 With our Kentucky rifles.
So he led us down to Cypress swamp,
 The ground was low and mucky;
There stood John Bull in martial pomp
 And here was old Kentucky.
                Oh Kentucky, &c.

A bank was rais'd to hide our breasts,
 Not that we thought of dying,
But that we always like to rest,
 Unless the game is flying.
Behind it stood our little force,
 None wished it to be greater,
For ev'ry man was half a horse,
 And half an alligator.
                Oh Kentucky, &c.

They did not let our patience tire,
 Before they show'd their faces;
We did not choose to waste our fire,
 So snugly kept our places.
But when so near we saw them wink,
 We thought it time to stop 'em,
And 'twould have done you good I think,
 To see Kentuckians drop 'em.
                Oh Kentucky, &c.

They found, at last, 'twas vain to fight,
 Where lead was all the booty,
And so they wisely took to flight,
 And left us all our beauty.
And now, if danger e'er annoys,
 Remember what our trade is,
Just send for us Kentucky boys,
 And we'll protect ye, ladies.
                Oh Kentucky, &c.

Sold wholesale & retail by William Rutter, No. 1, Snow's Wharf, Boston.

Figure 5.1. "Hunters of Kentucky, or Half Horse and Half Alligator," Boston (probably from the early 1820s). Dozens of versions of these broadsides were printed mostly in the 1820s but also in later decades. Several of them featured these types of images of half horse half alligators clearly a reference to the emerging impressions of western vocabulary and western manhood. Library of Congress, https://www.loc.gov/item/amss .as105650/.

in a few eastern newspapers in 1821 and 1822, Noah Ludlow, an itinerant performer, received a clipping of them by mail from his brother, who had seen them in a New York paper. In 1822 Ludlow performed it as a treat for a New Orleans audience of rivermen. On a whim, he also decided to dance and sing the ditty that night dressed, he recalled, "in a buckskin hunting-shirt and leggins . . . and with moccasins on my feet, and an old slouched hat on my head, and a rifle on my shoulder." In this respect, Ludlow was probably inspired by engravings of Daniel Boone that he had previously sold to make ends meet while out of work. Ludlow's performance drew raves from the rivermen, who at one point cheered him with "a shout and an Indian yell." Subsequently, Ludlow began performing the song regularly to enthusiastic audiences across the western country, and from there it spread to the rest of the nation.[46] The embrace of the song signaled that the rowdy, virile, and violent western men captured by the phrase alligator-horse had become the natives of the western country, no less so—as least as far as white audiences were concerned—than the Indians they were so good at fighting as well as imitating.

Ludlow recalled that in 1822 while touring with his group across the old southwest, he was practically *"compelled* to sing the Hunters of Kentucky almost every night." Sometimes, "the audience would leave the theatre" only after he sang it "twice or thrice." Inspired by Ludlow, entertainers in Baltimore, Philadelphia, New York, Boston, and elsewhere perfected rousing renditions of the song, and by the mid-1820s each town boasted a local specialist who perfected a boisterous performance. It became a mainstay at shows that included demonstrations of horsemanship skills, which was typically among the varied fare of performances in local theaters and circuses catering to common folk. In what can be described as a dialectical, reinforcing relationship with the song's live performances, it circulated over the 1820s, from New Orleans back to New York (where it was written), with the lyrics reproduced in newspapers, songsters, broadsides, almanacs, and other published materials. Although newspapers initially attributed the song to Samuel Woodworth, as when first introduced, by the end of 1822 newspapers and other printed materials added "as sung by N. M. Ludlow in New Orleans."[47]

Thus, "The Hunters of Kentucky" emerged as perhaps the first prominent artifact of a nascent American popular culture, the product of an expanding echo chamber that relied on reinforcing cycles of print, stage performances, and ultimately everyday amusement. Indeed, much like "Yankee Doodle," it was "so popular that," according to Ludlow, "you could hear it sung or whistled almost any day, as you passed along the principal thoroughfares of the city." An article in a Philadelphia paper reported an incident that occurred "at 2 o'clock in the morning" involving drunkards being arrested for "singing the Hunters of Kentucky, with all their might, and most horribly out of tune."[48] Unlike "Yankee Doodle," however, "The Hunters of Kentucky" was not a product of vernacular culture that grew in popularity over many decades and then exploded, in that instance around the revolution. Although touching on vernacular themes, Woodworth's song was a product of a novel popular culture as well as a touchstone of national identity for many years after the War of 1812.

Eleven years after the Battle of New Orleans, the fifth toast at a local celebration of the New York National Guard extolled "*The 8th of January, 1815—The day which added another proof to an unbelieving world that citizen soldiers were invincible, when fighting in the sacred cause of liberty.*" The attendees followed it with a rendition of "The Hunters of Kentucky."[49] Perhaps even more telling of its success as a new form of popular culture was the lament of one New England Brahmin over the lure of the western country for young New Englanders in the 1820s, a phenomenon he attributed as part and parcel of the song's vulgar comic appeal. "The rude strain of the song of the 'Hunters of Kentucky' have more charms for the ears of the rough and patriotic race whom they [New England youth] celebrate, than have the graceful stanzas of Moore or the deep poetry of Byron."[50] Indeed, the success of "The Hunters of Kentucky" was not only a local affair but signaled the emergence of a new phenomenon of hit songs that would sweep the United States, including Federalist New England, in the decades following 1820. The song would become a central component of the first robust and widespread national culture of the modern era.[51]

If "Yankee Doodle" enshrined the American country clown alongside George Washington as American icons of the revolutionary generation, "The Hunters of Kentucky" cemented the frontier jester as the natural companion to Andrew Jackson in the decades following the War of 1812. As before, it was the injection of raucous mirth into the symbolism of the nation that helped cohere the national community around an unapologetic commitment to common, anti-elitist themes. Woodworth's song and later cultural products from the era pointed to the United States turning into a nation of jovial, common men. Of course, it also yoked egalitarian sensibilities with a zeal for violent and masculine performances as central to the vitality of the nation.

Republicanism and the West

The success of "The Hunters of Kentucky" and its genealogy captured the cross-regional character of Americans' resurgent nationalism. After all, it had been written by a one-time New Englander who moved to New York, yet was first performed in New Orleans by a New York–born actor who became synonymous with western theater. In contrast to the many histories of the period that highlight the centrifugal forces undermining a unified idea of the nation in the antebellum era, the song's popularity revealed the existence of numerous cultural brokers working to shape a multilayered, compelling, and broadly resonant nationalism across regional, class, and partisan divides. It also helps explain how insofar as the increased nationalism of the period was cross-regional, it coalesced around the euphoric mythology of the western country.[52]

The broader historical context of the period's economic and political ruptures helps explain the affinity of so many Americans, north, south, east, and west, for the violent and boisterous westerners and the "The Hunters of Kentucky." James Kirke Paulding serves well as a travel guide. After the War of 1812, Paulding's good standing with President Madison and his journalistic support for the US Navy secured him a position as part of the administration's patronage network, serving as secretary of the Board of Navy Commissioners. Soon after, however, he felt his health waning, and during the second half of 1816 took a leisurely tour through Virginia to revive his spirits. Upon his return, he delved into preparing yet another broadside at the British, the following year publishing a travel account of his journey.[53]

Although Paulding never ventured far inland during his travels, and despite his account being titled *Letters from the South* (1817), the missives in it discuss the character of the people of the western country just as much, if not more than, they do those of the south. Regardless of the initial subject matter of his letters, he usually ends up in a long-winded disquisition about the two items that interested him most: lambasting the British, and everything associated with them, and upholding the character of America, especially its western inhabitants. In this regard, his diatribes gravitate toward castigating the eastern establishment for "hankering after Johnny Bull's cast of clothes"—that is, imitating British fashions—and against what he perceives as the European-derived financial malpractice of the country, such as the "torrent of speculation" and the "paper system." In contrast, he turns to the "almost uninhabited Eden in the west, whose bosom is opened to the industrious and enterprising," as a source of vitality for the nation. In another letter, he opens by declaring that "young nations, like children, seem destined to endure certain diseases," and subsequently notes that the "disease . . . goes at present by the name of *speculation* . . . and extends to every article of sale or purchase." A few pages in, he turns to the topic of the western country observing, "The more active and enterprising—the people who partake of youth, enterprise, and hardihood, and who increase the actual productions of the earth by their labours, are looking more and more to the west." Seemingly following the trajectory of Andrew Jackson's career, he continues by portraying a typical frontiersman who first "builds him a log cabin" and later adds "an addition to his cabin and last of all, builds him a stately house, and becomes a judge, a general, or a member of Congress.[54]

Though Paulding offers quite serious commentary in his letters, his writing style resembles the formula of Laurence Sterne's whimsical-if-sincere *A Sentimental Journey* (1768), beloved by all self-styled traveling bachelors. He imbues his characterization of the western country with considerable doses of mirth, at one point taking after Schultz and Irving by introducing his favored western specimens as "half horse, half alligator" and "part earthquake and a little of the steam boat." He describes a western household as a "family of giants, seven in number . . . an old man whose countenance . . . was not quite so amiable . . . and six young fellows, that looked as if the forest itself would bow before them." Although at one point he anxiously concedes that he "did not like the looks of three of four rifles, displayed rather ostentatiously" and quips uneasily of his determination "to look at the sheets to see if they were not bloody," he also enthuses, "These are the lads to go in front of the great caravan of man, in his progress to the west." Such passages reveal Paulding's peculiar position as an easterner: though a member of the coastal elite and committed to refined modes of discourse and comportment, he seeks vitality for himself and the nation elsewhere. Ill at ease with his own class and suffering from a general malaise of spirit, he toured a southern section of the western country in search of able-bodied men as a source of rejuvenation. Thus, what would typically be ridicule—and at times is quite ambivalent—turns into uneasy adoration.[55]

Such reliance on western themes became even more urgent as republican anxieties surged with the financial meltdown of 1818/19. Indeed, Paulding's assault on monied interests—the banks, speculation, and paper money at the heart of finance capitalism—appears prescient of the sentiments that would erupt almost a year later as a backlash to the Panic of 1819. In the realm of economic policy, no American commentator commanded a larger audience than Hezekiah Niles during the 1810s and 1820s. Established as the preeminent magazine of political economy, *Niles' Weekly Register* led the charge against, as he put it in one account of the panic, "the excess of the paper system" and "the rage for British goods" led by "men . . . too weak to resist the temptation of making great fortunes." According to Niles the fault lay with "certain great proprietors of the stock of the bank of the United States" and "with other speculators . . . to whose benefit the welfare of the *nation*" had been "prostrated." Together they wrought a "curse that will divest the people not only of their property, but of their liberty, and transform them into a herd of underlings and slaves . . . just as in England." "Gracious heaven!" he exclaimed, "are such things to be that fifty men may 'ride rough shod' over a ruined people—a great gallant nation the pride of the world and hope of posterity?"[56]

Surprisingly, Republicans of very different stripes sounded similar alarm bells. Although Niles viewed John Taylor of Caroline as his intellectual foe, he here sounds very much like the revered Jeffersonian thinker, who stood for opposition to the monied interests at all costs. Despite Niles being a passionate promoter of a protective tariff, and much of Taylor's writing hinging on his fiery opposition to protectionist measures, both could agree on their opposition to what Taylor calls in a rather Marxist-sounding tone the "avarice of the capitalist, monied or paper interest."[57] Indeed, contentious republican traditions came together for a time around the Panic of 1819 to castigate Americans, in the words of another angry commentator "for embracing phantoms for realities, and running mad schemes of refinement, tastes, pleasures, wealth and power."[58]

Likewise, they could for the most part also agree on the solution for these tendencies within the ranks of the country's class of capitalists, if not the strategy through which to achieve it. For Taylor, the only source of comfort and sound political economy had to issue from the productive elements in society, by which he usually meant agriculturalists, whom he also at one point refers to suggestively as the "yeomenry of the forest."[59] For Niles, the time would eventually come when "honest men would get into fashion," and when "solidly chartered companies would seek to do business with plain, economical, and productive men, instead of speculating madmen and visionary schemers." Imagining a time when "Mr. Jack plane's daughter" will "have as much respect in the ball room . . . as Mr. Note-maker's or Mr. Land-dealer's," he declares, "let the productive people . . . the sinews of every country, the true patriots of every land . . . command the deference in the national and state legislatures," that has been "denied them from twenty years past."[60] For Niles, it was clear that much of these types of specimens would increasingly reside out west. This was, after all, the same editor who launched the first issue of his magazine with "The Western Country," a piece casting Ohio and Kentucky as newly opened vital lands in which the "yell of the savage had given place to the cheerful note of the sailor."[61] Over the next decade, nationalist orators like Taylor, Niles, and Paulding would increasingly look west when seeking to stir pride in their country.

A similar argument regarding western expansion could be made for the threat of political disunion in the wake of the famous congressional amendment introduced by David Talmadge in February 1819. As Talmadge's proposal that slavery not be permitted in the new state of Missouri threw the country into turmoil, nationalists glimpsed what they had long feared: the impending dissolution of the Union. Although the growing hankering for the western country bled into and exacerbated the emerging sectional crisis over Missouri, the lands to the west also became a source of respite from the frightening debates over the fate of the Union. Thus, during the 1820s, ideologues on both sides of the emerging partisan divide would increasingly look westward and argue in ways that defied easy sectional divides as they considered policies to best suit expansion in that direction. In fact, the partisan divide that developed during the 1820s and 1830s, as many have noted, helped hold the country together for the next thirty years or so; it did so by focusing much of the partisan conflict on different formulas for western expansion, thus skirting the sectional divide laid bare by Talmadge's amendment. Niles emerged as one of the leading voices in the 1820s advocating the economic nationalism that would become the most important tenet of the emerging Whig Party and its members' vision of what they called an American system that led west. Likewise, following the teachings of John Taylor of Caroline, the Democrats would argue that western expansion with minimal federal intervention would best bring the promise of democracy to the masses. Both sides envisioned the lands to the west as the natural domain for the success of the most vital forces in America.[62]

The Lion of the West

Even before Jackson rode the success of "The Hunters of Kentucky" into the White House, a fellow Tennessean by the name of David Crockett pioneered a style of politicking during the 1820s that combined whimsical braggart tales with a common man's charisma that celebrated the provincial frontiersman. A man famous for a jumbled and crude vernacular at a time when the eloquent oratory of the likes of John Randolph and Henry Clay dominated American politics, Crockett might have been the first populist politician in the full sense of the word in American history in his persistent commitment to the common man's agenda, but even more so in his style. After serving under Andrew Jackson in the War of 1812, the extroverted Crockett cut his political teeth in the public life of the frontier, earning a reputation as an enthusiastic and convivial yarn spinner known for his tall tales of frontier adventures. His conspicuous comportment won him local renown at such community events as militia musters, gatherings for corn shucking, and house raisings and eventually on the frontier campaign trail. Indeed, after several years as an officeholder at the county level, Crockett decided to run for the Tennessee House of Representatives in 1821. He won and served two sessions in the state legislature as a spokesperson for frontier interests before running for Congress. Winning on his second attempt, he took his seat in the House of Representatives for a western Tennessee district in 1827.[63]

Crockett's reputation as a prototypical backwoodsman and hunter known for spinning tales in crude western jargon preceded him in Washington. In particular, it appears that while a county and state politician, Crockett developed a talent for injecting the aggrandizing mythology of the frontier into his speeches at campaign gatherings, which would often become merry drinking affairs. Thus, by the time Crockett reached Washington, he had emerged as the foremost figure associated with the comic and virile image of "The Hunters of Kentucky," and papers around the country ran stories on him. "One of the most amusing members of the House of Representatives," reported a New Hampshire paper in 1828, "is Mr. Crockett of Tennessee." Mocking as well as celebrating Crockett, stories presented readers with choice quotes invoking the tone and syntax familiar from alligator-horse anecdotes: "'I don't know why' says Mr. C. 'I should be afraid to rise and address the House of Representatives, for I can whip any man in it.'—and his appearance promises a fulfillment of his words. This is the gentleman who sometime since boasted that he could 'wade the Mississippi, carry a steamboat on his back and whip his weight in wild cats.'"[64]

Crockett served two more congressional terms, gaining notoriety for his maverick contrarianism as he left the Jacksonians to join the National Republicans (later Whigs). Indeed, in later years he became known for his long anti-Jacksonian tirades. Although he initially felt self-conscious about his provincialism, by his last congressional term he seemed much more comfortable in his own skin. During his last years, Crockett enjoyed the patronage of the Whigs, who helped propagate his image as an icon and, in turn, drew on his popularity for their own political ends. When he lost his 1835 congressional run to the Jacksonians, he embarked on the westward trip that would seal his immortality. Joining the struggle for Texas's independence from Mexico, Crockett was probably executed after falling prisoner in the Battle of the Alamo near San Antonio de Béxar in 1836.[65]

Whereas Crockett's rise to fame in the late 1820s and 1830s signaled the passing of the baton from the Yankee to the frontier jester as the preeminent American clown trope of the period, the famed actor James Hackett made the transition quite literally.[66] After several years of great success performing Yankee characters on stage, Hackett, looking for fresh material, placed an advertisement in the *New York Evening Post* in April 1830 offering a prize of $250 for the best comedy "dramatizing the manners and peculiarities of our own country."[67] Inspired by the news of Crockett sitting in Congress, James Kirke Paulding rose to the challenge and wrote *The Lion of the West*, a play tailored for Hackett in the lead role. Paulding won the competition. Trying to avoid a direct link with Crockett—perhaps to spare being challenged to a duel—Paulding crafted his character as Nimrod Wildfire from Kentucky and even sent a message to Crockett reassuring him that despite "rumors which lately appeared in newspapers," he did not mean "an outrage on the feelings of any Gentleman." To all, however, including to Crockett, it was abundantly clear that Crockett was the model for Nimrod Wildfire.[68]

Paulding's play debuted before a full house at New York's Park Theater in April 1831. The most thorough record of the original production is an extensive review published in a New York paper.[69] The reviewer commended Paulding for "an extremely racy representation of western blood, a perfect *non-pareil*—half steam-boat, half alligator, &c... The body and soul of Col. Wildfire was Kentuckian—ardent, generous, daring, witty, blunt, and original." The reviewer concluded, "the amusing extravagances and strange features of character which have grown up in the western states, are perhaps *unique* in the world itself." Though satirical, as we have come to expect from Paulding, this doubtless, was a favorable representation of the frontier jester.[70]

The Lion of the West, later revised and renamed *The Kentuckian or a Trip to New York in 1815*, was a success on both sides of the Atlantic. It uses well-worn formulas, employing themes common in Yankee theater, but pays more attention to the iteration of the provincial American yokel newly reimagined as a western jester. Like Royall Tyler's *The Contrast*, for example, it is a comedy of manners, of sorts, that juxtaposes the simplistic integrity of the Americans with the genteel affectation of the British.[71] Hackett's production, however, was first and foremost an opportunity for him to show off his comedic skills, and secondarily the chance to deliver sentimental moral commentary. Indeed, despite the romantic narrative of sensibility that held the play together—to which Nimrod Wildfire was not a part—the frontiersman was the hero of the play, and audiences attended primarily for Hackett's performance. The play cast the crude American as something of a buffoon, but he was a good-natured fool, who—unlike the artifice of the foppish genteel sort—presented American simplicity in a positive light, as overflowing with manly vitality. Also, like Yankee theater, it purported to use a genuine vernacular, boasting a combination of bits of quotes that drew from Crockett's tall tales with an added flair of creative interpretation. Thus, one finds the swaggering tone and syntax associated with Crockett and alligator-horse vocabulary every time Wildfire has the opportunity to show off his idiosyncratic speech, especially when bragging of his virility. "Of all the fellers either side the Allegheny hills," boasted Wildfire in a typical moment, "I myself can jump higher, squat lower, dive deeper, stay longer under and come out drier."[72]

Once again, the emergent popular culture machine, combining mass print publications with stage performances, pounced on the new material. Following the success of Paulding's play, several publications appeared that purported to present the real David Crockett to American audiences. Among them was one by James Strange French, who without Crockett's knowledge, released *Sketches and Eccentricities of Colonel David Crockett of West Tennessee* (1833), which underwent several printings. In light of the various publications about him, Crockett, with the help of his more erudite friend Thomas Chilton, set out to write his own biography, *A Narrative of the Life of David Crockett of the State of Tennessee* (1834). This positive and whimsical rendition of Crockett's life proved a great success with Americans, playing to the strengths of his persona in featuring a medley of anecdotes, droll sayings, and real biographical details, all dressed in a morality tale of homespun American virtue. Crockett then went on a much-publicized tour to promote his book, drawing big audiences wherever he went.[73]

For the most part, however, the representations of Crockett that truly enshrined him in American mythology were produced after his death, in 1836. A driving force behind the myth making appeared, however, two years earlier, in 1834, when the Boston printer Samuel Dickson published the first

Davy Crockett's Almanac, which according to one historian, championed Crockett as a "comic Hercules." Typical of the print industry of the period, several rival versions soon followed under various titles, all attempting to capitalize on the growing legend of Crockett and its jocular mass appeal.[74] Between 1834 and 1856, various printers issued numerous editions of at least 45 almanacs, putting millions of copies in circulation.[75] The almanacs, more than any other print material, made Crockett a household name across the country in the decades following his death. Furthermore, after Crockett's death, his publishers released a fabricated diary, *Col. Crockett's Exploits and Adventures in Texas*, allegedly found after the Battle of the Alamo. Rife with the comic devices that made Crockett an icon, it sold 10,000 copies in the first year of publication. In short, following Crockett's death, myriad Americans produced an unending parade of representations of him, creating an unceasing gristmill of Davy Crockett anecdotes, stories, and imagery that transformed him into the closest thing the American West had to a patron saint or a Greek demigod, though with a uniquely American comic twist.[76]

Thus, during the 1830s, and even more so in the following decades, Americans contrived a rich and national popular mythology of provincial America that upheld the western country as a terrain fit for the comical and uninhibited structure of feelings they associated with freeborn, rural white men. These western backwoodsmen had emerged from the frontier crucible victorious and ebullient in the face of Indian terror and Eastern Seaboard elitism. Indeed, though uneasy around such people, Americans in urban centers or of more genteel standing found themselves tapping into the western country and its inhabitants for vitality and regeneration. Thus, for many, Crockett and his ilk became a favored medium through which to celebrate the glory of both self and nation. Davy Crockett and fellow famous frontiersmen, such as Mike Fink, Jed Smith, Kit Carson, and many more, were the shock troops of this new American sensibility, rendering white common men indigenous to the American environment. They were all the sons of Andrew Jackson and his Hunters of Kentucky. By the same token, this would exclude from the United States the actual Indigenous peoples of North America as well as Americans of African descent.[77]

PART THREE

A TALE OF TWO CLOWNS

The song "Backside Albany" celebrates the US victory in the Battle of Plattsburgh (1814), one of a few cherished American successes in the War of 1812. Although numerous patriotic songs partook in and reinforced the nationalist uproar of the period—most notably "The Star-Spangled Banner" (1814)[1]—"Backside Albany" was the first to do so in Black dialect. Indeed, scholars often regard "Backside Albany" as the first American written Black dialect song to achieve wide success; it was widely reproduced in print and premiered on stage in the fall of 1814. The song's use of a clownish narrator, a Black American sailor who botches every other word, initially appears a confounding choice, since aside from the dialect itself, the lyrics do not appear to mock or even deal with Blacks. In fact, the narrator is one of the victors in the battle. When one considers the increased interest at that time in policing the nation's borders around whiteness, however, it becomes clear that "Backside Albany" was aimed at reinforcing a racially inflected construction of US nationalism. It did so explicitly by celebrating an American victory against the British enemy, but also implicitly by reifying the racial category of blackness. Thus, through an appeal to levity and play, it employed humor to draw racial boundaries for the national community.[2]

Another Black dialect song, sometimes titled "The Guinea Boy" and written in the spring of 1815, has largely eluded historians, but it better illustrates the ways black dialect songs contributed to racial nationalism.[3] This songwriter likely borrowed the idea of employing Black dialect from "Backside Albany" and then applied it to the song structure of "Negro and Buckra Man," a comical song from the British Atlantic Black dialect tradition that explores the experience of Africans kidnapped into slavery from the coast of "Guinea."[4] The case of "The Guinea Boy" requires little analytical heft to demonstrate the ways in which it underscored resurgent racial nationalism because the Black narrator is perfectly integrated into the main point the song sought to make. Using scare quotes, the introduction to the song claims that it was composed by "one of the 'brave black patriots,' who so nobly 'volunteered' their services" to the British after running away from their Chesapeake plantations. The song itself tells the narrative of the Battle of New Orleans (1815) from the perspective of the runaway slave. Here are the first four stanzas:

> When me leetle boy, den me sum from Guinea,
> Buckra man teal me, bring me to Virginia;
> Dare me very much work
> Great big fence-rail toat-e—
> But British man he come,
> He give me find red coat-e
>
> Captain money give, very much I tank he,
> But de sojer man call me dam black Yankee;
> Admiral clever, good,
> He give me port and bean-e
> I go long wid him
> For take New-Orlean-e
>
> When we come ashore, great big gun we shoot-e
> For make Yankee run, den we could get de "booty"
> But de backwood Yankee,
> He not much good nater,
> He say he "one half horse,
> Half an alligator!"
>
> General he much swear, make de mortar thunder,
> Old Hickory man for scare, till we get de plunder;
> Den wid pretty garl,
> We'll have plenty fun-e—
> But Old Hickory man
> Debil a step would run-e[5]

Though "The Guinea Boy" never attained the same degree of popularity as "Backside Albany," it appeared in at least eight different newspapers and a few broadsides, almanacs, and songsters. It was no surprise that white Americans took a liking to the satirical song, for not only did it delight in the new heroes of the war—Jackson as Old Hickory and the "backwood Yankee," referred to as "half horse / half an alligator"—but it also painted runaway slaves who joined the British as despicable fools and the British as corrupt race traitors.[6] As "The Star Spangle Banner" reveals with its infamous reference to the "hireling and the slave," runaway slaves escaping to British ships in the Chesapeake, often joining the British armed forces, was a sore point during the war.[7]

"The Guinea Boy" demonstrates how several years before "The Hunters of Kentucky" (1821) launched American popular culture in the 1820s, Americans were already hard at work rescripting the narrative of the War of 1812 and the Battle of New Orleans into a usable synthesis of racial nationalism that cast white militiamen protecting American femininity from Black and Native marauders. Like so many American culture productions before it and since, the song employed mirth and levity—in this case the conceit of the white author assuming Black dialect and perspectives—to discipline the borders of the national collective so that only white men could feel fully at ease in their "own" nation. Unlike "Backside Albany," however, "The Guinea Boy" ditty eminently makes clear that along with the British, escaped Black slaves deluded by their promises, and supposedly hyped for plundering and pillaging, were the butt of the joke. Of course, it was just as clear who got to join in the mirth generated by this Black dialect song—first and foremost white men.[8]

"The Guinea Boy" also captured the nature of the emergent genre of blackface minstrelsy, a novel form of popular culture that functioned as a backlash to Black self-assertion, in this case to slaves daring to run away and take up arms against the country that permitted their enslavement. Black Americans would assert themselves in a variety of ways in the antebellum period. Some would mount other militant challenges, such as attacking white enslavers, most famously in Nat Turner's Rebellion in 1831 and during the Civil War. Others, especially in the northern states, took to the public sphere, demanding to be treated as legitimate members of the community and calling for the immediate abolition of slavery in the south. White Americans contrived an array of responses in the face of such challenges to American racial nationalism, one of the most salient being the cohering genre of blackface minstrelsy.

The following two chapters discuss the surging popular and jovial culture of the antebellum period to trace the emergence of a white man's democracy—the particular and paradoxical combination of racial nationalism and democracy that emerged in the United States. Chapter six traces the origins and context of blackface minstrelsy to the conceptual disturbance caused by the failure of the traditional equation between blackness and slavery to explain the new realities in the northern states as they abolished slavery during this period. As an alternative to the traditional connection between blackness and slavery and in response to Black demands for equality and dignity, white Americans during this period rendered blackness a comical and degraded category. Chapter seven looks at the Black minstrel and the frontier ruffian, the iconic clownish prototypes of the antebellum period who played outsized roles as foils in the emerging popular culture, in particular the frontiersman turned jester Davy Crockett. As "The Guinea Boy" anticipated, the degraded Black buffoon and the giddy backwoods jester would offer exceptional vehicles for outlining the borders of the nation around white manhood. Though both were innately comical and theoretically giddy and uninhibited in their manhood, in America white freedom rested on using unchecked impunity to curb and co-opt Black virility and respectability. Only white men got to be truly merry and free as they expanded westward into a landscape, and a national future, they made their own.

CHAPTER SIX

A Black Clown for a White Nation

The Origins and Context of Blackface Minstrelsy

Blackface minstrelsy, cast broadly, is best understood as a host of cartoonish and disparaging impressions that white people concocted regarding Black people. It can best be assessed by how it proliferated across a variety of media and, in turn how, these constituted a national popular culture that deeply shaped the American imagination. Moreover, it is largely an American genre, in that it differs from earlier portrayals and tropes that circulated in the Atlantic world regarding Black people. This far more virulent imagery emerged in the United States in the early nineteenth century in response to three novel and interlocking developments: (1) the rise of democratic convictions; (2) the emergence of an assertive and vocal free Black community in the northern states that demanded full equality; and (3) the formation of a vigorous, if embattled, radical abolitionist movement consisting of vocal and indefatigable Black and white reformers. To these developments one might add the ongoing fear of Black rebellion among white Americans, especially in the wake of the Haitian Revolution (1791–1804), the most successful slave revolt in history, and Nat Turner's Rebellion (1831) in Virginia that stirred widespread panic.

Though traditionally scholars have cast blackface minstrelsy as a genre defined by live musical and comical performances and marked by its sudden breakout success in the United States around 1830, blackface minstrelsy extended beyond the blackface minstrel show. In fact, much of the material from which actors developed their early blackface performances in the 1830s was already well established in the minds of white Americans through the interplay of print culture and theater in the preceding decades. Thus, one can better assess the characteristics of this uniquely American genre by focusing on its origins: the use of Black dialect and degrading print imagery of Black Americans in the years leading up to the emergence of blackface minstrel shows in the 1830s.[1] Moreover, for most Americans, blackface minstrelsy would continue to be a genre they encountered mostly through the pages of newspapers, magazines, songsters, almanacs, broadsides, and other print materials that carried the bulk of national popular culture for decades to come. This is not to say that live blackface minstrel shows or other stage performances were marginal to this genre, for surely they were not; the impression of one live performance, especially during the antebellum period, roughly 1815 to 1860, could outweigh mounds of textual references. Nevertheless, while live performances would in time become the most famous and definitively American form of the genre, they were only one facet of it.

Building on themes developed in previous chapters, this chapter traces how the growth of democracy in the United States paradoxically engendered hardened racial categories.[2] Once traditional European social hierarchies were no longer viewed as innate, a more virulent strand of racism emerged to explain to Americans why only white men should, and would, get to enjoy the democratic promise and vision for which the United States increasingly stood. Once more, Americans turned to humor, this time in the form of blackface minstrelsy, to sort out and naturalize who could partake in its communion and who would not be allowed rightful membership in the national community.

This also explains the emergence of blackface minstrelsy in the urban north in the 1820s and 1830s. Although the institution of slavery would continue to help southerners organize their social hierarchies, the rise of democratic ideas posed a new challenge for white Americans in the northern states, where a growing Black community sought to assert its rights to participate in American democracy as free and equal citizens. Thus, when by the late 1820s such Black Americans as Samuel Cornish, Hosea Easton, and David Walker articulated an unapologetic and even militant stance toward their rights as free Americans, blackface minstrelsy emerged by the next decade as a counter, fully cohering as a genre that enjoyed unprecedented success on the stage and in print. In short, the humor of blackface minstrelsy functioned as a convenient tool for making whiteness a necessary condition for true citizenship or belonging. According to the logic of the genre, whatever the Declaration of Independence had to say about "unalienable rights," it was self-evident that only white men got to be free and equal in America.

The most influential studies of blackface minstrelsy, written in the 1990s, represented an extension of a growing interest in social history and bottom-up approaches to the past. Inspired by growing emphasis on the agency of the underclasses and on vernacular cultures, as opposed to cultural forms ushered in by capitalism, several influential scholars in this tradition tended to view blackface minstrelsy with some sympathy as an American vernacular tradition that boasted a cross-racial, working-class, and therefore rebellious, promise. At least early on, during the 1830s, argued most scholars of the genre, it was the fighting music of the working classes against haughty urban elites. It was only the corruption associated with the cooptation of blackface minstrelsy by market forces beginning in the 1840s that transformed it into a racist genre and an expression of white supremacy.[3]

Taken together, these studies have complicated blackface minstrelsy's stature as a racist genre, especially during its early, supposedly vernacular, beginnings. By contrast, assessing the emerging genre of blackface minstrelsy along the lines of a nationwide "humor event"—an approach that prioritizes context and impact over authorial intention or innate character—reveals that the cultural work performed by the genre was in fact largely in the service of an ascending racial nationalism. That is, it continued and reinforced the tradition of white settler humor that helped designate the American landscape as the exclusive domain of white men. Though this multivocal genre enlisted mirth and play, including carnivalesque humor, that cut in many different directions and was composed by a variety of historical actors with a host of agendas, when assessed in terms of its contribution to the political culture, there is far less room for ambiguity than many scholars of the genre would have one believe.[4]

Many scholars, due to their avid interest in class, missed what should have been obvious. More than an era of class conflict, the 1830s were a high point for racial hostility and tensions in the United States with an ascending synthesis of racial nationalism taking shape. This is not to say that class never figured in the elaborate cultural web woven by and around blackface minstrelsy. Rather, scholars have errantly prioritized class and concerns arising from the market revolution when examining a period in which the work of nationalism took center stage in the minds of a critical mass of white

American men. In sum, the preponderance of the evidence suggests that blackface minstrelsy—the array of comical forms that more than any cultural product of its day shaped the "black image in the white mind"—served racial nationalism far more than any other agenda to which it might have also, at times, contributed.[5]

Atlantic Origins

Generally speaking, European impressions of sub-Saharan African peoples and their descendants developed over centuries of colonialism and slavery beginning in the fifteenth century, but in the English-speaking world they primarily took shape during the eighteenth century. By then a combination of travel accounts, plays, novels, and many other print materials—as well as firsthand contact and experiences with Black people, whose presence had become common in the major cities, Merchant Marine, and Navy and on plantations—had left virtually all members of the British commonwealth with notions of blackness. Most importantly, their perception of blackness became associated with slavery, as opposed to whiteness, which stood as a marker of freedom. Moreover, since claims of inferiority and "savagery" associated with Africa figured in the various ways Europeans legitimized slavery and discussed blackness, the racial markers associated with African descent also implied a lesser degree of civilization.[6]

In Britain and its American colonies, where strict social hierarchies were the norm and considered self-evident, it was still quite viable to account for blackness by relying on earlier tropes associated with social inferiority. As with explorations of numerous other social categories and their significance, such as gender, ethnicity, or class, a good number of portrayals of Black people took comical forms similar to other comical tropes. Thus, during the eighteenth century, the most familiar prototype of a Black person—usually enslaved, though not always—was a comical clown grafted onto earlier clown imagery, typically the Irish clown. As these tropes developed by the turn of the nineteenth century, white Britons and Americans "knew well" what to expect of Black people, especially when they appeared in a comic setting in print or on stage. If the Irish were marked with such typical Irish names as Teague or Paddy, Black people had their own distinct names, among them Sambo, Cuffy, or the comically ostentatious Pompey, Caesar, and the like. The Irish spoke their typical brogue, while Black people had their own recognizable dialect. Thus, in jestbooks from the period, one finds jokes featuring

Irish or Black clowns, often in similar situations, involved in dynamics common to most clowns from the period. Although both characters were often the butt of the joke, as jesters they could at times evade the full brunt of the humor. Besides, as with the Irish, country, and Yankee clowns, black jesters enjoyed the common inclination of viewing the lowest members of society as simple-minded folk who did not traffic in the corrupt ostentation and deceit of the upper classes.[7]

Take, for instance, the following anecdote from a 1789 Philadelphia jest collection about a "clergyman" who owns a "Negro by the name of *Quash*, who was by no means fond of working" and who even "conceived it a hardship, 'dat he poor negar man mus worke so hard, and massa do noting.' You are mistaken Quash," said the clergyman, "my labour is more fatiguing than Your's; I do head work, and your's is merely bodily exercise." The next day, instead of Quash gathering wood as instructed, the clergyman finds him "astride on a large maple log in a pensive attitude." Upon the clergyman's inquiry, Quash rubs his "midnight brow, oh! massa me—me have been doing head work . . . Suppose massa, here be five pigeons on dis tree, and you take a gun and foot two of den, how many dere be left? Why three, you old sinner.—No massa, dem toder tree fly away." This anecdote, having fun with the lazy and crude, if savvy Black clown, could just as well have been told about an Irish servant and his master. Both were often depicted as similarly buffoonish types who could nevertheless outwit members of the upper classes if they handled their underlings carelessly.[8]

Indeed, in such anecdotes, half the point was enjoying the comical dialect of the simpleton characters. In the case of Black dialect, however, there appears to be even more avid interest in caricaturing speech attributed to people of African descent. While Irish brogue exhibited a few favored turns of phrase, such as "by my shoul," Black dialect—or rather, white impressions of Black speech—boasted by the turn of the nineteenth century a richer dialect that included a more broken English as well as the constant obsequious, if at moments cunning, use of "massa" to address any white man. Aware of the potential appeal of the clownish Black fool and his entertaining dialect as a form of comical reprieve, several plays from the period featured Black clowns in place of or alongside other clownish tropes. Since many of these plays involved merry ditties, songs with Black dialect began to appear in print and in live performances by actors usually in blackface. In fact, *The*

Disappointment: or, the Force of Credulity (ca. 1767), a pseudonymously written "comic opera" penned in America, prominently features a clownish "old debauchee" of clearly Black or mixed race who, interestingly, sings a version of "Yankee Doodle" in broken English. A Philadelphia theater company even planned to stage the play—in which case presumably the actor, playing a Black fop version of Yankee Doodle Dandy, would have belted the famous song in Black dialect; the production was ultimately canceled, however, never to see the light of day. Comical versions of the free Black dandy would later become common in the 1830s, the most famous being the character Zip Coon.[9]

More typically, however, by the 1790s one found Black jesters in traditional clown roles that had up until then been played by Irish clowns, or in America in the wake of the success of *The Contrast*, Yankee clowns. *Love and Friendship, or Yankee Notions* (1809), a clumsily composed play published in New York, outdid them all, featuring three Yankees and two comical Black characters, the latter introduced in the dramatis personae as "Harry, *a black boy*" and "Phillis, *a black woman*." As was typical of such plays, the clownish archetypes were not in this instance part of the main plot. Nevertheless, featuring as much Black and Yankee dialect as possible was clearly central to this particular play. Although Black clowns figured as the butt of the crowd's humor, as with other clown tropes, they at times also played the role of lower-class simpletons, who could either trick their upper-class interlocutors or, as symbols of simplicity, embody a more morally sound position. One British play, *Laugh When You Can* (1799), went as far as to cast the Black servant Sambo, a freed slave who stayed on with his master, as the moral arbiter of the plot.[10]

Indeed, in the first decade of the nineteenth century, almost all imagery of Black people in Britain and the United States—the latter still predominantly reliant on British sources for its cultural consumption—relegated them to the margins of the action. Aside from some early antislavery texts, such as the captivity narrative by Olaudah Equinao, an enslaved African turned abolitionist, or the exceptional case of Shakespeare's *Othello*, the voices and agency of Black people in theater and in novels largely constituted a comical reprieve that was rarely integrated into the main action. This started to change in the United States around the War of 1812, as nationalist interest in local American themes and characters converged with democratization on the one hand and the growing presence of assertive free Black Americans in the northern states on the other.

Northern Origins

As revolutionary principles contested social hierarchies in America, earlier ready-made British tropes no longer fully addressed new social and political realities. Not surprisingly perhaps, problems first arose where the equation between slavery and blackness and whiteness and freedom no longer organized social and political realities. In this vein, most accounts of black-face minstrelsy rightly emphasize the northern and urban origins of the genre, but they often offer a quite sentimentalized version of them. According to most scholarship, the genre emerged from an early period in which lower-class whites and Blacks in northern cities cultivated an interracial vernacular culture in the 1830s, or what one scholar called a "new underclass alliance," that challenged middle-class values. Thus, many scholars cast Blackface minstrelsy in its origins as a working-class counterweight to high-brow theater performances in more respectable venues. These supposedly heady times came to an end when larger market forces co-opted this vernacular street culture and transformed it into commercialized popular culture that sought to racially divide and conquer the working classes during the 1840s and beyond.[11]

Although such accounts convey realities from the period, they tend to mischaracterize the dominant tensions of the period. No doubt, there were moments of interracial exchanges and tacit solidarity, even many such moments in the urban "frontier" of the early nineteenth century. As with the western borderlands, however, in the urban environment of the early republic, the more Black and white working-class people lived near each other and resembled each other, at least in some respects, the more tensions and hatred simmered and at times erupted into riots to reestablish racial divides. The closer the two groups became, the more it animated the racial anxiety of white northerners, especially urbanites in racially mixed, lower-class neighborhoods. Indeed, from what historians know of the period, there was more resentment between the races than camaraderie and more efforts to segregate and marginalize Black Americans, as well as Native peoples, than attempts to cultivate lasting multiracial communities.[12]

Such dynamics became even more evident around 1830, as militant Black American voices and actions started to reverberate across the country, most famously in David Walker's *Appeal to the Colored Citizens of the World* (1829) and in Nat Turner's Rebellion (1831), the latter soon followed by *The Confessions of Nat Turner* (1831). For many contemporaries and historians alike,

Walker's prophecy—"the Lord our God . . . will give you a Hannibal"—and urging of Black Americans to "give him your support and let him go his length, and behold in him the salvation of your God" anticipated Nat Turner, whose *Confessions* painted his violent rebellion as inspired by deep Christian convictions. Black Americans and their white allies had tried their hands at publishing antislavery newspapers during the 1820s, and the decade also saw attempts by Black northerners to assert their presence in public life by establishing social organizations and annually commemorating the abolition of the Atlantic slave trade with public events. The early 1830s were therefore watershed years in the history of the abolition movement. In 1831 William Lloyd Garrison founded the *Liberator*, which would become the preeminent antislavery paper over the next two decades. The paper featured an array of Black authors and unequivocally expressed the most important Black American position of the day: full-throated opposition to colonization and the immediate abolition of slavery. Thus, in many ways, the *Liberator* was in no small way an expression of genuine Black voices and agendas for Black abolitionists—as well as in the eyes of their foes. It was no coincidence, therefore, that the 1830s and 1840s were also an era of race riots and anti-abolitionist violence.[13]

Since race riots represent an extreme expression of resentment, it is quite telling how often racial tensions boiled over into outright violence. In fact, by most historical accounts of public violence, the 1830s—especially between 1833 and 1838, the years that saw blackface minstrel performances' early success—were the highpoint of racial violence before the 1850s and the Civil War. Hezekiah Niles, one of the most authoritative journalistic voices of the day, wrote that given the amount of rioting in the country, he tended to "suppress" reports of rioting, "though some cases of peculiar atrocity must be inserted." He did so, he professed, because "we cannot consent to hold up our country to contempt and scorn of the old world." According to one study of rioting during this period, the *Niles' Weekly Register*, even under what might have been an editorial regime of news suppression, published reports of 48 different instances of anti-Black or anti-abolitionist violence during the 1830s and 1840s, 73 percent of them between 1833 and 1838. Another study counted 43 racial riots of note between 1824 and 1849, with 25 of them, or 58 percent, between 1833 and 1838.[14] Meanwhile, the most thorough study of rioting found that in 1835 alone, "there were 46 proslavery riots (35 against abolitionists and 11 in response to insurrection scares and 15 racial riots, 11 of those against blacks, 3 in aid of fugitive slaves, and 1 by blacks)."[15]

Of importance, although the period saw several other forms of mob violence, and race riots were predominantly a northern phenomenon—the southern equivalent being slave rebellions and violent retaliation to suspected conspiracies—the only recurring form of violence across broad sections of the country was racial. In the northern states abolitionists and Black communities faced mobs, while in the southern states, both authorities and vigilantes purged abolitionist literature, lynched suspected abolitionists, and promised hefty monetary rewards for the heads of leading abolitionists. Moreover, in the wake of Nat Turner's Rebellion in 1831, southern states experienced a period of heightened vigilance and terror against the slave majority and free Black minority.[16]

Despite the 1830s being years of increasing conviction and activism within radical abolitionist circles, these vocal Black and white activists remained an embattled and persecuted minority, and would remain outside of the mainstream of even northern political culture for some fifteen years, until around the Mexican-American War (1846–48).[17] Abolitionism would only start to emerge as a political force in the United during the second half of the 1840s. At that point, it truly became a mass movement with its own popular culture often casting their own forms of sentimental middle-class culture as an alternative to what it viewed as the proslavery appeal of blackface minstrelsy. Curiously, during these years, the middle classes to some degree co-opted blackface minstrelsy for their own purposes and even for the antislavery agenda.[18] In any event, between the War of 1812 and the late 1840s, deprecating accounts of Blacks in print, on stage, and in the streets would be at the center of a popular culture that transcended party, section, or class, representing an extension of the anti-Black and anti-abolitionist violence of the period.

Indeed, policing the borders of society was not an agenda only shared by mobs, which consisted of people from an array of backgrounds, nor solely by the lower classes.[19] Elites expressed outrage against the regime of mobocracy that at times seemed to grip the country and complained about racy blackface minstrel performances, but they also often expressed an even more severe opposition to the specter of "amalgamation" of the races.[20] After the War of 1812, anxiety over an emerging free Black population rose exponentially across the northern and mid-Atlantic states. Within more polite circles, the increased popularity of colonization schemes probably best captured this phenomenon. It was no coincidence that the African Colonization Society (ACS) was founded in 1816 as the major national organization devoted to colonizing free Black Americans in Africa, and that within a few more years, the United States government would secure the colony of Liberia in Africa as the official site for colonization. Despite the ACS casting itself as an antislavery movement, and although certain activists in the movement seemed quite genuine about its potential to help eliminate slavery in due time, much of the support for the organization stemmed from anxieties over racial mixing in what most white Americans thought should be a white nation. The overwhelming popularity of colonization efforts among elite circles crossed party and region; almost every prominent political figure from the antebellum period outside of the Deep South—from James Madison to Andrew Jackson to Abraham Lincoln—professed support for colonization.[21]

The emergent consensus that Black Americans should be clearly designated as a separate category of people and outside the bounds of the nation was reinforced in the realm of politics in the wake of the Missouri Compromise (1820). It was then that political brokers ensured that the nation would remain a synthesis of both free and slave states, unified around a commitment to slavery as a central American institution, even if only in certain regions. More tacitly, the compromise between pro-slavery and colonization advocates suggested a national commitment to white supremacy; all could agree that the nation should benefit its white citizenry. The political order's commitment to sweep the question of slavery under the carpet would become more blatant in the 1830s with the introduction of the gag rule. Passed during each session of Congress with the support of northern representatives from 1836 to 1844, the resolution largely prohibited petitions challenging slavery in the national halls of power.[22]

In intellectual and scientific circles, the period from 1820 to 1840 marked a shift in ideas on race toward new scientific and biological currents that viewed it as an innate and fixed condition. Most men of letters and science in America had previously considered supposed racial characteristics and behaviors as the products of distinct environments and believed that they could be altered under different conditions. The growing appeal of phrenology was but one symptom of the shift to viewing race as innate. Similarly, the American government transitioned from a "civilizing" approach to Native populations—attempting to transform them into white Christians and assimilate them—to ethnic cleansing, removing them from their land to areas at great distances from white settlements. Many officials believed there could be no real future for "racial amalgamation." As with arguments in support of colonization, it was deemed in the best interest of the Indians, as an inferior race of humans, to be as far away as possible from white people, with whom they could never live as equals.[23]

This context explains a new wave of print culture painting Black people as woefully incapable of joining the citizenry of the United States. Even before the War of 1812, a spattering of material was in circulation that deprecated Black dialect, mocking attempts at political participation and polite and respectable comportment. For example, in 1804 several newspapers published a poem in which the characters Sambo and Pompey discuss upcoming gubernatorial elections in New York. Casting the two as deliberating between the George Clintonian faction and Aaron Burr's faction, known as the Little Band, it begins,

> In kitchen clean one eve of late,
> Sambo and Pompey, (friends of state)
> Open'd their meeting with debate.
> Says Sambo section time's at hand,
> And I'll support de "Little Band";
> Fore I've three years been democrat,
> To massa Clinton rais'd my hat,
> Thinking he'd gib me office, sir,
> He gib me none—I vote for Burr.[24]

The two go back and forth, referencing many of the political scuffles surrounding the candidates' electioneering. The afterword maintains the conceit of a supposedly formal discussion by a respectable society of refined gentlemen by adding, "Resolved that the proceedings of this meeting be published. Quashy Quankum, chairman. Cuffy Quashy, Secretary. Cellar Kitchen, March 28, 1804."[25]

While this mockery of blackness was relatively tame, an 1810 newspaper article demonstrated the more acerbic and degrading quality of some of this humor. In this case, the vehicle was a supposed letter from Sambo to his friend Mungo "on the interesting subject of corsets." "Dear Mungo," it begins, "Turrer [the other] day I meet misse Phillisee in de street, she strut like a turkey wis [with] he tail spread; trait [strait] like a lamps; her head so high she no able for see de patent [pavement], she stumble over de tep tone [step stones], she broke her toe and de side walk." Explaining to Mungo why she was walking in such a weird manner, Sambo says, "She had on a gossip, or fossip, or cossup [a corset], or what you call dem tings de buckram lady wear before, for make him hold up she head." So on and on, the ridiculous conversation goes, as both Sambo and Phillis demonstrate their incapacity to appropriate white respectability, in writing letters and wearing a corset.[26]

This type of text was a hybrid, incorporating some more general British Atlantic themes and dialects with more local American ones. For example, the reference to "buckram lady" was part of an Atlantic tradition of Black dialect in which the term *buckram* or *buckra* denoted white people, while the name Phillis was of local origin. Indeed, an undated broadside published this particular anecdote alongside a song in Black dialect from the same tradition that similarly disparaged Black Americans for entertaining notions of respectability. In the song, "Chinger Ring," the Black narrator urges his Black brethren to leave "Buckra lan" (the United States) for "Hettee" (Haiti), where they would be fetted like "Lafatee" (Lafayette) and enjoy a life of leisure. There they would "smok de hes segar, fech from de Habannah," "hab partys big," and "in a gran saloon" dance with "de blushing damsel."[27] While anecdotes such as the one on New York elections tended to be less scathing and more in line with the broader treatment of the clown trope, mocking depictions of Blacks became more pointed and degrading over time. The increasing amount of broken Black dialect in written texts was one result of this attempt at more vitriolic contempt, as for instance, demonstrated by Sambo's letter compared to the earlier political anecdote.

These early precedents of blackface minstrelsy, appearing in newspapers, jestbooks, and almanacs—spaces not strictly devoted to deprecating Blacks—foreshadowed a new type of print material dedicated to mocking Black American advocacy for abolition and other efforts at legitimacy in the public sphere. Scholars usually refer to the first print series to deal exclusively with Black Americans as "bobolition" broadsides, which mocked the "bobolition," or abolition, of the slave trade.[28] Such broadsides, published from 1816 into the early 1830s, mostly in Boston and later in New York, were produced in response to attempts by Black societies and organizations to assert their presence in the public sphere. Printed in bulk and sold cheaply, the annual appearance of these prints—often tied to the yearly parades commemorating the abolition of the Atlantic slave trade in the United States in 1808—spoke to their popularity. Newspapers, always in search of comic materials, copied content from the broadsides, disseminating parts of them to reading audiences far and wide.

If these broadsides are any measure, the abolition parades were one of the most abrasive forms of Black self-assertion in the eyes of resentful white northerners. The first parades appear to have occurred on January 1, 1808, in Philadelphia and New York, and on July 14, 1808, in Boston. These marches, typically followed by orations and toasts—in the mode of many contemporary celebrations—for some years became an annual event and the focal point of organized public action by Black Americans. They were indicative of how Black communities grew and gained confidence by organizing formal institutions, such as the Free African Society, founded in 1787 in Philadelphia; the African Society, established in 1796 in Boston; and the African Society for Mutual Relief, founded in 1808 in New York. While early Black institutions were nominally fraternal organizations, mutual aid societies, schools, and churches, their founders and members were the most committed proponents of abolition and maintained close contact with early white abolitionist institutions, such as the Pennsylvania Society for the Abolition of Slavery and the New York Manumission Society.[29]

Birth of a New Genre

As a reactionary backlash to a vocal and assertive Black presence in the public sphere, bobolition broadsides attempted to burlesque the most salient of such efforts, the yearly abolition parades, by degrading them as buffoonish mimicry of white practices (figure 6.1). What better way for contemptuous whites to do so than to co-opt Black voices and stereotype the condition of Black people as intrinsically comical and unfit for participation in the processes of democratic self-rule? Black dialect texts of the broader Atlantic world might present an occasional song, anecdote, or stage cameo using the dialect and clownish tropes to ratchet up humor and levity. By contrast, the significant volume of verbiage, the new subject matter of mocking Black respectability, and the new medium of yearly broadsides exclusively in Black dialect marked bobolition broadsides as the beginnings of blackface minstrelsy as a distinct genre of humor in the early United States. It grew from a new era characterized by a concerted interest in marginalizing Black Americans in response to abolition in the northern states and to Black demands for equality and dignity nationally.

In the early stages of Black minstrelsy, white portrayals of Black people in the nascent popular culture of the period were concerned much of the time with casting attempts at upward social mobility and an assertive presence in the public sphere as clownish. This was hardly a new concern or trope in the Anglophone world, nor was the specific iteration of this trope as a Black urban clown unique. In fact, it appeared in America in the eighteenth century, notably with *The Disappointment* and also in print and on stage around the

Figure 6.1. "Grand Celebration! Of the Abolition of the Slave Trade. General Order," 1817, Boston. A "bobolition" broadside mocking yearly parades in Boston in which the Black community celebrated Congress's abolition of the Atlantic slave trade in 1808. The year 1817 marked the second known year for such publications. Early American Imprints, ser. 2, suppl. 1. Reproduced courtesy of the American Antiquarian Society, accessed through Readex.

turn of the nineteenth century. Nevertheless, bobolition broadsides were an important bridge between such early scattered impressions and the appearance of the blackface minstrel dandy in Zip Coon and other characters in the 1830s.

Moreover, 1810s and 1820s bobolition broadsides engendered additional broadsides and other ephemera, inspired by the success of Black mockery. One example of materials in the same tradition was broadsides featuring songs in Black dialect, such as "Backside Albany" and "The Guinea Boy." Another was a series of broadsides featuring sermons in Black dialect that mocked autonomous Black Christianity as yet another version of inadequate Black respectability. In this vein, the broadside "Rev. Mr. Sambo's Sarmont," which appeared in several different formats, ridiculed Black interpretations of Christianity as crude and a far cry from true religiosity (figure 6.2). As with much else from this earlier period, such materials would later become a mainstay of blackface minstrel performances, which over time developed and offered white audiences an increasing array of skits, including, on many occasions, a mock Black dialect sermon largely modeled after these early examples.

Bobolition broadsides and their offshoots expanded the subject matter and genre of Black dialect, but they also offered opportunities to further develop the traditional form of Black dialect songs that would continue to dominate the genre of blackface minstrelsy throughout its century-long run. Indeed, as part of the fictional information for a celebration, bobolition broadsides, in keeping with actual common practice, noted songs, either in short references, such as noting the title of the song the band should play before the next toast, or in full, providing audiences the lyrics to a new Black dialect song. Thus, for instance, an 1817 broadside offered a number of short little racist ditties: "O dear, dear, tell us what besen be / Dat poor negur is usen dus worse den a dog / O dear, dear, can all de resen be / Dat he scul and e hair look juss like he hog!" or "When old negur hab money he merry / And will molsen he clay wid good flip / But when he none he look sulkee and sorry / You may judge by de fall of de lip" (figure 6.1).[30] Such silly, often barely legible songs, aimed at a generally giddy mood in which Black people supposedly made fun of their bodies, became common fare in white representation of Black Americans in years to come and on the minstrel stage. It reinforced blackness as grotesque to distinguish it more clearly from whiteness and to dehumanize. Similar themes would often paint Black people as atavistic, or even outright animalistic, and therefore deserving of scorn and outside the democratic community

Figure 6.2. "Rev. Mr. Sambo's Sarmont," undated, from the 1820s, Boston. A broadside featuring a mock sermon, part of the wave of "bobolition" broadsides that mocked different facets of Black self-assertion in the public sphere, in this case, the increasing presence of autonomous Black churches. Harris Broadsides Collection, Brown Digital Repository, Brown University Library, https://repository.library.brown.edu/studio/item/bdr:287921/.

of men. They made it easier to cast Black people as a logical exception to the democratic rule that equated manhood with citizenship.

One sub-genre of Black dialect songs that clearly developed and found increasing traction within bobolition broadsides were comical love songs that mocked courting and romance between Black people, usually with a woman named Phillis as the love interest. In fact, one can draw connections between several love songs appearing on a few different bobolition broadsides and what historians consider the first American blackface minstrel stage performance, of the mock love song "Coal Black Rose" in 1829. While silly love songs by a variety of clown types appeared in many previous occasions, including a whole genre of widely successful Yankee mock love songs around 1800, the inclusion of such songs on bobolition broadsides that on their face had no relation to such subject matter suggest their appeal to white audiences thirsty for new material featuring antics by Blacks.[31] An 1822 bobolition broadside, for instance, found an opportunity to oblige readers with such a song after toasting "De Africum Fair Sex—May every true son of Africa crasp to he trobbing bosom de brushing virgin he adore." The first two of the four stanzas are as follows:

O love is like de pepper-corn,
It make one act so cute,
It make de bosom feel so warm,
And eye shine like new boot.
I meet Miss Phillis tudder day,
In berry pensive mood;
She almost cry her eye away,
For Pomp's ingratitude

O lucky brushing maid, say I,
What makee look so sad?
Ah Scip, de booteous virgin cry,
I feel mose deblish bad
For Pomp he stole my heart away,
Me taught him very good,
But he no lub me now he say,
Chah! what ingratitude.[32]

The particular genealogy of this song about the romance between Phillis and Pompey is suggestive of how deeply engaged these texts were with current affairs and concerns. In this particular case, it appears to directly reference the Boston broadside "Riot on Negro Hill," likely published just a few weeks after the first bobolition broadside came out in Boston, in July 1816. The Boston broadside featured a poem supposedly composed by Phillis, a resident of the largely Black neighborhood in the West End called Negro Hill. It relates to a riot during which a white mob rampaged through the neighborhood. Such violent attacks appear to have been recurring events when Negro Hill was referred to by one contemporary as a "sink of sin," with "scenes of iniquity and debauchery too dreadful to be named," and was a target of white resentment.[33] Riots along the route of the yearly abolition processions erupted on occasion and at an increasing rate in all the cities hosting such parades. Clearly, bobolition broadsides and anti-Black and anti-abolitionist race riots were joined at the hip.[34]

While the song in the 1816 broadside was somewhat sympathetic to the plight of Phillis and her family, it was clear who the humor was directed at: the Black inhabitants of West End, who had attempted to make their voices heard as a legitimate community to be reckoned with in Boston. The name of the woman protagonist of the events described and the chosen medium of poetry to relate the narrative, allegedly in her own voice, was a clear reference to Phillis Wheatley, the famous Black American poet, who had become a topic of contention in discussions over race. Wheatley stood out as the best example of the potential for "racial uplift" among proponents of the proposition that Black Americans were fully capable of becoming virtuous citizens of the republic and that one day Black and white folks could live side by side and perhaps even intermarry. For opponents of these ideas—the majority of white Americans at this time—Wheatley became the target of condemnation and mockery. Thus, crude poetry by a woman named Phillis, who attempted to appear respectable and genteel clearly sought to make the idea of black equality appear preposterous. Moreover, much of the song relates to the destruction of Phillis's upscale furnishings—"My hogan [mahogany] Desk . . . ," "My Coffee Urn and pipe of Wine" and "My husband's spensive Library." Phillis then concludes, "By de great detruction of my Furniture, you will perceve my house was pretty genteely furnish—common Furniture will do in de country, but in Bosson if a body wish to be reckon any ting they muss conform to de fashon of de place!"[35]

Not only was this particular broadside quite successful—eliciting at least one other print run that very year, as well as a few others over the years—it also led to several spin-offs, including the above love song about Phillis and

Pompey, and was part of the rise in the popularity of the name Phillis in mocking depictions of Black women during the first several decades of the nineteenth century. Thus, when in 1824 an anti-Black riot hit the Hard Scrabble neighborhood in Providence, Rhode Island, a rejoinder to this 1816 broadside, "Hard Scrabble, Or Miss Philises Bobolition" included similar scenes. The penultimate stanza warns,

> "So Miss Boston keep home your lazy black rabble.
> Nor compel them seek shelter again at Hard Scrabble,
> For every maggot should stick to he core;
> For should they visit us gain they may find it foul weather
> We've plenty of Tar and de ground cover'd wid Fether
> And we've Pitch to pitch you all out door.[36]

Here again, anti-Black riots and Black dialect in print were extensions of each other.

The increasing use of comical Black romance and derogatory impressions of Black women found an even more popular expression in *The Forest Rose* (1825), by Samuel Woodworth. One of the most successful Yankee theater productions, it also features a Black woman named Lid Rose, after whom the play is titled. As with many of the era's comedies of manners, of which Yankee theater was a subgenre, the play's ultimate joke was on the character of the fop. Importantly, however, the joke played on him by the Yankee couple Jonathan and Sally is that he ends up kissing the Black servant Lid Rose instead of the virtuous, and lily white, Harriet. To top that off, Jonathan's recurring and memorable line in the play is "I would not serve a negro so," spoken to the audience in a knowing way, given that the main joke of the plot is to serve a Black woman up to the fop. The play was so popular that it appeared to have inspired the blackface minstrel stage performance of "Coal Black Rose," likely a riff on the character of Lid Rose, at one point referred to as "Black Rose" in *The Forest Rose*.[37]

Featuring for the first time a significant amount of verbiage exclusively in Black dialect, bobolition broadsides also anticipated how regardless of the exact agenda behind the humor, inevitably the authors lost some control over the text. While this is common to any genre, these dynamics are heightened in comedic genres, where the allure of humor and whimsy are often too hard to resist, even if they do not exactly comport with the overall thrust of the text, leading it to wander. As giddy energy builds, it seems to find numerous avenues for comic expressions that flow in a host of directions. Take for instance the second extant bobolition broadside, published in Boston in 1817, which has a straightforward title: "Grand Celebration! Of the Abolition of the Slave Trade; General Order." The Black dialect begins in the main body of the text, stating, "To de culur peeple ob ebery occupation, decription, profeshon, and denomenation: Plese Notis, De Annuel Birth Day ob de Affricum Bosson Bobalition ob Slave Importation, will be celebrate to-morrow-de gemmen [general or gentlemen] Committey hab made ebery possable derangement [arrangement] de shortness ob time wood alou." So far this was simply a broken English representation of what one might expect from such broadsides. By the end of the paragraph, however, the writer also introduces ludicrous instructions to begin the events of the day: "Gemmen Officers of de presses yeer," will eat a meal of "hot tripe and lobster-claw supe, while in pressen of he Honor Lieut. Brigade-Major-Captin General Pomp, and he Honor de High-Depety-Grand-Marshel Scip." The outrageous ranks of the two Black honorees—who were served a poor man's soup of lobster-claw and tripe soup, which combined seemed particularly crude—suggest how, try as they might, they could never emulate the refinement and rank to which they aspired (figure 6.1).

Much of the remainder of the text is in this vein, ridiculing the supposed ostentation of Black people. Yet on occasion, the sheer giddy energy released by such buffoonery lets loose with humor that cuts in a range of directions. For instance, when the broadside calls for a set of toasts to be made, the first one is indeed a cheap shot at Black people, suggesting that they would be better off enslaved: "Dis day ob our Bobolition we celebrate—may it neber be forgot or dispected while we hab a single pisareen in our pocket, and when we git so poorer as dis tis better to be a well fed Slave den a dam poor half starve Free negur." The third toast is quite ambiguous, however, seeming directed at the state of Virginia, whose savage use of and behavior toward slaves led many freed and runaway slaves to find refuge in the North: "De Tate of Virginee—de Merican Purgatory, where de poor Affrican Emegrant muss endure Purgation and Laceration to make um fit citizen for Bosson Tate." Some later toasts also seemed to take the side of Blacks, if only for a fleeting moment, such as a toast that mocked, the Speaker of the House and proponent of the fatuous project of colonization, "Massa Henry Clay" and his "motion to Congres—to send all de Virgene people of culur back to Affreka," and a cheeky pseudo-patriotic toast to "De tirteen Merican Stripe—may day ever be display pon top gallant-mass head, and not pin [upon] our backs!" Indeed, the raucous, carnivalesque, and topsy-turvy momentum built up over the text took jabs at a host of targets, alongside Blacks, as part of its attempt to maintain its heady energy.

Here, however, one must proceed with caution. Carnivalesque humor of this kind is impossible to fully control. The author and audience are in no mood to stanch the giddy rush, even if the humor starts cutting in new directions. Nevertheless, one should not confuse this tendency of humor with the objectives of the intended humor, and certainly not with the workings of this humor in the context of racial nationalism. Here is where circling back to the framework of humor as a social event is required. Humor has no wholly inherent or self-evident logic. It derives its full meaning from its cultural, social, and political contexts. If American audiences could interpret the humor surrounding the Yankee clown as self-affirming, regardless of the agenda behind it, they could and did employ riots and myriad forms of discrimination to ensure that the last laugh would be on Black people and not with them, especially because so much of it was bursting with vitriol. To discern this, humor must be situated in the context of the rising racial tensions at the time, in the South and even more importantly in the North, where the majority of white Americans lived and where, even as slavery disappeared, racism endured and racial notions hardened.

Indeed, many recent studies of racial relations and more broadly on racial thinking have emphasized the fraught nature of the emancipation period in the northern states, all of which approved measures for immediate or gradual emancipation between the revolution and 1804.[38] New Jersey was the last of the northeastern states to pass emancipation laws, in 1804. With emancipation, however, the problem of entrenched racial thinking in a purportedly democratic society proved ever more urgent, especially as the free Black population in the North tripled in twenty years, from 27,034 in 1790 to 75,156 in 1810. Consequently, northerners also instituted legislation that addressed the position of free Black people in the North, almost always casting them as second-class citizens regarding such issues, among others, as voting, residency rights, and testimony in courts. Historians have aptly regarded this wave of legislation as anti-Black laws and precursors to Jim Crow segregation laws that would be instituted decades later by southern states.[39] The increasing presence of derogatory Black dialect in the North in this regard comprised the cultural rejoinder to such legislation, helping to instinctively explain to a population largely committed to democratic ideas why free Black northerners could never be full and legitimate participants in the United States' democratic society and culture. Thus, viewing free Blacks as outside the bounds of American society and politics became second nature to most white northerners.

While the increasing amount of verbiage in Black dialect released carnivalesque energies ripe with opportunities for subversion, it was into a political environment that devoted immense efforts to ensuring that the interpretation of such humor would remain unequivocal. The effort proved quite successful and in part explains the desire within abolitionist circles to promote opposing dignified and assertive Black voices in abolitionist newspapers like the *Liberator*. "When I was young," before the *Liberator* featured "speeches by intelligent colored men and women," remembered one abolitionist, "there were no allusions to colored people in newspapers, unless it was some grotesque caricature, pretending to be 'Cuffe's Speech at the Great Bobolition Meeting.'"[40] In 1837, when the Reverend Hosea Easton, a Black man, explained how American children were inculcated into racial attitudes, he observed that this kind of "education is not altogether oral. Cuts and placards descriptive of the negroe's deformity are everywhere displayed in the North to the observation of the young, with corresponding broken lingo, the very character of which is marked with design."[41]

Indeed, during the late 1820s and 1830s, the "next generation" of blackface minstrelsy saw an intensification of Black mockery as part of a contentious and increasingly visible dialogue between Black Americans and their allies, on the one hand, and the forces of racial nationalism, on the other. The increasing appearance of Black dialect, and during the 1830s of degrading Black imagery and blackface minstrel performances, stood as a direct response to emboldened Black voices who demanded immediate abolition and, in response to advocates of colonization, even insisted that Black people were truer Americans than their white brethren.[42] Ultimately, the embrace of the seductive effects of blackface minstrelsy by many white Americans reveals that far from being subversive, the genre offered authors and audiences, as intended, more moments of levity on account of Blacks rather than with them. These degrading representations helped relieve white anxieties about Black demands for equality and visibility and policed the borders of the young republic.

Graphic Illustrations

While the Black image in the white mind was to some degree reliant on real interactions between white and Black Americans, as the antebellum period wore on, it increasingly rested on mocking and degrading constructions of blackness that became central to the period's emerging popular culture. White Americans could read about Blacks or discuss their perceptions of blackness in various settings and contexts; it was not a subject new to them. What changed was the growing popularity of comical and deprecating imagery of blackness, eventually emerging as the dominant representation of blackness for the nation. Before the 1820s, print culture exposed Americans to comical representations of blackness, usually organized around the device of Black dialect. In the antebellum era, not only did Black dialect become ubiquitous, these comical textual representations of blackness were increasingly reinforced by mocking graphic illustrations. In the 1820s and the 1830s, such imagery became more widespread and cheaper and increasingly adjoined textual representations of blackness. In short, the antebellum period ushered in a new development in the history of race whereby blackness intrinsically elicited humor across media.[43]

Once more, bobolition broadsides, most of which contained coarse illustrations of Black people, were a key medium for some of the earliest mutually reinforcing combinations of comical text and graphic images.[44] Usually appearing at the top of the page above the title, many of the illustrations featured a group of Black soldiers, presumably marching as the main feature of the yearly abolition parade (see, for example, figures 6.1 and 6.2). Much of this imagery was not inherently comical or degrading. What lent this imagery its deprecating bent was the content of the text and that the images were colored in Black. While Black Americans encountered in real life invariably looked very different from each other, casting them as a group with one common feature—their blackness—reified their condition as a people apart, who, in the context of the broadside's text, acted, spoke, walked, and looked pretty much the same. They were all of a kind, and all were comical, especially when they tried to transcend their innate condition of difference. Blackness had originally been associated with slavery and emerged as a visible quality for a society eager to police enslaved people. In the early republic, especially in the North, where these equations no longer fully held, white Americans constructed blackness as a buffoonish condition.

Thus, from the earliest, when Americans consumed visual images of blackness, it almost always involved stock Black characters often represented as grotesque, if not through an image, then in adjoining text. With time, as visual technologies became cheaper and more widespread, particular forms of grotesque bodily stereotypes and clownish gait originally primarily in textual form, became more standard in illustrations as well. For example, while the aforementioned 1817 bobolition broadside boasted the ditty about "de fall of de lip," a New York bobolition print from 1828 featured a stock Black character with cartoonishly large lips (figure 6.3). Ultimately, in the reader's imagination, the distinction between textual and visual imagery collapsed and, with them, distinctions between representations of Black people in print and reality dissolved as well.

Just as the Bostonian tradition of printing bobolition broadsides ebbed toward the late 1820s, Life in Philadelphia, a popular series of racist illustrations, took off in Philadelphia. Drawn and engraved by Edward Williams Clay and printed in several different runs between 1828 and 1837, these illustrations turned to vivid visual images to disparage alleged Black ostentation in public life. A similar series, also engraved by Clay and published around 1830, enacted similar themes in New York. These were not the first elaborately drawn racist illustrations published in the United States. For instance, earlier engravings by the Philadelphia-based artist and actor David Claypoole Johnston disparaged Black organizations, such as an illustration of "A meeting of the Free & Independent Chimney Sweepers, Wood-Sawyers, Boot-Cleaners, Porters, &c" (figure 6.4). The widespread success and recurring themes, however, appearing in numerous different comical settings, of the 1828 Philadelphia and then 1830 New York series made them a far more influential milestone in racist illustrations of blackness than anything until then printed in the United States. There is much evidence to suggest that they circulated widely across the country and even in major European cities, including Paris and London. Indeed, they were so influential that they were picked up, copied, and elaborated on by London-based engravers and printers during the 1830s. In one case, a British engraver drew an illustration of a celebration of the "Bobolotion ob African slabery" as part of his own elaboration of Life in Philadelphia prints, demonstrating the broad appeal of both the series and bobolition broadsides as well as how they converged in the contemporary imagination.[45]

In Life in Philadelphia, Clay and those who copied him drew numerous contexts in which Black Americans attempted respectability in the urban landscape. It included scenes in the street, parlors, shops, and ballrooms, where Black Americans acted with ostentatious airs that mimicked white mores of etiquette, dress, and comportment. In each case, the artist cast them

Figure 6.3. "De Interestin Accoun ob de Last Meetin ob de Bobolition Society in 1828," 1828, New York. A "bobolition" broadside featuring degrading images of Black Americans in mocking the annual New York City parade celebrating the abolition of the Atlantic slave trade. Such broadsides started in Boston, but later spread to other places. American Broadsides and Ephemera. Reproduced courtesy of the American Antiquarian Society.

Figure 6.4. "A Meeting of the Free & Independent Chimney-Sweepers, Wood-Sawyers, Boot-Cleaners, Porters, &c . . . ," by David Claypoole Johnston, 1819, Philadelphia. A caricature mocking Black respectability in response to the rise of publicly visible organizations representing free Black Americans. Reproduced courtesy of the American Antiquarian Society.

as being out of their element by employing a combination of cartoonish features, a smattering of Black dialect (usually in speech bubbles), and gauche clothing and gait. As with bobolition broadsides, even as Clay's humor concentrated on the allegedly flamboyant airs of free Black people, it did not stop there. Clay also occasionally mocked white ostentation in Life in Philadelphia, usually on separate prints but at times alongside Black people. For instance, in one engraving, he painted a scene of a fashionably dressed Black woman asking for "flesh coloured silk stockings" from a white sales clerk in an upscale shop who himself appears excessively flamboyant in his dress and mannerisms. In addition, he responds to the woman in a mix of French and English, "Oui Madame! here is von pair of de first qualité!" Thus, both figures in the engraving mark themselves as un-American: the

Figure 6.5. "Life in Philadelphia, Have you any flesh coloured silk stockings . . . ?," by Edward Williams Clay, ca. 1830, Philadelphia. Part of a series of images degrading free Black Americans and their increased presence in the public sphere in northern states. Reproduced courtesy of the Library Company of Philadelphia.

Black woman was out of her lane in such a shop, and the salesclerk of high-end items was a Frenchified effeminate dandy deserving of derision in an American landscape where such "old world" affectations were a form of deviancy (figure 6.5).[46]

Yet again, however, one should not deduce from the barbed humor cutting in different directions that the broadside was not fundamentally racially motivated or not largely concerned with demeaning Black Americans. It was also not primarily a working-class attack on elite pretensions and only secondarily an attack on Black people, as some have insinuated. Clay's commentary is largely about Blacks and couched in a broader political environment deeply engaged in marginalizing Black Americans. Clay's cartoons and others like them clearly revealed white people's resentfulness at attempts by Black people to inject meaning into their position in American society and contest their role as second-class citizens. They responded in many ways, including rioting, passing legislation to marginalize Black people and prevent them from immigrating to northern states, and launching fanciful initiatives to ship Black people to Africa. To complement such designs, in the realm of culture, they turned to humor as a complementary way to police the nation's borders.

Similar to Black dialect and comical and demeaning illustrations merging to create a more vivid image of Black people in the white imagination, so too did popular culture in print and popular culture on the antebellum stage. Indeed, when George Washington Dixon debuted on stage in 1834 as a Black dandy named Zip Coon, he represented an extension of the numerous images regularly conjured by and for white Americans in print culture, such as Clay's Life in Philadelphia series. In turn, as performances of blackface minstrels became increasingly popular in the 1830s, print culture began producing even harsher imagery of Black people, clearly inspired by vivid theatrical staging. By then, print illustrations had become ubiquitous in various media, appearing on broadsides, songsters, song sheets, almanacs, newspapers, magazines, playbills, novels, valentine sheets, trade cards, and more. When printers needed a cheap image to enliven various print products, they often turned to previously used images stored in-house. Thus, many images that first appeared on 1810s and 1820s bobolition broadsides found second lives in the 1830s alongside newer deprecating images of Black people.

Toward the Minstrel Stage

Although stage performance and print production are entirely different formats, approaching them separately prevents one from fully understanding the cultural influence they exerted in the antebellum United States through their mutual reinforcement of one another. Charles Mathews and his 1820s imitations on the London stage of various American peoples, including Black

Americans, offer a window onto the dialectical and reciprocal relationships between media that gave rise to blackface minstrelsy as a broad genre. In the one-man show *Trip to America*, he reenacted encounters during his travels, inviting the audience to join him on his adventures. Often considered a precursor to the more famous blackface minstrels of the 1830s, Mathews might have been the first white actor to specialize in songs, comportment, and speech mocking and imitating Black Americans. Although Mathews's presentations of blackness appeared on the British stage, his enactments of Black people were based on research he conducted for his show in the United States in the early 1820s. In turn, printed accounts of these shows became popular in the United States starting in 1824, which subsequently influenced early blackface stage performers in America.

When Mathews arrived in the United States in the summer of 1822, he was expecting to encounter a variety of local peoples, as he had during previous trips, which provided him with materials for earlier performances. After several brief encounters with lower-class Americans, however, he was sure he wanted little to do with them, finding them "unendurable." Instead, in letters to his wife explaining why he had found little material so far, he made excuses: "As to the lower orders," he proclaimed, "I know not where they are to be found. I know no bait that will tempt them from their lurking places." Fortunately, since his primary host, Stephen Price, managed the New York Park Theater, and Washington Irving provided him with numerous letters of introduction, he was never short on genteel company in America. Thus, in contrast to the lower orders, whom he never looked very hard for in the first place, he spent his spare time with the "upper orders of society," the members of which, he confessed, were "very pleasing, and infinitely more polished than it is the fashion to believe in Europe." [47]

Ultimately, instead of collecting most of his materials from firsthand impressions, he relied on his American friends and on the local print culture for his assessment of American characters. To be sure, Mathews's fine ear for the occasional local colloquialism did contribute to his account of some Americanisms in his performances. Yet the most memorable and successful segments of *Trip to America* involved his portrayal of Yankee and Black characters he encountered in print, rather than reality, and developed for the stage. Since he was in close contact with local actors and theater managers, it takes little effort to deduce from where he drew his Yankee materials. Indeed, Yankee theater was coming into its own in the 1820s, with several actors specializing in Yankee characters and mannerisms.

Identifying the source of his portrayal of Black Americans, however, requires a bit more digging to uncover. The clearest indication that he relied on contemporary portrayals of Black dialect in the print culture of the period was his inclusion of the aforementioned love poem about Phillis and Pompey in one of his letters to his collaborator, James Smith, regarding possible material for his show. He was in the United States from the summer of 1822 to the spring of 1823, when bobolition broadsides would have been in vogue, so it seems reasonable to infer that he borrowed the poem from one of the several bobolition prints that featured it, and probably considered such broadsides as potential resource for future shows.[48]

The content of *Trip to America*, which Mathews began performing upon his return home, provided additional evidence that he relied to a large degree on American print culture. For one of the Black characters he portrayed was a clownish Black actor at a Black theater who in broken dialect butchers parts of Shakespeare's *Richard III* and *Hamlet*, including "to be or not to be dat is him question." Here it appears that rather than a real visit to New York's Black theater, the Minor Theater, sometimes called the African Theatre or African Grove, his inspiration was Price, who at the time sought to shut down the Minor because it was competing with the nearby Park Theater. In fact, Price had enlisted the services of Mordecai Noah, New York's sheriff—who also happened to be a close friend, local newspaper editor (of the *National Advocate*), and playwright—to help shutter the bothersome and, to him, reprehensible attempts by Black managers and performers to undercut the Park Theater's dominance. Noah was also a pioneer in Black dialect, whose attacks on New York's Black community ranged from lobbying in his paper to limit Black suffrage to mocking them in Black dialect. Indeed, on one such occasion, about a year before Mathews's visit, in September of 1821, Noah lambasted the Minor in a scathing review for his paper. The column at one point painted a comic scene of a Black actor performing a soliloquy from *Richard III* in broken Black dialect. This piece, most likely, inspired Mathews. In Noah's case, as in others, a resentful white person assumes the voice of Black Americans in mocking derision in response to the growing Black presence in American life—here in the form of the Minor Theater, a venue for respectable Black entertainment and leisure, owned operated, and attended by Black Americans in the heart of New York City.[49]

Thus, local American Black dialect in print inspired an early precursor of blackface minstrelsy in England. Indeed, at one point Mathews burst out singing in the combination of black dialect and dance that would become so popular in the United States just a few years later. When he butchered Hamlet's famous lines in the crude soliloquy noted above, Mathews at one point said "opossum," Black dialect for "oppose em." Once he invoked the word "opossum," however, the Black theater's crowd—Mathew was enacting a scene supposedly witnessed at a Black theater—started chanting "opossum, opossum, opossum." At this point, to the imaginary crowd's request, Mathews broke out in a wild ditty called "Opossum up a Gum Tree," signaling that this type of music and dance jibed far better with the tastes of Black theater goers than any Shakespearean soliloquy. Curiously, this proved to be no less of a hit with real English audiences, who laughed at the notion of a Black crowd requesting the song as they themselves reveled in the comical representation of Black mannerisms and dialect. It is telling that of all the black dialect songs swirling around the United States at the time, Mathews chose "Opossum up a Gum Tree" for his show. While songs such as the one he copied in his letter, about Phillis and Pompey, and "Backside Albany" and "The Guinea Boy" were considered at the time "negro songs," "Opossum" was the only widely referenced song during these years that might have actually been a true vernacular tune sung by Black Americans.[50]

While there is no clarity on the origin of "Opossum," contemporary texts from the 1810s, the earliest references known, usually refer to the song as a typical Black jig. Mathews and his collaborator, Thomas Phillipps, who helped arrange the song and lyrics, certainly seemed to think so. Apart from references to its title, however, there are no extant earlier versions of this song before Mathews, but the title's reference to an opossum, native to America, suggests its roots. Mathews and Phillipps, to some degree at least, fabricated the lyrics and the tune to make it sound "Black"; Phillipps said that after searching for the origins of the song without success, he made up the tune. In sum, when Mathews sought to strike up a ditty that appeared to him to be the most authentically Black—one that would best represent the purportedly more primal nature of Blacks—he chose "Opossum up a Gum Tree." Here is the song from an 1824 Philadelphia-printed version of Mathews's *Trip to America*:

> Opossum up a gum tree,
> On de branch him lie;
> Opossum up a gum tree,
> Him tink no one is by.
> Opossum up a gum tree,

Nigger him much bewail;
Opossum up a gum tree,
He pulls him down by the tail.
Opussum, &c.

Opossum up a gum tree,
Him know not what to follow;
Opossum up a gum tree,
With Nigger in de hollow.
Opossum up a gum tree,
Him know not what him ail;
But Nigger go up de gum tree,
And pull him down by de tail
Opossum, &c.

Opossum up a gum tree,
Have no fear at all,
Opossum up a gum tree,
Him never tink to fall.
Opossum up a gum tree,
Him hop and skip and rail;
But Nigger him too cunning,
So he pull him down by de tail.
Opossum, &c.[51]

Several other versions of the song with similar lyrics began circulating both in the United States and in the United Kingdom at about the same time Mathews started performing it, suggesting that Mathews popularized it for white audiences.

In sum, when in the summer of 1829 George Washington Dixon popularized "Coal Black Rose" to raving crowds, he drew on a rich tradition of Black dialect and Black imagery in print and on the stage that demeaned and marginalized Black Americans.[52] The lyrics are usually attributed to White Snyder, and the air was appropriated from a British ballad. Dixon's racy rendition became the first broadly popular blackface minstrel performance of a Black dialect song in America. By the late 1820s, there were numerous "Negro songs" in print, most of them in Black dialect, as well as songs touted as authentic Negro songs, such as "Opossum up a Gum Tree," including accounts of Charles Mathews performing such songs on the British stage.

Dixon's "Coal Black Rose" clearly packaged numerous established comic elements into a performance that appealed to a wide array of Americans bred on racist impressions of Black Americans and eager for more.

As performance, the first popular blackface minstrel acts must also be situated within the ongoing experimentation with new modes of audience engagement in the United States. Noah Ludlow, the itinerant actor who popularized "The Hunters of Kentucky," and several who followed in his footsteps had become particularly adept at catering to American crowds with energetic song and dance routines, part of a new, more raucous theater scene developing across the country. Performers would usually try out new material in small towns, then, once they honed the material, and if it proved popular, they would present it in major cities. At the time, even more highbrow venues like the Park Theater in New York would have offered a diverse array of materials on most nights. Thus, much of the new material seemed to come out of the western country, as in the case of "The Hunters of Kentucky," "Cole Black Rose," and "Jim Crow." Dixon's performance of "Cole Black Rose" was probably inspired in part by his long experience as a performer in the circus, which often featured blackface mimes and other blackface acts providing highly engaged audiences with low-brow fare.[53] The result was a song about a comical love triangle, in which Sambo and Cuffee fought over Coal Black Rose (figure 6.6).[54] First Sambo goes to Rose's house:

> Lubly Rosa, Sambo cum,
> Don't you hear de banjo—tum, tum, tum;
> Lubly Rosa Sambo cum,
> Don't you hear de banjo—tum, tum, tum;
> Oh, Rose, de coal black Rose,
> I wish I may be cortch'd if I don't lub Rose,
> Oh, Rose de coal black Rose.

Rose asks him to wait a second:

> Tay a little Sambo, I cum soon
> As I make a fire in de back room,
> Tay a little Sambo, I cum soon
> As I make a fire in de back room.
> Oh, Rose de coal black Rose,
> I wish I may be burnt if I don't lub Rose.
> Oh, Rose, &c.

Figure 6.6. "Coal Black Rose," 1832–37, Boston. A broadside featuring lyrics for the popular song and a racist image of a Black woman similar to those found on "bobolition" broadsides, demonstrating the connection between bobolition broadsides and blackface minstrel songs. Reproduced courtesy of the American Antiquarian Society.

Later Sambo pledges his love in comical terms:

> I laugh to tink if you was mine, lubly Rose,
> I'd gib you a plenty the Lord above knows,
> Ob possum fat, and homminy, and sometime rice,
> Cow heel an sugar cane, an ebery ting nice;
> Oh, Rose, bress, dat Rose!
> I wish I may shute if I don't lub Rose.
> Oh, Rose, &c.

Suddenly, Sambo notices Cuffee in the room:

> What in de corner dare, dat I py?
> I know dat nigger Cuffee, be de white ob he eye;
> Dat not Cuffee, 'tis a tic ob wood, sure;
> A tic ob wood wid tocking on, you tell me dat, pshaw;
> Oh Rose take care, Rose!
> I wish I may be burnt if I don't hate Rose.
> Oh, Rose, you blacka snake Rose.

Sambo rushes at Cuffee as Cuffee runs away:

> Let go my arm, Rose, let me at him rush.
> I swella his two lips like a blacka balla brush;
> Let go my arm an let me top his win,
> Let go my arm Rose, while I kick him on de shin.
> Oh, Rose, take care Rose!
> I wish I may be burnt if I don't hate Rose,
> Oh, Rose you blacka snake Rose![55]

According to most scholars of blackface minstrelsy, "Coal Black Rose" introduced a new hybrid of black and white folk cultures. As the evidence above implies, however, "Coal Black Rose" captured white impressions of blackness and was hardly a meeting of authentic vernacular traditions.[56] Dixon's next famous gambit, "Zip Coon," reinforced the sense that the audience's white gaze and white agendas played a far greater role in determining the character and meaning of these early hit performances than any genuine Black traditions. Part of an established discourse and imagery that deprecated Black attempts at respectability, "Zip Coon" is a song about a Black dandy that Dixon started performing in 1834.[57] It proved even more successful than "Coal Black Rose" and rivaled "Jim Crow" for popularity in the

1830s. The first stanza introduces Zip Coon as well as some of the recurring gibberish throughout the song (figure 6.7):

> I went down to Sandy holler t'other arternoon, / [×3]
>
> An de first man I chanc'd to meet war old Zip Coon,
>
> Ole Zip Coon he is a larn'd scholar, / [×3]
>
> For he plays upon de banjo, "Cooney in de hollar"
>
> Tudle tadle, tudle, tadle, tuadellel dump,
>
> O tuadellel, tuadellel, tuadellel dump,
>
> Ri tum tuadellel, tuadelleldee.

After Zip Coon introduces himself, his rivalry with Jim Crow, and his current love interest, he comments on contemporary politics, including the following stanza, where he preposterously claims that he might become president:

> Away down south dare close to the moon, / [×3]
>
> Dare lives a nullifier wha they call Calhoun,
>
> When gineral Jackson kills Calhoun / [×3]
>
> Why de berry next President be ole Zip Coon

Finally, the ditty ends with Zip Coon's plans for his presidency, including a reference to the period's most famous frontier jester, Davy Crocket:

> Oh if I was president ob dese Nited States, / [×3]
>
> I'd lick lasses candy and swing upon de gates,
>
> And does I dina like what I strike em off de docket, / [×3]
>
> De way I ns'd em up was a sin to Davy Crocket.[58]

Early blackface performers such as Dixon or Thomas Dartmouth Rice, who started performing "Jim Crow" in the early 1830s, perhaps as early as the summer of 1830, were master synthesizers, blending these traditions and impressions into the type of performances that captured the imagination of American audiences.[59] While their contributions were surely innovative, especially in their ability to channel all these resources into a new medium of stage performance, they were expanding on an emerging tradition of comical representations of blackness by pioneering a new, more engaging version of it.

In the case of Rice, it appears that he was influenced by his experience performing with Ludlow's theater troupe and other itinerant troupes in the 1820s and by a culture increasingly interested in impersonating Black

ZIP COON

ON THE GO-AHEAD PRINCIPLE.

Sold wholesale and retail, by L. DEMING, at the sign of the Barber's Pole, No. 62, Hanover Street, Boston, and at MIDDLEBURY, Vt.

I went down to Sandy hollar t'other arternoon,
'I went down to Sandy hollar t'other arternoon,
I went down to Sandy hollar t'other arternoon,
An de first man I chanc'd to meet war ole Zip Coon,
Ole Zip Coon he is a larn'd scholar,
Ole Zip Coon he is a larn'd scholar,
Ole Zip Coon he is a larn'd scholar,
For he plays upon de banjo, "Cooney in de hollar."
Tudle tadle, tudle, tadle, tuadellel dump,
O tuadellel, tuadellel, tuadellel dump,
Ri tum tuadellel, tuadelleldee.

Cooney in de hollar an racoon up a stump,
Cooney in de hollar, &c.
And all dose 'tickler tunes Zip use to jump.
Oh de Buffo Dixon he beat Tom Rice,—(repeat.)
And he walk into Jim Crow a little too nice.

Ole Sukey Blueskin she is in love with me,
Ole Sukey Blueskin, &c.
An I went to Suke's house all for to drink tea,
An what do you think Sue and I had for supper,
An what do you think, &c.
Why possum fat an hominy, without any butter.

My old missus she's mad wid me,
My ole missus, &c.
Kase I wouldn't go wid her into Tennessee.
Massa build him a barn to put in fodder,
Massa build him, &c.
'Twas dis ting an dat ting, one thing or odder.

Did you eber see he wild goose sailing on a ocean,
Did you eber, &c.
De wild goose motion is a mighty pretty notion,
De wild goose wink and he beacon to de swallow,
De wild goose wink, &c.
An de wild goose hollar google, google gollar.

I spose you heard ob de battle New Orleans,
I spose you heard, &c.
Whar ole gineral Jackson gib de British beans;
Dare the Yankee boys de de job so slick,
Dare de Yankee, &c.
For dey cotch Pakenham, an row'd him up de creek.

Away down south dare close to the moon,
Away down, &c.
Dare lives a nullifier what they call Calhoun,
When gineral Jackson kills Calhoun,
When gineral, &c.
Why de berry next President be ole Zip Coon.

He try to run ole Hickory down,
He try to run, &c.
But he strike a snag an run aground,
Dis snag by gum war a wapper,
Dis snag by, &c.
And sent him into dock to get a new copper.

In Phil a del fie is old Biddle's Bank,
In Phil a del fie, &c.
Ole Hickory zamin'd him an found him rather crank
He tell Nick to go and not make a muss,
He tell Nick to go, &c.
So hurrah for Jackson he's de boy for us.

Possum on a log play wid im toes,
Possum on a log, &c.
Up comes a guinea hog and off he goes,
Buffalo in cane break, ole owl in a bush,
Buffalo in a canebreak, &c.
Laffin at de blacksnake trying to eat mush.

Nice corn's a growing, Sukey loves gin,
Nice corn's a growing, &c.
Rooster's done crowing at ole niggars shin,
Oh Coone's in de hollar and a Possum in de stubble,
Oh Coone's in the hollar, &c.
And its walk chalk ginger blue, jump double trouble.

Oh a bullfrog sot an watch an alligator,
Oh a bullfrog sot, &c.
An jump upon a stump an offer him a tater;
De alligator grinned an tried for to blush,
De alligator grinned, &c.
An de bullfrog laughed an cried oh hush.

Oh if I was president ob dese Nited States,
Oh if I was, &c.
I'd lick lasses candy and swing upon de gates,
An does I dina like why I strike em off de docket,
An does I dina like, &c.
De way I ns'd em up was a sin to Davy Crocket.

[1832—1837]

Figure 6.7. "Zip Coon on the Go-Ahead Principle," 1832–37, Boston. A broadside featuring lyrics for the popular song "Zip Coon" and an image taken from earlier "bobolition" broadsides of black soldiers marching, demonstrating the connection between bobolition broadsides and blackface minstrel songs in the popular imagination. Reproduced courtesy of the American Antiquarian Society.

people.[60] While "Coal Black Rose" and "Zip Coon" drew more from the established tradition of Black dialect and imagery in the theater and in print, "Jim Crow" synthesized these impulses with the logic behind "Opossum up a Gum Tree" and other attempts at Black verisimilitude. Rice's innovative contribution, even more so than Dixon, was his claim to authenticity, although this was borrowed from Mathews, who had also proclaimed the authenticity of his renditions of blackness in *Trip to America*. In this vein, rather than provide any clear plot line or set lyrics, Rice channeled the open-ended, rambunctious—indeed, supposedly atavistic—quality of "Opossum" and other Black vernacular songs, or at least impressions that white performers had of those songs, whose echoes proved increasingly seductive for performers seeking to find their footing in an emerging popular entertainment landscape.

As scholar of minstrelsy W. T. Lhamon, Jr., suggested, this was probably a process of "social osmosis" over time, usually captured by the apocryphal story that had Rice learning the song and dance from a slave hand who went by the name Jim Crow.[61] Where Lhamon and others highlight the significance of Black vernacular traditions in the making of "Jim Crow"—such as a song about a buzzard and a crow, that reads a bit like the song "Opossum"—it is important to recall how little Rice and most other white folks knew of these traditions and how much white-invented content and themes were grafted onto them.[62] "Jim Crow"—whose name, as in "Opossum" and later "Zip Coon" also features an animal—sounded like a Black vernacular song, and probably was an echo of one, but the lyrics largely combine the degrading tradition of Black dialect with a focus on national affairs. Here are the three opening stanzas from some of the earliest published "Jim Crow" lyrics that meander through some American national lore in good fun. Rice would sing the stanzas and then engage in his iconic Jim Crow "jump," shuffle moves, during the chorus (figure 6.8):

> Here come de sussy nigger, and I want you all to know
> That he'll feel about, and turn about and jump Jim Crow
>
> Chorus:
> Weell about, and turn about and do jis so,
> Ebery time I weel about I jump Jim Crow
>
> I was born in cane break and cradled in a trough
> I swam the Mississippi and cotch'd the hoopen cough

JIM CROW.

OLD JIM CROW'S come agin, as you must all know,
And ebery body say I cum to jump Jim Crow.

CHORUS.—Weel about and turn about, and do jis so.
Ebery time I weel about, I jump Jim Crow.

My name is Daddy Rice, as you berry well do know,
And none in de Nited States like me, can jump Jim Crow.

I was born in a cane brake, and cradled in a trough,
Swam de Mississippi, whar I cotch'd de hoopen coff.

To whip my weight in wild cats, eat an alligator,
And drink de Mississippi dry, I'm de very critter.

I went to de woods, heard a debil of a howl,
I look'd up a tree, and saw a great owl.

I off wid my hat, stuck my heel in de ground,
And then went to work to grin the owl down.

I grinn'd wid my eyes open, and den wid um shut,
But I could not dishiver dat I stirred de owl a foot.

Den I grinn'd slantendicular, den wid one eye,
'Twould have done your soul good to see de feathers fly.

Den I climb'd up de tree, and I wish I may be shot,
If I had'nt been grinning at a great pine knot.

I'm like de frost in de December, git my foot widin de ground,
Takes a hook and ladder company to try to pull me down.

And eben when you get me down, I melt and run about,
You'll hab to send for engine, to cum and put me out.

Though you tink you get me out, some heat dar will remain,
Nex morning, bright and early, I'll be blazing up agin.

I've been to ole Kentucky, whar I hab you for to know,
Dat all de pretty ladies dar lub Jim Crow.

I've been to Philadelphia, New York and Baltimore,
But when I got to Bosto,, it beat all I'd seen before.

Dey build most all dar houses out ob brick and stone,
Dey run em up so high, dey almost reach de moon.

Dey talk ob de Philadelphia markets, an de New York markets, loud,
But de ole market, here in Boston, will be seen among de crowd.

No matter what is wantin, in de market you can buy
From a quarter of an ox, down to a punkin pie.

Dare is someting I gwaing to tell you, which I want you all to know,
Dare is a pretty lady here, in lub wid Jim Crow.

Lor bless de lubly creature, I teach dem how to dance,
And show dem de new step, just arrived from France.

Dis is de style ob Alabama, what dey trike upon de heel,
And dis is Louisiana, whar dey trike upon de heel.

Here's Virginny double trouble, whar dey dance de cora chuck,
And dare's de real scientific, what dey hab in Kentuck.

Here's de long Island ube, or de hunck ober dee,
And here's de Georgia step, by de double rule ob tree.

Here's de kneel to Carleton's daughter, what dev hab in Indi-an,
And here's de ole Mississippi step, and fetch it if you can.

And dare is ole Virginny, she cut a pretty figger,
I neber go dar, kase dey don't respect de nigger.

It was twelve o'clock de udder night, or somewhere dare about,
I took my finger for de snuffers, and put de candle out.

De debil take de noise when de nigger is so tire,
When along came watchman, and boilar, fire!! fire!!

O, I got out ob de bed, put on my close widout much fright,
And started for de fire, in de middle ob de night.

When I got to de fire, I did'nt know what to do.
But I heard a gemman cry, lay hold ob No. 2.

I went up up to de Colonel, and ax'd how he'd ben,
He say, you sassy nigger, you lay hold ob No. 10.

I work hard at de engine, den de foreman send for rum,
Jolly, how my eye glisten, wen I see it cum.

When I saw de eatables a comin, says I, if you please,
I'll thank you for a stiffer, and hunk ob bread and chêese.

I take one horn, and den I take anoder,
When I drink more, white man call me brudder.

Den I went down to Ann Street, de niggers had a hop,
And dey took me to de watch house, and I couldn't get away.

And de tin pot alley, de niggers had a hop,
I went in a little while, didn't mean to stop.

The house was topsy turvey, all turned upside down,
And de niggers had de dance ten foot under groun.

De wite folks get a barrel of flour, and knock'd de head in,
And den de way dey cried fire. I'm sure it was a sin.

De niggers rushed out, as if it was a shower,
And when dey got up stair, dey let 'em hab de flour.

And such a set ob niggers, 'm sure was neber seen,
And such fun in white folk, I tink was berry mean.

I was liv'd in ole Virginny, and dey used to gib me
Hoe cakes, sassafras, and shangalanga tea.

De way dey bake de hoe cake, in ole Virginny neber tire,
Dey put de cake upon de foot, and hold de foot to de fire.

If nature make me black man, and oder folks white,
I went to ole Boston, where dey learn me left and right.

I went into de cradle, where dey rock'd sweet Liberty,
And dare I saw de names ob those who made their country free.

I went across to Charlestown, and on to Bunker Hill,
Which once de British tried to climb, but found it diffikil.

'Twas dare I saw de Navy Yard, likewise de Dry Dock,
'Twas lin'd by de best ob stone, dng out ob Quincy Rock.

Near it lay de ship ob war, among dem de Constitution,
Which our brave heroes sail'd in, and put England in confusion.

De finest fun dat eber happened, was in de city ob New York,
When dey told de British soger it was time to walk and talk.

Dey did'nt know what to tink ob it, when dey found dey must be gone,
Kase dey hab no shoe or tocking on, and cold wedder comin on.

So dey gaddered up dare fixeds, and 'gan to march away,
And sailed for land ob Johnny Bull, about de brake ob day.

When dey got back to England dey didn't fear de debbil,
But dey rader be excused, dan fight wid Yankee rebel.

For dey are like a piece ob India rubber, you may hit 'em on de sconce,
De harder dat you knock 'em down, de higher up they bounce.

Dare's a place dey call de Boson, once fought for liberty,
Dey'd throw de nullifiers overboard, as once dey did de tea.

Dar's two ole sogers, whose names me no forget,
One was massa George Washington, de oder Laughayit.

De war was ober, and ebery ting content,
De people make George Washington de great President.

Den he put all de States togedder, and tied a string around,
And when de string is broken, boys, dey'll tumble to de ground.

When dev was first set up, dare was only a dozen and one,
But now dare is twenty-four, and a number more to cum.

Dese twenty-four children belong to Uncle Sam,
And hab been bery dutiful, except now and den.

You all know who Uncle Sam is, from de captain to de mate,
He's de fader ob de children ob dese Nited State.

He's got a handsome fortune by industry's made,
And now his chief concern is, to gib his children a trade.

He's got one sassy daughter, her name is Caroline,
I'm 'fraid he'll hab to tie her up and gib her 39.

Now as for South Carlina, she'd better keep her passion in,
Or else she'll get a licken now, before she does begin.

Johnny C. Calhoun is courting her, dey say he's got de wedding ring.
And when de wedding' ober, dey are going to make him king.

When he walks up to Caroline, her sun-bright hand to take,
Be careful de wedding don't turn out to be an Irish wake.

Dey say South Carolina is a fool, and as for Johnny C. Calhoun,
He'll be worse dan Davy Crockett, when he tried to fool de coon.

Oh, he took up his crooked gun, and fired round de maple tree,
De ball came back in de same place, and hit him on de knee.

O, wite folks, wite folks, please to let me go,
I'm bery much afraid dat you neber get snuff.

Now wite folks, wite folks, please to let me go,
And I'll cum back anuder night and jump JIM CROW.

Sold, wholesale and retail, by LEONARD DEMING, at the Sign of the Barber's Pole, No. 61, Hanover Street, Boston, and at Middlebury, Vt.

Figure 6.8. "Jim Crow," 1837–1840, Boston and Middlebury, VT. A broadside featuring lyrics for the popular song and a stock image similar to earlier ones from "boboltion" broadsides. American Broadsides and Ephemera. Reproduced courtesy of the American Antiquarian Society.

Dares two ole sogers who's name me nier forget,
One was massa George Washington, de oder Laughayit.

Chorus . . .

When de war was over and ebry ting content.
De people made George washington de great big President,
Den he put all de states togedder and tied a string around,
And ven de tring be broken boys day tumble to de ground.

Chorus . . .

Ven dey vas virst set up dare vas only a dosin and one'
But now dare is twenty four and a number more to cum;
Dese twenty-four children belong to Uncle Sam,
And have been berry dutifull except now and den.[63]

These were typical stanzas, but far from definitive. As with "Yankee Doodle," "Jim Crow" did not have established lyrics, aside from the chorus, and thus amassed a long list of stanzas written by Rice or others for any occasion or theme that came to mind, though much of the material dealt with contemporary national themes. In most early versions of the song, one recurring line stands out as though to orient the song's logic. Toward the end of the song, Jim Crow bids farewell to the white audience:

Now wite folks, wite folks, pleas to let me go,
I'll cum back again nudder night and jump Jim Crow.[64]

Thus, early "Jim Crow" lyrics identify the community generated by such humor—white people. To be sure, the song encouraged white audiences to visit and plumb the alleged authentic and primal carnivalesque energies of Black people. Since white minstrels mocked black people by harnessing an established tradition of racist humor, however, and since they performed almost exclusively before other white people in an era of high racial tensions, it was ultimately a celebration of whiteness on account of black folks.[65]

Much has been made of the significance of cross-cultural and interracial encounters in New York's Catherine Market. According to numerous accounts, Rice imbibed in African American culture during his youth in and around New York City's Catherine Market only to later develop his own "Jim Crow" jig. While several accounts and even a famous illustration depict young Black people "dancing for Eels," or a quick buck, in the market, and dance challenges were meeting places for both Black and European vernacular traditions, there remains little evidence that white audiences fully plumbed or understood Black song traditions. Clearly, members of the white and Black working classes, who lived in close proximity, influenced each other, but the cultural divide between Black and white vernacular cultures was still quite vast, and especially for white onlookers, not very legible.[66]

Studies of Black culture in the free North and the plantation South, where different traditions emerged, have shown that Black vernacular culture was in fact a largely segregated sphere, and though there were significant cultural exchanges, a good amount remained out of reach to white people and therefore was poorly understood by them. Thus, for example, it was only in the late nineteenth century that white Americans learned of the trickster stories associated with Br'er Rabbit and other trickster characters, one of the richest veins of Black vernacular culture. Moreover, though they seemed able to retrieve some elements of Black vernacular music, such as what scholars of folk culture sometimes call "nonsense" elements or improvisation, most other facets of Black folk music—its call and response rhythms, its communal and sacred character, its interest in work and nature cycles—were lost on most of early white "Negro delineators," as these performers often called themselves. Similarly, although in time performers incorporated instruments until then used almost exclusively by Black musicians, such as the banjo and the bone castanets, the music itself was still largely European.[67]

There is another facet of Black freedom and white reactions to it. As Black Americans gained freedom in the North, their newfound attempts to inject meaning into their new status as free Americans were not limited to attaining respectability in the public sphere. The historian Shane White showed that free Black northerners in the first decades of the nineteenth century cultivated a new and robust tradition of dancing that "reclaimed their bodies as instruments of pleasure, not toil." Blending various Black traditions with European music and jigs as well as European instruments, including the fiddle, an urban vernacular culture emerged and thrived in the seedier parts of town in cellars and oyster bars, largely segregated spaces where Black men and women could define their freedom, on their own terms. "For the most part," White explained, "this music and dancing occurred away from the gaze of white New Yorkers, and deliberately so, which partly explains why it is so hard for historians to find material on it and on the world of which it had become a part." In time, as white voyeurs increasingly witnessed glimmers of these exotic, sexualized dances—or read about them in the newspapers as a dangerous if tantalizing new phenomenon—they became inspiration for the dance element of blackface minstrelsy, as pioneered by Rice and other early so-called Black delineators of the 1830s.[68]

Here one also sees the limits of white voyeurism. Although some of the dance elements of "Jim Crow" and other blackface minstrel routines were probably influenced by underground Black dancing in urban areas, likely visible to white New Yorkers at Catherine Market, the lyrics for many songs that became mainstays appear to have been inspired by rural southern Black culture. Clearly white voyeurs like Rice had little inkling that Black urban culture in the North and Black plantation culture in the South were quite different; for them Black dancing in New York City cellars and on the plantation were one and the same. After all, Jim Crow was a weird hodgepodge: a slave hand out of the West who somehow danced just like free Blacks did in New York City while discussing national politics. White observers demonstrated an avid interest in Black culture to both deride it and explore its exotic pleasures, but they usually only got to see the tip of the iceberg. Unlike Black Americans, who had to understand white culture because they had to navigate it, whites largely avoided Black establishments, except when they had an itch to observe something that intrigued them. For instance, during a visit to New York in 1842, Charles Dickens explored the seedier parts of town, including a dance establishment, where he witnessed a "regular breakdown" in the infamous Five Points neighborhood. White voyeurs had little genuine interest in Black culture, although they certainly exhibited a vested interest in representing it in highly racialized and often derisive terms as they enjoyed its exotic pleasures. To be sure, as demonstrated by the underground dancing scene—a hybrid of white and Black traditions—there were indeed exchanges, especially starting in the 1820s, when some establishments emerged as venues where Black and white dancers competed over their manhood. These did not, however, typify the nature of blackface minstrelsy as a genre nor its meaning as a humor event.[69]

Ultimately, it appears most likely that Rice incorporated hazy Black vernacular themes gleaned at Catherine Market or in working-class dancing establishments into what he was more familiar with: contemporary white performances and imitations of blackness. While Rice lived close to Black people, he did not, as far as anyone knows, spend a significant amount of time with them. Indeed, Rice was far more familiar with the tradition of Irish jigs and other contemporary white traditions performed at the time by innovative popular entertainers such as Ludlow, Dixon, Mathews and others, from whom Rice learned his craft. After all, Rice had previously performed "Coal Black Rose," numerous Irish jigs, and cut his teeth with Ludlow's troupe while he developed his iconic "Jim Crow."[70]

The greatest genius of "Jim Crow" was that it felt real. Although the focus of its lyrics was national and its music British in origin, enough wishful thinking and a dance element that might have been somewhat authentic was enough to feel genuine.[71] It invited white audiences to dive into an imagined realm of authentic premodern carnivalesque pleasures, and Rice's specialty, as with all successful blackface minstrel performers, was to give white audiences what they thirsted for most. To provide them with the experience they craved, Rice offered a particular racy blend of dance and song that employed twists, jerks, shuffles, and jumps, joined with ever changing lyrics that addressed every subject under the sun. Probably containing echoes of authentic traditions of Black music and dance, Rice's savvy synthesis excited the imagination of his white audiences, who reveled in the semblance of Black authenticity, by then established by many white observers as closer to nature than the supposedly more civilized white Americans.

The infamous New York riots in the summer of 1834, in which crowds of angry, white working-class men in Five Points wreaked havoc on the Black community and symbols of abolitionism in the city, further reinforced the racism of blackface minstrelsy during its early stages in the 1830s. They were more race riots than class riots, as all too often depicted in blackface minstrelsy literature. As the historian Brian Roberts aptly noted, when the crowd at one point organized an impromptu mock "bobolition" meeting—straight out of the pages of the era's boboltion broadsides, and ended the comical proceeding by singing and dancing "Jim Crow"—they made the connection between racial violence and blackface minstrelsy quite explicit. Similar reports suggest that when on the same evening the riots bled into the Bowery Theater, the manager, Thomas Hamblin, had to oblige the audience with a similar demand—a performance of "Zip Coon."[72]

Indeed, the two most popular songs of the 1830s, "Jim Crow" and "Zip Coon," and their contexts make it quite clear that when the revelry ended, the carnivalesque world they conjured would revert to the reaffirmed reality in which white people got to enjoy an immersive and regenerative experience, as well as a good laugh, both on account of Black people. Although there was some admission that Black song and dance were a throwback to a preindustrial order that reveled in unchecked carnivalesque, even virile, energies, it was also made quite clear where the racial slippage stopped. If white audiences tapped the heady spirit of the Black carnival, or their mocking impressions of it, in the context of a period that saw ongoing campaigns to marginalize Black communities, they also made clear in painstaking terms what the humor meant and at whom the violence innate to such humor was directed—Black people.[73]

To be sure, for many in the audience, carnivalesque interventions in the social order were also directed against other social foes, such as the pretentious upper classes, who often cast blackface minstrel performances as uncouth and beneath them. Blackface minstrelsy was a double-edged sword, however, because American elites at the time were just as interested in finding ways to distinguish themselves from the working classes during a period that saw the subversion of traditional hierarchies. Indeed, Lawrence Levine has persuasively argued that in the 1830s class divides in the United States were more unsettled than ever before or since in its history. During this period, elites sought to redraw class distinctions by honing divisions between highbrow and lowbrow cultural forms and venues. There is even evidence that elite Americans who viewed themselves above mass culture events, nonetheless entertained their guests privately with blackface minstrel acts.[74] Ultimately, blackface minstrelsy emerged for them as an easily identifiable target for the work of distancing themselves from the masses. Blackface minstrelsy, then, was also a terrain in which emerging working classes and new middle-class elites negotiated the developing democratic landscape, but this was only a secondary feature of the genre, not the primary one. In sum, blackface minstrel shows were useful for white Americans in multiple ways—largely on account of Black Americans and rarely in solidarity with them.[75]

Thus, in the context of the 1830s, blackface minstrelsy as a broadly defined genre contained some nuance and complexity. These, however, are secondary concerns for the purposes here. The primary work blackface minstrel shows performed when couched in the context of the nation first, and class second—which is a more accurate reading of the period—was as a backlash to Black voices and Black agency.

CHAPTER SEVEN

American Foils

Black and White Jesters in Antebellum Popular Culture

Both the frontier jester and the Black minstrel, as icons in the American imagination, rose to prominent positions in the United States' nascent popular culture during the two decades following the War of 1812. Aside from that and their general comical affinity, however, they appeared to share little in common. One, the Black minstrel, was a new more degraded and highly racialized American variation of the European clown trope, while the other, the frontier jester, was a descendent of the so-called white Indian and a champion of a newfound American virility. Davy Crockett and his ilk were also somewhat derivative of Yankee or Irish clowns, but they stood as largely American inventions who, as Constance Rourke put it, were the closest thing Americans had to pagan "demigod[s]." In *Moby-Dick* (1851), Herman Melville even described Hercules as "that antique Crockett," while others cast his tall tales as something closer to an American version of the beloved Baron Munchausen stories.[1] In short, one was a maligned social subaltern, while the other was a representative of the prominent positions eked out by white common men largely for themselves. Nevertheless, several early moments in the development of these tropes hint at a deeper connection between the two.

A stanza of the "The Guinea Boy" (1815), a Black dialect song, brings the two characters together shortly after the War of 1812:

When we come ashore, great big gun we shoot-e
For make Yankee run, den we could get de "booty"
But de backwood Yankee,
He not much good nater,
He say he "one half horse,
Half an alligator!"[2]

Here, the antihero narrator of the song, a runaway slave, encounters and is defeated by the "backwood Yankee," who claims to be "one half horse / half an alligator!" In the song's retelling of the Battle of New Orleans, the two were counterpoised as the degraded Black buffoon, who fled his plantation and was seduced by British promises of "beauty and booty," and the heroic backwoods militiaman, who saved New Orleans and white womanhood from plunder and pillage. By the 1830s, however, the two would occasionally appear as extensions of one another as in a stanza of "Zip Coon," a popular blackface song, and as follows in the opening lyrics of the blackface minstrel song "Jim Crow":

My name is Daddy Rice, as you berry well do know.
And none in de Nited States like me, can jump Jim Crow
I was born in a cane brake, and cradled in a trough
Swam the Mississippi, what I cotch'd de hoopen coff.
To whip my weight in wild cats, eat an alligator
And drink de Mississippi dry, I'm de very critter.[3]

Here, Jim Crow sounds rather similar to the frontier braggart, who in the character of Nimrod Wildfire in *The Lion of the West* (1831), the play by James Kirke Plauding, says of himself, "I'm half horse, half alligator, a touch of the airthe-quake, with a sprinkling of the steamboat!"[4] In fact, the similarity between the two was such that Hans Nathan, one of the earliest historians of blackface minstrelsy, declared Mike Fink, a fabled riverman closely associated in the public imagination with Crockett, and the famed frontiersman Davy Crockett "models" for blackface minstrels.[5] This should not be surprising given that both fictional characters were entertainers, and in that vein, could easily be discussed in the same breath. Thus, for instance, an 1832 newspaper depicted both of them as centerpieces of the wild live entertainment scene in Philadelphia in the midst of a cholera outbreak: "In Philadelphia, Mr. Hackett, at Arch-street, is dashing as Col. Nimrod Wildfire;—while at the Chestnut-street, Mr. Rice is exciting laughter as Jim Crow. Tears and smiles, Cholera or no Cholera, the world will roll on much after the old fashion." In the eyes of contemporaries, as well as scholars of the period, the two seemed to share an unbridled manhood that offered audiences a vicarious experience of freedom from inhibitions.[6]

What should one make of this curious overlap between two very different clown tropes? How should one characterize a burgeoning national and popular culture so prominently featuring these two rowdy, jubilant, and blustering icons? Scholars have traditionally cited such similarities as evidence of the unique nature of American humor as an expression of a democratic and multiracial national character—at least as far as its folk origins are concerned. Put another way, why should Jim Crow and Davy Crockett not be understood as latter-day Yankee Doodles, contributing to the same leveling culture of self-deprecating humor as in the revolutionary era, when Americans appropriated the Yankee Doodle Dandy from the British? As historians well know, context is everything. The precise context within which this humor operated and its overall contribution, here considered a humor event, explains how white men were able to control the humor of the period so that there would be little doubt over who was a buffoonish outsider and who was a lovable, if violent and crude, comical superhero and icon of white manhood.

Indeed, the varied forms of proximity between these two vibrant characters reflected the racial and national contours of the popular culture at the time. It was novel, multiracial, and democratic, but also tense and violent, and it helped inure white Americans to race-based slavery and to salient racial hierarchies within a white man's democracy. The two icons, with their curious, ying-yang dynamic proved central to the United States' early popular culture during their heyday in the 1830s and 1840s.

As this curious pairing suggests, in the heady rush of carnivalesque laughter, there were moments when racial divisions eased or even blurred. When understood as a humor event, however—against the backdrop of a racial caste system and slave-based economy as well as amid broad concerns over the fate of the Union—when the laughter stopped, racial divisions resurfaced, more real and more central than before. Indeed, racial anxieties rose to unprecedented levels during the antebellum period, when the United States became both a democracy, at least as far as white men were concerned, and by the 1850s the largest slave society in the world. On the one hand, the slave population in the South increased exponentially, as part of the expansion of slavery westward into the so-called cotton belt, while cotton production became the backbone of the nation's economy. On the other hand, as the northern states gradually abolished slavery, the increasing number of free Black people stood out as an oxymoronic proposition for many white Americans. Adding Nat Turner's Rebellion (1831) to the mix, alongside a rejuvenated abolitionist movement that elevated eloquent Black spokespersons, resulted in a recipe for a national popular culture deeply enmeshed in racial concerns.[7]

As with the interracial frontier of the day, the closer lower-class white men came to free Black men—in the gritty reality of burgeoning urban centers as well as the contemporary imagination—the more the racial difference between the two emerged as the most important identity touchstone for them and for the nation. As in the case of "The Guinea Boy," when on occasion the two met in print culture, there was no doubt who was superior—who was Black and who was white, who was a fully entitled native and citizen of the United States, who was a degraded, marginalized scapegoat.

Moreover, although Black vernacular traditions made their way into popular culture, it was largely in the form of white creations for white consumption with the purpose of ensuring that white men could feel fully comfortable in their own skins as the "true" masters of "their" vast continent; this they did in part by inhabiting Black bodies and tapping into perceived Black virility. As white manhood, now synonymous with citizenship, achieved a prominent position in American life, the stakes for maintaining control over those two crucial forms of capital, manhood and whiteness, emerged as the predominant concern of the period's popular culture. By contrast, Black women but especially Black men—whose supposed wild, uninhibited ways had always preoccupied and haunted white manhood in America—could only fit into roles typecast for them by white Americans. Thus, representations of Black manhood honed in on formulas that enabled white men to co-opt the supposed atavistic and thrilling promise of Black masculinity, even as Black men appeared buffoonish, amusing, and, perhaps most importantly, unthreatening. In this regard, constructing blackness as a buffoonish and therefore innocuous category—even as events such as the Haitian Revolution and Nat Turner's Rebellion proved otherwise—was key. Similarly, in response to demands for dignity and respect from such imposing and dignified Black male abolitionists—most famously, Fredrick Douglass—white Americans instead preferred to imagine Black Americans as uncouth simpletons.

Defusing the threat of Black manhood and interpreting white manhood as the definition of uninhibited freedom, American popular culture forged a national landscape befitting a white man's democracy, where the land of

Crockett and Boone out west played a crucial role. Thus the west, now hold-ing immense symbolic significance for the vitality of the nation and its future, emerged in the American imagination as a carnival-scape in which only white men could feel masters of the continent. There they could shed the sti-fling, inhibition-laden superego of the eastern middle class reformers and revel in unending mirth and play. This was true freedom: the promise of America for white men, or at least a good part of it.

A National Popular Culture

A popular culture as it emerged in the antebellum period was the field in which entrepreneurs and business operations seeking to tap the financial po-tential of emerging, large, and widespread audiences produced novel cultural artifacts that shaped meaning for a broad, in effect national, audience that transcended class and regional divides. Thus, for instance, it was quite com-mon for audiences of diverse backgrounds to watch a Shakespeare performance and a blackface minstrel show on the same night, as part of the same ticket.[8] Moreover, where once theater performances were limited to a few large cit-ies on the Eastern Seaboard, by the 1820s and 1830s, theaters had opened in growing cities like Buffalo, Cincinnati, and New Orleans, and itinerant troupes and circuses visited smaller towns on circuits. Meanwhile, print products, including newspapers, almanacs, and songsters, became cheaper and more available to a growing reading audience nationwide.[9]

Much of the scholarship on culture and popular culture in the nineteenth century in Europe and the United States has viewed them from the perspec-tive of the rise of capitalism and the making of class in the modern world; the main interventions here are nation and race. This does not imply that class conflict was not intrinsic to popular culture, but rather that although conflict, including class conflict, was ubiquitous in American popular cul-ture, the terms of the conflict helped underscore the national community along with what was possible and impossible within it. As it turned out, the comical foils of the frontier jester and the Black minstrel implicated a na-tional popular culture that underscored the supremacy of white men. How power would be divided within this framework was up for grabs, but not the fundamental racial and gender assumptions of the young republic.[10]

The brokers of popular culture in the antebellum United States were rel-atively small operations when compared with those of the late nineteenth century and beyond. Although these businesses and entrepreneurs experi-mented with new ways of engagement—such as tapping new technologies, pioneering new types of publications, and developing new forms of stage performances—they were still rather tentative, individual or family-run outfits that did not require large amounts of capital and labor.[11] Nevertheless, a deep divide separated them from earlier stage performers and print operations, most importantly in their combination of a national and popular orientation while seeking commercial success. Historians of antebellum popular culture, in addition to focusing on blackface minstrelsy, have traditionally also taken into account the culture and business rationale that surrounded the spectacle and exhibitions fostered by the likes of P. T. Barnum and the print pioneers of the "penny press" in New York. While devoting attention to early blackface minstrelsy, the focus here is on other forms of popular print culture, in particular mass-produced comic almanacs and songsters.

Blackface Minstrelsy in Songsters

Blackface minstrel performances emerged as one of the most influential and novel forms of the new American popular culture. Traditionally, scholars argued that blackface minstrelsy emerged in no small part from authentic Black American folk music traditions. As demonstrated in the previous chapter, however, although some elements of Black vernacular traditions made their way into the genre early on, they were largely co-opted by performers not particularly interested in Black traditions in and of themselves. In sum, blackface minstrelsy as a genre was not a form of vernacular culture, but a novel form of popular culture far more interested in representations of blackness that matched the national mood during the heyday of slavery and the rapid increase in the population of free Black Americans in the northern states.

"Coal Black Rose" (1829) the first popular blackface minstrel song, relied completely on British music and song, and its success led blackface performers to search for more Black materials for their shows. Inspired by the song's success, Thomas Dartmouth Rice, the most famous blackface performer of the 1830s, seemed to have become familiar with some Black vernacular traditions of dance and lyrics and incorporated them in a song that largely discussed national topics, resulting in the song "Jim Crow." With the help of popular print publications, "Jim Crow," perhaps the first true hit song in US history, became so quickly well known that within a year or two of its first performance on stage, there were racehorses and ships named Jim Crow, and it became part of common parlance, as, for example, when an author accused his political enemies of jumping "Jim Crow," or switching to the opposition.[12]

In searching for vernacular materials, a growing cohort of early blackface performers followed in the footsteps of Rice and George Washington Dixon, the first famous blackface minstrel during the 1830s who was associated with the popular songs "Coal Black Rose" and "Zip Coon." Most scholars of blackface minstrelsy have argued that the performances of the 1830s were expressions of deep cross-cultural interactions, but it appears, in fact, that the originators of these cultural hybrids were largely entrepreneurs on the make, their biographies even alluding to their ongoing search for Black vernacular materials. One scholar described the quest as effectively "what would later be called participant-observation ethnomusicology." These culture brokers "went out to the wharves, docks, canals, and frontier towns; they watched, learned from and imitated black players, and they brought those observations back for an urban working-class audience."[13]

These performers, who usually cut their teeth on the performance culture of itinerant theater troupes and circuses, merged their growing, though still rather limited, familiarity with Black vernacular and British performance traditions to create the first blackface minstrel songs and acts. As Black folklore scholar Shirley Moody-Turner notes, "Rice's contemporaries regarded him not only as a performer of black folk material, but also as an ethnographer translator, and representative of authentic Negro life."[14] Since so much of the act was ridicule—and white crowds were all too willing to suspend disbelief when it came to mocking Black people—these hybrids of British jigs with Black vernacular elements proved highly compelling vehicles for supposedly tapping "authentic" Black virility while at the same defusing it as a threat to the nation. Thus, before the Civil War, largely only white men were allowed on stage as "Black" performers. The stakes were far too high to permit real Black performers to take the stage with instructions to release their unbridled masculinity. After all, Nat Turner might turn up instead of the Jim Crow.[15]

Much work has gone into tracing the biographies of some of these blackface pioneers, but less attention has been devoted to tracing the emergence of blackface minstrelsy through the medium of songsters, which had become quite popular by the antebellum period.[16] One benefit of examining songsters is that they constitute a corpus of lyrics, as opposed to biographies or newspaper advertisements of blackface performances that usually offer little by way of lyrics. Another advantage is that although songs tended to appear in songsters a few years after they were first performed, they were usually dated—especially those printed before 1840[17]—allowing the possible construction of a genealogy of a song and its lyrics, as opposed to broadsides and song sheets, which were often undated. Songsters had been around for decades before the War of 1812, but by the 1820s an interest in patriotic songs surrounding the conflict, as well as the availability of cheaper printing technologies, made songsters one of the most popular print publications, delivering popular song lyrics to an expanding continental audience. Pocket sized—no larger than the palm of one's hand, averaging three by four and a half inches—some of them nonetheless contained hundreds of pages of text. Lacking musical notations, printing songsters proved far cheaper than producing song sheets. They emerged as a central commodity in a burgeoning market of cheap popular print materials that also included broadsides, almanacs, children's literature, cookbooks, cheap novels, trade cards, valentines, and rewards of merit for students.[18] Some songsters noted that 150,000 copies of the edition had been printed. Although a relatively small group of printing establishments in eastern cities published most songsters, they were nevertheless sold far and wide, distributed in bulk through a network of itinerant peddlers who traveled to small outposts, as well as stores in small and mid-sized towns. This infrastructure allowed a minstrel song like "Oh Susanna," (1848) to become a national sensation in short order, including in the goldmining areas of California.[19]

Reviewing songsters published between 1820 and 1850 in the United States with an eye to Black dialect, one can observe a growing repertoire of minstrel songs. The years 1830 and 1840 being watersheds.[20] The first locally written Black dialect songs—"Backside Albany" (1814) and "The Guinea Boy"(1815)—began appearing occasionally in songsters during the 1820s. Some earlier songs arriving from the broader British Atlantic world had made it into songsters before that, but for the most part, there were still relatively few Black dialect songs recorded of any kind until 1830,[21] after which the flood gates opened with a marked increase in Black dialect materials almost yearly. The first appearances of "Coal Black Rose" were in 1830 in a songster published in Baltimore and in 1831 in one from New York; "Jim Crow" first appeared in a New York songster in 1833.[22] Over the 1830s, one finds an increasing variety of Black dialect songs, some of which became famous while others appeared only a handful of times and failed to attract much attention. Another turning point emerged around 1840, with the first songsters devoted exclusively to Black minstrel songs or grouped under the heading "Nigger Songs" or "Nigga Songs," alongside other categories, such as "Patriotic Songs," "Sentimental Songs," and "Irish Songs." By then songsters featuring Black minstrel songs boasted a wide array of versions, including derivative songs and variations on familiar songs like "Jim Crow" and "Zip Coon."

Nonetheless, by the 1840s minstrel songs still mainly consisted of two very different kinds. On the one hand were the most popular songs, offering full-fledged white representations of blackness and rehearsing such themes as Black dandies ("Zip Coon," "Jim Brown," "Long Tail Blue"), mock romance and crude depictions of Black femininity ("Coal Black Rose," "Dinah Crow," "Ginger Blue, "Who's dat Nigga dar a Peepin'?"), and several popular Black simpletons ("Jim Crow," "Jim Along Josey," "Ole Dan Tucker"). On the other hand were the slightly less popular songs, a bit more mysterious in their origin, usually featuring nature and work rhythm and routines, and reminiscent of "Opossum up a Gum Tree," suggesting Black vernacular origins. These included "Clar de Kitchen," "Gumbo Chaff," "Blue Tail Fly," "Bee Gum," "Old Wurgginy," "Jenny Git Your Hoe Cake Done," "De Old Jaw Bone," and "Sitting on a Rail," which for the most part, did not betray the centrality of the white gaze nearly as blatantly as the other group. Somewhat limited in their appeal, they never attained the popularity of "Jim Crow," "Old Dan Tucker," or "Oh Susanna," but they added depth to the genre in its early stages.

It appears that aside from forging racist songs out of materials already available in the public sphere, performers and publishers felt a need to diversify their output to sustain the genre's momentum. Such songs as "Clar de Kitchen," "Blue Tail Fly," and "Gumbo Chaff" can be traced to some of the famous blackface performers of the period,[23] but other songs probably made their way into the canon as publishers and performers searched for Black vernacular songs and snatched up and incorporated whatever they could get their hands on. This seems to be the case of "Bee Gum," which first appeared in an 1829 songster with the additional information that it was "written expressly for the Universal Songster." Whoever contrived this particular song seemed to follow the model of "Opossum up a Gum Tree," in this case telling the story of a simple slave, "nigger Bob," who after eating too much honey gets stuck in a bee gum, a hollowed gum tree where bees hive, and then is chased away by a hungry bear. "Bee Gum" appears too close in form and content to Charles Mathews's version of "Opossum" to be a real folk song. At best an echo of a Black song, "Bee Gum," nevertheless, attempts, with some success, a verisimilitude of Black folklore through its allusion to local customs and local flora and fauna, such as the gum tree, a raccoon, an alligator, and a bear, which Bob encounters in his escapades. In the song's later appearance on a song sheet from 1833, the publisher alleges Black vernacular origins from South Carolina. By then, in the era after "Jim Crow," claiming Black folk origins had clearly become an asset.[24]

As they zigzagged the continent, performers and publishers interested in uncovering Black song and dance traditions encountered new materials and incorporated them into their shows, songsters, or song sheets. They did not do this out of genuine interest in Black culture, but because of the success of such materials in the period's racially inflected and increasingly national public sphere. Indeed, Both Rice and Dixon, the two most prominent performers of the 1830s, designed short plays that allowed them to feature a few blackface song and dance routines that catered to the growing thirst for them across the country and even in Europe.[25] It is often hard to trace the transition of a Black vernacular song into a feature of blackface performances in this period, but "Opossum up a Gum Tree" and "Jim Crow" were definitely two of the first of these hybrid songs that leaned on Black materials yet, especially in the case of "Jim Crow," were largely attuned to white audiences.[26]

The transformation of "Jim Crow" from its origins into Rice's version is a bit muddled. The extant lyrics are probably far removed from Black vernacular traditions, and tracing dance routines is elusive at best. The lyrics to the less popular "Clar de Kitchen" betray a bit more of this process. The 1834 songster lyrics, the earliest found in a songster for this study, appear to remain quite close to the song's vernacular origins. They do not resonate at all with contemporary blackface materials and seem evocative of what little is known to be common among Black vernacular materials, such as references to animals and the rhythms of work life and nature, and since it contained virtually no derogatory language. Here are the first two stanzas:

> An old bay horse lay in the road,
> And on his hip-bone sat a toad:
> He raised his voice to the woods around,
> "Hark from the tombs a doleful sound,"
> So clar de kitchen, old folks, young folks,
> Clar de kitchen, old folks, young folks,
> Old Virginia never tire!
>
> A little old man came riding by,
> Says he, Old man, your horse will die;
> Well, if he dies I'll tan his skin,
> But if he lives I'll ride him agin;
> So clar de kitchen, old folks, young folks,

Clar de kitchen, old folks, young folks,

Old Virginia never tire!

Here are the last two stanzas:

As I went to market t'other day,

I got so drunk that I lost my way,

My master says, Where have you been,

The way I lights on you's a sin:

So clar de kitchen, old folk, young folk,

Old Virginia never tire!

A jay-bird sat on a swinging limb,

He winked at me, and I winked at him,

I cocked my gun, and split his shin,

And left the arrow sticking in:

So clar de kitchen, old folk, young folk,

Clar de kitchen, old folk, young folk,

Old Virginia never tire![27]

"Clar de Kitchen" is hardly a Black dialect song at all, and as with much that comes from folk tradition, its origins and meaning remain mysterious and largely opaque today. The same song in a similarly titled songster—published by the same publisher five years later and whose title suggestively alludes to Davy Crockett—features similar lyrics, but it includes a bit more Black dialect as well as the following cross references to "Jim Crow" and "Coal Black Rose":

I went to de creek, I cou'dn't get across,

I'd nobody wid me but an old blind horse;

But old Jim Crow come riding by,

Says he, old fellow your horse will die.

Oh Clare de kitchen, &c.

Dis love is a ticklish ting you know,

It makes a body feel al over so;

I put de question to Coal Black Rose,

She's as black as ten of spades, and got a lubly flat nose.[28]

Appearing on multiple songsters, broadsides, and song sheets, this version became the most common one and a mainstay of early blackface minstrelsy (figure 7.1). Given this, it seems likely that one of the blackface pioneers of the

CLAR DE KITCHEN!

IN old Kentucky, in de arternoon,
We sweep de kitchen wid a bran new broom :
And arter dat we form a ring,
And dis de song dat we do sing.
 O! clar de kitchen ole folks, young folks,
  Ole Virginny neber tire.

I came to a creek and could'nt get across,
I'd nobody wid me but a ole blind horse ;
But ole Jim Crow came riding by,
Says he, ole fellow ! your horse'll die.
 It's clar de kitchen, &c.

A jay-bird sot on a hickory limb,
He winked at me, and I looked at him ;
I up wid a stone and hit him on de chin,
And dat's de way I suck'd him in.
 He clar'd de kitchen, &c.

A bull-frog, dress'd in soger's clothes,
Went in de field to drill some crows ;
His first lieutenant was a wood-chuck,
Who had more mettle than Curnel Pluck.
 So clar de kitchen, &c.

Den I went down wid Cato Moore,
To see de steam-boat come a shore ;
Eb'ry man for himself, so I pick'd up a trunk,
"Let off," said de Captain, "or I burn you wid a chunk,"
 And clar de kitchen, &c.

I hab a sweet-heart in dis town,
Who dresses in a green silk gown ;
And when she walks de streets around,
De hollow ob her foot makes a hole in de ground.
 Now clar de kitchen, &c.

Dis lub is a ticklish ting, you know,
It makes de fair sec feel ober so ;
Dare's schooner-head Sambo, who lubs black Rose,
Wants to cum possum ober Dina, I spose.
 And clar de kitchen, &c.

One day, as I walk'd in Chesnut Street,
My lubly Dina I did meet ; ·
I winked—she blushed like a bag ob sut,
Roll'd de white ob her eye, and gib a great strut.
 To clar de kitchen, &c.

"Go away," says she, " wid your cowcumber chin,
If you come here again, I'll stick you wid a pin ;"
So I turn'd on my heel, and bid her good bye,
And arter I was gone, she began for to cry.
 O! clar de kitchen, &c.

I wish I was back in ole Kentuck,
For since I left dare I had no luck ;
De galls, dey so proud, dey won't eat mush,
And when you go to court'em, dey say, "O! HUSH ! !
 Now clar de kitchen ole folks, young folks,
  Ole Virginny neber tire.

Sold, wholesale and retail, by L. Deming, No. 62, Hanover Street, Boston.

⌐1833–1837⌐

Figure 7.1. "Clar de Kitchen," 1832–37, Boston. A broadside featuring lyrics for the popular song and image of a Black soldier taken from earlier "bobolition" broadsides and an intriguing image of what appears to be a white woman, probably as a result of a print culture at times including random images held in-house. American Broadsides and Ephemera. Reproduced courtesy of the American Antiquarian Society.

day—perhaps Rice or Dixon, both of whom sang it as early as 1832—stumbled across this song and refashioned it for their performances. Thus, they rendered it part of the early canon by adding a few new stanzas, sprinkling in a bit more Black dialect, inserting references to known characters like Jim Crow, and amping up the derogatory language. In "Clar de Kitchen," allusions to animals, Black dialect, and what some scholars have called "nonsense" elements, central to many vernacular traditions, sound authentic, but the references to the broader blackface oeuvre signal the version to be part and parcel of a tantalizing new genre that white audiences could never get enough of.[29]

Similarly, "Jenny Git the Hoe Cake Done" follows the ebbs and flows of life on a plantation alongside what appear to be natural rhythms and allusions to animals. Taken together with "Clar de Kitchen," they suggest that some contemporary white performers and publishers actually identified genuine veins of Black vernacular folk songs. There were many points of contact where one could glean a sense of Black song traditions, perhaps nowhere more so than on plantations in the South, where the vast majority of Black Americans lived and forged a common culture. Indeed, with time, more and more "Negro songs" seemed to convey the work cycles and settings of plantations and the South more generally. In both these songs, however, it appears that the process of cooptation involved some additions and changes that helped performers cast them within the broader mold of blackface minstrelsy, thus providing more material for songsters and for the stage. The following stanzas from "Jenny Get the Hoe Cake Done" demonstrate some semblances to themes and style from "Clar de Kitchen":

Forty weight of gunger bread and fifty weight of cheese,
A great big pumpkin and a band box of peas,
An de Indian pudding and a pumpkin pie,
De white cat kicked out the grey cat's eye.
O, Jenny get, &c.
Dare was a frog jump'd out de spring,
It was so cold he couldn't sing,
He tied his tail to a hickory stump,
He rared an pitched but he couldn't make a jump.
O, Jenny get, &c.[30]

Interestingly, all the versions of the song have the following stanza suggestive of genuine yearnings:

Old massa and Misses promist me,
When they died they'd set me free;
But now they both are dead and gone,
And here is old Sambo hillin up corn
Oh Jenny etc.[31]

Nevertheless, most versions end with the familiar cue, probably added by performers to bracket the song's meaning and to place it within the blackface canon, in which Black musicians—in reality white performers in blackface, of course—performed for the entertainment of white audiences:

Now white folks, I'd hab you to know
Dare is no music like de old banjo,
And if you want to hear it ring,
Jist watch dis finger on de string,
Oh Jenny etc.[32]

"Gumbo Chaff," another favorite from the early blackface oeuvre, also appeared to tap into some Black folk traditions. As with several other songs that appeared vernacular in origin, Gumbo Chaff, the narrator, is a buffoonish Black minstrel out for an adventure—and not to be confused (or perhaps *to be* confused) with the Gumbo Cuff protagonist of T. D. Rice's blackface minstrel play *Oh! Hush!* (1833). Although similar in style to "Bee Gum," which tracks the escapades of a clownish Black slave, "Gumbo Chaff" conveys a more freewheeling spirit as the narrator lives in Indiana, a free state, and is enjoying his freedom after his master's death. Gumbo Chaff, nevertheless, continues to roam the Mississippi and Ohio Rivers, embarking on various adventures on his way to and from New Orleans. Still, Gumbo Chaff, whose musical skills helped him entertain white audiences, did not fundamentally challenge the white gaze, and at the end of the song, as in the case of "Jim Crow," he reminds the audience that the racial divisions that marked both sides of the Ohio River Valley remain intact. Indeed, this is how he frames the narrative in the last stanza, reinforcing for his audience the racial categories that rule supreme in the antebellum United States:

Now I'rive on our farm on de Ohio bluff,
An' I tink of fun an' frolic ole Gumbo's had enough;
Oh! de wite folks at home wery much amuse,
When I sind dis song, an' tell 'em all de news;

So we'd music all night,

An' dey set up sich a laff

When I introduce'd de niggers to Mrs. Gumbo Chaff.[33]

"Jim Crow" established the tradition of cues of racial divisions at the end of minstrel songs as important framing devices for the so-called Negro delineators, and "Gumbo Chaff" follows in this tradition.

"Sitting on a Rail, or the Raccoon Hunt" and "Blue Tail Fly" are two lesser-known songs in the early blackface canon that stand out somewhat as exceptions to the rule that early blackface minstrel songs largely reinforced racial nationalism. In both songs, the clownish slave is a witness, and even perhaps an accomplice, to the death of his master. Whereas "Gumbo Chaff" was less clear on the particulars of the master's death, serving more as a device in the narrative, in these, the master's death is the culmination and focus of the narrative. Humor, never clear-cut, is often attached to social tensions, finding in them a giddy excitement in authority compromised or confirmed. Rather than viewing these two songs as representative of racial nationalism, they instead can be considered the meeting point of the white thirst for Black folklore—which imparted subversive trickster elements and yearned for the death of masters—and a democratic culture eager to see the downtrodden exact their revenge on the mighty.[34]

Songs like "Blue Tail Fly" or "Sitting on a Rail" captured the multivocal nature of blackface minstrelsy, and of humor more broadly, but they should also be considered within the context of the era's overwhelming thrust of racial nationalism given the preponderance of the evidence at hand. Similarly, occasional stanzas of "Jim Crow" cut against the prevailing themes of Black mockery and buffoonery, where Jim Crow emerged more the trickster and less the bumpkin or even voiced sympathy for slaves, but they were far from representative. In the end, when white people went to see blackface shows or read through the "Nigga Songs" section in their favorite songsters, they were confronted with the overwhelming sense of blackness as degraded and comical, if virile, and therefore regenerative. Publishers often reinforced this message in songsters, broadsides, and song sheets by supplementing the content with mocking comical engravings of Black characters drawn from the broader print culture (figure 7.2). Altogether, such imagery rendered blackface minstrelsy a genre that highlighted supposed Black virility while casting Black men as unthreatening buffoons.

Figure 7.2. Title page of *Nickerson's Humorous, Sentimental and Naval Songster* (Baltimore, 1837). Artwork typifying the cartoonish and degrading racist images in widespread circulation during the 1830s and 1840s, in this case for a songster that includes only a few popular minstrel songs, such as "Coal Black Rose," "Clar de Kitchen," and "Jim Crow." Reproduced courtesy of the American Antiquarian Society.

Based on this early phase of blackface minstrelsy and its growing representation in songsters over the course of the 1830s, it appears that stage performances provided the impetus behind white people's increased interest in the genre. White audiences, it turned out, could not laugh enough at alleged accounts of Black Americans by performers who presented them with what they thought, or wanted to believe, were authentic Black traditions. Thus, insofar as genuine Black vernacular traditions made their way onto the early blackface stage, they were often echoes designed to mock Black Americans. On occasion, genuinely subversive trickster elements seeped into the hectic performances given the complex cultural appropriation in conjunction with currents that served other agendas flowing from the novel democratic landscape of the 1830s.[35] The hodgepodge that was the theater scene of the day—where performers enacted plays followed by farces and interspersed them with short cameo appearances for the entertainment of diverse audiences—made it all too easy for such slippages to occur. This does not, however, mean that blackface minstrelsy on the whole, or much of the period's cultural output in general, shied from active participation in the project of trying to maintain unassailable racial divides, just as keeping the fast-growing nation together proved ever more challenging.

Whereas the 1830s were a period in which ambitious performers concocted notions about blackness from whatever uneven blend of materials they could find or out of prevailing ideas and attitudes, the 1840s saw even more driven entrepreneurs transform blackface minstrelsy into a truly national genre. Curiously, as it became a national staple, it also grew increasingly fractious and polyphonic, both exacerbating and reconciling North-South divisions. On the one hand, negotiating the tensions between South and North was on the minds of many contemporary nationalists, who strove to keep tensions over slavery at bay. In this vein, historians often view the two-party system, which held through the 1840s largely intact, as alleviating sectional tensions. Blackface minstrelsy, as a tacit tribute to white supremacy across sections, parties, and regions, was an expression of such nationalist commitments. At the same time, however, performers, seeking to engage more genteel middle-class audiences, often found it more expedient to express sympathy with slaves, therefore reinforcing sectional tensions. Indeed, such reinforcing and soothing at the same time became a confusing and often contradictory part of the political culture of the time.[36]

Flipping through songsters published in the late 1830s and early 1840s conveys the shift in the location and subject matter of the songs, which increasingly invoked slavery and the South, especially Virginia, the symbol of plantation slavery, boasting the largest slave population on the eve of civil war. Perhaps because blackface minstrelsy as a genre originated in the

North, this turn toward the South signaled the nationalization of the genre. While most earlier songs were set in the North ("Coal Black Rose" and "Zip Coon") or in the West ("Jim Crow" or "Gumbo Chaff"), "Clar de Kitchen," "Blue Tail Fly," "Sitting on a Rail," and "Jenny Git the Hoe Cake Done" focused on plantation life. Other songs, among them "De Carolina Crew" and "Old Wirginny," explicitly mention the South.[37]

The shift in the associated setting of blackface minstrelsy to southern plantation life and slavery was consolidated by the establishment of blackface minstrelsy as a more stable genre with the breakout success of the Virginia Minstrels in 1843 (figure 7.3). It would peak with Stephen Foster's plantation sentimentalism in the late 1840s and into the 1850s. Starting in 1843, a long list of minstrel bands, modeled after the Virginia Minstrels, toured the country and performed in various types of venues, from circuses to museums to public gardens to large theater halls.[38] In the larger cities in the 1840s, the new daily newspapers notified readers of at least one, though often several, minstrel bands performing that evening with promises of genuine Black music and dance. Thus, in 1843, one of the first accounts of the Virginia Minstrels in a New York paper portrayed the performance as a "variety of songs and choruses, after the manner of the Negroes of the South . . . an entirely new and original entertainment." Similarly, two years later one of the many copycat troupes of the day published an advertisement that promised to feature genuine Black instruments "from the banjo to the bones" and "ending with an old Virginia breakdown, in imitation of the southern niggers on a plantation." Within a few more years, in January 1848, Christy's Minstrels, who became even more successful than the Virginia Minstrels, reported that they had performed 879 concerts and made a net profit of almost $25,000. "This is doing pretty well . . . and we trust they will continue in this money making strain," reported the *New York Herald*.[39]

During the 1840s, as debates over slavery and western expansion intensified, blackface became an American staple and associated with slavery and plantation life. In time, these trends within blackface minstrelsy would allow even white reformers to co-opt it for their purposes, most famously with the transition of *Uncle Tom's Cabin* from a novel into a sentimental blackface musical in the 1850s. Indeed, tapping an emerging thirst for sentimental materials by a broadening middle-class culture of Christian reform with plenty of money to spend, blackface minstrels suddenly affected contemporary sentimental attitudes with the same gusto they had once reserved for humor

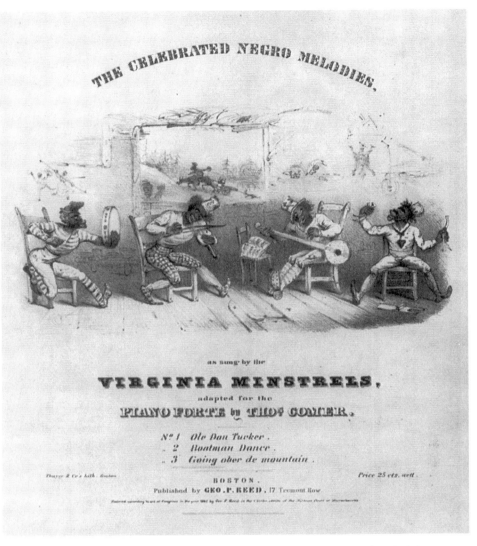

Figure 7.3. Cover page of "The Celebrated Negro Melodies, as Sung by the Virginia Minstrels, adopted for the Piano Forte," circa 1843, Boston. A song sheet featuring the Virginia Minstrels, the first popular blackface minstrel troupe, which starting in 1843 pioneered the full-length blackface minstrel show that included song, dance, music, and sketches performed by the troupe. Library of Congress, https://www.loc.gov/item /2016647558/.

and play. One magazine article, "Dark Prospects of the Darkies" (1852), comically lamented this new state of affairs. "There once was a day, 'Jim Crow' in his prime was then / And fun and delight the theme of each rhyme was then." In these "dismal times," by contrast, "when each vest must be Lilly white, / a burnt cork made up Nigger, transformed from a silly white, / Breaks our heart with his howlings, disturb the stilly night, / Lamenting the death of his love!"[40]

Thus, blackface minstrelsy became a national genre, transcending sections and classes, and simultaneously emerged as an arena of conflict over slavery and the future of the nation. Audiences from New York to San Francisco, straddling the Ohio and Mississippi rivers, from Pittsburgh to New Orleans, could revel in the raucous "Dan Tucker" as sung by the Virginia Minstrels or enjoy Foster's blend of cheerful sentimentalism in "Oh Susanna." Indeed, blackface minstrelsy demonstrated that sectionalism and American nationalism, with its intrinsic racial undertones, were not mutually exclusive. During the 1850s, one could celebrate nationalism by doubling down on slavery as a national staple or sympathize with poor Uncle Tom and hope for a future without slavery. In both cases, however, the racial divide remained as clear as ever. Aside from a small cohort of truly radical abolitionists, most white northerners still hoped that the West—the future of the nation—would be the domain of white men. Thus, for example, the Black couple in *Uncle Tom's Cabin*, Eliza and George, made their way at the end of the novel to Liberia, not San Francisco.[41]

Davy Crockett's Almanacs

Print culture as a medium not only helped distribute new songs, whose tropes percolated broadly, and provided such showmen as P. T. Barnum advertising spaces, as ever, it also allowed publishers to pioneer new kinds of cultural artifacts in their ongoing effort to satisfy the growing thirst of a national reading audience for fun and funny print materials. One scholar cast the print culture of the decades leading up to the Civil War as an age of "print exuberance" that challenged "serious intellectual pursuits" through "pleasure and laughter"—it was "carnival on the page."[42] Thus for instance, publishers helped transform Valentine's Day into the first fully fledged commercialized holiday. Through advertisements, the printing houses of Turner & Fisher, Thomas Strong, and a few others urged Americans of all walks of life to send valentine missives to anyone they might fancy, catering to audiences far beyond the traditional focus on young couples during Valentine's Day. Thus, printers offered an increasing array of materials for sale, from valentine sheets to booklets whose contents ran the gamut from sentimental love poetry to uncouth jokes (usually as part of an adjacent genre of mock-valentines that at times also featured deprecating Black imagery), engaging a fast-growing nation of eager consumers. Under this new order, what had originally been a folk holiday, increasingly stretched from one day, February 14, to a valentine "season" that started with an uptick in advertisements in mid-January and stretched into March.[43]

Comic almanacs were another emergent genre devised by print businesses as they took a more ambitious entrepreneurial approach to publishing. Starting in 1830, comic almanacs, a new type of almanac, gained in popularity. This new genre built and elaborated on the success of long-standing almanac publications that included a smattering of entertaining asides and had their origins in the eighteenth century, such as the *Old Farmer's Almanac*, and before that, Benjamin Franklin's *Poor Richard's Almanac*. Indeed, by the late 1830s, comic almanacs became in essence a halfway house between the older tradition of almanacs and jestbooks of the eighteenth century and the dime novels of the post–Civil War years. Offering readers comical and racy reading entertainment accompanied by vivid and vulgar engravings, publishers reimagined the traditional almanac, now more a collection of jests and stories with intermittent astronomical information and a calendar, rather than the other way around.[44]

By offering unprecedented amounts of entertaining print materials, Turner & Fisher, one the most ambitious publishing houses of the day, proved to be as central to the period's burgeoning popular culture as the more familiar P. T. Barnum and Rice. It would make the Davy Crockett almanac a wildly popular publication celebrating unchecked American manhood and westward expansion. Between 1834, when *Davy Crockett's Almanack* appeared, while its namesake was still alive, and 1855, twenty years after his death, several different publishers issued at least forty-five different almanacs co-opting his name. No one knows how many were published in each edition, but they were among the more ubiquitous print materials of the time, with the overall number in circulation in the millions. Whereas a Turner & Fisher trade catalog sold most of its fare in bulk by the dozen or the hundred, when it came to comic almanacs, they offered them by the thousands quite cheaply. For instance, for Crockett almanacs, publishers charged middlemen a rate of 1,000 copies for $30, 2,500 copies for $68, and 5,000 copies for $120. One study found that a popular comic almanac for one particular year sold at least 150,000 copies in the early 1830s; almanacs came out on a yearly basis, providing pertinent calendric and astronomical information for the coming year, typically also for a certain region. Likely then, a Turner & Fisher Crockett almanac during the peak of the Davy Crockett craze in the 1840s offered cheaply and in bulk would have sold, at least, in the hundreds of thousands.[45] Indeed, if one were to regard all the Davy Crockett almanacs in distribution together as a uniform publication, they were perhaps the most popular and widely available print materials in the antebellum United States, save Bibles. More than any other cultural artifact of the period, they were the purveyors of the Davy Crockett myth and formative of the ways Americans came to think about the West and white manhood. Arguably, few cultural products in American history have shaped the character of U.S. settler colonialism and racial nationalism so profoundly.[46]

While early Davy Crockett comic almanacs remained somewhat close to the real-life Crockett, by the 1840s—especially in the hands of Turner & Fisher and their derivative companies, which took control of the Davy Crockett almanacs market—they became even more fanciful and wild. By then, any connection between them and the historical Crockett was long lost. For instance, the almanac for 1837 (figure 7.4), the first one after the historical Crockett died, opened with a preface accounting for forthcoming almanacs by explaining that Crockett had made preparations before "he went to Texas" so that "two or three years should not prevent the Almanac's being published." Thus, the editors ran with the conceit that as they put it, "from a careful perusal of his manuscript writings, there is enough to make six almanacs after the present one." This ruse, however, was not too far from the surface, and the reader was brought in regularly on the joke, as for instance, when the introduction to the 1838 almanac contended that the engravings in the almanac, much like its content, relied on Crockett's "posthumous papers" "and are mostly taken from his drawings, which are very spirited. He drew on birch bark with a burnt stick."[47] By the 1839 almanac, the publishers had switched to a new explanatory device. This time, Ben Harding—supposedly a friend of Davy Crockett, who like him, spoke in a comical western dialect and told wild tales—assumed publication of the almanacs. Upon hearing "how my old friend the Kurnel had a run agin a snag, as he used to call it," Harding explained, "I went on a cruise down into Kentuck, and there I cum across the Kurnel's papers" and "I tout I would keep up the Allmynick out of respect to the old Kurnel." By the 1841 almanac, however, Harding reported that Crockett was really still alive, and later almanacs dropped any attempts to account for the supposed veracity of the story.[48]

Figure 7.4. Cover page of *Davy Crockett's Almanack of Wild Sports in the West, Life in the Backwoods, & Sketches of Texas* (Nashville, TN, 1836). The almanac, probably produced in Boston by Charles Ellms, claimed to be published in Nashville as part of the conceit of its association with the real Davy Crockett and his family. The reference to "The Hunters of Kentucky" in the caption shows the deep connection between the Crockett mythology and the popular song that changed the view of the western frontier among Americans. Gale, Sabin Americana. Reproduced courtesy of the American Antiquarian Society.

At this stage, seeking to outdo the fanciful accounts of earlier publishers, in the Turner & Fisher publications of the 1840s Crockett was just as likely to fight dangerous animals as he was to make them into his pets. In the 1846 almanac, for example, Crockett "called all my wild pets together that I had tamed into perfect civilization" and taught them to dance the polka (figure 7.5). At other times, he rode animals, like his "pet barr" "Death Hug," at a speed of "about twenty miles an hour, with some important news for General Houston," or, as covered by the 1847 almanac, fleeing "[a] obscropolous grate catamount [presumably a wild cat]" while riding on the back "of a catawampus grate wolf." To up the ante, the subsequent story related how Crockett once blew up a pirate ship with a flash of lightening from his eyes.[49]

By the early 1840s, with more ambitious publishers, and against a backdrop of tensions with Mexico and then the outbreak of the Mexican-American War (1846–1848), the tall tales grew not only more unhinged in their content, but also more uninhibited in their racism and ribald nationalism. If early

CROCKETT, THE PET BEAR, AND ALLIGATOR, DANCING THE POLKA.

Figure 7.5. "Crockett, the Pet Bear, and Alligator, Dancing the Polka," *Crockett's Almanac for 1846: Scenes in River Life, Feats on the Lakes, Manners in the Back Woods, Adventures in Texas, &c, &c.* (Philadelphia: Turner & Fisher, 1845). The humor became ever more silly and absurd at the Davy Crockett almanacs' height of popularity.
Internet Archive, https://archive.org/details/crockettalmanacc1846croc/mode/2up. Reproduced courtesy of the Boston Public Library.

references to racial others, such as Black and Native peoples, were usually derogatory, they rarely made racist vilification the focus of the narrative. Thus, for instance, the 1836 almanac makes a passing reference to a "little nigger," who helped officiate a boat race between Crockett and a Yankee who "was at least seven foot high, and as broad between the two eyes as a New-Orleans cat-fish." Similarly, in the 1839 almanac, Crockett, in an offhand manner, refers to his slave as "nigger b'y Dough-boy, what I give three hundred dollars for," yet again without making him his antagonist. Since Indians were some of Crockett's "natural foes" out West, early almanacs plied readers with stories of "scrapes" with "injuns," who Crockett would call "red skin varmints," but they never seemed particularly intent, as later almanacs would, on degrading them. In fact, in the 1840 almanac, a somewhat sympathetic story, "Indian Notion," relates the tale of an Indian who once confided in Crockett about a dream in which he had met his former wife in the land of the dead, to which Crockett admitted, "but if I didn't drop tears as big as a bullet, I hope I may be shot." To be sure, Crockett bracketed the story with derisive language and mockery, explaining that "injuns are a pesky set of het-hens" and "beleeve that a raccoon or a painter, or a rock has a sole, and are to be found in tother world, like a Kristian what worships God and fites for his country." Nevertheless, that such a story appeared in the same almanac alongside a later story that related a "scrape with the Indians" betrays a different emphasis from later Crockett almanacs. At this point, the almanacs certainly contained nationalist themes and occasionally racist invective, but not conveyed in shrill chauvinistic and belligerent tones.[50]

After Turner & Fisher took over the Crockett almanac market, the tone changed. As early as 1841, in the 1842 almanac, Crockett fought with a Black man whom he suspected of being a runaway slave, explaining at one point that he attacked his foe after "Mr. Nig" "grinned rite in my face. I never allowed a nigger to do that, nor I wouldn't stand it before I war a member of congress," he explained. Thus, he killed him—though not before announcing, "His smell war most clanderniferrous and quite unpleasant." The story was accompanied by a vivid racist image of the struggle between the two (figure 7.6). Just a couple of years later, the 1844 Turner & Fisher almanac continued its attack on racial outsiders by castigating any readers who might have had doubts about "injun character," explaining that "for as nigger will be nigger, so injun will be injun, the tarnal head cutter, blood drinken, rum drinkin, humanity cookin varmints . . . Why thar boasted humanity is a little

THE BULL NIGGER'S TRAP.

Figure 7.6. Ben Hardin's Crockett Almanac for 1842: Rows-Sprees and Scrapes in the West: Life and Manners in the Backwoods: and Terrible Adventures in the Ocean (Boston: James Fisher, 1841). Such racist images as Davy Crockett fighting a "monstracious hyperbolicle nigger" were common in Crockett almanacs from the 1840s.
Reproduced courtesy of the American Antiquarian Society.

bit thinner than city milk, and they like a drink of white baby's blood nearly as well as whiskey, an the only reason why they don't eat up each other is bekase they're of the buzzard disposition, and couldn't begin to stomach their own."[51]

Finally, by the mid-1840s, Crockett was just as likely to fight Indians and Black people, as well as racially malign Mexicans, especially during the Mexican-American War, as he was to fight animals. In 1845, at the height of the Crockett almanac rage and the recent success of the more elaborate blackface minstrel shows by the Virginia Minstrels and their competitors, Turner & Fisher offered both a racy and extra racist Davy Crockett almanac, as well as an even more racist "De Darkie's Comic Al-Me-Nig," devoted entirely to the mockery of Black Americans.[52] Indeed, by publishing Davy Crockett almanacs and most of the period's songsters devoted exclusively to blackface minstrel songs, Turner & Fisher had become specialists in churning out such materials with ever-greater regularity. Thus, with Turner & Fisher leading the way, during the 1840s the language and imagery of the period's popular culture spiraled into unabashed racist and nationalist ribaldry.

To be sure, the almanacs of the 1840s to some degree simply stretched the logic of earlier almanacs farther. In the attempt to sustain the giddy and carnivalesque energy of the genre, they made fun of everyone, including a comical taxonomy of all types of white Americans, such as Yankees (New England), Pukes (Missouri), Wolverines (Michigan), Hoosiers (Indiana), and so on. As before, however, the particular bite and cruelty with which nonwhites were discussed, but even more importantly the context of the period, brought the work of the almanacs into full (comic?) relief. Moreover, the focus of the almanacs was national, and between escapades about fighting Indians, often included added references to national sites of memory, such as the 1843 Turner & Fisher almanac that included engravings, songs, and stories about the Pilgrims and the Battles of Bunker Hill and of Lexington and Concord. In short, the almanacs became a key feature of the period's heightened racial nationalism.[53]

Manhood

To fully plumb the context in which Davy Crockett almanacs performed the work of racial nationalism, one must contend with the nature of the struggles and challenges surrounding manhood and honor in antebellum America. The early United States was a strange beast—a nation committed to democratic values, even as it tightly held on to, as well as recast, hierarchies, especially along the lines of race and gender. The result was a tightly wound, if contradictory, intersection of whiteness and manhood that most contemporaries would probably instinctively understand as also deeply enmeshed with the slippery construct of "honor." What exactly honor was, however, or what it was worth, compared to, say, financial capital was not always clear.[54] Above all else, however, to the vast majority of Americans, it was abundantly clear that only white men could fully realize their manhood; the increasing population of Black men in the North and the South made white manhood even more significant, yet also more volatile. Indeed, the more white men amassed capital in the form of whiteness and manhood, the more they felt considerable anxiety around the prospect of losing honor, which they associated with effeminacy, slavery, and blackness—everything that white men were not supposed to be.[55]

In attempting to sort out this fluid and tumultuous landscape, the historian Amy Greenberg proposed construing manhood in the period along two parallel tracks: "martial" and "restrained". While martial manhood signifies an honor system that champions the absence of restraint, such as when men turned to violence to demonstrate their manhood, restrained manhood frames honor as the embrace of restraint, such as channeling the struggle for power into the economic and political realms, where "honorable" men—at least according to the restrained constructions of manhood—establish their power and authority. While martial manhood champions dominance in more explicit and belligerent terms, restrained manhood recasts domination in more subtle terms. Whereas middle-class northern Christian reformers were the most influential brokers of restrained manhood, martial manhood was associated with the West, Andrew Jackson, and, by the 1840s, perhaps most of all with Davy Crockett and his ilk. Ultimately, however, as Greenberg notes, few if any men of the period embodied and abided exclusively by one of these constructions of manhood, and they should be viewed as abstractions that in reality figured in a host of complex, contradictory, and overlapping ways into men's lives.[56]

There is a catch intrinsic to this landscape of masculinity, however: how were white men to hold on to two very different, indeed contradictory, forms of capital—civilization and manhood? As Americans cultivated restrained manhood, an American variation on colonial genteel constructions of masculinity, those who sought to tap it could never fully shake off the specter of effeminacy, as it had historically emerged in conjunction with a stadial theory of culture and civilization, that viewed polite and refined men, especially in the proximity of women, as more civilized. What Scottish Enlightenment thinkers who developed such ideas could not fully anticipate, however, was that there would be a tradeoff for civilization, especially in the United States, where older forms of hierarchy would hold less sway. In the New World," the more civilized one was, the less certainty one had regarding his virility. Stadial views of progress and civilization cast crude and more uninhibited formulations of masculinity as inferior—usually associated with the lower classes or with manhood in more "savage" civilizations, as in Africa or America—while restrained men, or men in their restrained moments, stood above the more unadulterated manhood of the savage state. In the United States, this proved particularly challenging and unnerving for northerners associated with middle-class and Christian reform when they encountered southern men who leaned into their performances of martial manhood. By the same token, martial men like Jackson struggled to assert their claim to civilization, a cornerstone of their claims to superiority over other races, even as they tapped into more primal forms of masculinity. Antebellum popular culture offered some resolutions to these complications.[57]

If Davy Crockett almanacs were a gateway into a fantastical universe that offered Americans reprieve, then it is particularly striking that such escapism took the form of a steady loss of politeness and refinement. The more a man headed west, in his imagination if not in reality, and immersed himself in the giddy, if ruthless, logic of the western country, the more he distanced himself from the trappings of middle-class society and the culture of Christian reform, which stressed temperance and restraint. Thus, one snooty literary critic pronounced the Crockett almanacs "as contemptible a mess of trash as ever disgraced the public press. They are devoid of sense, of wit, of delicacy—are filled with matter of the lowest and most vulgar cast—profane, licentious, and demoralizing in its tendency." This was even before the more virulent almanacs of the 1840s appeared. The same writer also linked the almanacs "to the introduction to the public eye of the most indecent engravings even on bank bills . . . so grossly offensive that decent females will hardly venture to make purchases where money is exchanged."[58] This was, of course, precisely the point. The western country, to some degree in reality, but more importantly in the American imagination, was no place for women. That was for the best, as far as the virility and vitality of the nation were concerned.

In the Anglo-American mind, the lands to the west represented incivility and savages living in a state of nature. It was a dog-eat-dog world, where men needed to be men to survive. Crockett almanacs were therefore a gleeful vehicle for temporarily escaping the civilized confines of the Eastern Seaboard to inhabit a world of violence. Thus, the period's popular culture cast the western region as one where men could enjoy manly escapades, uninhibited by the stifling trappings of civilization that prevented them from acting out their manhood. In this vein, the subtitles of the Crockett almanacs enticed readers with promises of "Life in the Backwoods," "Rows on the Mississippi," "Exploits, Sprees, & Scrapes in the West," "Scenes in River Life, Feats on the Lakes," "Manners of Warfare in the West; Feats on the Prairies, in Texas and in Oregon," and more. The western country itself, therefore, became a territory suspended from habits and restrictions, where men would never be henpecked by their wives and coddled into polite and effeminate leisure—at least, when visited through the pages of the Crockett almanacs, where laughter and fury, levity and incivility, and uninhibited manhood were joined at the hip. Much like blackface minstrelsy, Davy Crockett almanacs offered American men a vicarious experience of the savage and unrestrained manhood for which they thirsted.[59]

The irony, of course, was that reading Crockett almanacs was a new form of cheap leisure in which all Americans could engage in the safety of their "civilized" environs. Scholars have often commented on this aspect of these almanacs and other frontier adventure tales, viewing them as safety valves of a sort that helped contemporaries relieve anxieties stemming from the up-heavals of market capitalism.[60] This, no doubt was true, but perhaps an even greater threat loomed over American men—the loss of unbridled viril-ity, even as they came to rely during the antebellum years on the manly brawn of slaves more than ever before and as more Black Americans lived as free men and women in the northern states. Indeed, what the historian David Brion Davis called the "animalization" of Black Americans in the white American imagination had a flip side. In the process of dehumanization nec-essary to reconcile themselves to slavery in the age of democracy, white Americans unwittingly conceded one key theme, which haunted them—Black Americans were a threat to their civilization. While animals were far below humans in the stadial imagination of Westerners who cherished their civilization above all else, they were also dangerous beasts, representative of nature's unchecked brute force, the ultimate danger to civilized life. As Kath-leen Brown noted "the robust, laboring, male body" had always loomed large in an Atlantic world that relied so heavily on plantation economies. It would be hard to overestimate the specter of Black manhood, both during an earlier period in which northern leaders preached unity and tried to bury the questions of slavery as well as during the 1840s and beyond, when the ques-tion of slavery reared its head once again.[61]

During the 1820s and 1830s, as American leaders committed the nation to unity across sectional divides and its economy to slavery, the prospect of Black manhood emerged with greater concern. When sectionalism rose dur-ing the 1840s, if anything, the prospect of Black manhood haunted the white American imagination even more, for now the question was front and center. Southerners accused northerners of putting their lives in danger by encouraging slaves to challenge authority, while northerners charged south-erners with dismissing the needs of common white men by prioritizing the labor of slaves over that of free men.[62] This of course, also meant that the Black slave's alleged savage manhood posed the threat of rebellion, making it the stuff of nightmares for white Americans. Indeed, Black manhood haunted the white American consciousness especially in the wake of Nat Turner's Rebellion (1831) and with the relatively recent precedent set by the Haitian Revolution (1791–1804). Southerners, as well as white Americans more broadly, lived a paradox. They constantly worried about a slave insurrection, even as they proclaimed their "slave population" to be, in the words of one southern author, "not only a happy one, but . . . contented, peaceful and harmless."[63]

One solution was to accuse white abolitionists of infecting the minds of the slaves with misplaced notions of freedom, while another was a pincer movement in the realm of popular culture. While Davy Crockett and his ilk relieved concerns about American men's innate virility, blackface minstrelsy eased anxieties about the virile Black men in their midst. The buffoonish and innocuous representations of Black manhood allowed white men to tap Black men's supposedly uninhibited savage state. Moreover, when Davy Crockett occasionally met one of the inferior "Black brutes," he made quick work of him.

During this period, violence against Black Americans was far more than mere representation in print. In fact, in September 1843, while out west, in Indiana, on the abolitionist lecture circuit, the Black orator and abolitionist Fredrick Douglass himself encountered a violent western mob led by a man in a coonskin cap, practically straight out of a Davy Crockett almanac. Douglass, who faced numerous white mobs in those days, would later cite his experiences in Indiana as the beginning of his turn away from Garrisonian nonviolence.[64]

It was not a coincidence that the 1840s saw the meteoric rise of Douglass, the most famous abolitionist, spokesperson on behalf of Black Americans, and counter-symbol to the Black minstrel. It was also not a coincidence that Douglass posed a special challenge for white men. That is what he had set out to do. Indeed, Black men also launched a pincer movement of their own in challenging white male supremacy: while Nat Turner and other militant slaves struck at the notion that Black men were innocuous buffoons through unbridled violence and militancy, genteel Black abolitionists assaulted the same tropes by embodying restrained manhood even more than white gentlemen. Perhaps the most vocal critic of blackface minstrelsy, and certainly the most famous Black man in America, Douglass modeled his presentation of self and of his manhood before the American public as an intervention and a response to blackface minstrelsy. Thus, starting in 1841, when Douglass's masculine baritone first stunned white audiences on the northern abolitionist lecture circuit, his dignified rebuke of American society and slavery, rife with witty sarcasm, was the polar opposite of the crude humor and broken English that most contemporary Americans had come to expect from Black men given the period's popular culture. In part at least, his success as an abolitionist lecturer and author—and as a spokesperson for his race, as he and others often thought of his life's work—was a testament to how deeply blackface minstrelsy had penetrated American notions of blackness and motivated Black Americans and their allies to find the best counterexample possible. When Douglass castigated blackface minstrel performers as the "filthy scum of white society, who have stolen from us a complexion denied to them by nature, in which to make money, and pander to the corrupt taste of their white fellow-citizens," he sought to embody the complete opposite in his very being. Indeed, Douglass strove to show white men that he could achieve the ideal of the self-made man better than any of them could. After all, he was a self-taught runaway slave who mastered the art of public speaking and writing and gained the reverence of the Western world, a feat no white man had accomplished.[65]

For most white Americans, free Black people, and especially assertive Black men, posed a threat to the nation. This was true for both elites, who mostly struggled to maintain unity and to make apologies for slavery during the 1820s and 1830s, as well as for the lower classes, some of whom lived in proximity to Black men and saw them as their potential foes, both in the marketplace and in the race riots common to the period.[66] James Fenimore Cooper's defense of "northern men" was typical. Northerners "had to do one of two things," Cooper explained: "separate their fortunes from a portion of their countrymen, to whom they were bound by the ties of fellowship, blood, common interests, and common descent, or submit to be parties to an union in which some of the other parties were slave holders." Thus, he submitted, any "reproach against the northern man . . . is more likely to be made by those who view the Union, and the continued harmony which pervades these vast regions, with unquiet jealousy, than by any reasoning and practical philanthropist." Black abolitionists were clearly part of the problem, not part of the solution. In fact, for most white Americans—until the sectional crisis reared its head again during the late 1840s—remarkable free Black men such as Fredrick Douglass, David Walker, and, for that matter, Nat Turner, who could potentially influence the masses of Black slaves to rebellion, posed the gravest threat to the Union.[67]

As the historian Joanne Pope Melish noted, white Americans viewed free Black Americans as "uncontrolled," as opposed to free white people, whom they viewed as "self-controlled." Thus, even leading abolitionists sometimes expressed "disappointment and frustration at the failure of the freed people to behave ... as abolitionists had promised they would."[68] In the end, the two very different styles and sensibilities of policing the borders of the nation—restrained and uninhibited—found commonality on many of the issues facing the nation, among them western expansion and commitment to a white man's democracy. Thus, for every Andrew Jackson, who expanded the physical borders of the country violently and at times illegally, there was a John Quincy Adams, who negotiated the Adams-Onís (1819) Treaty, which capitalized on Jackson's military success in Florida, or an Abraham Lincoln, whose Homestead Act (1862) cast settlers of lands cleared of Native peoples as the ultimate beneficiaries of the process of western expansion.

In the South, of course, the politics surrounding Black bodies had long been the focal point of the commitment to white supremacy. There, domination over the labor, mobility, and lives of Black Americans stood at the heart of the social compact that elevated white men over the rest. In the slave states, even more ruthlessly and explicitly than in the North, laws and local vigilante traditions combined to ensure supremacy, and safety, for white Americans.[69] Thus, in restrained and orderly, as well as in martial and unchecked ways, Americans, in both the slave and free states, contributed to a social order that rendered white men supreme through a zero-sum calculus that rested on the denigration of Black Americans, with a pointed emphasis on Black men. In the end, white men would strive to ensure that only they would be able to act like Davy Crockett, disorderly and uninhibited, all the while remaining vigilant to ensure that Black men, supposedly predisposed to act in those same ways, would never dare to do so. This logic would in later years find its most insidious conclusion in the reign of lynch law.[70]

In this regard, as far as white men are concerned, one might think of martial and restrained constructions of manhood as just as often being mutually complementary—part of the same structure of feeling—rather than inherently in tension with each other. Much as manifest destiny was a facade, the superego overlaying a violent expansionist id, restrained manhood was the superego to the unrestrained id captured by martial expressions of manhood. Whereas in the 1820s, James Fenimore Cooper's novels offered Natty Bumppo, the stoic frontiersman who warned Americans of their "wasty ways"—and lamented his friends, the "last of the Mohicans," as a noble and restrained version of American manhood—the popular culture offered Americans the Black minstrel and Davy Crockett as effective rejoinders. Blackface minstrelsy served as an invitation for Americans to visit the supposedly unrestrained id of Black Americans, even as they mocked their manhood as incompetent. Meanwhile, Davy Crockett allowed Americans to revel in the uninhibited martial and violent manhood so often associated with Black people or Native Americans, without any of the consequences of "rough living." There is a tendency all too often to group Americans along class or regional lines, when the lines were just as likely in their psyches. American culture and manhood catered to Americans in different moods and moments, just as much as it catered to distinct class and regional divides.

The need to delve into a fantasy of the "Wild West," as it would later be called, was not only a sensibility shared by Eastern Seaboard urbanites. The western country that Jefferson hoped would offer Americans a safety valve for generations to come was closing far faster than anyone imagined. As Alexis de Tocqueville noticed during his visit to the United States, by the 1830s, "The man you left in New-York you find again in almost impenetrable solitudes: same clothes, same attitude, same language, same habits, same pleasures. Nothing rustic, nothing naive, nothing which smells of the wilderness." To be sure, there were pockets of rough-and tumble living, but those were too few and quickly incorporated into a market economy that transformed the American landscape with merciless rapidity. Davy Crockett almanacs, therefore, helped extend the frontier both in time and space to whomever felt the need to indulge in its carnivalesque and unrestrained manhood for a short while.[71]

Challenging Manhood through Dance

The cultural medium of challenge dancing—exceptional in that Black and white men and women competed in front of mixed-raced audiences—suggests that struggles over manhood were ubiquitous during the antebellum years. Indeed, particularly for the urban working and lower classes, dancing competitions were probably the most appealing, genuinely cross-racial form of vernacular culture. Often intersecting with blackface minstrel performances, which incorporated the dance moves and some of the famous jig dancers themselves into their routines, challenge dancing was nevertheless a distinct form of culture that grew out of two separate folk traditions: Irish jigs and Black "break down" traditions, both of which included competitive dancing elements. During the first few decades of the nineteenth century, some urban locales increasingly offered opportunities for exposure to new cultural modes and cross-cultural pollination. Thus, it appears to have emerged in taverns, markets, and street corners in northern cities, especially where Black and white people lived in close proximity.[72] Even here, as part of a cultural phenomenon that historian April Matsen described as a "medium for confrontation without conflict," competition over manhood took center stage.

Typically, crowds would bet on the representative of their community and size up the manhood of their rivals. Although women could participate as well, the heart of the tradition was a competition over dance moves between men, who sought to demonstrate their superior dexterity and stamina and, by implication, the manhood of their community, somewhat akin to the boxing matches of later days that could also play out along racial lines. Indeed, it was precisely the tensions of the period that made the medium an appealing avenue for gauging neighboring communities and releasing racial tensions. In one particularly suggestive moment, when the famed white dancer John Diamond beat the most famous Black dancer of the day, Juba, an observer noted, "one of the colored boys yelled out 'He's a white man, sure . . . but he's got a nigger in his heels.'"[73]

By the 1840s, under the hands of entrepreneurs like P. T. Barnum, challenge dancing had spread to more commercial venues, emerging as part of the period's vibrant popular culture scene. At that stage, it tended to reproduce the logic of blackface minstrelsy and either explicitly or implicitly became a high-profile competition between white and Black men. By then, the dances were called Negro jigs or Negro dancing, and through this association with Black traditions, complemented the conceit that blackface minstrel songs were genuine Black folk traditions. Thus, white dancers who specialized in this genre became known as "Negro dancers" and wore blackface costumes. Turner & Fisher was quick to pounce on the fame of the most renowned Negro dancer of the day, John Diamond, naming the first songster devoted exclusively to Black dialect songs *The Black Diamond Songster* (1840 or 1841). As with blackface minstrelsy, the European origins of challenge dancing—now called Negro dancing, even though largely performed by white "delineators"— were erased, or at least obscured, in favor of Black verisimilitude.[74]

This is also the context in which white audiences could countenance a Black performer, rather than exclusively white performers in blackface. The only prominent Black performer of the period who appeared on stages across the country was the aforementioned Juba, a free Black man whose real name was William Henry Lane. Historians of dance regard Lane as one of the most important precursors of the dancing tradition that with time would become tap dancing and a key figure in brining genuine Black dance traditions into the early American mainstream. Patronized by Barnum after Diamond escaped his grip, Barnum touted Lane as "Master Juba, the king of Negro dancers." Juba, or the Pat Juba, had by that time also become the name of the most famous Black dance style, as well as a common name for a Black slave, all of which made it even more appealing as a stage name for the only famous Black performer of the day. Lane also paired up with white opponents in blackface, as described in the above anecdote when he competed with Diamond over who was the better "Negro dancer." At the same time, they also challenged each other to plumb uninhibited manhood.[75]

For white audiences, these racially loaded dances afforded them a chance to root for the white challengers to show that they could beat Black dancers at their own game. Furthermore, when white Negro dancers performed on their own, rather than in a formal competition, as they often did once jig dancing become a common feature of the more elaborate blackface minstrel performances of the 1840s, they demonstrated flair in what observers believed were Black dance moves. If Black men were regarded as particularly virile and unfettered by the restraints of western civilization, white men took to minstrel and dancing traditions to demonstrate their superior abilities here as well. Thus, when the Virginia Minstrels began performing in 1843, they allegedly incorporated three distinct genuine Black traditions into their performances—Black songs, Black music, and Black dance—and claimed to do it just as good or even better than any Black person the audience had ever seen. In the end, the point was that white men got to have their cake and eat it too. Much like Daniel Boone, Davy Crockett, and, later, Buffalo Bill supposedly outperformed Indians in their own way of fighting, white dancers in blackface could equal or even outlast Black men at their own rowdy and uninhibited folk traditions.[76]

The Whigs

The history of the Whig Party offers some of the best examples of the thirst for martial versions of manhood and the populist sensibilities that accompanied them, particularly since historians often associate it with Christian reform, restrained manhood, and middle-class sentimentalism. In addition, the party cast itself as an alternative to Andrew Jackson, the standard bearer of unrestrained manhood. During the 1830s, however, as the congealing Whig Party sought political success and attempted to assume the mantle of a party of the people, freeing itself of associations with elitism and Federalism, it all too often borrowed pages from the Jacksonian playbook. In fact, its leaders outdid the Jacksonians at their own game and embraced as an early standard bearer a crude, populist young politician from Tennessee, Andrew Jackson's home state, by the name of Davy Crockett. They doubled down on this approach when they nominated William Henry Harrison, perhaps the second most famous Indian fighter of the day (after Jackson, of course), as their presidential nominee for the 1836 elections and then again in 1840. First, they reinvented the retired general and statesmen as "Old Tippicanoe," or "Old Tip," for short, a reference to the Battle of Tippicanoe (1811), where forces under Harrison's command supposedly defeated a good portion of the northwestern Indian confederacy then taking shape under Tecumseh; in reality the battle was far from a clear victory for Harrison. Old Tippicanoe also sounded very much like "Old Hickory," Jackson's popular nickname. Next, they cast him as a folk hero from the frontier, in the mold of Crockett and Jackson with a log-cabin and coonskin cap to boot. Thus, in old age, William Henry Harrison, the scion of one of Virginia's leading families, turned into America's favorite common man and frontiersman. While schisms within the Whig Party and the flush economic times denied Harrison victory in 1836, he would win the presidency for the Whigs in 1840.[77]

Yet the Whig Party's most famous gambit in the effort to capture the presidency was to incorporate the rambunctious logic of the period's popular culture into the 1840 presidential campaign, despite portraying themselves as the standard bearers of Christian reform. By injecting the giddy self-deprecating humor that white American men had made their own over the past century, they cast themselves as the true embodiment of the nation. Print culture, jokes, songs, and merriment became Whig calling cards, making for a memorable campaign. The party sought to convince Americans that they had to be a Harrison man to be among the in-crowd. Ironically, to the Whigs' delight, it was a Jacksonian Democrat who provided them with their most famous piece of propaganda for their 1840 presidential campaign. Casting Harrison as an old man best fit for retirement, one Jacksonian reporter exclaimed, "Give him a barrel of hard cider and settle a pension of two thousand a year on him and my word for it, he will sit the remainder of his days in a log cabin by the side of a 'sea coal' fire." Whig campaigners pounced on his jest. Tapping the American vernacular tradition of self-deprecating, yet edifying, provincial humor when responding to urbane condescension, they injected humorous and rambunctious themes into their campaign, championing Harrison as the "log cabin and hard cider" candidate. Thus, Harrison's campaign became a large-scale celebration of crude and provincial western origins, as Tippicanoe and Log Cabin and Cider clubs cropped up across the nation to rally behind the Whig Party and its celebrated candidate, usually operating out of hastily built symbolic log cabins.[78]

The Whig campaigners also outdid the Jacksonians in their use of popular print culture. They issued at least 25 partisan songsters during that year—by contrast, only one Democratic songster has been identified from that year— at least five different almanacs, including a Davy Crockett comic almanac dedicated to Harrison (figure 7.7), and a weekly campaign sheet entitled the

Figure 7.7. Cover of *Crockett's Harrison Almanac, 1841* (New York: Elton, 1840). This Davy Crockett almanac was wholly devoted to William Henry Harrison's 1840 presidential campaign, demonstrating the commitment of the Whig Party to harness the popular culture of the period for their campaign. Reproduced courtesy of the American Antiquarian Society.

Log Cabin, edited by a talented young editor, Horace Greeley, circulating 80,000 copies a week. Greeley, a committed advocate of temperance and reform, might have written many of the campaign songs, which included numerous allusions to hard cider and were printed on the backside of the *Log Cabin*.[79]

The Whigs' campaign events drew huge crowds on a regular basis, numbering in the tens of thousands. They paraded around with coonskin caps, by then associated with Daniel Boone, Davy Crockett, and their ilk. They drank hard cider and other hard beverages, such as Log Cabin Whiskey sold in log cabin–shaped bottles (figure 7.8) despite the general popular push for reform and temperance with which the Whigs were usually associated, and they sang some of the one hundred–plus campaign songs.[80] In preparation for a pro-Whig convention in Columbus, Ohio, on February 22, 1840—the birthday of "the *immortal Washington*"—organizers came up with "Old-Tippecanoe," which delivered comical allusions the crowds came to expect:

> Ye jolly young Whigs of Ohio,
> And ye sick "Democrats" too,
> Come out from among the foul party,
> And vote for Old Tippecanoe
> They say that he lived in a cabin,
> And lived on old hard cider too;
> Well, what if he did? I'm certain
> He's the Hero of Tippecanoe.
> And if we get any ways thirsty,
> I'll tell you what we can do;
> We'll bring down a keg of hard cider,
> And drink to Old Tippecanoe.[81]

At the same time, much as the Jacksonian Democrats had done to them in past, the Whigs cast their opponent, Van Buren, as an urbane aristocrat, whose effeminate demeanor was anathema to the true, crude American manhood of Harrison. Relishing fun slogans and puns, such as "Van Van Van— Van's a used-up man" and "Down with Martin Van Ruin!"—the crowd's thirst for humor in support of their cause seemed all encompassing.[82]

Not surprisingly given the contemporary success of Black dialect songs and of racism more broadly, the Whigs co-opted them as vehicles as well. One song in Black dialect and modeled after "Jim Along Josey" wove together hate for the Loco Focos—a faction of the Democrats, but used here as a

Figure 7.8. Log cabin bottle with cork, 1840, glass, cork, 5 ½ × 3 ¾ × 2 ¾ inches. This whiskey bottle was among the print and material culture items associated with the 1840 presidential campaign of Whig candidate William Henry Harrison. Bearing "Tippecanoe" (on reverse side), in reference to the battle won against a Native confederacy and his eponymous nickname, it exemplifies the popular fascination with the wild and rowdy western frontier. New-York Historical Society 1953.373. Gift of Clarence G. Michalis. Photo reproduced with permission of the New-York Historical Society.

derogatory byword for Democrat—and a champagne-drinking Martin Van Buren. Former Democratic vice president and the man who killed Tecumseh, Richard Mentor Johnson, received a hefty dose of slander as well in this racially charged song for committing one of the worst sins against his own race: promoting amalgamation. Johnson had a common law Black wife and treated his mixed-race daughters as his legitimate heirs. Indeed, the Whigs were hardly above race baiting, often making the case that a vote for Van Buren and Johnson was a vote for a mixed-race nation. Here are four of the ten stanzas:

I suppose you know the Whigs next fall,
Are gwoin to stop de Look ball;
Gin'rawl Harr'sin he too strong for Martin,
And at de lexshun will beat him sartin:
Hey cum along, &c.

De Lokos say he drink hard cider,
Bud dey only spread his fame de wider;
And dey may ober dere shampane
Make fun ob him, but it's all in wane:
Hey cum along, &c.

Yes, let um laf and call him granny,
But it's well for you my little Vanney,
Dat he draw de Injuns and British far
While you were talkin 'ginst de war:
Hey cum, along, &c.

And he who at 'Cumsey pull de trigger,
Whose wife was cousin to dis nigger;
Eben dat wont save him for de nashun
Say hey not for amalamation.
Hey, cum along, &c.[83]

Perhaps most impressively, the election turnout was the highest to date, around 80 percent, setting a new bar for engaging American voters. In this regard, the election of 1840 stands out as a no less notable watershed moment in the trajectory of the American polity than that of Andrew Jackson as president in 1828, which for many had marked the arrival of American democracy. If Jackson was the first populist president who stressed his common origins and signaled the arrival of the era of the common man, Harrison's great electioneering success in 1840 signaled the demise of genteel authority in American history. Even the elite holdouts of society succumbed to the exigencies of democracy, and they did so with populist and comical flair. Democracy—that is, a boisterous white man's democracy—had won out.[84]

One more anecdote brings several of the threads in this chapter together. In the 1841 *Crockett's Harrison Almanac*—which contained a half-baked biography of William Henry Harrison in the racy Crockett frontier dialect—the story "Tippecanoe and the Nigger" related what supposedly happened when "a pesky nigger . . . [t]his infernal stinking, traytor run off to the injuns, and aggreed to kill Old Tip." Designed as comic relief between stories largely concerned with establishing Harrison's chops as an Indian fighter, the writer went out of his way to animalize Black Americans.

"The night be4 the battle of Tippecanoe war fout," according to this fictitious narrative of the battle that lent Harrison his Indian fighting credentials, "on offsir seed sumthing on the ground that lookt like a monstracious grate black snake. He crepp up to it softly, and seed its heel, and then he knowed it war a nigger." They caught the would-be assassin and "sentenced him to be chawed up and turned over the wurms," but then "Old Tip's hart" turned "kynder soft, and he began to want to save his life." In the end, Harrison heeds the advice of one of his officers, who suggested that the "nigger better be saved seeing as he war not much better than a wild varmint, and couldn't expected to have no more conshence then a bare." Thus, the story closes on the note that Harrison is as "generous as he is brave."

A very curious version of restrained manhood had won the day in Davy Crockett's universe. If only Harrison had shown such restraint on the day he assumed office in 1841. After stubbornly plowing through a particularly long inauguration speech from the Capitol steps on a bitterly cold and rainy day—perhaps to further his overhyped reputation as a virile American man—Harrison died a month later from a cold that developed into pneumonia.[85]

Epilogue

Laughter and Fury from the Klan to January 6, 2021

> These tricks enjoyed only a brief vogue; the novelty soon wore off
> and even the most gullible freedman was not apt to be taken in
> by very many of these performances. The stories, however, lived
> on and on, repeated and laughed over by generations of whites.
> They comprise one of the most cherished parts of the Klan saga.
> —Allen Trelease, *White Terror: The Ku Klux Klan Conspiracy*
> *and Southern Reconstruction* (1971)

Until the civil rights movement forced the US government to action on behalf of all its denizens in the 1960s, the Civil War and Reconstruction appeared as aberrations on the national landscape. For about a decade following the Emancipation Proclamation, issued January 1, 1863, Black Americans and their well-being were one of the chief concerns of the government. This did not, however, signal the end of a white man's democracy in the United States. In fact, precisely because of this aberration, the most famous white supremacist organization in American history took shape during this period, and it did so with carnivalesque flair. In the aftermath of the Civil War (1861–65), and especially after congressional, or radical, Reconstruction (1867–76) got underway, white southerners felt their world turned upside down. The war had eliminated racial slavery, the "corner-stone" of the Confederacy, as its vice president, Alexander Stephens, famously put it. In response, white southerners sought to reclaim the South after experiencing humiliation and defeat. They also found themselves in need of laughter, preferably on account of the freed slaves. The Ku Klux Klan provided them with both.[1]

Formed by six young Confederate veterans in Pulaski, Tennessee, in May 1866, the Reconstruction-era Klan seemed to have originated as a semi-clandestine fraternal association whose ultimate shape and purpose emerged over the next two years in the context of increasingly organized opposition to the Union presence across the South. It was semi-clandestine in that it operated relatively secretly but flaunted the idea of its secrecy; ostentatiously reveling in its own conceit, they made themselves known to the public through a variety of media. In fact, as in other similar types of humor conceits, such as the Whiskey Rebellion's Tom the Tinker, it operated as a joke or prank to which only select members of the community were privy, having knowledge of organizational inner workings and the people behind them. Much of the humor in the early days of the Klan—before it became a terror organization—hinged on the mysterious and ostentatious, yet inane names associated with it, starting with the name of the organization itself: Ku Klux. Thus, those who fully shared in the mirth knew that the nonsensical and ostentatious language Klan members used, such as the titles of its leaders—Grand Wizard, Grand Cyclops, or Grand Dragon—were in the spirit of a prank; everyone else, those left out, could only guess at the full meaning and significance of the vocabulary they adopted. When the Klan transitioned into a terror organization, visiting violence in masquerade on the recently freed Black Americans and those associated with their cause, it drew on these dynamics, infusing fury with laughter.[2]

As a militant organization seeking to reclaim the South for white men through widespread terror and violence, the Klan had to compete with other organizations of similar origins and design, among them the Knights of the White Camellia, the White Brotherhood, and the Ghouls. Ultimately, it might have succeeded more than other similar organizations of the late 1860s and early 1870s because it was more compelling. With its mysterious names and carnivalesque performative culture, it excited the southern and northern imaginations more than its competitors. Indeed, it was so compelling that it remained etched in both southern and northern memory for decades, leading to later applications of the conceit, most famously and successfully during the 1920s. Ultimately, the Ku Klux Klan became southerners' favored vehicle for opposing radical Reconstruction: It was both a militant organization and a joke shared by white southerners on account of Unionists and Black Americans.

The Klan's success revealed how important it was for white men to transform the scarred landscape of the South in the wake of the war. Under

Union occupation and without racial slavery, the landscape itself felt strange, alien, and depressing. This new land was mired with inhibitions, a far cry from what they remembered and would continue to remember as the good old days, before the Yankees crushed southern freedoms. As an occupied territory where new laws uplifting Black Americans limited white privilege, the South was no longer a place where white men could dominate others. This was not the promise of America, where freedom reigned supreme and where real men, white men, could act with impunity. Surely, this was no way to live. As the historian Elaine Frantz Parsons has noted, southern white men struggling to make sense of their new surroundings were quick to turn to amusements of various sorts. Indeed, she traced the origins of the Klan to a cultural moment in which young elite southerners struggled to infuse what seemed like meaningless daily drudgery with mirth and play. Striking a rich vein of carnivalesque levity, they contrived a new clandestine association with fanciful names and elaborate and quaint rituals. Designed to reclaim their surroundings, the logical next step was to turn it into a white supremacist terror organization. In a further twist, by the mid-1870s, as the nation's centennial drew close, they viewed themselves as rekindling the spirit of the revolution itself. Linking themselves to a vaunted American tradition, they were the new yeomanry rallying against insidious and oppressive tyrannical forces.[3]

During 1868, as Klan activity increased in violence, it also grew more elaborate and funnier—to the community of participants and more broadly to southern whites, who reveled in the lurid tales surrounding such performances of violence against freed people and Unionists. By the time white vigilantes across the South took up the identity and theatrics first contrived in Pulaski, Tennessee, as they carried out violence against Black southerners and their white allies, they often touted themselves as ghosts of the Confederate dead come back to haunt the living. In this vein, some told their victims that they had come from Hell, while other Klan vigilantes cast themselves in the mold of rural vigilantes from an earlier period—as howling Indian savages.[4] The Ku Klux, as they called themselves, wore a variety of different carnivalesque costumes, but as in the case of the revolutionary-era vigilantes who dressed as Indians to take control of their landscape, the messaging behind the masquerade extended far beyond the simple need to hide one's identity to avoid Union prosecution. It was their way of signaling—often as much to themselves as to their victims and to the broader national community—that they were asserting control of the southern landscape and rendering it a place where only those in on the conceit could feel comfortable in it and in the knowledge of its underpinnings.

Humor positively shores up communal bonds through the communion of shared mirth, but also negatively by excluding those not fully in on the joke's humor or, worse, who are its targets. Reports, for instance, often portrayed the Ku Klux as trying to capitalize on the alleged superstition of freed people by highlighting and supposedly demonstrating supernatural traits and powers. Thus, Ku Klux raiders often employed pranks, such as rigging a hose under their disguise that allowed them to appear to consume several buckets of water in front of what they hoped would be gullible victims.[5] Surely, a spirit of levity and mirth animated the preparation for these performances and gave the raiders much to unpack and enjoy when they related accounts of their antics to their community of insiders. While such "practical jokes" and "tricks," as the historian Alan Trelease called them, probably played some role in amping up the terror experienced by Black southerners and their allies, when weighed against the scope of real violence—during a period in which white vigilantes murdered and abused thousands—they appear trivial and superfluous. Nevertheless, the ubiquity of such practices demonstrates how significant it was for southern white men to engage in combinations of violence and glee, largely for their own benefit as a tool of communal cohesion, as they moved to reclaim the South.[6]

As with the Black Boys of Pennsylvania, the White Indians of Main, and the Whiskey Rebels, many Klan vigilantes made use of written notices in public spaces, such as town centers, and in newspapers. The purpose of the announcements was to induce terror in the local Black community and any others mentioned in them or associated with what southerners would in time call "Black rule." No less importantly, however, such notices—often written as part of elaborate performative schemes, such as an author masquerading as the ghost of a dead soldier and using cryptic language—and other comical devices gave rise to a heady sense of elation stemming from being in the know and therefore feeling in control of the landscape. Thus, such notices followed up by action, or even just parades where Klan members came out in full regalia, helped white men reclaim the South for themselves. The wide appeal of such actions across so many communities in the South that had little contact with one another suggests the importance of Klan symbolism complementing the real violence exacted by Klan members on so many Black victims between 1868 and 1871, the peak years of Klan activity.[7]

Although contemporary depictions of the Klan, as well as those by some of the earliest historians of the group, took the Klan at its word in casting it as hierarchical, organized, and largely centralized, more recent historians have explained the Reconstruction-era Klan as a more spontaneous phenomenon that emerged across many of the former Confederate states with little coordination. Starting in 1868, in response to the passage of the Reconstruction Acts (1867–68) and the national elections of 1868—in which Black men stood to vote in large numbers for the first time—Klansmen emerged for their night raids in a host of ghoulish costumes to exact violence on freed people and their allies. While some Klan "dens" and regional networks for certain periods of time in some areas demonstrated considerable organization and coordination, many others who cast themselves as Ku Klux were local initiatives that harnessed the humor and mystique of the Klan as they assumed the mantle of white supremacy in their particular communities, with little or no relationship to a broader organization structure. In this way, as Parsons put it, "they self-consciously drew on a translocal grammar" surrounding the Klan and applied it to "local cultural ideas and meaning." In the first half of 1868, as stories of the Klan circulated in the local and national press, local vigilantes found the conceit of a supposedly broad and clandestine organization the best solution to the challenges they faced. Already committed in a variety of ways to resisting the new order imposed on them by northerners, many southern men turned to the blueprint of violence and theatrics associated with the Klan.[8]

The Ku Klux Klan, in its various iterations and in memory, emerged as the most iconic form of home-grown white supremacy after the Civil War. As noted, it was also a meeting point between humor and violence. The particular nature of Reconstruction-era Klan violence and masquerade also offers an apt moment to reconsider the various cultural registers of humor discussed throughout this book—elite, vernacular, and popular—as they represent a hybrid of all three. As something of a social organization for elites along the lines of such outfits as the Free Masons, including references to Latin and Greek—the name Ku Klux is a modification of the Greek *kuklos*, meaning "ring" or "circle"—its origins and some of its symbolism conformed to certain modes of elite culture. Nevertheless, much of its use of violence and terror drew on white American vernacular traditions, such as rough music and regulation, and seemed steeped in premodern notions of the carnival and in the idea of the community as a corporation bound by timeless traditions.

Much of Klan activity did not, however, depend on oral transmission for its spread, as is usually the case with vernacular cultural traditions, but largely relied on a modern print culture that became obsessed with the Klan and often lent the Klan a much more coordinated and elaborate aura than warranted. Indeed, the Klan owed much to the national press for its rapid spread across the South and for lending it the mystique of clandestine calculation and organization though only loosely based in reality.[9] This Reconstruction-era white supremacist organization was, therefore, very much in tune with American culture and its various cultural registers about a century into the United States' experiment in self-rule, tapping into its cultural history in many of its diverse iterations. This suggests that the Klan's uniquely American marriage of violence and humor was here to stay. Propagated, sensationalized, and fed to an eager northern reading audience, who grew obsessed with the Klan and its mystery, its approach appealed to white Americans across class and even sectional divides.

The carnivalesque humor of the Klan would appear once more in later years, in different forms that suited the particular moment within which they occurred. For the purposes here, what appears most striking when surveying the cultural landscape constructed by white American men since the late nineteenth century is the thirst for enacting fantasies of militant and aggressive manhood, preferably in the wilderness. Ranging from extremely violent and horrific acts, such as night rides, to far less violent ones (at least for humans), such as hunting, many rituals of manhood over the last 150 years seem connected to militant fantasies offering white men a way to contend with developments in demographics, politics, and culture that caused them anxiety. Fantasies of violence enacted to mollify conservative anxieties appeared enticing to white men of all walks of American life, and included the Ivy League and imperialist sensibilities of Theodore Roosevelt's Rough Riders, the respectable, even wholesome, veneer of the 1920s Klan, and the rural paramilitary outlook of the white power insurgents of the 1990s militia movement.[10]

While Klan membership in the 1920s peaked at four million, and estimates of the broader reach of the networks and culture surrounding the 1990s militia movement extended into the millions, overtly militant phenomena should be seen for the most part as extreme outcomes of a much deeper and more widespread culture of feeling.[11] In this regard, broadly practiced male rituals of bonding, many of them in the "great outdoors"—from the Boy Scouts to hunting and fishing to off-roading—forge a sense of entitlement to the landscape. Proving foundational to white men's sense of self, place, community, and nation, such activities appear somewhat akin to the militia musters of old.[12] Moreover, even if they did not carry out violence themselves, decades of witnessing extra-legal (lynching) and legal (police) violence against Black men and benefitting from a legal system and culture that upheld their right to control their families and dependents led them to view freedom as a zero-sum game. Freedom in America, according to the historian Jefferson Cowie, emerged in the early national period as an "expression of power," with lynching the ultimate example of the "right to dominate even on a whim." This formative and intuitive interpretation of freedom—one of several competing interpretations of freedom in American history—reared its head every time white male hegemony faced perceived or real threats, from the period of Reconstruction to the era of Donald Trump.[13]

The last 150 years have also been the era of mass media when a defiantly American construction of freedom increasingly rested on new formulas of popular culture that made white male violence iconic. In particular, westerns, in their many iterations and permutations, explained the historian Richard Slotkin, became the vehicle for frontier mythology, affirming the United States as a "gunfighter nation," where violence itself became mythologized. Thus, the same zero-sum racial logic that animated dime novels and Wild West shows during the late nineteenth century seemed to aminate American soldiers during the Cold War as they headed into the Vietnamese jungles, the twentieth-century version of Indian country.[14] A similar racial logic also underscored the developing war on drugs. In lockstep, during the late twentieth century, popular TV shows like the "Dukes of Hazzard" and "Cops" emerged, and merged, to deliver very clear lessons: illegal acts committed by white men and those taken by racialized minorities portended very different consequences. In this vein, white boys playing Indians and cowboys could under the right circumstances—say, the impression of urban uprisings by minorities—make the leap by adulthood to training in the woods as part of a self-appointed militia in preparation for a race war or an attempt to bring down a government supposedly controlled by cabals of Jews, communists, or pedophiles. Notably, for white men animated by a combination of righteous anger against the enemies of freedom and steeped in mirth and play, any consequences for taking actions they deem necessary appear so remote as to be unthinkable. Indeed, from the Black Legion of the 1930s to the militia movement of the 1990s to the January 6, 2021, insurrectionists, white men who commit crimes against the state have appeared unprepared for the potential consequences of their violent plans and actions. It would be hard to imagine such naivete among circles of militant minorities. The Black Legion, a secretive white supremacist offshoot of the 1920s Klan, organized tens of thousands of men into militia units to enact vigilante justice against Catholics, Jews, Blacks, and communists. In their flights of fancy, they also imagined themselves mounting an insurrection against a New Deal government that they believed had been taken over by communists and Jews. Invoking the memory of the Boston Tea Party and the Minutemen, and wearing elaborate black regalia in their rituals, they trained for battle and adopted the codeword, Lixto, to signal when to take up arms and descend on Washington. So long as Black Legion members committed violence against communists or Black folks, they were left to their own devices. When they, however, killed Charles Poole, a white Catholic Works Progress Administration worker, state repression caught up with them and triggered alarm about the rise of fascism in the country. At the ensuing trials, the defendants appeared genuinely mortified to learn that anyone would view their insurrectionist plans as traitorous or somehow un-American.[15]

Similarly, in the 1990s, militias organized by the tens of thousands across the United States to take down what they deemed to be a hostile, un-American government, including those led by Republican Presidents Ronald Reagan and George H. W. Bush. In fact, as Robert Churchill has noted, it might have been the startling revelation that the state would dare to regulate white men that drove them over the edge, from marginal white supremacist militias in the 1980s to a mass movement in the 1990s. In the wake of government actions at Ruby Ridge in 1992 and Waco in 1993, when federal agents employed paramilitary violence—first applied against minorities during the so-called war on drugs in the 1980s—to curtail the illegal activities of white militants in the 1990s, many white men expressed fury and indignation. Increasingly anti-statist, conspiratorial, and, indeed, fantastical in their thinking, they drew once more from the history and myth of the revolution as they amassed guns, organized as militias, and planned a new revolution. After a white power militant carried out the Oklahoma City bombing on April 19, 1995—220th anniversary of the Battles of Lexington and Concord—killing 168 people and injuring hundreds, there was a genuine sense of confusion among some leaders of the militia movement over how they could have wrought such a thing. Several decades later, with the Oklahoma City bombing consigned to the distant past, the call to action came yet again on January 6, 2021, incredibly from a sitting American president—Trump. Shrouded in fantasy and carnivalesque glee, many of the insurgents seemed confused about how to actually enact the violence they committed when it was no longer innocuous play and befuddled when they learned that there would be consequences.[16]

Clearly, there is something to Patrick Wolfe's dictum that settler colonialism is a structure, not an event.[17] These structures, in societies and psyches, have resulted time and again in violent and dangerous reactionary movements, often appropriating some of the most deeply held myths of American nationhood toward horrific ends. Mostly led by white men, these forces have often turned to humor and play to naturalize violence as well as themselves as the true inheritors of the American landscape. Simultaneously, humor and play also helped obfuscate these processes, preventing Americans from reckoning with their history. Indeed, perhaps the most insidious part of settler colonial ideology is that it hides its true nature from the settler collective it serves. This process is multilayered, involving a particular regimen of sensibilities that have come to shape Americans' sense of self such that they cannot fully grasp its inner workings. The self-affirming American structure of feeling—with humor and play as its id and more lofty constructions, such as manifest destiny, as its super ego—has animated the United States as it committed extreme acts of violence over its 250-year history. Thus, the rangers who dressed as Indians to fight Indians in the distant past were truly predecessors of generations of US Army Rangers who smudged their faces with war colors and headed into Vietnam, Afghanistan, and Iraq as well as self-styled militiamen who trained in the woods in preparation for a race war.

While historians rarely get to shape the world as policymakers, they are perhaps uniquely equipped to address Americans' ongoing struggles with the mythology surrounding their country. That requires recognizing the limits to what one can and what one should do. Too often historians seem attracted by the prospect of molding mythic memory anew—in more productive ways and toward more progressive ends. It would perhaps be wiser, however, if they played to their strengths: focus on dispelling mythologies and shedding light on the relationship between myth, culture, and nations, rather than affirming versions of them that they believe they can control. It does not serve history, for example, to pretend that the Second Amendment was not, in part, influenced by the myth of spontaneously organized freedom-loving militiamen. Unfortunately, the truth is that self-styled militias and gun advocates have not been wholly wrong in their interpretation of the Second Amendment. It also does not serve history, as some have recently tried, to teach yet another generation of Americans the self-affirming notion that for all the faults of the United States, it has been committed to the process of increasing democratization. Historians have been at their best when they dispel myths, not when they seek to recalibrate them. *American Laughter, American Fury* is an attempt at the former.

More narrowly, I hope this study makes a case for historians to better understand the nature of humor in American history and to refuse to view it as a largely innocuous mode of culture or, as so many comics do, as a uniquely protected form of speech that holds intrinsic positive qualities. Indeed, recognizing this problem in 2005, the comedian Dave Chapelle walked away from comedy (and gobs of money) when he could not tell whether he was "dancing or shuffling," a clear allusion to blackface minstrelsy.[18] Thus, even if before telling a joke someone asks themselves whether they are punching up or down, the answer is not up to them. Unfortunately, the audience usually has the final say.

The greatest problem for many, nevertheless, is to recognize up from down, and settler colonial nations seem to be some of the least adept at such a task. Unfortunately, this appears all too urgent a problem in the United States as well as in another settler colonial country—my homeland, Israel. Here, too, historians can be of use. In the United States, with significant numbers of white men coming to view themselves as an embattled minority, many historians have sought in recent years to disturb such short-sighted grievances by shedding light on the histories of race and power in American history. I hope this book contributes to this important goal. Given the immensity of the crisis in Gaza, I cannot abstain from a quick comment on the subject at hand. As I wrote these words, Israel was punching down under the genuine confusion that it is punching up, with the United States offering it invaluable financial and moral support to do so. Thus, the shared settler colonial affinity between the "leader of the free world" and the "only democracy in the Middle East" once more spells disaster for many.

As an exploited laborer at a mismanaged public university and a union leader on campus, I had initially intended to use this space for a tirade about the state of academia and my profession. The more I thought about the many people who helped create this book, however, the more I realized how fortunate I was to receive the assistance and feedback that made it possible. Since so many in the discipline of history and adjoining fields, such as archivists and librarians, are overstretched, overworked, underpaid, and underappreciated, I feel all the more indebted to those who have given their time, energy, and sheer goodwill to support a project that is not their own.

Since my teaching and research highlight history from the "bottom up," it seems fitting to express my gratitude first to the librarians and archivists who contributed to this book. Thousands of hours of labor over centuries went into obtaining, organizing, and maintaining the texts I relied on for my research. What a profound labor of love. It is truly moving that someone would devote so much effort so that others might benefit from it not only during their lifetime, but also at some future date, maybe hundreds of years down the line. I am humbled by the effort, a great deal of it not fully rewarded but nonetheless ongoing, by the many archivists and librarians who have contributed to the production of historical knowledge and in particular to this book. I would especially like to thank the archivists and staff at the archives that I have most relied on over the years: the New-York Historical Society, the Library Company of Philadelphia, the Library of Congress, the Massachusetts Historical Society, and, most of all, the American Antiquarian Society, where I spent a month as a fellow. They are the unsung heroes of the study of history.

Next, I would like to single out a few mentors who have aided and taught me, offering guidance in the scholarship of history and serving as role models for how to teach history. At Tel Aviv University, it was in Michael Zakim's classes that I first encountered the thrill of studying the fascinating and disturbing subject of American history. In some ways, the first paper I wrote in my first class with Professor Zakim remained a work in progress, and this book yet another installment in my many attempts to capture the contradictions of American history I encountered in his classes. Milette Shamir, also at Tel Aviv University, showed me the delights of American studies and literary history, which became an important source of inspiration for my scholarship.

At the University of California, Davis, I found a new mentor in Clarence Walker, who was most generous with his time and advice. Over meals and drinks, we discussed at great length dozens of books and scholars and their respective contributions to the field. In Clarence, who has now sadly passed away, I had found someone with whom I could heatedly engage any topic in ways that made an overly argumentative Israeli feel at home. Perhaps above all else, Walker taught me the importance, and delights, of irreverence and iconoclasm as a form of intervention in a field that sometimes suffers from stultifying assumptions and preoccupations. My most important mentors at UC Davis, however, were perhaps my fellow graduate students, who taught me more than they can know. They also put up with me and my contrarian tendencies. I would especially like to thank Elad Alyagon, Logan Clendening, Andrew Higgins, Juan Carlos Medel Toro, Brenda Medina-Hernandez, Nick Perrone, Rachel Reeves, Marco Rosales, Jordan Scavo, David Stenner, and Laura Tavolacci.

Over these past several years, David Waldstreicher has been another mentor and a guide in the field, ever since I worked with him on an article for the *Journal of the Early Republic*, in his capacity as the journal's editor at that time, and, more recently, as a reader for this book. David's willingness to engage with my ideas and find ways to provide constructive feedback was a revelation, demonstrating how scholarship can be a collaborative endeavor even when it feels quite lonely. Indeed, a good number of folks contributed to this book by reading chapters or providing helpful feedback in other ways. They made the book far better than it would have been otherwise. In this regard, I would like to thank the anonymous reader for Johns Hopkins University Press as well as Elad Alyagon, Boaz Berger, Billy Coleman, Greg Downs, Sean Gallagher, Nick Guyatt, Karen Halttunen, Jonathan Karp, Ari Kelman, Michael Mortimer, Catherine O'Donnell, Ray Raphael, David Roediger, Jordan Scavo, Manisha Sinha, John Smolenski, Alan Taylor, Nan Wolverton, Rosie Zagarri, Michael Zakim, and Nadine Zimmerli. Last but not least, thanks are in order to Robert Brown, Laura Davulis, and Ezra Rodriguez, and everyone else from Johns Hopkins University Press for their time, effort, and faith in the project, and to Robin Surratt for copyediting my manuscript.

I am grateful to my colleagues at California State University, Chico, who have helped make Chico a home as well as a stimulating intellectual environment. I am honored to be part of a faculty that strives to provide students with the best possible education, even though our workloads and working conditions are far from optimal. The department chairs during my time at Chico, Steve Lewis and Robert Tinkler, have supported my work materially and intellectually, while Alisa Wade, the "historiography ninja," has been a comrade in all things early American. In these troubling times, when programs for diversity, equity, and inclusion have come under heinous attack, it feels meaningful to give thanks to READI (Research in Equity, Antiracism, Diversity, and Inclusion), a Chico State program that supported my work with a generous grant.

Most of all, I am greatly indebted to my family, an anchor for this wandering Jew who is not sure what exactly he is. When I came to live in the United States for graduate school, the support and friendship of my aunt and uncle Tamar and Matt and their kids, Eli and Tali, sustained me through a rough start. They have also had a profound influence on my intellectual growth over the years. My sister and brother, Iris and Yuval, and their spouses and kids, Maor, Ariel, Alma, Liana, Maya, and Carmel, have been constant beams of sunshine in my life as we somehow manage to keep close even while physically far apart. My parents, Debbie and Natti, have always been a backbone in all the ways a son could hope. Their love, care, and guidance have been as invaluable from afar as they were when I was closer by. This book is in no small part a product of all that they have instilled in me.

Throughout this journey, my immediate family, who surround me day in and day out, have made everything I do possible. Without them I would be lost. I would like first to thank three furry family members who made my life happier and richer while I worked on this project: Maverick, now deceased, and Connolly and Leon, who have filled my life with so much genuine joy. Finally, I would not have been able to write this book without the constant support of Robin Marie, my best friend as well as my partner in history and activism, a form of crime, I suppose. Morally, intellectually, and in many other ways, she has been my co-thinker and really a co-author. No less important, her love and support have made it possible for me to find the peace of mind and sense of purpose necessary to write this book. I love you, always.

Introduction

1. Mikhail Bakhtin, *Rabelais and His World*, trans. Hélène Iswolski (Bloomington: Indiana University Press, 1984).

2. By "limited violence," I am not suggesting that no violence occurred; several people died that day. Nevertheless, the violence was limited when compared to what took place at Lexington and Concord or what one might expect from a genuine uprising by armed militiamen.

3. For contemporary analysis highlighting the white male profile of the protestors, see Caroline Kitchener, "What Happened at the Capitol Was 'Pure White Male Privilege,'" *Washington Post*, January 6, 2021, https://www.washingtonpost.com/gender-identity/what-happened-at-the-capitol-was-pure-white-male-privilege/; and Catherine Muni, Soroya Chemaly, and Undark, "How Science Explains Trump's Grip on White Males," *Scientific American*, January 14, 2021, https://www.scientificamerican.com/article/how-science-explains-trumps-grip-on-white-males/.

4. For structures of feeling, see Raymond Williams, *Marxism and Literature* (New York: Oxford University Press, 1977), 128–35.

5. For more on violence and Indian play, see chapter four. For more on the masquerade of the Ku Klux Klan, see the epilogue.

6. Edmund S. Morgan, *American Slavery, American Freedom: The Ordeal of Colonial Virginia* (New York: W. W. Norton, 1975), 4. Barbara Fields, "Slavery Race and Ideology in the United States of America," *New Left Review* 181 (May 1990): 113–15. For a similar view in regard to gender ideologies, see Rosemarie Zagarri, *Revolutionary Backlash: Women and Politics in the Early American Republic* (Philadelphia: University of Pennsylvania Press, 2007). For insightful discussions of this paradox in the context of settler colonialism, see Aziz Rana, *The Two Faces of American Freedom* (Cambridge, MA: Harvard University Press, 2010); and Adam Dahl, *Empire of the People: Settler Colonialism and the Foundations of Modern Democratic Thought* (Lawrence: University Press of Kansas, 2018).

7. For nationalism in the early United States, see David Waldstreicher, *In the Midst of Perpetual Fetes: The Making of American Nationalism, 1776–1820* (Chapel Hill: University of North Carolina Press, 1997); Andrew Robertson, "'Look on This Picture . . . And on This!' Nationalism, Localism, and Partisan Images of Otherness in

the United States, 1787–1820," *American Historical Review* 106, no. 4 (Fall 2001): 1263–80; Len Travers, *Celebrating the Fourth: Independence Day and the Rites of Nationalism in the Early Republic* (Amherst: University of Massachusetts Press, 1997). For a broad survey of the question of nationalism in the early United States, see Eran Zelnik, "Self-Evident Walls: Reckoning with Recent Histories of Race and Nation," *Journal of the Early Republic* 41, no. 1 (Spring 2021): 1–38.

8. For more on this, see chapter one.

9. For the Boston Tea Party, see chapter one; for "Jim Crow," see chapter six.

10. Benedict Anderson, *Imagined Communities: Reflections on the Origin and Spread of Nationalism* (London: Verso, 1983).

11. Williams, *Marxism and Literature*, 128–35, quote on 132.

12. Jenette Tandy, *Crackerbox Philosophers in American Humor and Satire* (New York: Columbia University Press, 1925); Constance Rourke, *American Humor: A Study of a National Character* (New York: Harcourt, Brace and Company, 1931); Walter Blair, *Horse Sense in American Humor, from Benjamin Franklin to Ogden Nash* (Chicago: University of Chicago Press, 1942).

13. Lorenzo Veracini, *Settler Colonialism: A Theoretical Overview* (New York: Palgrave Macmillan, 2010), 18. Like Veracini's thinking, my views on settler colonialism have been largely influenced by the work of Patrick Wolfe. See especially Patrick Wolfe, *Settler Colonialism and the Transformation of Anthropology: The Politics and Poetics of an Ethnographic Event* (London: Cassell, 1999); idem, "Settler Colonialism and the Elimination of the Native," *Journal of Genocide Research* 8, no. 4 (December 2006): 387–409; and idem, *Traces of History: Elementary Structures of Race* (London: Verso, 2016). For settler colonialism in North America, see Rana, *Two Faces of American Freedom*; Walter L. Hixson, *American Settler Colonialism: A History* (New York: Palgrave Macmillan, 2013); Dahl, *Empire of the People*; and Jeffrey Ostler and Nancy Shoemaker, "Settler Colonialism in Early American History: Introduction," *William and Mary Quarterly* 76, no. 3 (July 2019): 361–450.

14. Sean Wilentz, *The Rise of American Democracy: Jefferson to Lincoln* (New York: W. W. Norton, 2005), Gordon S. Wood, *The Radicalism of the American Revolution* (New York: Vintage Books, 1992).

15. Morgan, *American Slavery, American Freedom*, 344 and 369 (emphases added).

16. Here I invoke the suggestive formulation of Jeffrey Ostler, *Surviving Genocide: Native Americans and the United States from the American Revolution to Bleeding Kansas* (New Haven, CT: Yale University Press, 2019).

17. Wolfe, "Settler Colonialism and the Elimination of the Native."

18. For this conceptualization of humor, I am especially indebted to Victor Raskin, ed., *The Primer of Humor Research* (Berlin: Mouton de Gruyter, 2008), and Victor Raskin, *Semantic Mechanisms of Humor* (Dordrecht: D. Riedel, 1984); and Mahadev Apte, *Humor and Laughter: An Anthropological Approach* (Ithaca, NY: Cornell University Press, 1985).

19. For "Yankee Doodle," see chapter one; for Royall Tyler and Seba Smith, see chapter three.

20. For a critique of the 1990s scholarship on blackface minstrelsy, see chapter six.

21. Louis Cazamian, *The Development of English Humor* (New York: AMS Press, 1965), 308–30, 387–413.

22. Natalie Zemon Davis, *Society and Culture in Early Modern France* (Stanford: Stanford University Press, 1975), 123.

23. In this conceptualization of vernacular culture, I have been particularly influenced by Alfred Young's scholarship of Euro-American vernacular traditions and Lawrence Levine's scholarship of Black vernacular culture in the early United States. See Alfred F. Young, "English Plebeian Culture and Eighteenth-Century American Radicalism," in *The Origins of Anglo-American Radicalism*, ed. Margaret C. Jacob, James R. Jacob (Boston: Globe Pequot Press, 1984), 185–212, and idem, *Liberty Tree: Ordinary People and the American Revolution* (New York: New York University Press, 2006); Lawrence W. Levine, *Black Culture and Black Consciousness: Afro-American Folk Thought from Slavery to Freedom* (New York: Oxford University Press, 1978).

24. For elite culture in the colonial and early national periods see, Richard Bushman, *The Refinement of America: Persons, Houses, Cities* (New York: Alfred A. Knopf, 1992); for the nineteenth-century United States, see Lawrence W. Levine, *Highbrow/Lowbrow: The Emergence of Cultural Hierarchy in America* (Cambridge, MA: Harvard University Press, 1988).

25. For discussions and examples that suggest the messiness surrounding the term popular culture, see Kathleen Franz and Susan Smulyan, eds., *Major Problems in American Popular Culture* (Boston: Cengage Learning, 2012), and John Storey, *Cultural Theory and Popular Culture: An Introduction* (New York: Routledge, 1997).

26. Zelnik, "Self-Evident Walls." The United States was at the forefront of a broad transition in the West from monarchies to popular forms of sovereignty and nation-states and from economies that mostly relied on the household to ones that increasingly hinged on market forces. For the relationship between structural changes and the rise of nation-states, see Ernst Gellner, *Nations and Nationalism* (Ithaca, NY: Cornell University Press, 1983).

27. For early mass culture, see Michael Denning, *Mechanic Accents: Dime Novels and Working-Class Culture in America* (New York: Verso, 1987), and Richard Ohmann, *Selling Culture: Magazines, Markets, and Class at the Turn of the Century* (New York: Verso, 1996), esp. 11–30.

Part I • Yankees and Gentlemen

1. Oliver Morton Dickinson, ed., *Boston under Military Rule, 1768–1769, as Revealed in* Journal of the Times (Boston: Chapman & Grimes, 1936), 1–2.

2. For Saratoga, see William Gordon, *The History of the Rise, Progress, and Establishment of the Independence of the United States of America*, 4 vols. (London, 1788), 2:574. Though myth has it that the British played "The World Turned Upside Down" as they marched in Yorktown, no contemporary account corroborates this. For the negotiations over the Articles of Capitulation and the attitude of British soldiers in defeat, see George F. Rankin and Hugh F. Scheer, *Rebels and Redcoats: The American Revolution through the Eyes of Those Who Fought and Lived It* (New York: Da Capo Press, 1957), 491–95. For contemporary papers reporting on "Yankee Doodle" at Yorktown, see, for example, "Fish-Kill November 1," *Continental Journal and Weekly Advertiser* (Boston), November 8, 1781.

3. For more on the history of "Yankee Doodle" and its role in the revolution, see Eran Zelnik, "Yankees, Doodles, Fops, and Cuckolds: Compromised Manhood and

Provincialism in the Revolutionary Period, 1740–1781," *Early American Studies* 16, no. 3 (Summer 2018), 514–44.

Chapter 1 • The Joyous Multitude

1. Many considered Lord Bute and George Grenville the forces behind the Stamp Act.

2. In order of appearance, "An Unknown Stamp Act Letter," *Proceedings of the Massachusetts Historical Society* 78 (1966): 140, and for accounts of a longer ditty, n. 4; "Boston, Aug. 19, 1765," in *Extracts from the Itineraries and Other Miscellanies of Ezra Stiles, D.D., LL.D, 1755–1794*, ed. Franklin Bowditch Dexter (New Haven, CT: Yale University Press, 1916), 436; "Extract of a Letter from Boston, in New England, August 26," in *A Collection of Interesting, Authentic Papers Relative to the Dispute between Great Britain and America*, ed. J. Almon (London, 1777), 10; John Rowe, *Letters and Diary of John Rowe*, ed. Anne Rowe Cunningham (Boston: Clarke Company, 1903), 89; "An Unknown Stamp Act Letter," 141.

The burned building was incorrectly thought to be the stamp office. For a summary of the whole affair see, Richard Archer, *As If an Enemy's Country: The British Occupation of Boston and the Origins of the American Revolution* (New York: Oxford University Press, 2010), 24–25. In addition to "joyous multitude," colonial Virginians also used the expression "giddy multitude." On this see, T. H. Breen, "A Changing Labor Force and Race Relations in Virginia," *Journal of Social History* 7, no. 1 (Autumn 1973): 3–25.

3. Pauline Maier, *From Resistance to Revolution: Colonial Radicals and the Development of American Opposition to Britain, 1765–1776* (New York: Norton, 1972), 5.

4. The Acts of Union (1706–7) turned the kingdoms of England and Scotland into Great Britain.

On the idea of a corporation, see Dirk Hoerder, *Crowd Action in Revolutionary Massachusetts, 1765–1780* (New York: Academic Press, 1977), 20–36. For the concept of regulation in North America, see, for example, Terry Bouton, *Taming Democracy: The People, the Founders, and the Troubled Ending of the American Revolution* (New York: Oxford University Press, 2007), 218–19.

5. Alfred F. Young, "English Plebeian Culture and Eighteenth-Century American Radicalism," in *The Origins of Anglo-American Radicalism*, ed. Margaret Jacob and James Jacob (Boston: Globe Pequot Press, 1984), 188.

6. For the resurgence of festive days in eighteenth-century England, see E. P. Thompson, "Patrician Society, Plebeian Culture," *Journal of Social History* 7, no. 4 (Summer 1974): 382–405. For the vitality of the joyous multitude in the eighteenth-century North American British colonies, see Young, "English Plebeian Culture."

7. Peter Oliver, *Origin and Progress of the American Rebellion*, ed. Douglass Adair and John Schutz (San Marino, CA: Huntington Library, 1961), 94.

8. Peter Shaw, *American Patriots and the Rituals of Revolution* (Cambridge, MA: Harvard University Press, 1981), 177–203; Brendan McConville, "Pope's Day Revisited, 'Popular' Culture Reconsidered," *Exploration in Early American Culture* 4 (2000): 258–80.

9. Mikhail Bakhtin, *Rabelais and His World*, trans. Hélène Iswolski (Bloomington: Indiana University Press, 1984), 8 and 11.

10. Bakhtin, *Rabelais and His World*, 10, 81, and 90. For the limits of elite hegemony and crowds in early modern England and Britain, see Peter Laslett, *The World We Have Lost* (New York: Scribner, 1966), 210–28; E. P. Thompson, *Customs in Common* (London: Merlin Press, 1991); George F. E. Rudé, *The Crowd in History: A Study of Popular Disturbances in France and England, 1730–1848* (New York: Wiley, 1964). New Left historians have typically cast Pope Day along the lines noted above. For a useful corrective that argues against over-idealization of Pope Day, see McConville, "Pope's Day Revisited." I tend to view Pope Day as a scene of conflict and negotiation.

11. Rowe, *Letters and Diary*, 114.

12. Shaw, *American Patriots and the Rituals of Revolution*, 177–203; McConville, "Pope's Day Revisited"; Alfred F. Young, "Pope's Day, Tar and Feathers, and 'Cornet Joyce, Jun.': From Ritual to Rebellion in Boston, 1745–1775," *Bulletin of the Society for the Study of Labour History* 27 (1973): 27–39; John Gilmary Shea, "Pope Day in America," *United States Catholic Historical Magazine, 1888*, vol. 2 (New York: Press of the Society, 1888), 1–7.

13. For these dynamics during the revolutionary period, see Maier, *From Resistance to Revolution*; Hoerder, *Crowd Action in Revolutionary Massachusetts*; Benjamin Carp, *Rebels Rising: Cities and the American Revolution* (New York: Oxford University Press, 2007).

14. Quotes from Shea, "Pope Day in America," 3–4; William Gordon, *The History of the Rise, Progress, and Establishment of the Independence of the United States of America*, 4 vols. (London, 1788), 1:177; Gouvernour Morris, *The Diary and Letters of Gouvernour Morris*, ed. Anne Cary Morris, vol. 1 (New York: Charles Scribner's Sons, 1888), 4.

15. Oliver, *Origin and Progress of the American Rebellion*, 94.

16. Shaw, *American Patriots and the Rituals of Revolution*, 21. See also Young, "English Plebeian Culture"; Gary B. Nash, *The Urban Crucible: The Northern Seaports and the Origins of the American Revolution* (Cambridge, MA: Harvard University Press, 1986), 165–66; Paul A. Gilje, *Road to Mobocracy: Popular Disorder in New York City, 1763–1834* (Chapel Hill: University of North Carolina Press, 1987), 16–30.

17. McConville, "Pope's Day Revisited," 274–77.

18. Nicholas Cresswell, *The Journal of Nicholas Cresswell* (New York: The Dial Press, 1924), 44, 128. For an account of Pope Day celebrations, see Shaw, *American Patriots and the Rituals of Revolution*, 177–203, and Shea, "Pope Day in America."

19. Letter from Governor Bernard to the Earl of Shelburne, Boston, March 19, 1768, *Letters to the Ministry from Governor Bernard, General Gage, and Commodore Hood* (Ann Arbor, MI: Ann Arbor Text Creation Partnership, 2011).https://quod.lib.umich.edu/e/evans/N08743.0001.001/1:2.7?rgn=div2;view=fulltext.

20. James Montresor, "The Montresor Journals," *Collections of the Historical Society of New York for the Year 1881* (New York, 1882), 371. Pitt was popular in the colonies and in Liberty Party circles across the British domain at the time. The pole became part of the symbolism surrounding John Wilkes, a radical and popular member of Parliament who stood in support of the colonists and opposition to the king. See, for example, Maier, *From Resistance to Revolution*, 161–97.

21. Alfred F. Young, "Liberty Tree: Made in America, Lost in America," *Liberty Tree: Ordinary People and the American Revolution* (New York: New York University Press, 2006), 325–94.

22. Roger D. Abrahams, "White Indians in Penn's City: The Loyal Sons of St. Tammany," in *Riot and Revelry in Early America*, ed. William Pencak, Matthew Dennis, and Simon P. Newman (University Park: Pennsylvania State University Press, 2002), 179–204.

23. "The Procession, with the Standard of Faction: A Cantata," New York, 1770, Library of Congress, www.loc.gov/item/rbpe.10401200/.

24. Young, "Liberty Tree," 347.

25. For oral traditions in colonial societies see Rhys Isaac, "Dramatizing the Ideology of Revolution: Popular Mobilization in Virginia, 1774–1776, *William and Mary Quarterly* 33, no. 3 (July 1976): 357–85. For the use of signs and symbols in colonial New England, see Robert Blair St. George, *Conversing by Signs: Poetics of Implication in Colonial New England Culture* (Chapel Hill: University of North Carolina Press, 1998).

26. See, for example, Archer, *As If an Enemy's Country*, 36–37.

27. Alfred F. Young, "Ebenezer Mackintosh: Boston's Captain General of the Liberty Tree," in *Revolutionary Founders: Rebels, Radicals, and Reformers in the Making of the Nation*, ed. Alfred F. Young, Gary B. Nash, and Ray Raphael (New York: Vintage Books, 2011), 25.

28. One commentator noted on August 10, 1766, that the Sons of Liberty referred to it as the "tree of liberty." See Montresor, "The Montresor Journals," 382.

29. John Lamb, *Memoir of the Life and Times of General John Lamb: An Officer of the Revolution*, ed. Isaac Q. Leake (Albany, NY, 1850), 37 for quotes, and also see 54–56.

30. "To the Printer," *New York Journal*, March 1, 1770, 1 (supplement).

31. Young, "English Plebeian Culture," 189–94; Benjamin H. Irvin, "Tar, Feathers, and the Enemies of American Liberties," 1768–1776, *New England Quarterly* 76, no. 2 (June 2003): 197–238.

32. *Virginia Gazette* (Williamsburg), July 13, 1769, 2.

33. Alfred F. Young, "Tar and Feathers and the Ghost of Oliver Cromwell: English Plebeian Culture and American Radicalism," *Liberty Tree*, 144–45.

34. Rowe, *Letters and Diary*, 202; Almon, *A Collection of Interesting, Authentic Papers*, 249. Another report put the duration of the affair at six hours. See John Adams, *Legal Papers of John Adams*, ed. L. Kinvin Wroth and Hiller B. Zobel, vol. 1 (Cambridge, MA: Harvard University Press, 1965), 39–40.

35. John Drayton, ed., *Memoirs of the American Revolution: From Its Commencement to the Year 1776, Inclusive*, 2 vols. (Charleston, 1821), 2:17.

36. Gordon, *The History of the Rise, Progress, and Establishment of the Independence of the United States of America*, 1:270

37. *Boston Gazette*, November 20, 1769.

38. Drayton, *Memoirs of the American Revolution*, 2:17

39. *Newport Mercury* (Rhode Island), July 17, 1775.

40. "New London, September 3," *Essex Journal* (Newbury Port, MA), September 14, 1774.

41. Joseph Spencer to Governour Trumbull, East Haddam, September 14, 1774, in *American Archives*, 4th ser., Containing a Documentary History of the English Colonies in North America . . . , ed. Peter Force (Washington, DC, 1837), 1:788.

42. See in Joan D. Dolmetsch, *Rebellion and Reconciliation: Satirical Prints on the Revolution at Williamsburg* (Williamsburg, VA: Colonial Williamsburg Foundation; Charlottesville: Distributed by University Press of Virginia, 1976), 63–64.

43. Morris, *The Diary and Letters of Gouvernour Morris*, 4.

44. Rowe, *Letters and Diary*, 194.

45. The moniker "Boston Tea Party" probably became widespread as part of nationalist American mythology in the 1830s. See Alfred F. Young, *The Shoemaker and the Tea Party: Memory and the American Revolution* (Boston: Beacon Press, 1999), esp. 155–65.

46. Benjamin L. Carp, *Defiance of the Patriots: The Boston Tea Party and the Making of America* (New Haven, CT: Yale University Press, 2010).

47. L. F. S Upton, ed., "Proceedings of Ye Body Respecting the Tea," *William and Mary Quarterly* 22, no. 2 (April 1965): 298.

48. Dr. Samuel Cooper to Dr. Benjamin Franklin, Boston, December 17, 1773, *Collections of the Massachusetts Historical Society*, 4th ser. (Boston, 1858), 4:375.

49. John Andrews to William Barrell, December 18, 1773, *Letters of John Andrews*, ed. Winthrop Sargent (Cambridge, MA,1866), 13.

50. George R. T. Hewes, *A Retrospect of the Boston Tea-Party, with a Memoir of George R. T. Hewes*, ed. James Hawkes (New York, 1834), 38.

51. Francis S. Drake, ed., *Tea Leaves: Being a Collection of Letters and Documents Relating to the Shipment of Tea to the American Colonies in the Year 1773* (Boston: A. O. Crane, 1884), lxxi–lxxii.

52. Carp, *Defiance of the Patriots*, 158.

53. Dr. Cooper to Dr. Franklin, 375; Mercy Warren, *Poems, Dramatic and Miscellaneous* (Boston, 1790), 204. Like the Mohawks, the Tuscarora were part of the League of Six Nations, or the Haudenosaunee Confederacy.

54. Drake, *Tea Leaves*, lxxxviii.

55. Carp, *Defiance of the Patriots*, 95–140.

56. In this chapter and the next, I lowercase *whig* in the context of the thought tradition to distinguish it from the American rebels of the same name and later the Whig Party of the antebellum period.

57. For Augustan humor, see Roger D. Lund, *Ridicule, Religion, and the Politics of Wit in Augustan England* (Burlington, VT: Ashgate, 2012).

58. For homespun humor in America, the classics are Jenette Tandy, *Crackerbox Philosophers in American Humor and Satire* (New York: Columbia University Press, 1925); Constance Rourke, *American Humor: A Study of a National Character* (New York: Harcourt, Brace and Company, 1931); Walter Blair, *Horse Sense in American Humor, from Benjamin Franklin to Ogden Nash* (Chicago: University of Chicago Press, 1942).

59. Carp, *Defiance of the Patriots*, 78–85.

60. According to a letter submitted for publication by loyalists in London, this might have been John Winthrop Jr. See February Meeting, 1898, *Proceedings of the Massachusetts Historical Society* 12, 2nd ser. (1899): 139–42. For more on Joyce Junior, see Young, "Pope's Day Tar and Feathers and 'Cornet Joyce Jun.,'" 29.

61. Young, "Tar and Feathers and the Ghost of Oliver Cromwell," 156–64.

62. For more on forms of Indian play, see chapters three and four.

63. William Bradford, *History of the Plymouth Plantation*, ed. Charles Deane (Boston, 1856), 237. The specter of Thomas Morton and Merry Mount continued to haunt New Englanders for many years, even making its way into Nathaniel Hawthorne's short story "The May-Pole of Merry Mount" (1832).

64. For the nature of settler anxieties and settler culture, see Lorenzo Veracini, *Settler Colonialism: A Theoretical Overview* (New York: Palgrave Macmillan, 2010).

65. Eran Zelnik, "Yankees, Doodles, Fops, and Cuckolds: Compromised Manhood and Provincialism in the Revolutionary Period, 1740–1781," *Early American Studies* 16, no. 3 (Summer 2018): 514–44.

66. Oliver Morton, ed., *Boston under Military Rule (1768–1769) as Revealed in* Journal of the Times (Boston: Chapman & Grimes, 1936), 1, 55, 118–19.

67. Jonathan Edwards, "The Perpetuity and Change of the Sabbath," *The Works of President Edwards*, 4 vols. (New York, 1843), 4:635.

68. Morton, *Boston under Military Rule*, 19–22, 42, 106, 118–19.

69. "Extract of a Letter from a Gentleman in Boston," *Newport (RI) Mercury*, March 27, 1775. See a similar and corroborating account in Sargent, *Letters of John Andrews*, 90.

70. "Description of Thomas Ditson," "Extract of a Letter from Boston to a Gentleman in New York, March 12, 1775," and "Remonstrance Presented by the Selectmen of Billerica to his Excellency General Gage, March 16, 1775," *American Archives*, 4th ser., ed. Peter Force (Washington, DC, 1839), 2:94, 121–22, 153; *Connecticut Courant* (Hartford), May 15, 1775.

71. Sargent, *Letters of John Andrews*, 87, 90. For references to plays from the period, see the discussion of John Burgoyne's "The Boston Blockade," below in this chapter, and in Sargent, *Letters of John Andrews*, 90.

72. John Lax and William Pencak, "The Knowles Riot," *Perspectives in American History* 10 (1976): 163–214.

73. Douglas Edward Leach, "Brothers in Arms? Anglo American Friction at Louisbourg, 1745–1746," *Proceedings of the Massachusetts Historical Society* 89 (1977): 52.

74. Beckles Willson ed., *The Life and Letters of James Wolfe* (London: William Heinemann, 1909), 397.

75. For camaraderie within the ranks of British regulars in the "American Army," see Sylvia Frey, *The British Soldier in America: A Social History of Military Life in the Revolutionary Period* (Austin: University of Texas Press, 1981), 112–32, and Stephen Brumwell, *Redcoats: The British Soldier and War in the Americas, 1755–1763* (Cambridge: Cambridge University Press, 2002), esp. 112–20.

76. Zelnik, "Yankees, Doodles, Fops, and Cuckolds."

77. John Trumbull, *M'Fingal: A Modern Epic Poem. Canto First; or, The Town Meeting* (Philadelphia, 1775), 25–26.

78. Trumbull, *M'Fingal*, 26.

79. Kenneth Silverman, *The Cultural History of the American Revolution: Painting, Music, Literature, and the Theatre in the Colonies and the United States from the Treaty of Paris to the Inauguration of Washington* (New York: Columbia University Press, 1976), 246–423; Bruce Ingham Granger, *Political Satire in the American Revolution, 1763–1783* (Ithaca, NY: Cornell University Press, 1960).

80. Robert Parkinson, *The Common Cause: Creating Race and Nation in the American Revolution* (Chapel Hill: University of North Carolina Press, 2016), 8.

81. Parkinson, *The Common Cause,* traces how racism helped forge the colonists' common cause. For a racial perspective of this period, see chapter four. On how culture helped unite the colonists in opposition to the British, see Ann Fairfax Withington, *Toward a More Perfect Union: Virtue and the Formation of American Republics* (New York: Oxford University Press, 1991).

82. For more on attacks on manhood in print and other media of the period, see Benjamin H. Irvin, *Clothed in Robes of Sovereignty: The Continental Congress and the People Out of Doors* (New York: Oxford University Press, 2011), esp. 52–74.

83. For a biography of Burgoyne, see Richard J. Hargrove, Jr., *General John Burgoyne* (Newark: University of Delaware Press, 1983).

84. Philip Morin Freneau, "A Voyage to Boston, A Poem," Philadelphia, 1775, 10, in reference to the inflated public exchange Burgoyne had with the patriot general Charles Lee through the pages of contemporary newspapers.

85. Philip Morin Freneau, *The Poems of Phillip Freneau* (Philadelphia, 1786), 75.

86. Freneau, "A Voyage to Boston" 21.

87. "A Vaudevil, Sung by the Characters at the Conclusion of a New Farce, called The Boston Blockade," 1776, Boston, ser. 1, Evans 15195, Early American Imprints.

88. Some scholars ascribe *The Blockheads* to Mercy Otis Warren, but there is no consensus.

89. *The Blockheads: Or, the Affrighted Officers* (Boston, 1776).

90. For the politics of virtue during the revolution from a cultural lens, see Withington, *Toward a More Perfect Union.*

91. *The Blockheads,* 10

92. *The Blockheads,* 17, 19.

93. *Pennsylvania Packet* (Philadelphia), January 1, 1776.

94. See, for instance, Gordon, *The History of the Rise, Progress, and Establishment of the Independence of the United States of America,* 279.

95. Wheeler Case, *Poems, Occasioned by Several Circumstances* (New Haven, CT, 1778), 12–16.

96. See, for example, "The Farmer and His Son's Return from a Visit to Camp Together with the Rose Tree," ser. 1, Evans 42034, Early American Imprints.

97. Barry Schwartz, *George Washington: The Making of an American Symbol* (New York: Free Press, 1987).

98. Bernard Bailyn, *The Ideological Origins of the American Revolution* (Cambridge, MA: Harvard University Press, 1992).

Chapter 2 • The Witty Few

1. For elite culture in eighteenth-century British America more broadly, see David Shields, *Civil Tongues and Polite Letters in British America* (Chapel Hill: University of North Carolina Press, 1997), and Richard Bushman, *The Refinement of America: Persons, Houses, Cities* (New York: Vintage Books, 1993).

2. For the Anchor Club, see Leo A Bressler, "The Anchor Club Defender of Federalism," *Pennsylvania Magazine of History and Biography* 80, no. 3 (July 1956): 312–19. For J. S. J. Gardiner, see T. A. Milford, *The Gardiners of Massachusetts:*

Provincial Ambition and the British-American Career (Durham: University of New Hampshire Press, 2005), 175–216. For Thomas Paine (of Boston and later known as Robert Treat Paine Jr.), see *The Works in Verse and Prose of Robert Treat Paine Jun. Esq., with Notes and Sketches of His Life, Character, and Writings* (Boston, 1812), xv–lxxxiv. For the Anthologists see, Catherine O'Donnell, *Men of Letters in the Early Republic: Cultivating Forums of Citizenship* (Chapel Hill: University of North Carolina Press, 2008), 184–215. For Joseph Dennie, see Harold M. Ellis, "Joseph Dennie and His Circle," *Texas Studies in English*, no. 3 (1972), and O'Donnell, *Men of Letters*, 114–83. For Washington Irving and his circle, see Brian Jay Jones, *Washington Irving: An American Original* (New York: Arcade Publishing, 2008), 51–76, and Andrew Burstein, *The Original Knickerbocker: The Life of Washington Irving* (New York: Basic Books, 2007), 47–65. For earlier clubs in the colonial period, see Shields, *Civil Tongues*, 175–208. While I focus on the way humor served elites' purposes, Shields argues that their use of humor and wit helped their goals appear innocuous to the state.

3. *Works of Fisher Ames, Compiled by a Number of His Friends* (Boston, 1809), 1:315.

4. "The Loiterer." *Monthly Anthology*, March 1804.

5. John Ward Fenno, introduction to William Cliffton, *Poems, Chiefly Occasional by the Late Mr. Cliffton*, ed. John Ward Fenno (New York, 1800), vii. For the eighteenth-century wits, "gothic" served as a byword for the collapse of aesthetic standards.

6. "Letters of Thomas Boylston Adams to William Smith Shaw, 1799–1823" Philadelphia, January 6, 1803, *Proceedings of the American Antiquarian Society* 27 (April–October 1917): 172.

7. D. Judson Milburn, *The Age of Wit, 1650–1750* (New York: Macmillan, 1966), 17.

8. Milburn, *The Age of Wit.*

9. I lowercase *whig* here to distinguish whig thought from the Whig Party and the Whigs of the American Revolution. The scholarship of British republicanism and whig thought is vast. For a few influential works, see Isaac Kramnick, *Bolingbroke and His Circle: The Politics of Nostalgia in the Age of Walpole* (Ithaca, NY: Cornell University Press, 1992), J. G. A. Pocock, *The Machiavellian Moment: Florentine Political Thought and the Atlantic Republican Tradition* (Princeton, NJ: Princeton University Press, 1975), and Lawrence Klein, *Shaftesbury and the Culture of Politeness: Moral Discourse and Cultural Politics in Early Eighteenth-Century England* (Cambridge: Cambridge University Press, 1994). For analysis of this historiography in the American context, see Robert E. Shalhope, "Toward a Republican Synthesis: The Emergence of an Understanding of Republicanism in American Historiography" *William and Mary Quarterly* 29, no. 1 (January 1972): 49–70.

10. Milburn, *The Age of Wit*; Shields, *Civil Tongues*, 175–208.

11. For a recent analysis of the 1688 Glorious Revolution, see Steve Pincus, *1688: The First Modern Revolution* (New Haven, CT: Yale University Press, 2009).

12. This class-oriented view of eighteenth-century republicanism combines the historiography of republicanism (see above, note 9) with E. P. Thompson's work. See, especially, E. P. Thompson, "Patrician Society, Plebeian Culture," *Journal of Social History* 7, no. 4 (Summer 1974): 382–405; Milburn, *The Age of Wit.*

13. See, for example, Peter Earle, *The Making of the English Middle Class: Business, Society, and Family Life in London, 1660–1730* (Berkeley: University of California Press, 1989).

14. O'Donnell, *Men of Letters*; Milburn, *The Age of Wit*, 185–225.

15. Linda Kerber, *Federalists in Dissent: Imagery and Ideology in Jeffersonian America* (Ithaca, NY: Cornell University Press, 1970), 2–3.

16. This was a new development in American colleges and owes much to the Hartford Wits, whose influence on the Yale curriculum would steer the college toward embracing more modern (seventeenth- and eighteenth-century) literary models as legitimate subjects. See Kenneth Silverman, *The Cultural History of the American Revolution: Painting, Music, Literature, and the Theatre in the Colonies and the United States from the Treaty of Paris to the Inauguration of Washington* (New York: Columbia University Press, 1976), 218–35.

17. Declaration of Independence, opening paragraph.

18. Leon Howard, *The Connecticut Wits* (Chicago: University of Chicago Press, 1943).

19. Howard, *The Connecticut Wits*, 37–78.

20. Edward J. Larson and Michal P. Winship, eds., *The Constitutional Convention: A Narrative History from the Notes of James Madison* (New York: The Modern Library, 2005), 18.

21. J. K. Van Dover, "The Design of Anarchy: *The Anarchiad*, 1786–1787," *Early American Literature* 24, no. 3 (1989): 238–47.

22. David Humphries, Joel Barlow, John Trumbull, and Dr. Lemuel Hopkins, *The Anarchiad: A New England Poem*, ed. Luther G. Riggs (New Haven, CT, 1862), 4

23. Van Dover, "The Design of Anarchy"; Howard, *The Connecticut Wits*, 169–205.

24. See discussion in James Engell, *The Committed Word: Literature and Public Values* (University Park, PA: Pennsylvania State University Press, 2010), 35–40.

25. David Humphries et al., *The Anarchiad*, 3–7.

26. William Cliffton, "Rhapsody on the Times," in *Poems, Chiefly Occasional by the Late Mr. Cliffton*, 31–32.

27. Cliffton, "Rhapsody on the Times," 32.

28. Cliffton, *Chimeriad*, in *Poems, Chiefly Occasional by the Late Mr. Cliffton*, 66.

29. Cliffton, *Chimeriad*, 66.

30. For partisan poetry in the early republic, see George L. Roth, "Verse Satire on 'Faction,' 1790–1815," *William and Mary Quarterly* 17, no. 4 (October 1960): 473–85; Judith Yaross Lee, "Republican Rhymes: Constitutional Controversy and the Democratization of Verse Satire, 1786–1799," *Studies in American Humor* 2, no. 6 (1988): 30–39; Colin Wells, *Poetry Wars: Verse and Politics in the American Revolution and Early Republic* (Philadelphia: University of Pennsylvania Press, 2018).

31. J. S. J. Gardiner, *Remarks on the Jacobiniad* (Boston, 1795), 7–8.

32. For the Democratic societies and Federalist responses, see David Waldstreicher, *In the Midst of Perpetual Fetes: The Making of American Nationalism, 1776–1820* (Chapel Hill: University of North Carolina Press, 1997), 126–41.

33. Gardiner, *Remarks on the Jacobiniad*, 17, 31, 36–37.

34. Benjamin Franklin's Silence Dogood letters and *Poor Richard's Almanac* essays from earlier in the century employed the same device. Like most of Franklin's other pieces of wit, however, it is hard to regard these as elitist pieces, even if Franklin did employ Augustan forms and at times mild condescension. For more on wit in the public sphere of the colonial era, including a discussion of Franklin's Silence Dogood persona, see Shields, *Civil Tongues*, 175–274.

35. As David Shields, *Civil Tongues*, 175–208, notes, for British literati during the Augustan period, casting themselves as noncommittal humorists also provided helpful cover in staving off state persecution of speech challenging state power. .

36. Joseph Dennie, *The Farrago*, ed. Bruce Ingham Granger (Delmar, NY: Scholars Facsimiles and Reprints, 1985), 10, 23.

37. James Kirke Paulding, William Irving, and Washington Irving, *Salmagundi: Or, the Whim-Whams and Opinions of Launcelot Longstaff, Esq. and Others*, vol. 1, 1814, 15–16. It is quite telling that the words *farrago* and *salmagundi* evoke similar ideas of a medley; both were suggestive of a commitment not to commit to any form of serious reporting.

38. Ellis, "Joseph Dennie and His Circle," 43–68; Jones, *Washington Irving*, 51–76; Burstein, *The Original Knickerbocker*, 47–65; Ralph M. Aderman, and Wayne R. Kime, *Advocate for America: The Life of James Kirke Paulding* (Selinsgrove, PA: Susquehanna University Press, 2003), 42–51.

39. Joseph Dennie, *The Letters of Joseph Dennie, 1768–1812*, ed. Laura Green Peddler (Orono: University of Maine Press, 1936), 158.

40. Ellis, "Joseph Dennie and His Circle," 84–109; O'Donnell, *Men of Letters*, 114–39.

41. Ellis, "Joseph Dennie and His Circle," 84–109; O'Donnell, *Men of Letters*, 114–39.

42. Milford, *The Gardiners of Massachusetts*, 175–216; Dennie, *The Letters of Joseph Dennie*, 182–85; Robert Treat Paine Jr., *The Works in Verse and Prose of the Late Robert Treat Paine Jun. Esq.* (Boston, 1812), lxxi.

43. Paine, *The Works*, lxx.

44. Thomas Robbins, *The Diary of Thomas Robbins*, ed. Increase N. Tarbox, 2 vols. (Boston: Beacon Press, 1886), 1:114, 118.

45. *Works of Fisher Ames*, 319, 328; Elkins and McKitrick, *The Age of Federalism*; Kerber, *Federalists in Dissent*; Joyce Appleby, *Capitalism and a New Social Order: The Republican Vision of the 1790s* (New York: New York University Press, 1984), 1–23.

46. See, especially, David Waldstreicher, *In the Midst of Perpetual Fetes*, and Andrew Robertson, "'Look on This Picture . . . and on This!' Nationalism, Localism, and Partisan Images of Otherness in the United States, 1787–1820," *American Historical Review* 106, no. 4 (Fall 2001): 1263–80.

47. For studies that stress sectionalism, see Trish Loughran, *The Republic in Print: Print Culture in the Age of U.S. Nation Building, 1770–1870* (New York: Columbia University Press, 2007), and Benjamin E. Park, *American Nationalisms: Imagining Union in the Age of Revolutions, 1783–1833* (New York: Cambridge University Press, 2018).

48. On Barlow, see Richard Buel Jr., *Joel Barlow: American Citizen in a Revolutionary World* (Baltimore: Johns Hopkins University Press, 2011).

49. Robert Edson Lee, "Timothy Dwight and the Boston Palladium," *New England Quarterly* 35, no. 2 (June 1962): 229–39.

50. Dennie, *The Letters of Joseph Dennie*, 159, 182–85.

51. For more on foreign views in this vein, see chapter five.

52. "Virginian" is a reference to Thomas Jefferson and James Madison. "The Lay Preacher," *Farmer's Weekly Museum* (Walpole, NH), January 19, 1796; "From the Shop of Mess. Colon and Spondee," *Farmer's Weekly Museum*, May 9, 1797, 4; "The Lay Preacher," *Farmer's Weekly Museum*, May 2, 1797, 4.

53. James Kirke Paulding, William Irving, and Washington Irving, *Salmagundi*, vol. 1, 1807, 11, 15–16.

54. Jones, *Washington Irving*, 51–76; Burstein, *The Original Knickerbocker*, 47–65; Aderman, and Kime, *Advocate for America*, 42–51.

55. "The Lay Preacher," *Farmer's Weekly Museum*, December 22, 1795; "Dr Franklin," *Farmer's Weekly Museum*, January 17, 1797.

56. Gordon Wood, *The Americanization of Benjamin Franklin* (New York: Penguin Books, 2004), 234; William Cobbett, *Porcupine's Works*, 12 vols. (London, 1801), 7:245; "The Remarker," *Monthly Anthology*, December 1805.

57. Wood, *The Americanization of Benjamin Franklin*, 230–35.

58. Appleby, *Capitalism and a New Social Order*; Gordon S. Wood, *The Radicalism of the American Revolution* (New York: Vintage Books, 1992); Drew McCoy, *The Elusive Republic: Political Economy in Jeffersonian America* (Chapel Hill: University of North Carolina Press, 1980).

59. Paine, *The Works*, xxxv–xxxvi, lxxiii.

60. "Posthumi," *New England Galaxy & Masonic Magazine*, vol. 1, no. 41, July 24, 1818, 2; Milford, *The Gardiners of Massachusetts*, 186–87.

61. Ellis, "Joseph Dennie and His Circle."

62. For Augustan satire employed by Federalists, see Kerber, *Federalists in Dissent*, 1–22, and William C. Dowling, *Literary Federalism in the Age of Jefferson: Joseph Dennie and the Port Folio, 1801–1812* (Columbia: University of South Carolina Press, 1999). For "arch Federalists," see the discussion of "old school" Federalist in David Hackett Fischer, *The Revolution of American Conservatism: The Federalist Party in the Era of Jeffersonian Democracy* (New York: Harper and Row, 1965), 1–28.

63. *Catalogue of the Honorary and Immediate Members and of the Library of the Porcellian Club of Harvard University* (Cambridge, MA: Allen and Farnham, 1850), 11. For college clubs during the colonial period, see Shields, *Civil Tongues*, 209–74.

64. Ellis, "Joseph Dennie and His Circle"; O'Donnell, *Men of Letters*, 114–83.

65. A clear example of Dennie's influence is Irving's growth as an essayist. Several years earlier, when writing his first, Irving had adopted the pseudonym Jonathan Oldstyle, inspired by Dennie's Oliver Oldschool persona.

66. "Levity," *The Port Folio*, vol. 6, no. 18, October 29, 1808, 8.

67. Jones, *Washington Irving*, 51–76; Burstein, *The Original Knickerbocker*, 47–65; Aderman, and Kime, *Advocate for America*, 42–51.

68. "Distressing," *Evening Post* (New York), October 26, 1809; "To the Editor of the Evening Post," *Evening Post* (New York), November 6, 1809.

69. For a literary analysis of *A History of New York*, see Marty Roth, *Comedy and America: The Lost World of Washington Irving* (Port Washington, NY: Kennikat Press, 1976), esp. 114–54.

70. Washington Irving, *A History of New York from the Beginning of the World to the End of the Dutch Dynasty, by Diedrich Knickerbocker*, 2 vols. (New York, 1809), 1:120.

71. Irving, *A History of New York*, 1:138–39.

72. Irving, *A History of New York*, 1:243–46.

73. Irving, *A History of New York*, 1:214.

74. Irving, *A History of New York*, 2:179–80.

75. For more on the conflict between Yorkers and Yankees, see Dixon Ryan Fox, *Yankees and Yorkers* (New York: New York University Press, 1940).

76. See, for example, the discussion of Irving as a mythmaker for New York in Edwin G. Burrows and Mike Wallace, *Gotham: A History of New York* (New York: Oxford University Press, 1999), xi–xxiv.

77. Washington Irving, *History, Tales, and Sketches* (New York: The Library of America, 1983), 783.

78. This theme continues in chapter five. For the recalibration of Federalist views in the wake of the War of 1812, see Marshall Foletta, *Coming to Terms with Democracy: Federalist Intellectuals and the Shaping of an American Culture, 1800–1828* (Charlottesville: University of Virginia Press, 2001).

Part II • From Backcountry to Frontier

1. Pierre Nora, "Between Memory and History: Les lieux de mémoire," *Representations* 26 (Spring 1989): 12. This discussion of memory is also inspired by Peter Fritzsche, *Stranded in the Present: Modern Time and the Melancholy of History* (Cambridge, MA: Harvard University Press, 2010).

2. For a comprehensive history of the memory of the American Revolution over the past 250 years, see Michael D. Hattem, *The Memory of '76: The Revolution in American History* (New Haven, CT: Yale University Press, 2024). For the memory of the revolution in the early national period, see Sarah J. Purcell, *Sealed with Blood: War, Sacrifice, and Memory in Revolutionary America* (Philadelphia: Pennsylvania University Press, 2002).

3. For the fiction and reality behind the myth of the minutemen, see John R. Galvin, *The Minute Men, The First Fight: Myths and Realities of the American Revolution* (Washington, DC: Potomac, 2006). Contrary to myth, the Massachusetts minutemen were well trained and on the whole more battle tested than their opponent, as many of them were veterans of the Seven Years' War; almost none of the British regulars had combat experience. Moreover, the minutemen had been training for precisely such a moment for a year or so, including several mobilization efforts in response to British probes that effectively functioned as dry runs in the lead up to April 19. They were also probably equipped equally as well as the British, with reliable muskets and ample ammunition and many with bayonets. The notion that the militias were heavily outnumbered by the British is inaccurate as well. Although numerically the minutemen, especially early on, were a smaller force, during the retreat from Concord back to Boston, they quickly outnumbered the British. By most estimates, by the time they reached Charles Town, there were 4,000 militiamen as opposed to some 1,500 British regulars. The original British force, before Percy's reinforcements arrived during the retreat, had only been about half that number.

Chapter 3 • Laughter in the Wilderness

1. For the myth and reality of these events, see Robert A. Gross, *The Minutemen and Their World* (New York: Hill and Wang, 1976), and John R. Galvin, *The Minute Men: The First Fight. Myths and Realities of the American Revolution* (Washington, DC: Potomac Books, 2006).

2. For the "joyous multitude," see chapter one. Thomas Gage to Earl of Dartmouth, September 2, 1774, Boston, *Documents of the American Revolution 1770–1783*, 21 vols., Colonial Office Series (Dublin, 1972–81), 8:182.

3. Frank Moore, *The Diary of the American Revolution* (Hartford, CT, 1876), 37–38.

4. For the Black Boys, see Patrick Spero, *Frontier Rebels: The Fight for Independence in the American West, 1765–1776* (New York: Norton, 2018). For the Paxton Boys, see Peter Silver, *Our Savage Neighbors: How Indian War Transformed Early America* (New York: Norton, 2008), 73–190, and Kevin Kenny, *Peaceable Kingdom Lost: The Paxton Boys and the Destruction of William Penn's Holy Experiment* (New York: Oxford University Press, 2009). For the Regulators, see Marjoleine Kars, *Breaking Loose Together: The Regulator Rebellion in Pre-Revolutionary North Carolina* (Chapel Hill: University of North Carolina Press, 2002). For Shays' Rebellion, see Leonard L. Richards, *Shays's Rebellion: The American Revolution's Final Battle* (Philadelphia: University of Pennsylvania Press, 2002). For the Whiskey Rebellion, see Thomas P. Slaughter, *The Whiskey Rebellion: Frontier Epilogue to the American Revolution* (New York: Oxford University Press, 1986).

5. For the New Jersey land riots, see Thomas L. Purvis, "Origins and Patters of Agrarian Unrest in New Jersey, 1735–1754," *William and Mary Quarterly* 39, no. 4 (October 1982): 600–627. For the New York anti-renters, see Sung Bok Kim, *Landlord and Tenant in Colonial New York Manorial Society, 1664–1775* (Chapel Hill: University of North Carolina Press, 1978). For the Green Mountain Boys, see Michael A. Bellesiles, *Revolutionary Outlaws: Ethan Allen and the Struggle for Independence on the Early American Frontier* (Charlottesville: University of Virginia Press, 1993). For the Wyoming controversy, see Paul B. Moyer, *Wild Yankees: The Struggle for Independence along Pennsylvania's Revolutionary Frontier* (Ithaca, NY: Cornell University Press, 2007). For Maine, see Alan Taylor, *Liberty Men and Great Proprietors: The Revolutionary Settlement on the Maine Frontier, 1760–1820* (Chapel Hill: University of North Carolina Press, 1990).

6. For a lengthier list of rural revolts that also analyzes them along different lines, see Taylor, *Liberty Men*, 4–7; Slaughter, *The Whiskey Rebellion*, 29–45.

7. One obvious outlier here is Bellesiles, *Revolutionary Outlaws*, which portrays the struggle of the Green Mountain Boys as largely successful by creating a democratic alternative in Vermont.

8. The most famous account of democratization in this vein is Gordon Wood, *The Radicalism of the American Revolution* (New York: Vintage Books, 1991). See also Joyce Appleby, *Inheriting the Revolution: The First Generation of Americans* (Cambridge, MA: Harvard University Press, 2000), and Sean Wilentz, *The Rise of American Democracy: Jefferson to Lincoln* (New York: Norton, 2005).

9. Raymond Williams, *Marxism and Literature* (Oxford: Oxford University Press, 1977), 128–35, quote on 132.

10. Eric Hobsbawm, *Bandits* (New York: Pantheon Books, 1981); Philip Deloria, *Playing Indian* (New Haven, CT: Yale University Press, 1998), 22; E. P. Thompson, *Whigs and Hunters: The Origin of the Black Act* (New York: Pantheon Books, 1975); Douglas Hay, "Poaching and the Game Laws on Cannock Chase," in *Albion's Fatal*

Tree: Crime and Society in Eighteenth Century England, ed. Douglas Hay et al. (New York: Pantheon Books, 1975), 189–253.

11. The legend of Robin Hood had been commonplace in English folklore, particularly in ballads, at least since the fifteenth century.

12. Deloria, *Playing Indian*, 10–37.

13. William Little, *History of Weare, New Hampshire, 1735–1888* (Lowell, MA, 1888), 191.

14. Jeremy Belknap, *The History of New Hampshire* (Carlisle, MA, 1784), 2:89–90; Isaac W. Hammond, *The State of New Hampshire, Miscellaneous Provincial and State Papers, 1725–1800* (Manchester, NH, 1890), 18:53. Also see, Joseph J. Malone, *Pine Trees and Politics: The Naval Stores and Forest Policy in Colonial New England, 1691–1775* (Seattle: University of Washington Press, 1965), 110–13.

15. Strother E. Roberts, "Pines, Profits, and Popular Politics: Responses to the White Pine Acts in the Colonial Connecticut River Valley," *New England Quarterly* 83, no. 1 (March 2010): 90–95.

16. Little, *History of Weare, New Hampshire*, 188–91.

17. Purvis, "Origins and Patterns of Agrarian Unrest in New Jersey," 600.

18. See note 5.

19. Taylor, *Liberty Men and Great Proprietors*, 181–207, and Moyer, *Wild Yankees*, 13–93.

20. Deloria, *Playing Indian*.

21. James Smith, "An Account of the Remarkable Occurrences in the Life and Travels of Col. James Smith, during His Captivity with the Indians," *Ohio Valley Historical Series*, no. 5 (Cincinnati, 1907), 110.

22. Smith, "An Account," 110–11; "Deposition of Lt. Charles Grant, 1765," *Pennsylvania Archives*, 1st ser., ed. Samuel Hazard (Philadelphia: J. Severns, 1852–56), 4:220–22; "Deposition of Leonard McGlashen, &c., 1765," in Hazard, *Pennsylvania Archives*, 1st ser., 4:233–36; "Extract of a Letter from Lieutenant Colonel Reid, June 4, 1765," *Pennsylvania Archives: Colonial Records* (Harrisburg, PA, 1851–53), 9:269.

23. "Deposition of Lt. Charles Grant, 1765," 4:221–22. According to the account Smith published years later, the prisoners held in Fort Loudon were released only after an exchange had been agreed upon. See Smith, "An Account," 111–12. Other accounts suggest they were released with bail. While Grant's deposition is suspiciously silent on these particulars, Colonel Read, his commanding officer, informed General Gage that they were "released upon bail." See "Extract of a Letter from Lt. Col. Reid," 9:269.

24. "A Letter from General Gage to the Governor New York, June 16, 1765," *Pennsylvania Archives: Colonial Records*, 9:267; "Sir William Johnson to Gov. Penn, April 12, 1765," in Hazard, *Pennsylvania Archives*, 1st ser., 4:215–16. For a broad examination of the affair, see Spero, *Frontier Rebels*.

25. "Sir William Johnson to Gov. Penn, April 12,1765," 4:215–16, and "Deposition of Lt. Grant, 1765," 4:221–22; "Extract of a Letter from Lt. Col. Reid, June 4, 1765," 9:268.

26. Smith, "An Account," 110, 120–23. For evidence of the raid on an Indian goods convoy, see "Philadelphia," *Pennsylvania Chronicle* (Philadelphia), August 14, 1769.

27. Bellesiles, *Revolutionary Outlaws*.

28. "Public Disorders Fomented by N. Hampshire," in *The Documentary History of the State of New York*, ed. E. B. O'Callaghan (Albany, NY, 1849–51), 4:420.

29. James Duane, *A Narrative of the Proceedings Subsequent to the Royal Adjudication, concerning Lands to be Westward of the Connecticut River, Lately Usurped by New Hampshire* (New York, 1773), 13.

30. "Deposition of Samuel Gardenier, of Wallumscock concerning the Injuries He Received from the Bennington Rioters," in Duane, *A Narrative of the Proceedings*, appendix.

31. Duane, *A Narrative of the Proceedings*, 15.

32. Ira Allen, *The Natural and Political History of the State of Vermont* (London, 1798), 29.

33. "Affidavits," in O'Callaghan, *The Documentary History of the State of New York*, 4:514.

34. For blasphemy in colonial America, see Susan Juster, *Sacred Violence in Early America* (Philadelphia: University of Pennsylvania Press, 2016), 126–91. For a broad discussion of the "speech economy" of colonial Massachusetts, see Kristin A. Olbertson, *The Dreadful Word: Speech Crime and Polite Gentlemen in Massachusetts, 1690–1776* (New York: Cambridge University Press, 2022).

35. O'Callaghan, *A Documentary History of the State of New York*, 4:453–54. For Ethan Allen's religious beliefs, see Bellesiles, *Revolutionary Outlaws*, esp. 217–44.

36. O'Callaghan, *A Documentary History of the State of New York*, 4:520–25.

37. "Advertisement," *Pennsylvania Archives: Colonial Records*, 9:271.

38. "Tom the Tinker's Notice to John Reed," *Pennsylvania Archives*, 2nd ser., ed. John B. Linn and William Henry Egle (Harrisburg, PA, 1874–90), 4:61–62.

39. H. H. Brackenridge, *Incidents of the Insurrection*, ed. Daniel Marder (New Haven, CT: College and University Press, 1972), 126–27.

40. Brackenridge, *Incidents of the Insurrection*, 169.

41. Taylor, *Liberty Men and Great Proprietors*, 189.

42. Taylor, *Liberty Men and Great Proprietors*, 186.

43. For frontier republicanism, see Bellesiles, *Revolutionary Outlaws*, 105–6; Taylor, *Liberty Men and Great Proprietors*, 89–114. For the Anglo-American revolutionary Atlantic and radical republicanism, see Isaac Kramnick, *Republicanism and Bourgeois Radicalism: Political Ideology in Late Eighteenth-Century England and America* (Ithaca, NY: Cornell University Press, 1990); and Seth Cotlar, *Tom Paine's America: The Rise and Fall of Transatlantic Radicalism in the Early Republic* (Charlottesville: University of Virginia Press, 2011). For the emergence of a self-described democratic creed in the 1790s, see Matthew Rainbow Hale, "Regenerating the World: The French Revolution, Civic Festivals, and the Forging of Modern American Democracy, 1793–1795," *Journal of American History* 103, no. 4 (March 2017): 891–920.

44. Ezekiel Russell, "A Bloody Butchery, by the British Troops: or, The Runaway Fight of the Regulars," 1775, ser. 1, Evans 13839, Early American Imprints.

45. "Letter II, Boston April 22, 1775," and "Extract of a letter from a Gentleman of Rank in New England, dated April 25, 1775," in *Letters on the American Revolution*, ed. Margaret Wheeler Willard (New York, 1925), 86–87, 92.

46. John Leacock, *The Fall of British Tyranny, or, American Liberty Triumphant* (Providence, RI, 1776), 32, 34. Leacock uses animals in the parable.

47. "Massachusetts Bay, Worcester, May 10," *Connecticut Courant* (Hartford), May 15, 1775.

48. John Trumbull, *M'fingal: A Modern Epic Poem. Canto First, or the Town Meeting* (Philadelphia, 1775), 1.

49. William Gordon, *The History of the Rise Progress and Establishment of the Independence of the United States of America*, 4 vols. (London, 1788), 1:481.

50. Mercy Otis Warren, *History of the Rise, Progress, and Termination of the American Revolution*, 3 vols. (Boston, 1805), 1:185–87.

51. Ralph Waldo Emerson, "Concord Hymn" (1836); Henry Wadsworth Longfellow, "Paul Revere's Ride" (1861). For emerging patterns of memory surrounding Lexington and Concord, see Sarah J. Purcell, *Sealed with Blood: War, Sacrifice, and Memory in Revolutionary America* (Philadelphia: Pennsylvania University Press, 2002), 41–44, 67–68, 125–26, 204–5.

52. Dorinda Outram, *Four Fools in the Age of Reason: Laughter, Cruelty, and Power in Early Modern Germany* (Charlottesville: University of Virginia Press, 2019), 2.

53. The classic study of the meanings and tensions surrounding city and country in the British tradition is Raymond Williams, *The Country and the City* (London: Oxford University Press, 1973).

54. The refrain "Yankee Doodle Dandy" probably became common during the revolutionary period. See Eran Zelnik, "Yankees, Doodles, Fops, and Cuckolds: Compromised Manhood and Provincialism in the Revolutionary Period, 1740–1781," *Early American Studies* 16, no. 3 (Summer 2018): 523–24. The earliest dated references to the stanza about Yankee Doodle coming to town riding on a pony and putting a feather in his hat are from the nineteenth century. It is possible, however, that the stanza was written in the 1780s, when the word *macaroni* was in use as a comical reference to elaborate wigs and by implication to outrageous cosmopolitan fops who traveled to Italy. O. G. Sonneck, *Report on the Star-Spangled Banner, Hail Columbia, America, and Yankee Doodle* (New York: Dover Publications, 1972), 125–30. The word *dandy* at the time was increasingly associated with the stereotype of the fop (alongside a host of other words with a similar meaning, such as *coxcomb, beau,* and *rake*) and by the mid-nineteenth century had become the most familiar term for such posturing.

55. Royall Tyler, *The Contrast: Manners, Morals, and Authority in the Early American Republic*, ed. Cynthia Kierner (New York: New York University Press, 2007). For a biography of Tyler, see Thomas G. Tanselle, *Royall Tyler* (Cambridge, MA: Harvard University Press, 1967), 21–23, for this episode.

56. By "sturgeons," Jonathan meant "insurgents." Tyler often has Jonathan mispronounce words as a comical device.

57. Tyler, *The Contrast*, 61–62. For a comprehensive discussion of Brother Jonathan as an American icon, see Winifred Morgan, *An American Icon: Brother Jonathan and American Identity* (Newark: University of Delaware Press, 1988).

58. For the man of feeling and sensibility in the American Revolution and the early republic, see Sarah Knott, *Sensibility and the American Revolution* (Chapel Hill: University of North Carolina Press, 2009).

59. Tyler, *The Contrast*, 56.

60. *The Daily Advertiser* (New York), April 14, 1787. For the comic tradition in early American theater, see Daniel F. Havens, *The Columbian Muse of Comedy: The Develop-

ment of a Native Tradition in Early American Social Comedy, 1787–1845 (Carbondale: Southern Illinois University Press, 1973), and Francis Hodge, *Yankee Theater: The Image of the American on Stage, 1825–1850* (Austin: University of Texas Press, 1964).

61. Jeffrey H. Richards, *Drama, Theatre, and Identity in the American New Republic* (New York: Cambridge University Press, 2005), 60–84, 188–210.

62. For *The Contrast* as a comedy of manners, see Donald T. Siebert Jr., "Royall Tyler's 'Bold Example': The Contrast and the English Comedy of Manners," *Early American Literature* 13, no. 1 (1978): 3–11.

63. For a discussion of various "Yankee Doodle" stanzas, see Sonneck, *Report on the Star-Spangled Banner*. For "as thick as mustard" and "the nation" in the play, see Tyler, *The Contrast*, 71–72.

64. Tyler, *The Contrast*, 75

65. Tyler, *The Contrast*, 73, 96.

66. See, for example, comments on *The Contrast* and Jonathan in William Dunlap, *History of the American Theatre* (London, 1833), 127, 137.

67. Hodge, *Yankee Theater*.

68. On this, see chapter five.

69. Seba Smith, *The Life and Writings of Major Jack Downing* (Boston, 1834), 56.

70. Smith, *The Life and Writings of Major Jack Downing*, 124.

71. See Milton Rickels and Patricia K. Rickels, *Seba Smith* (Boston: Twayne Publishers, 1977), 24–71.

72. John William Ward, *Andrew Jackson, Symbol for an Age* (New York: Oxford University Press, 1955), 79–91, and Rickels and Rickels, *Seba Smith*.

73. On Jackson's reaction, see Rickels and Rickels, *Seba Smith*, 54. Supporting the argument on anti-intellectualism and the *Jack Downing Letters*, see Ward *Andrew Jackson, Symbol for an Age*, 79–91.

Chapter 4 • The Laughter and the Fury

1. "Extract of an Authentic Letter from an Officer of the Army at Boston, to a Friend in London, Dated April 20, 1775," and "Letter II," in *Letters on the American Revolution*, ed. Margaret Wheeler Willard (New York: Houghton Mifflin, 1925), 76–77, 84–85.

2. For the *"rage militaire"* of 1775, see Charles Royster, *A Revolutionary People at War: The Continental Army and American Character, 1775–1783* (Chapel Hill: University of North Carolina Press, 1979), 25–53.

3. "Extract of Letter from Philadelphia, April 28," and "Extract of a Letter from a Gentleman in Stafford County, Virginia to His Friend in London, Dated Aug. 20, 1775," in Willard, *Letters on the American Revolution*, 95, 202.

4. John Grenier, *The First Way of War: American War Making on the Frontier, 1607–1814* (New York: Cambridge University Press, 2005), 5. For the concept of the skulking way of war, see Patrick M. Malone, *The Skulking Way of War: Technology and Tactics among the New England Indians* (London: Madison Books, 1991).

5. Wayne E. Lee, *The Cutting-Off Way: Indigenous Warfare in Eastern North America, 1500–1800* (Chapel Hill: University of North Carolina Press, 2023), esp. 15–69.

6. Patrick Wolfe, "Settler Colonialism and the Elimination of the Native," *Journal of Genocide Research* 8, no. 4 (December 2006): 387–409.

7. See, for example, Sharon V. Salinger, *Taverns and Drinking in Early America* (Baltimore: Johns Hopkins University Press, 2002), 74–75, 125. On such behavior during the revolution, see Philip Vickers Fithian, *Journal 1775–1776: Written on the Virginia-Pennsylvania Frontier and in the Army around New York*, ed. Robert Greenhalgh Albion and Leonidas Dodson (Princeton, NJ: Princeton University Press, 1934), 158.

8. *The Life of Timothy Pickering*, ed. Octavius Pickering (Boston, 1867), 1:26–27.

9. This is in part inspired by the conceptualization of the relationship between the German notion of *heimat* and the nation in Alon Confino, *The Nation as a Local Metaphor: Württemberg, Imperial Germany, and National Memory, 1871–1918* (Chapel Hill: University of North Carolina Press, 1997).

10. For the militia in republican American and British thought, see Robert Churchill, *To Shake Their Guns in the Tyrant's Face: Libertarian Political Violence and the Origins of the Militia Movement* (Ann Arbor: University of Michigan Press, 2009), 27–56; Noah Shusterman, *Armed Citizens: The Road from Ancient Rome to the Second Amendment* (Charlottesville: University of Virginia Press, 2020).

11. Grenier, *The First Way of War*; Kyle Zelner, *A Rabble in Arms: Massachusetts Towns and Militiamen during King Philip's War* (New York: New York University Press, 2009).

12. Fred Anderson, *A People's Army: Massachusetts Soldiers and Society in the Seven Years' War* (Chapel Hill: University of North Carolina Press, 1984), 27.

13. Anderson, *A People's Army*.

14. "Extract of a Letter from New York, Dated May 2," in Willard, *Letters on the American Revolution*, 99; H. H. Brackenridge, *The Battle of Bunker Hill: A Dramatic Piece in Five Acts* (Philadelphia, 1776), 12. See discussion of the enthusiasm surrounding riflemen in Royster, *A Revolutionary People at War*, 34.

15. See, for example, George Washington to John Hancock, September 25, 1776, *Founders Online*, National Archives, https://founders.archives.gov/documents/Washington/03-06-02-0305. For the challenges the militia posed for patriot leaders in Virginia, see Michael A. McDonell, *The Politics of War: Race, Class, and Conflict in Revolutionary Virginia* (Chapel Hill: University of North Carolina Press, 2007). For Andrew Jackson and the militia tradition, see chapter five.

16. Grenier, *The First Way of War*, 16–52. Lee, *The Cutting-Off Way*, 15–34, offers an important corrective: although modeled after Native ways of war, the guerrilla warfare the settlers adopted was in fact a hybrid that combined assumptions of European objectives and values regarding warfare with Native methods of fighting in the eastern woodlands.

17. Grenier, *The First Way of War*, 53–86, 115–45.

18. "New York, April 3," *Penn Gazette* (Philadelphia), April 6, 1758.

19. "The Virginia Centinel, no. XVI," *Penn Gazette* (Philadelphia), March 17, 1757.

20. Benjamin Franklin, "The Autobiography," in *A Benjamin Franklin Reader*, ed. Walter Isaacson (New York: Simon and Schuster, 2003), 522–53.

21. "The Speech of his Excellency William Franklin, Burlington, November 16, 1763," *New Jersey Archives*, 1st ser., ed. William Nelson (Patterson, NJ, 1902), 24: 277.

22. "Narrative of Ensign D'Bernicre," *American Archives,* 4th ser., ed. Peter Force (Washington, DC, 1833), 1:1265–66.

23. Daniel P. Martson, "Swift and Bold: The 60th Regiment and Warfare in North America" (master's thesis, McGill University, 1997).

24. Jeffrey Amherst, *Amherst and the Conquest of Canada*, ed. Richard Middleton (Stroud, UK: Army Records Society, 2003), 17. For the makeup of the 80th, see John Richard Alden, *General Gage in America: Being Principally a History of His Role in the American Revolution* (Baton Rouge: Louisiana State University Press, 1948), 42.

25. George Washington to Henry Bouquet, July 3, 1758, *Founders Online*, National Archives, https://founders.archives.gov/documents/Washington/02-05-02-0199. For more on changing British military tactics and adoption of ranger warfare during the period, see Steve Brumwell, "'A Service Truly Critical': The British Army and Warfare with the North American Indians, 1755–1764, *War in History* 5, no. 2 (April 1998): 146–75; Matthew C Ward, "'The European Method of Warring Is Not Practiced Here': The Failure of the British Military Policy in the Ohio Valley, 1755–1759," *War in History* 4, no. 3 (July 1997): 247–63; David L. Preston, "'Make Indians of Our White Men': British Soldiers and Indian Warriors from Braddock's to Forbes's Campaigns, 1755–1758," *Pennsylvania History* 74, no. 3 (Summer 2007): 280–306; Grenier, *The First Way of War*, 115–45.

26. Colonel Henry Bouquet to Colonel Adam Stephen, July 4, 1764, *The Papers of Henry Bouquet*, ed. Sylvester K. Stevens and Donald H. Kent (Harrisburg, PA: Pennsylvania Department of Public Instruction 1941), 14:7, 32–33.

27. *Letters of John Andrews Esq. of Boston*, ed. Winthrop Sargent (Cambridge, MA, 1866), 58.

28. Fithian, *Journal 1775–1776*, 24.

29. Frank Moore, *Diary of the American Revolution from Newspapers and Original Documents* (New York, 1860), 1:121–22.

30. Moore, *Diary of the American Revolution from Newspapers and Original Documents*, 1:122–23.

31. "Extract of a Letter from Norfolk, Virginia, July 19," in Willard, *Letters on the American Revolution*, 171. For more on the rage militaire, see Royster, *A Revolutionary People at War*, 25–53.

32. For more on the triangular settler colonial structure and its implications, see Lorenzo Veracini, *Settler Colonialism: A Theoretical Overview* (New York: Palgrave Macmillan, 2010).

33. Kathleen Brown, "The Anglo-Algonquian Gender Frontier," in *Negotiators of Change: Historical Perspectives on Native American Women*, ed. Nancy Shoemaker (New York: Routledge, 1995), 27.

34. Fortescue Cummings, "Sketches of a Tour to the Western Country," in *Early Western Travels, 1748–1846*, ed. Reuben Gold Thwaites (Cleveland: Arthur H. Clark Company, 1904–7), 4:137.

35. For scholarship on gender encounters, see Theda Perdue, *Cherokee Women: Gender and Culture Change, 1700–1835* (Lincoln: University of Nebraska Press, 1998); Gail D. Danvers, "Gendered Encounters: Warriors, Women, and William Johnson," *Journal of American Studies* 35, no. 2 (2001): 187–202; Nancy Shoemaker, *A Strange Likeness: Becoming Red and White in Eighteenth-Century North America* (New York: Oxford University Press, 2004); Ann Little, *Abraham in Arms: War and Gender in*

Colonial New England (Philadelphia: University of Pennsylvania Press, 2007); Juliana Barr, *Peace Came in the Form of a Woman: Indians and Spaniards in the Texas Borderlands* (Chapel Hill: University of North Carolina Press, 2007); Michelle LeMaster, *Brothers Born of One Mother: British-Native American Relations in the Colonial Southeast* (Charlottesville: University of Virginia Press, 2012); Alejandra Dubcovsky, *Talking Back: Native Women and the Making of the Early South* (New Haven, CT: Yale University Press, 2023).

36. John Bricknell, "The Captivity of John Bricknell," *American Pioneer* 1 (1842): 48; Charles Fredrick Post, "Two Journals of Western Tours," *Early Western Travels, 1748–1846*, 1:203. For manhood and frontier warfare, see Little, *Abraham in Arms*, 12–90; LeMaster, *Brothers Born of One Mother*, 51–83.

37. Cummings, "Sketches of a Tour to the Western Country," 134.

38. Honor Sachs, *Home Rule: Household Manhood and National Expansion on the Eighteenth-Century Kentucky Frontier* (New Haven, CT: Yale University Press, 2015), 62.

39. For evaluating the changing positions of women in Native American societies or the rise warriors and war chiefs, see Theda Perdue, *Cherokee Women*; Jan V. Noel, "Revisiting Gender in Iroquoia," in *Gender and Sexuality in Indigenous North America, 1400–1850*, ed. Sandra Slater and Fay A. Yarbrough (Columbia: University of South Carolina Press, 2011), 54–74; Little, *Abraham in Arms*; Danvers, "Gender Encounters," 196–202; Pekka Hämäläinen, *The Comanche Empire* (New Haven, CT: Yale University Press, 2009), 209–71; Lee, *The Cutting-Off Way*, 92–97.

40. See Gunlog Fur, *A Nation of Women: Gender and Colonial Encounters among the Delaware Indians* (Philadelphia: University of Pennsylvania Press, 2009).

41. Fur, *A Nation of Women*; Danvers, "Gender Encounters."

42. "At a Conference Held at Lancaster," *Pennsylvania Archives: Colonial Records* (Harrisburg, PA, 1851–53), 7:521–22.

43. Colin Calloway, *Pen and Ink Witchcraft: Treaties and Treaty Making in American Indian History* (New York: Oxford University Press, 2013), 49–95; Eric Hinderaker, *Elusive Empires: Constructing Colonialism in the Ohio Valley, 1673–1800* (New York: Cambridge University Press, 1997), 161–75.

44. James Smith, "An Account of the Remarkable Occurrences in the Life and Travels of Col. James Smith, during His Captivity with the Indians," *Ohio Valley Historical Series*, no. 5 (Cincinnati, OH, 1907), 45.

45. Robert Rogers, *Ponteach, or, the Savages of America: A Tragedy* (London, 1766), 38; John Long and Milo Milton Quaife, *John Long's Voyages and Travels in the Years 1768–1788* (Chicago: The Lakeside Press, 1922), 48–49.

46. William Clarke, *Observations on the Late and Present Conduct of the French, with Regard to Their Encroachments upon the Colonies of North America* (Boston, 1755), 20–21; Ann Maury, *Memoirs of a Huguenot Family*, trans. and comp. James Fontaine (New York, 1853), 366–67.

47. For Native American humor, see Kenneth Lincoln, *Indi'n Humor: Bicultural Play in Native America* (New York: Oxford University, 1993), and Vine Deloria Jr., *Custer Died for Your Sins: An Indian Manifesto* (New York: Macmillan, 1970), 146–67.

48. For the symbolism of the woods for Natives and frontier settlers, see James Merrell, *Into the American Woods: Negotiators on the Pennsylvania Frontier* (New

York: Norton, 1999). For the yearning to inhabit the Indian body and environment, see Philip Deloria, *Playing Indian* (New Haven, CT: Yale University Press, 1998), and Richard Slotkin, *Regeneration through Violence: The Mythology of the American Frontier, 1600–1860* (Middletown, CT: Wesleyan University Press, 1973).

49. For difference and similarity, see Nancy Shoemaker, *A Strange Likeness: Becoming Red and White in Eighteenth-Century North America* (New York: Oxford University Press, 2004). For violence in the Ohio Valley and West Pennsylvania during the period, see Peter Silver, *Our Savage Neighbors: How Indian War Transformed Early America* (New York: Norton, 2008); Patrick Griffin, *American Leviathan: Empire, Nation and Revolutionary Frontier* (New York: Hill and Wang, 2008); Kevin Kenny, *Peaceable Kingdom Lost: The Paxton Boys and the Destruction of William Penn's Holy Experiment* (New York: Oxford University Press, 2009). For pan-Indian constructions, see Gregory Evans Dowd, *War under Heaven: Pontiac, the Indian Nations, & the British Empire* (Baltimore: Johns Hopkins University Press, 2002).

50. Smith, "An Account," 108. For the broader story of James Smith and his men, see Patrick Spero, *Frontier Rebels: The Fight for Independence in the American West, 1765–1776* (New York: Norton, 2018).

51. John Mack Faragher, *Daniel Boone: The Life and Legend of an American Pioneer* (New York: Macmillan, 1992), 154–204, quote on 181.

52. John Filson, *The Discovery, Settlement and Present State of Kentucke and an Essay Towards the Topography, and Natural History of That Important Country: To Which Is Added, an Appendix, Containing, The Adventures of Col. Daniel Boon, One of the First Settlers* (Wilmington, DE, 1784). For Daniel Boone and frontier mythology, see Slotkin, *Regeneration through Violence*, and Faragher, *Daniel Boone*.

53. For a similar perspective, see Sachs, *Home Rule*, 25. Tellingly, in *The Last of the Mohicans* the white damsel in distress, Alice, is alive and well at the end of the narrative and marries a British officer, while Cora, her not fully white half-sister, is killed. For the significance of Jane McCrae's death, see, Robert Parkinson, *The Common Cause: Creating Race and Nation in the American Revolution* (Chapel Hill: University of North Carolina Press, 2016), 340–50.

54. Filson, *The Adventures of Col. Daniel Boon*, 50.

55. Phillip W. Hoffman, *Simon Girty, Turncoat Hero: The Most Hated Man on the Early American Frontier* (Franklin, TN: American History Press, 2008).

56. Hoffman, *Simon Girty*.

57. Hoffman, *Simon Girty* .

58. Dr. John Knight, "Narrative of Dr. Knight," in *Narratives of a Late Expedition*, ed. H. H. Brackenridge (Philadelphia, 1783), 9–12; Hoffman, *Simon Girty*.

59. The classic text on the preference white captives had for life in Native communities and the disturbing implications for white society is James Axtell, "The White Indians of Colonial America," *William and Mary Quarterly* 32, no. 1 (January 1975): 55–88.

60. Silver, *Our Savage Neighbors*, 39–71. For similar dynamics in seventeenth-century New England, see Jill Lepore, *The Name of War: King Philip's War and the Origins of American Identity* (New York: Vintage Books, 1999).

61. Theodorus Frielinghuysen, "Wars and Rumors of Wars, Heavens Decree over the World" (New York, 1755), 10.

62. Grenier, *The First Way of War.*

63. "Extract of a Letter from Carlisle," *Pennsylvania Gazette* (Philadelphia), September 29, 1763.

64. Riflemen made excellent guerrilla fighters because the absence of bayonets relieved them of charging, and the range and accuracy of their rifles were greater than those of muskets. These same elements also prohibited them from taking part in the traditional schemes and tactics of the period, such as line formations and of course bayonet charges.

65. See James Graham, *The Life of Daniel Morgan, of the Virginia Line of the Army of the United States* (New York, 1856), 63–64.

66. Orders to Col. Daniel Morgan, June 13, 1777, *Founders Online*, National Archives, https://founders.archives.gov/documents/Washington/03-10-02-0026.

67. George Washington to Major General Israel Putnam, August 16, 1777, *Founders Online*, National Archives, https://founders.archives.gov/documents/Washington/03-10-02-0626; George Washington to Major General Horatio Gates, August 20, 1777, *Founders Online*, National Archives, https://founders.archives.gov/documents/Washington/03-11-02-0012.

68. *George Rogers Clark Papers, Collections of the Illinois State Historical Library*, ed. Clarence Walworth Alvord (Springfield, IL, 1912), 8:274 (punctuation added).

69. Col. Brodhead to Pres. Reed, 1779, Col Brodhead to Gen. Washington, 1779, Col. Brodhead to Gen. Sullivan, 1779, Col. Brodhead to Gov. Reed, 1780, *Pennsylvania Archives*, 1st ser., ed. J. Severns (Philadelphia, 1852–6), 7:505; 12:131,155; 8:559.

70. John Romeyn Brodhead, ed., *Documents Relative to the Colonial History of New York* (Albany, 1853), 3:714.

71. Victor W. Turner, *The Ritual Process: Structure and Anti-Structure* (Chicago: Aldine Publishing, 1969), attributes his conceptualization of liminality to the work of Arnold Van Gannep. Mikhail Bakhtin, *Rabelais and His World*, trans. Hélène Iswolski (Bloomington: Indiana University Press, 1984), identifies a similar dynamic in the premodern European carnival. Deloria, *Playing Indian*, employs both the work of Bakhtin and Turner in his analysis. For Native war preparations in eastern woodlands societies, see Lee, *The Cutting-Off Way*, 83–86.

72. Here I allude to formulations in Kathleen Brown, *Good Wives, Nasty Wenches, and Anxious Patriarchs: Gender, Race, and Power in Colonial Virginia* (Chapel Hill: University of North Carolina Press, for the Institute of Early American History and Culture, 1996).

73. Bakhtin, *Rabelais and His World*, 90. Turner, *The Ritual Process*, esp. 94–130.

74. Deloria, *Playing Indian*, 7.

75. See, for example, Roger Abrahams, "Introduction: A Folklore Perspective," in *Riot and Revelry in Early America*, ed. William Pencak, Matthew Dennis, and Simon P. Newman (University Park: Pennsylvania State University Press, 2002), 23. For an example of anthropological scholarship that casts the liminal moment as perpetuating power structures, see Meyer Fortes, "Ritual and Office," in *Essays on the Ritual of Social Relation*, ed. Max Gluckman (Manchester, UK: Manchester University Press, 1962). In contrast, Turner, *The Ritual Process*, 94–130, suggests that recognition of the power structure can prove both inversive or even subversive, but does not have to be either.

76. Walter L. Hixson, *American Settler Colonialism: A History* (New York, 2013), viii, makes a similar point. On the Gnadenhutten massacre, see Rob Harper, "Looking the Other Way: The Gnadenhutten Massacre and the Contextual Interpretation of Violence," *William and Mary Quarterly* 64, no. 3 (2007): 621–44; Silver, *Our Savage Neighbors*, 261–80; Leonard Sadosky, "Rethinking the Gnadenhutten Massacre: The Contest for Power in the Public World of the Revolutionary Pennsylvania Frontier," in *The Sixty Years' War for the Great Lakes, 1754–1814*, ed. David C. Skaggs and Larry Nelson (East Lansing: Michigan State University Press, 2001), 187–214. On the role of corporate bonds and a democratic spirit in the making of settler colonial sovereignty, see Veracini, *Settler Colonialism*, 55–74.

77. The Secretary of the Treasury to President Washington, August 5, 1794, *Pennsylvania Archives*, 2nd ser., ed. Samuel Hazard (Harrisburg, PA, 1876), 4:84, 101.

78. H. H. Brackenridge, *Incidents of the Insurrection*, ed. Daniel Marder (New Haven, CT: College and University Press, 1972), 17.

79. Brackenridge, *Incidents of the Insurrection*, 101–2, 104. On anti-authoritarian misrule, see chapter three.

80. Edmund Morgan, *Inventing the People: The Rise of Popular Sovereignty in England and America* (New York: Norton, 1988), 153.

81. For the making of the people and nationalism in early America, see David Waldstreicher, *In the Midst of Perpetual Fetes: The Making of American Nationalism, 1776–1820* (Chapel Hill: University of North Carolina Press, 1997); Andrew Robertson, "'Look on This Picture . . . and on This!' Nationalism, Localism, and Partisan Images of Otherness in the United States, 1787–1820," *American Historical Review* 106, no. 4 (Fall 2001): 1263–80; Benjamin Irvin, *Clothed in Robes of Sovereignty: The Continental Congress and the People Out of Doors* (New York: Oxford University Press, 2011); and John L. Brooke, *Columbia Rising: Civil Life on the Upper Hudson from the Revolution to the Age of Jackson* (Chapel Hill: University of North Carolina Press, 2010). All of these studies, as well as my own insights here, rely to some degree on the influential Benedict Anderson, *Imagined Communities: Reflections on the Origin and Spread of Nationalism* (New York: Verso, 1983).

82. Churchill, *To Shake Their Guns in the Tyrant's Face*.

83. It was also the two-year anniversary of the attack on the Branch Davidians compound in Waco, Texas. After Waco, McVeigh grew even more obsessed with April 19 as the mythic date of Lexington and Concord. Finding the coincidence with the attack on the Waco compound compelling, he chose it for the date of his attack. For the significance of Lexington and Concord to the modern militia movement, see Churchill, *To Shake Their Guns in the Tyrant's Face*, 256–65. For the significance of the memory of the American Revolution for twentieth-century right-wing militants, see Michael D. Hattem, *The Memory of '76: The Revolution in American History* (New Haven, CT: Yale University Press, 2024), 215–31, 276–87. For McVeigh's interest in revolutionary history and symbolism, see, for example, Tom Kenworthy, "Anti-Government Writings in McVeigh's Car, Agent Says," *Washington Post*, April 28, 1997.

84. See the discussion on nationalism and race in Eran Zelnik, "Self-Evident Walls: Reckoning with Recent Histories of Race and Nation," *Journal of the Early Republic* 41, no. 1 (Spring 2021): 1–38.

85. Matthew Frye Jacobsen, *Whiteness of a Different Color: European Immigrants and the Alchemy of Race* (Cambridge, MA: Harvard University Press, 1998), 13–38.

86. *Acts Passed at the First Session of the Second Congress of the United States of America* (Philadelphia, 1792), 128.

Chapter 5 • *Alligator-Horses*

1. Dona Brown, "Travel Books," *An Extensive Republic: Print, Culture, and Society in the New Nation, History of the Book in America*, ed. Robert Gross and Mary Kelley (Chapel Hill: University of North Carolina Press in association with the American Antiquarian Society, 2010), 2:449–58.

2. J. Hector St. John de Crèvecœur's, *Letters from an American Farmer* (1782), and Alexis de Tocqueville, *Democracy in America* (1835, 1840).

3. James Fenimore Cooper, *Notions of the Americans: Picked up by a Traveling Bachelor*, 2 vols. (London, 1828), 1:423. Some of the infamous anti-American texts from the period include Isaac Weld Jr., *Travels through the States of North America and the Provinces of Upper and Lower Canada during the Years 1795, 1796, and 1797* (London, 1799); John Davis, *Travels of Four Years and a Half in the States of America during 1798–1799, 1800, 1801, and 1802* (London, 1803); Richard Parkinson, *A Tour in America in 1798, 1799, and 1800* (London, 1805); Charles Williams Janson, *The Stranger in America* (London, 1807); Thomas Ashe, *Travels in America Performed in 1806* (London, 1808); John Lambert, *Travels through Canada, and the United States of North America in the Years 1806, 1807, and 1808* (London, 1813).

4. James Kirke Paulding, *Letters from the South by a Northern Man*, 2 vols. (New York, 1835 [1817]), 2:100, 109–10.

5. Alexis de Tocqueville, *Democracy in America: Part the Second, The Social Influence of Democracy*, trans. Henry Reeve (New York, 1840), 238.

6. Joseph Eaton, *The Anglo-American Paper War: Debates about the New Republic, 1800–1825* (London: Palgrave Macmillan, 2012), and Frank Luther Mott, *A History of American Magazines, 1741–1850* (Cambridge, MA: Harvard University Press, 1966), 183–211.

7. Robert V. Haynes, *The Mississippi Territory and the Southwest Frontier, 1795–1817* (Lexington: University Press of Kentucky, 2010), 2; "For the Aurora," *Aurora General Advertiser* (Philadelphia), March 23, 1805.

8. Thaddeus Mason Harris, *Journal of a Tour into the Territory Northwest of the Allegheny Mountains* (Boston, 1805), 59.

9. Timothy Dwight, *Travels in New England and New York*, 4 vols. (New Haven, 1821), 2:459.

10. Fisher Ames to Thomas Dwight, October 31, 1803, *Works of Fisher Ames*, ed. Seth Ames (Boston, 1854), 1:329.

11. For Federalism after the elections of 1800, which the Federalists lost, see Linda Kerber, *Federalists in Dissent: Imagery and Ideology in Jeffersonian America* (Ithaca, NY: Cornell University Press, 1970), and David Hackett Fischer, *The Revolution of American Conservatism: The Federalist Party in the Era of Jeffersonian Democracy* (New York: Harper & Row, 1965).

12. Thomas Ashe, *Travels in America, Performed in 1806*, 3 vols. (London, 1808), 2:125, and for his impressions of Marietta, 1:292–96; Weld, *Travels through the States of North America*, 234–35.

13. François A. F. La Rochefoucauld-Liancourt, *Travels through the United States of North America, the Country of the Iroquois, and Upper Canada, in the Years 1795, 1796, and 1797*, 4 vols. (London, 1800), 4:528.

14. "Inchiquen's Favorable View of the United States," *Quarterly Review* 10, no. 20 (January 1814): 515.

15. For some of these figures, see Steven Watts, *The Republic Reborn: War and the Making of Liberal America, 1790–1820* (Baltimore: Johns Hopkins University Press, 1987).

16. William Meigs, *The Life of Charles Jared Ingersoll* (Philadelphia, 1897), 45.

17. Charles Jared Ingersoll, *Inchiquin the Jesuit's Letters, during a Late Residence in the United States of America* (New York, 1810), 6, 17, 18, 28.

18. Ingersoll, *Inchiquin*, 110–11.

19. Ingersoll, *Inchiquin*, 117, 121n.

20. George Fowler, *The Wandering Philanthropist, or Letters from a Chinese Written during His Residence in the United States* (Philadelphia, 1810), 9–11.

21. John Quincy Adams to Abigail Adams, June 30, 1811, in *Writings of John Quincy Adams*, ed. Worthington Chauncey Ford (New York: Greenwood Press, 1968), 4:127–28. For republican anxieties, see Watts, *The Republic Reborn*.

22. Richard Slotkin, *Regeneration through Violence: The Mythology of the American Frontier, 1600–1860* (Middletown, CT: Wesleyan University Press, 1973); Charles Jared Ingersoll, *An Oration, Delivered at Mr. Harvey's, Spring Garden, before a Very Numerous Meeting of Democratic Citizens, July 4, 1812* (Philadelphia, 1812), 8; Watts, *The Republic Reborn*, xix. For more on the role of emotions in the War of 1812, see Nicole Eustace, *1812: War and the Passions of Patriotism* (Philadelphia: University of Pennsylvania Press, 2012).

23. See Michael Paul Rogin, *Fathers and Children: Andrew Jackson and the Subjugation of the American Indian* (New York: Transaction Publishers, 1991), and Andrew Burstein, *The Passions of Andrew Jackson* (New York: Vintage Books, 2003), 72.

24. Andrew Jackson, "Address to the Citizens of Nashville, January 15, 1809," in *The Papers of Andrew Jackson*, ed. Sam B. Smith et al. (Knoxville: University of Tennessee Press, 1980), 2:210.

25. Andrew Jackson to William Henry Harrison, November 28, 1811, in Smith et al., *The Papers of Andrew Jackson*, 2:270.

26. Tom Kanon, *Tennesseans at War, 1812–1815: Andrew Jackson, the Creek War, and the Battle of New Orleans* (Tuscaloosa: University of Alabama Press, 2014); Rogin, *Fathers and Children*.

27. The classic text on the fabrication of the Battle of New Orleans as myth is John William Ward, *Andrew Jackson, Symbol for an Age* (New York: Oxford University Press, 1955), 3–29.

28. "To the Natchez Volunteer Rifle Corps," 1815, Natchez, ser. 2, Shaw and Shoemaker 35392, Early American Imprints.

29. "Victory of Orleans," *Western Courier* (Lexington, KY), February 16, 1815.

30. "From the Aurora," *Daily National Intelligencer* (Washington, DC), February 16, 1815, taken from the *Niles' Weekly Register* (Baltimore), February 25, 1815, 415. For more on the memory of the Battle of New Orleans in the wake of the war, see Joseph Stoltz III, *A Bloodless Victory: The Battle of New Orleans in History and Memory* (Baltimore: Johns Hopkins University Press, 2017), esp. 13–29. For the memory of the revolution during the Era of 1812, see Sarah J. Purcell, *Sealed with Blood: War, Sacrifice, and Memory in Revolutionary America* (Philadelphia: Pennsylvania University Press, 2002), 150–70, and Michael D. Hattem, *The Memory of '76: The Revolution in American History* (New Haven, CT: Yale University Press, 2024), 32–36. "I came, I saw. I conquered" is a reference to the famous Julius Caesar quote alluding to the mythology of the Roman citizen soldier and its greatest general.

31. Elliott Gorn, "'Gouge and Bite, Pull Hair and Scratch': The Social Significance of Fighting in the Southern Backcountry," *American Historical Review* 90, no. 1 (February 1985): 18; Thomas Anburey, *Travels through the Interior Parts of America in a Series of Letters by an Officer* (London, 1789), 2:349.

32. Weld, *Travels through North America*, 192. Ashe, *Travels in America Performed in 1806*, 1:223–32; Fortescue Cuming, *Sketches of a Tour to the Western Country, through the States of Ohio and Kentucky* (Pittsburgh, 1810), 137.

33. "Saturday, July 9," *New York Evening Post*, July 9, 1808, 2.

34. Washington Irving, *A History of New York from the Beginning of the World to the End of the Dutch Dynasty* (New York, 1809), 85.

35. Christian Schultz, *Travels on an Inland Voyage through the States of New-York, Pennsylvania, Virginia, Ohio, Kentucky and Tennessee Performed in the Years 1807 and 1808; Including a Tour of Nearly Six Thousand Miles* (New York, 1810), 2:145–46.

36. Robert Stubbs, *The Kentucky Farmer's Almanac, for the Year 1814* (Lexington, 1813). For a discussion of "Yankee Doodle," see chapters one and three.

37. Chapter four investigates this theme in depth.

38. For examples of settler views on the weight of the Long Knives moniker, see John Filson, *The Discovery, Settlement and Present State of Kentucke and an Essay towards the Topography, and Natural History of That Important Country: To Which Is Added, an Appendix, Containing The Adventures of Col. Daniel Boon, One of the First Settlers* (Wilmington, DE, 1784), 48, and James Smith, "An Account of the Remarkable Occurrences in the Life and Travels of Col. James Smith, during His Captivity with the Indians," *Ohio Valley Historical Series*, no. 5 (Cincinnati, 1907), 105. For the Native interpretation of "Long Knives" from the late eighteenth century, see Daniel Richter, "Onas the Long Knife: Pennsylvanians and Indians, 1783–1794," in *Native Americans in the Early Republic*, ed. Fredrick E. Hoxie, Ronald Hoffman, and Peter J. Albert (Charlottesville: University of Virginia Press, 1999), 125–61.

39. On the other hand, few westerners enlisted in the army. See J. C. A. Stagg, "Enlisted Men in the United States Army, 1812–1815: A Preliminary Survey," *William and Mary Quarterly* 43, no. 4 (1986): 615–45.

40. For the significance of the militia in Tennessee and Kentucky in and around the War of 1812, see C. Edward Skeen, *Citizen Soldiers in the War of 1812* (Lexington: University Press of Kentucky, 1999); Harry S. Laver, *Citizens More Than Soldiers: The Kentucky Militia and Society in the Early Republic* (Lincoln: University of Nebraska Press, 2007); Kanon, *Tennesseans at War*.

41. "To the 2nd Division, March 7, 1812," in Smith et al., *The Papers of Andrew Jackson*, 2:290.

42. For an example of Jackson's criticism of militia laws before the war, see Andrew Jackson to Willie Blount, February 15, 1810, in Smith et al., *The Papers of Andrew Jackson*, 2:236–38.

43. See, for example, "Poetry," *New Jersey Journal* (Elizabethtown), April 25, 1815. For more on this poem, see part three.

44. "Hunters of Kentucky, or Half Horse and Half Alligator," n.d., Boston, Library of Congress, https://www.loc.gov/item/amss.as105650/.

45. Ward, *Andrew Jackson*, 3–29.

46. Ward, *Andrew Jackson*, 3–29. The song probably first appeared under the title "New-Orleans" in the New York journal *Ladies' Garland* 3, no. 14 (1821): 112. Noah M. Ludlow, *Dramatic Life as I Found It: A Record of Personal Experience* (St. Louis, 1880), 237–38.

47. For a few examples of entertainers who sang "The Hunters of Kentucky" in East Coast cities, see "Performed by Mr. Drake at the Baltimore Theatre," *American Commercial Daily Advertiser* (Baltimore), May 11, 1824; "This Evening, Performed by Mr. Stickney," *New York Evening Post*, July 5, 1825; "Performed This Evening by Mr. Simonds" *Commercial Advertiser* (New York), July 30, 1825.

48. Ludlow, *Dramatic Life as I Found It*, 241, 250; "Items," *Daily Chronicle*, February 18, 1829 (Philadelphia), 2.

49. "Target Firing," *Commercial Advertiser* (New York), August 8, 1826.

50. "Police Office," *Poulson's American Daily Advertiser* (Philadelphia), November 22, 1825, 3.

51. For more on hit songs as part of national popular culture, see chapters six and seven. For the early United States as the first paradigmatic nation, see Eran Zelnik, "Self-Evident Walls: Reckoning with Recent Histories of Race and Nation," *Journal of the Early Republic* 41, no. 1 (Spring 2021): 1–38.

52. For recent studies stressing the fractured nature of the antebellum era, see Benjamin Park, *American Nationalisms: Imagining Union in the Age of Revolutions, 1783–1833* (New York: Cambridge University Press, 2018); Stephen Hahn, *A Nation without Borders: The United States and Its World in the Age of Civil Wars, 1830–1910* (New York: Penguin Books, 2016); Trish Loughran, *The Republic in Print: Print Culture in the Age of U.S. Nation Building, 1770–1870* (New York: Columbia University Press, 2007).

53. Aderman and Kime, *Advocate for America*, 62–72.

54. Paulding, *Letters from the South*, 2:121, 2:57, 2:79, 1:67–72.

55. Paulding, *Letters from the South*, 1:139, 2:71.

56. "The Times," *Niles' Weekly Register* (Baltimore), June 5, 1819, 1–2, and "Money Matters," *Niles' Weekly Register* (Baltimore), April 10, 1819, 2–3.

57. John Taylor, *Arator, Being a Series of Agricultural Essays* (Baltimore, 1817), 16.

58. *Cause of and Cure for Hard Times: Containing a Definition of the Attributes and Qualities Indispensable in Money* (New York, 1818), iv.

59. Taylor, *Arator*, 16

60. "The Times," *Niles' Weekly Register* (Baltimore), June 5, 1819, 2–3.

61. "The Western Country," *Niles' Weekly Register* (Baltimore), September 7, 1811, 9–10.

62. The best account of the emerging Second Party System and its national impetus is still George Dangerfield, *The Awakening of American Nationalism, 1815–1828* (New York: Harper and Row, 1965). For a broad synthesis of the period that highlights the significance of the period's party system see Daniel Walker Howe, *What Hath God Wrought: The Transformation of America, 1815–1848* (New York: Oxford University Press, 2007).

63. Mark Derr, *The Frontiersman: The Real Life and the Many Legends of Davy Crockett* (New York: William Morrow, 1993), 95–144.

64. This example is from "Washington Correspondence," *New Hampshire Sentinel* (Keene), February 29, 1828.

65. Derr, *The Frontiersman*, 189–248.

66. Though the Yankee would continue to appear on stage and in print throughout the century, and his image would become the blueprint for the character of Uncle Sam, he could not compete with the frontier jester in popularity and mythic significance. The most famous representation of the Yankee during the next few decades would be Seba Smith's Jack Downing stories.

67. Ralph M. Aderman, and Wayne R. Kime, *Advocate for America*, 132.

68. Aderman and Kime, *Advocate for America*, 136. See also Derr, *The Frontiersman*, 189–91.

69. The play underwent several revisions, and the version that Hackett revised for British audiences several years later is the only one extant.

70. James Kirke Paulding, *The Lion of the West and the Bucktails*, ed. Frack Gado (Oxford: Rowman & Littlefield, 2003), 87.

71. For an in-depth discussion of *The Contrast,* see chapter three.

72. Paulding, *The Lion of the West*, 111.

73. Derr, *The Frontiersman*, 197–203.

74. Derr, *The Frontiersman*, 254.

75. Michael Winship estimated that around this period, a typical edition of a comic almanac published by Charles Ellms would have sold at least 150,000 copies nationwide. As Winship also noted, Crockett's almanacs were just as popular as Ellms's *Comic Almanac*, and in fact, Ellms might have been the originator of the early Crockett almanacs as well; they probably saw similar distribution methods. See Winship, "Pirates, Shipwrecks, and Comic Almanacs: Charles Ellms Packages Books in Nineteenth-Century America," *Printing History*, no. 9 (January 2011): 8.

76. Derr, *The Frontiersman*, 253–69; Paul Andrew Hutton, "'Going to Congress and Making Allmynacks Is My Trade': Davy Crockett, His Almanacs, and the Evolution of a Frontier Legend," *Journal of the West* 37, no. 2 (1998): 10–22. For more on the booming industry of publications related to the tales of Crockett and other frontiersmen, see chapter 7.

77. For the consumption of the frontiersman and western mythology as a response to market capitalism and urbanization, see Richard Slotkin, *The Fatal Environment: The Myth of the Frontier in the Age of Industrialization, 1800–1890* (New York: Atheneum, 1985), and Daniel Herman, "The Other Daniel Boone: The Nascence of a Middle-Class Hunter Hero," *Journal of the Early Republic* 18, no. 3 (Fall 1998): 429–57.

Part III • A Tale of Two Clowns

1. "The Star-Spangled Banner" was known during this period, but only decades later did it emerge as the most memorable song from the War of 1812 to become enshrined as the national anthem in the twentieth century.

2. For a compelling case for placing "Backside Albany" squarely within the "reinvention of American nationhood" during the "era of 1812," see David Waldstreicher, "Minstrelization and Nationhood: 'Backside Albany,' Backlash, and the Wartime Origins of Blackface Minstrelsy," *Warring for America: Cultural Contests in the Era of 1812*, ed. Nicole Eustace and Fredrika J. Teute (Chapel Hill: University of North Carolina Press, 2017), 33.

3. I have found no recent scholarship that cites this song. There is brief discussion of it in S. Foster Damon, "The Negro in Early American Songsters," *The Papers of the Bibliographical Society of America* 28 (1934): 144–145, and, by referencing Damon, in Hans Nathan, *Dan Emmett and the Rise of Early Negro Minstrelsy* (Norman: University of Oklahoma Press, 1962), 34–35.

4. See, for example, "Negro and Buckra Man," *The American Muse or Songsters Companion* (New York, 1814), 67–68. The oldest extant version of "Negro and Buckra Man" in America is from 1811, see Damon, "The Negro in Early American Songsters," 133–38.

5. "Poetry," *New Jersey Journal* (Elizabethtown), April 25, 1815. I counted at least eight different newspapers that printed this song in April and May 1815. It appears to have first been published in the *American Volunteer* (Carlisle, PA). It was also published in at least one almanac: David Richardson, *The Virginia Pocket Almanac and Farmer's Companion for 1819* (Richmond, 1818), 3. "Chinger Ring" or "Sambo's Dress to He Bredren," another Black dialect song in this tradition probably written in the 1820s, also partakes in explicit Black mockery. See, for example, the broadside "Chinger Ring," ser. 1, vol. 2, no. 207, American Song Sheets, Rare Books and Special Collections, Library of Congress.

6. For a discussion of the half horse–half alligator, see chapter five.

7. Alan Taylor, *The Internal Enemy: Slavery and War in Virginia, 1772–1832* (New York: W. W. Norton & Company, 2013), 175–349.

8. For similar accounts of racial nationalism in the War of 1812, see Nicole Eustace, *1812: War and the Passions of Patriotism* (Philadelphia: University of Pennsylvania Press, 2012), and Waldstreicher, "Minstrelization and Nationhood." Eustace discusses at length the myth surrounding the purported promise made by the British to runaway slaves of "beauty and booty" as a touchstone for race-baiting. Note in the song above the reference to "booty" in this vein.

Chapter 6 • A Black Clown for a White Nation

1. Much of these print materials were interwoven with a blend of impressions and realities of Atlantic slavery and the Atlantic world more broadly. See Katrina Dyonne Thompson, *Ring Shout and Wheel About: The Racial Politics of Music and Dance in North American Slavery* (Urbana: University of Illinois Press, 2014).

2. See especially chapter four. For the connection between democracy and race, see Barbara Fields, "Slavery Race and Ideology in the United States of America," *New Left Review* 181 (May 1990): 113–15, and James Brewer Stewart, "The Emergence of

Racial Modernity and the Rise of the White North, 1776–1840," *Journal of the Early Republic* 18, no. 2 (Summer 1998): 181–217.

3. The most influential account of blackface minstrelsy in this vein is still Eric Lott, *Love and Theft: Blackface Minstrelsy and the American Working Class* (New York: Oxford University Press, 1993). Lott does not shy away from the racism of the genre, but he complicates it nevertheless with a suggestive postmodern flair in calling it "a mixed erotic economy of celebration and exploitation" and describing it as white "theft" of genuine Black vernacular tradition (40). For two other influential studies that treated blackface minstrelsy even more sympathetically, see W. T. Lhamon Jr., *Raising Cain: Blackface Performance from Jim Crow to Hip Hop* (Cambridge, MA: Harvard University Press, 1998), and Dale Cockrell's, *Demons of Disorder: Early Blackface Minstrels and Their World* (New York: Cambridge University Press, 1997). In *Raising Cain*, Lhamon describes the iconic early minstrel song "Jim Crow" as a performance that "moved toward cross-racial affiliation." Therefore, he concludes, "The pre-career of Jim Crow is opposite to the received, segregative meaning the term has today" (151). For Cockrell, the broader context of interracial vernacular culture emanating from urban centers was key: "the evidence, in total, suggests that urban life during the Jacksonian period was most highly integrated racially among the lower classes. It is conceivable that this time and place found the races living together as easily as any before and perhaps more so than any since." Thus "Jim Crow" is "much like a carnival, for it is of the common people (and not), of social criticism (and centers of power), of hope (and control), noise (and music)" (86, 89). For more sympathetic treatments of blackface minstrelsy, see Robert Nowatzki, *Representing African Americans in Transatlantic Abolitionism and Blackface Minstrelsy* (Baton Rouge: Louisiana State University Press, 2010); and Christopher J. Smith, *The Creolization of American Culture: William Sidney Mount and the Roots of Blackface Minstrelsy* (Urbana: University of Illinois Press, 2013).

4. On a humor event, see the introduction.

5. George Fredrickson, *The Black Image in the White Mind: The Debate on Afro-American Character and Destiny* (New York: Harper and Row, 1971). This interpretation of blackface minstrelsy has been influenced by and is mostly in agreement with David Roediger, *The Wages of Whiteness: Race and the Making of the American Working Class* (New York: Verso, 1991), and Brian Roberts, *Blackface Nation: Race, Reform, and Identity in American Popular Music, 1812–1925* (Chicago: University of Chicago Press, 2017). Both, however, still cast market forces and working-class alienation as playing a crucial role in the creation of the genre. Roberts discusses the "racial state," which parallels racial nationalism. For a more wholistic critical take on blackface minstrelsy, as part of the "rise of the white republic," see Alexander Saxton, *The Rise and Fall of the White Republic: Class Politics and Mass Culture in Nineteenth-Century America* (New York: Verso, 1990), 165–82. Two important exceptions to focusing on class are David Waldstreicher, "Minstrelization and Nationhood: 'Backside Albany,' Backlash, and the Wartime Origins of Blackface Minstrelsy," in *Warring for America: Cultural Contests in the Era of 1812*, ed. Nicole Eustace and Fredrika J. Teute (Williamsburg, VA: Omohundro Institute of Early American History and Culture; Chapel Hill: University of North Carolina Press, 2017), 29–55, and Thompson, *Ring Shout and Wheel About*.

6. The classic study of racialization in the Atlantic context is Winthrop Jordan, *White over Black: American Attitudes towards the Negro, 1550–1812* (Chapel Hill: University of North Carolina Press, 1968). For an important corrective and critique of Jordan's essentialist views of race, see Harvey R. Neptune, "'The Baby of Biological Race': The Issue of Racial Science in Winthrop Jordan's *White over Black*," *Journal of the Early Republic* 43, no. 2 (Summer 2023): 199–243. The classic study highlighting the emerging association between blackness and slavery and whiteness and freedom is Edmund Morgan, *American Slavery, American Freedom: The Ordeal of Colonial Virginia* (New York: Norton, 1975).

7. Joseph Boskin, *Sambo: The Rise and Demise of an American Jester* (New York: Oxford University Press, 1986), 17–64.

8. *The American Jest Book: Containing a Curious Variety of Jests,* 2 vols. (Philadelphia, 1789), 1:43.

9. Incidentally, Raccoon, or Coon for short, from *The Disappointment* was an antecedent for Zip Coon. See Mary D. Shepard, "Forrest's Curious Old Play: or, Hopkinson's Disappointment," *Papers of the Bibliographical Society of America* 88 (1994): 37–52.

10. Boskin, *Sambo,* 65–74; Cockrell, *Demons of Disorder,* 13–28.

11. Lhamon, *Raising Cain,* 151–52. This is largely the argument in Lott, *Love and Theft*; Cockrell, *Demons of Disorder*; Lhamon, *Raising Cain*; and William J. Mahar, *Behind the Burnt Cork Mask: Early Blackface Minstrelsy and Antebellum Popular Culture* (Urbana: University of Illinois Press, 1999). For less sentimentalized accounts of the Black northern origins of blackface minstrelsy, see Shane White, *Stories of Freedom in Black New York* (Cambridge, MA: Harvard University Press, 2002), esp. 185–218; Shane White and Graham White, *Stylin': African American Expressive Culture from Its Beginnings to the Zoot Suit* (Ithaca, NY: Cornell University Press, 1998), 85–124; and Jean H. Baker, *Affairs of Party: The Political Culture of Northern Democrats in the Mid Nineteenth Century* (Ithaca, NY: Cornell University Press, 1983), 212–58.

12. This dynamic was not new, of course, but is somehow still neglected by many scholars of blackface minstrelsy. For the classic accounts of how physical and social proximity reenforced racial divides in the nineteenth century, see Roediger, *The Wages of Whiteness*; Noel Ignatiev, *How the Irish Became White* (New York: Routledge, 1995); and Matthew Frye Jacobson, *Whiteness of a Different Color: European Immigrants and the Alchemy of Race* (Cambridge, MA: Harvard University Press, 1998).

13. David Walker, *Walker's Appeal in Four Articles Together with a Preamble to the Colored Citizens of the World* (Boston, 1830), 22. For the 1830s as a watershed in the history of an "authoritative Black voice," see Bruce Dickson, *The Origins of African American Literature, 1680–1865* (Charlottesville: University of Virginia Press, 2001), 175–210.

14. Leonard Richards, *Gentlemen of Property and Standing: Anti-Abolition Mobs in Jacksonian America* (New York: Oxford University Press, 1970), 12–13, quote and figures; John M. Werner, *Reaping the Bloody Harvest: Race Riots in the United States during the Age of Jackson, 1824–1849* (New York: Garland, 1986), 298, app. 1.

15. David Grimsted, *American Mobbing, 1828–1861: Toward Civil War* (New York: Oxford University Press, 1998), 4, who counts riots in the North and the South.

16. Richards, *Gentlemen of Property and Standing*. For the southern forms of violence, see Grimsted, *American Mobbing*, 85–113.

17. On occasion, early on and with increasing frequency in the lead up to the Civil War, Blacks and white abolitionists would riot in attempts to protect runaway slaves. Before the 1850s, these were only a small fraction of the race-related violence of the antebellum years. For more on the broader culture of riots in the antebellum period and how to evaluate racial violence in this context, see Paul Gilje, *Road to Mobocracy: Popular Disorder in New York City, 1763–1834* (Bloomington: University of Indiana Press, 1996), 121–70, and Grimsted, *American Mobbing*.

18. For antislavery music as popular culture, see Roberts, *Blackface Nation*, 127–56, 187–213. For cultural analysis of the transition into forms of antislavery popular culture, including blackface minstrelsy, see John L. Brooke, *"There Is a North": Fugitive Slaves, Political Crisis, and Cultural Transformation in the Coming of the Civil War* (Boston: University of Massachusetts Press, 2019), esp. 89–201.

19. For example, many organized anti-abolitionist riots largely consisted of "gentlemen of property and standing," frustrating simple class generalizations. For the makeup of race riots, see Richards, *Gentlemen of Property and Standing*, 82–155.

20. At the time, the word *amalgamation* expressed the notion of racial mixing and effectively functioned as a polite form of race baiting.

21. John Wood Sweet, *Bodies Politic: Negotiating Race in the American North, 1730–1830* (Baltimore: Johns Hopkins University Press, 2003), 271–409; Nicholas Guyatt, *Bind Us Apart: How Enlightened Americans Invented Racial Segregation* (New York: Oxford University Press, 2016).

22. Brewer, "The Emergence of Racial Modernity."

23. Reginald Horseman, *Race and Manifest Destiny: The Origins of American Racial Anglo-Saxonism* (Cambridge, MA: Harvard University Press, 1981), esp. 116–38.

24. "Poetry," *Albany Register*, April 6, 1804.

25. "Poetry," *Albany Register*, April 6, 1804.

26. "From Sambo, on the Interesting Subject of Corsets," *Portsmouth (NH) Oracle*, October 20, 1810.

27. "Chinger Ring," *American Song Sheets*, ser. 1, vol. 2, no. 207, Rare Books and Special Collections, Library of Congress. This song is probably from the 1820s, after Lafayette's visit to the United States in 1824. It is clearly inspired by bobolition literature as well as the song "The Guinea Boy" and other buckra song traditions that include the addition of *e* or *ee* at the end of the bars of the stanza. Later versions of the song that appeared after the success of blackface minstrel songs in the 1830s are titled "Sambo Dress to He Bredren." Interestingly, the chorus "chinger ring," or some variety of that combination, would become a mainstay in many other blackface minstrel songs. On the preference for the name Phillis in black dialect songs, see below, in this chapter.

28. "Invitation, Addressed to the Marshals of the 'Africum Shocietee,' at the Commemoration of the 'Abolition of the Slave Trade,'" 1816, Salem, MA, Boston Public Library.

29. For more on Black Americans and the early American public sphere, including discussions of bobolition broadsides, see David Waldstreicher, *In the Midst of Perpetual Fetes: The Making of American Nationalism, 1776–1820* (Chapel Hill:

University of North Carolina Press, 1997), 304–48; Shane White, "'It Was a Proud Day': African Americans, Festivals, and Parades in the North, 1741–1834," *Journal of American History* 81, no. 1 (June 1994): 13–50; White and White, *Stylin'*, 85–124.

30. "Grand Celebration! Of the Abolition of the Slave Trade. General Order," 1817, Boston, ser. 2, Shaw and Shoemaker, suppl. 1, Early American Imprints.

31. For comical Yankee love poetry, see Thomas Green Fessenden, "(The Country Lovers) Jonathan's Courtship, A Merry Tale," ser. 1, Evans 49771, Early American Imprints.

32. "Grand & Splendid Bobolition of Slavery, and Great Anniversary Fussible, by de Africum Shocietee of Bosson," 1822, Boston, Houghton Library, Harvard University, https://nrs.lib.harvard.edu/urn-3:fhcl.hough:101412375. For another love song between Phillis and Pomp, see "Grand Bobalition or Great Anniversary Fussible," 1821, Boston, Library of Congress, https://lccn.loc.gov/2008661721.

33. George A. Levesque, *Black Boston: African American Life and Culture in Urban America, 1750–1860* (New York: Garland, 1994), 4:382.

34. White, "It Was a Proud Day," 33–41.

35. "Dreadful Riot on Negro Hill!" 1816, Boston, Library Company of Philadelphia.

36. "Hard Scrabble, or Miss Philises Bobolition," 1824, Boston, Brown Digital Repository, Brown University, https://repository.library.brown.edu/studio/item/bdr:303827/.

37. For *The Forest Rose* as a precursor in blackface minstrelsy, see Saxton, *The Rise and Fall of the White Republic*, 121–23.

38. A short list of some studies in this vein include Joanne Pope Melish, *Disowning Slavery, Gradual Emancipation and Race in New England, 1780–1860* (Ithaca, NY: Cornell University Press, 1998); Brewer, "The Emergence of Racial Modernity"; White, "It Was a Proud Day"; White, *Stories of Freedom in Black New York*; Roediger, *The Wages of Whiteness*; Saxton, *The Rise and Fall of the White Republic*; and Sweet, *Bodies Politic*.

39. For the fight against anti-Black laws in the North, see Kate Masur, *Until Justice Be Done: America's First Civil Rights Movement, from the Revolution to Reconstruction* (New York: W. W. Norton & Company, 2021), 9.

40. Dickson, *The Origins of African American Literature*, 194.

41. Hosea Easton, *A Treatise on the Intellectual Character and Civil and Political Condition of the Colored People of the U.S. and the Prejudice Exercised towards Them* (Boston, 1837), 41.

42. See for example, Walker, *Walker's Appeal*, 70–71.

43. Erika Piola, "The Rise of Early American Lithography and Antebellum Visual Culture," *Winterthur Portfolio* 48, nos. 2/3 (Summer/Autumn 2014): 125–38.

44. Bobolition broadsides were not the first widely circulating print representations that denigrated blackness. Already in the eighteenth century, advertisements for the sale of slaves featured combinations of text and imagery that cast Black people as crude. Although many were highly stereotyped, they were not intended in mockery per se. See Barbara E. Lacey, "Visual Images of Blacks in Early American Imprints," *William and Mary Quarterly* 53, no. 1 (January 1996): 137–45.

45. I. Harris, "Life in Philadelphia, Grand celebration ob de bobalition ob African slabery," ca. 1833, London, Library Company of Philadelphia.

46. Edward Williams Clay, "Life in Philadelphia, Have you any flesh coloured silk stockings . . . ?, " plate 11, ca. 1830, Philadelphia, Library Company of Philadelphia.

47. Anne Mathews, *The Memoir of Charles Mathews*, 4 vols. (London, 1839), 3:315 and 354

48. This analysis largely relies on Robert Michael Lewis, "Speaking Black, 1824: Charles Mathews' Trip to America Revisited," *Nineteenth Century Theatre and Film* 43, no. 1 (May 2016): 46–48.

49. Lewis, "Speaking Black." For Stephen Price and Mordecai Noah's assault on New York's Black theater, see Marvin McAllister, *White People Do Not Know How to Behave at Entertainments Designed for Ladies and Gentlemen of Colour* (Chapel Hill: University of North Carolina Press, 2003), 131–66. See also, White, *Stories of Freedom*, 202–10, and Michael Warner, "A Soliloquy 'Lately Spoken at the African Theatre': Race and the Public Sphere in New York City, 1821," in *Publics and Counterpublics*, ed. Michael Warner (New York: Zone Books, 2002), 225–68, both of whom cast the print culture of the period as a hostile dialogue.

50. Lewis, "Speaking Black," 49–51.

51. "Opossum up a Gum Tree," *The London Mathews; Containing an Account of This Celebrated Comedian's Trip to America* (Philadelphia, 1824), 27.

52. The first established performance of "Coal Black Rose" in the records is in the summer of 1829 in New York theaters, but there is some evidence that suggests Dixon had earlier been working on his performance, before his breakout 1829 performances in New York. Cockrell, *Demons of Disorder*, 96–97.

53. For the democratic tradition in antebellum theaters, see Bruce McConachie, *Melodramatic Formation: American Theatre and Society, 1820–1870* (Iowa City: University of Iowa Press, 1992), 68–156; Rosemarie K. Bank, *Theatre Culture in America, 1825–1860* (New York: Cambridge University Press, 1997); Walter J. Meserve, *Heralds of Promise: The Drama of the American People during the Age of Jackson, 1829–1849* (New York: Greenwood Press, 1986). For Dixon's biography see Cockrell, *Demons of Disorder*, 94–139.

54. By contrast, Cockrell, *Demons of Disorder*, tries to distinguish between the racism of the *The Forest Rose* and the supposed racial solidarity that underscores "Coal Black Rose." Cockrell argues, unconvincingly, that the former was a product of the theater, and therefore elite culture, while the latter was an extension of street vernacular culture.

55. "Coal Black Rose," *The Universal Comic Songster: Being the Most Complete Collection Ever Published* (New York, 1831), 3–5. Later versions have Sambo challenging Cuffee to a duel rather than Cuffee running away.

56. Lott, *Love and Theft*, 40.

57. Dixon likely did not write "Zip Coon," although he became closely associated with it. Robert Farrell was the earliest known performer of "Zip Coon." See Cockrell, *Demons of Disorder*, 99.

58. "Zip Coon on the Go-Ahead Principle," 1832–37, Boston, American Antiquarian Society.

59. For speculation about Rice's first "Jim Crow" performances, see Cockrell, *Demons of Disorder*, 63–65.

60. For Rice's biography, see Cockrell, *Demons of Disorder*, 62–91, and Lhamon, *Raising Cain*, 151–208.

61. Lhamon, *Raising Cain*, 185.

62. For the Black vernacular song that might have been the origin of "Jim Crow," see Lhamon, *Raising Cain*, 180–88.

63. "Jim Crow," *The Singer's Own Book: Being a Choice Collection of the Newest and Most Popular Songs* (Woodstock, VT, 1833), 54–55.

64. "Jim Crow," *The Singer's Own Book*, 55.

65. For whiteness as a form of cultural capital that emerged in and around blackface minstrel performances, see Roediger, *Wages of Whiteness*. There is certainly some indication that Blacks attended such shows, usually limited to seats in the higher tiers, depending on segregation rules in different venues. The vast majority of audience members were white. See Bank, *Theater Culture in America*, 49–51.

66. For early blackface minstrelsy as the culmination of cross racial exchanges, especially at Catherine Market, see Lott, *Love and Theft*, 40–62; Cockrell, *Demons of Disorder*, esp. 30–61; Lhamon, *Raising Cain*, 1–55, 151–208. On the musical origins, see Toll, *Blacking Up*, 27.

67. For Black folklore and the politics surrounding it, see John Roberts, *From Trickster to Badman: The Black Folk Hero in Slavery and in Freedom* (Philadelphia: University of Pennsylvania Press, 1989), and Shirley Moody-Turner, *Black Folklore and the Politics of Representation* (Jackson: University Press of Mississippi, 2013). The classic study of Black culture is Lawrence Levine, *Black Culture and Black Consciousness: Afro-American Folk Thought From Slavery to Freedom* (New York: Oxford University Press, 1978). See also the editor's introduction to Gilbert Osofsky ed., *Puttin' On Ole Massa: Slave Narratives of Henry Bibb, William Wells Brown, and Solomon Northrup* (New York: Harper and Row, 1969), 9–48. For Black songs and music, see Dana J. Epstein, *Sinful Tunes and Spirituals: Black Folk Music to the Civil War* (Urbana: University of Illinois Press, 1977) and Roberts, *Blackface Nation*, 103–26.

68. Shane White, "The Death of James Johnson," *American Quarterly* 51, no. 4 (December 1999): 777 and 768.

69. Charles Dickens, *American Notes* (New York, 1842), 36, and White, "The Death of James Johnson." See also White, "'It was a Proud Day'"; White and White, *Stylin'*, 85–124; Douglas A. Jones, *The Captive Stage: Performance and the Proslavery Imagination of the Antebellum North* (Ann Arbor: University of Michigan Press, 2014), 50–74; McAllister, *White People*; Melish, *Disowning Slavery*, 163–209. For dancing as competitions over manhood, see chapter seven.

70. For the connection between Ludlow and Rice, see Louis Gerteis, "Blackface Minstrelsy and the Construction of Race in Nineteenth-Century America," in *Union and Emancipation: Essays on Politics and Race in the Civil War Era*, ed. David W. Blight and Brooks D. Simpson (Kent, OH: Kent State University Press, 1997), 79–104. For Rice as largely unfamiliar with Black vernacular culture, see Brian Roberts, *Blackface Nation*, 92–98. For a biographical examination of Rice's background, see Cockrell, *Demons of Disorder*, 62–91, and Lhamon, *Raising Cain*, 151–208. For the significance of Irish, as well as Black traditions, in antebellum dance culture, see April F. Masten, "Challenge Dancing in Antebellum America: Sporting Men, Vulgar Women, and Blacked-Up Boys," *Journal of Social History* 48, no. 3 (Spring 2015): 605–34.

71. For a musical analysis of Jim Crow, see Nathan, *Dan Emmett*, 166–71. For the origins of the dance element, see Nathan, *Dan Emmett*, 50–57, 87–94.

72. Roberts, *Blackface Nation*, 157–58. See, for instance, *The Man* (New York), July 16, 1834. For the riot, see Bank, *Theatre Culture in America*, 155–58; Lott, *Love and Theft*, 127–35; Cockrell, *Demons of Disorder*, 99–101; and Lhamon, *Raising Cain*, 30–31. All acknowledge that it was an anti-abolitionist riot, but Cockrell highlights the class dimensions of obliging the crowd with "Zip Coon," while Lhamon casts anti-abolitionist sentiment as a class conflict between elite abolitionists and the working classes.

73. Roberts, *Blackface Nation*, makes a similar point, casting the early United States as a "racial state."

74. See Baker, *Affairs of Party*, 217.

75. Lawrence Levine, *High Brow/Low Brow: The Emergence of Cultural Hierarchy in America* (Cambridge, MA: Harvard University Press, 1988). Roberts, *Blackface Nation*, paints blackface minstrelsy as a genre elites shied away from as part of their increasing commitments to abolitionism. I view their castigation of blackface minstrelsy as a strategy employed to claim superiority by cultivating high-brow culture. In other words, much of the disposition within elite circles to claim the mantle of abolitionism according to what Pierre Bordieu called "distinction," rather than a genuine commitment to support Black people. See Pierre Bordieu, *Distinction: A Social Critique of the Judgement of Taste*, trans. Richard Nice (Cambridge, MA: Harvard University Press, 1984). To be sure, a small cohort of abolitionists were genuine supporters of abolitionist reform and racial equality, but they were a small minority, at least until the late 1840s, and even then, much of the antislavery impetus in the North in the 1850s was not genuinely supportive of racial equality.

Chapter 7 • American Foil

1. Constance Rourke, *American Humor: A Study of National Character* (New York: Harcourt, Brace and Company, 1931), 58; Herman Melville, *Moby-Dick, or the White Whale* (Boston, 1892), 343; Walter Blair, "A German Connection: Raspe's Baron Munchausen," in *Essays on American Humor: Blair through the Ages*, ed. Hamlin Hill (Madison: University of Wisconsin Press, 1993), 57–71.

2. "Poetry," *New Jersey Journal* (Elizabethtown), April 25, 1815. For more on "The Guinea Boy," see the introduction to part three.

3. "Jim Crow," ser. 1, vol. 5, no. 669, American Song Sheets, Rare Books and Special Collections, Library of Congress. For more on "Zip Coon" and "Jim Crow," see chapter six.

4. James Kirke Paulding, *The Lion of the West and the Bucktails*, ed. Frank Gado (London: Rowman & Littlefield, 1994), 99.

5. Hans Nathan, *Dan Emmet and the Rise of Early Negro Minstrelsy* (Norman: University of Oklahoma Press, 1962), 52.

6. *New York American*, October 19, 1832.

7. For Nat Turner's Rebellion and abolitionism's influence on South Carolina, see Manisha Sinha, *The Counterrevolution of Slavery: Politics and Ideology in Antebellum South Carolina* (Chapel Hill: University of North Carolina Press, 2000), 9–62. For

Virginia, see Alison G. Freehling, *Drift toward Dissolution: The Virginia Slavery Debate of 1831–1832* (Baton Rouge: Louisiana State University Press, 1982).

8. Lawrence Levine, *Low Brow / High Brow: The Emergence of Cultural Hierarchy in America* (Cambridge, MA: Harvard University Press 1988), 11–82.

9. For the growth of print culture in the period, see Robert A. Gross and Mary Kelley, eds., *A History of the Book in America*, vol. 2, *An Extensive Republic: Print Culture and Society in the New Nation, 1790–1840* (Chapel Hill: University of North Carolina Press, 2010). I found no comprehensive study of the expansion of theaters into smaller cities, but for theater during this period in general, see Walter J. Meserve, *Heralds of Promise: The Drama of the American People during the Age of Jackson, 1829–1849* (New York: Greenwood Press, 1986).

10. For distinctions between popular culture, vernacular or folk culture, and elite culture, see the introduction. For a recent cultural history that traces how white men in the early United States negotiated power dynamics among themselves, see Kenneth Cohen, *They Will Have Their Game: Sporting Culture and the Making of the Early American Republic* (Ithaca, NY: Cornell University Press, 2017).

11. For example, Abraham Fisher—who along with Fredrick Turner oversaw Turner & Fisher, one of the largest publishing houses of the day—reported a personal estate valued at $30,000 and two servants in the 1860 census. No doubt, Fisher was a man of some means, but his was a far cry from the kind of wealth associated with P. T. Barnum, who during the 1850s reportedly earned $500,000 from Jenny Lind's tour of the United States. *Philadelphia on Stone Biographical Dictionary of Lithographers*, s.v. "Turner & Fisher," https://digital.librarycompany.org/islandora/object /digitool%3A79871.

12. *Richmond Enquirer*, June 3, 1831, 3.

13. Christopher J. Smith, "Blacks and Irish on the Riverine Frontiers: The Roots of American Popular Music," *Southern Cultures* 17, no. 1 (Spring 2011): 76. For biographies of Dixon, Rice, and others, see Dale Cockrell, *Demons of Disorder: Early Blackface Minstrels and Their World* (New York: Cambridge University Press, 1997), 62–162; W. T. Lhamon, Jr., *Raising Cain, Blackface Performance from Jim Crow to Hip Hop* (Cambridge, MA: Harvard University Press, 1998) 151–208; Robert C. Toll, *Blacking Up: The Minstrel Show in Nineteenth-Century America* (New York: Oxford University Press, 1974), 43–52; Ken Emerson, *Doo-dah! Stephen Foster and the Rise of American Popular Culture* (New York: Simon & Schuster, 1997); Nathan, *Dan Emmett and the Rise of Early Negro Minstrelsy*, 98–158.

14. Shirley Moody-Turner, *Black Folklore and the Politics of Racial Representation* (Jackson: University Press of Mississippi, 2013), 32.

15. The exceptions included Master Juba and at least one Black troupe as early as 1849 according to Fredrick Douglass, "Gavitt's Original Ethiopian Serenaders," *North Star* (Rochester), June 29, 1849, 2.

16. The only sustained examinations of blackface minstrelsy through songsters appears to be S. Foster Damon, "The Negro in Early American Songsters," *Papers of the Bibliographical Society of America* 28 (1934): 132–63, which is limited to songsters published up to 1830, and William J. Mahar, *Behind the Burnt Cork Mask: Early Blackface Minstrelsy and Antebellum Popular Culture* (Urbana: University of Illinois

Press, 1999), limited to songsters published after 1840 that specialized in blackface minstrel songs.

17. After 1840 most publishers relied on undated stereotypes for publishing their cheap print materials.

18. For rewards of merit, see Patricia Fenn and Alfred P. Malpa, *Rewards of Merit: Tokens of a Child's Progress and a Teacher's Esteem as an Enduring Aspect of American Religious and Secular Education* (Hong Kong: Ephemera Society of America, 1994). For valentines' centrality to the new popular culture, see Leigh Eric Schmidt, *Consumer Rites: The Buying and Selling of American Holidays* (Princeton, NJ: Princeton University Press, 1995), 38–104.

19. Norm Cohen, "The Forget-Me-Not Songsters and Their Role in the American Folksong Tradition," *American Music* 23, no. 2 (Summer 2005): 137–219, and Norm Cohen, "American Secular Songsters in the Nineteenth Century," *Cheap Print and Popular Song in the Nineteenth Century: A Cultural History of the Songster*, ed. Paul Watt, Derek B. Scott, and Patrick Spedding (New York: Cambridge University Press, 2017), 11–31. For an example of print material offerings, see the advertisement in the back of *Charlie White's Black Apollo Songster* (New York and Philadelphia: Turner & Fisher, n.d. [probably 1840s]), and "Catalogue of Plays, Song Books, and Juvenile Works, Offered by Turner & Fisher: At Their Dramatic World and Song Repository, Almanack and Toy Book Warehouse, 52 Chatham Street, New York," n.d. (probably early 1840s).

20. I examined ninety-one songster titles and editions published between 1820 and 1850 whose titles appeared pertinent to my research, mostly at the American Antiquarian Society but also at the Library Company of Philadelphia, the Library of Congress, the John Hay Library at Brown University, the Massachusetts Historical Society, and the New York Historical Society.

21. This is in line with Damon, "The Negro in Early American Songsters," which offers a precise account of all Black dialect and African-themed songs in songsters before 1830 in the library collections at Brown University.

22. *The Universal Comic Songster: Being the Most Complete Collection Ever Published* (New York, 1831), 3–5 (American Antiquarian Society). *The Singer's Own Book: Being a Choice Collection of the Newest and Most Popular Songs* (Woodstock, VT, 1833), 54–55 (American Antiquarian Society). For the 1830 publication, see Damon, "The Negro in Early American Songsters," 148.

23. See W. T. Lhamon, Jr., *Jump Jim Crow: Lost Plays, Lyrics, and Street Prose of the First Atlantic Popular Culture* (Cambridge, MA: Harvard University Press, 2003).

24. "The Bee Gum—A Negro Song," *The Universal and Theatrical Songster; Or Museum of Mirth* (Baltimore, 1829), 17 (American Antiquarian Society); Geo. Willig Jr., "The Bee-Gum," 1833 (Baltimore), box 18, item 17, Lester S. Levy Sheet Music Collection, Johns Hopkins University, https://levysheetmusic.mse.jhu.edu/collection/018/017. On Mathews and "Opossum up a Gum Tree," see chapter six.

25. For Dixon's biography, see Cockrell, *Demons of Disorder*, 92–139. For Rice's plays, see Lhamon, *Jump Jim Crow*, 148–383.

26. For the process of composing "Opossum" and "Jim Crow" for white audiences, see chapter six.

27. "Clar de Kitchen," *The Free and Easy Song Book: Comic, Sentimental, Amatory, Patriotic, Naval, Anacreontic, Sporting, Scotch, Irish and Western* (Philadelphia, 1834), 73–75 (American Antiquarian Society).

28. "Clar de Kitchen," *Crockett's Free and Easy Song Book: A New Collection of the Most Popular Stage Songs . . .* (Philadelphia, 1839), 29–30 (American Antiquarian Society). Some variations of this version had probably been around at least since 1833, but it would take time for it to make it into the songsters. See, for example, a version that seems to be somewhere between the original and this more polished version in the *Macon (GA) Weekly Telegraph*, April 10, 1833, 1.

29. For an early advertisement for "Clar de Kitchen" performed by Rice, see "Chestnut Street Theater," *Philadelphia Inquirer*, September 29, 1832, 3. For Black vernacular songs, see Lawrence Levine, *Black Culture and Black Consciousness: Afro-American Folk Thought from Slavery to Freedom* (New York: Oxford University Press, 1978), esp. 5–55, 190–221; Dana J. Epstein, *Sinful Tunes and Spirituals: Black Folk Music to the Civil War* (Urbana: University of Illinois Press, 1977); Brian Roberts, *Blackface Nation: Race, Reform, and Identity in American Popular Music* (Chicago: University of Chicago Press, 2017), 103–26.

30. "Jenny Get the Hoe Cake Done," *The Black Diamond Songster* (New York and Philadelphia: Turner & Fisher, n.d. [probably 1840 or 1841, based on song variety]), n.p. (American Antiquarian Society).

31. "Jenny Get the Hoe Cake Done," *The Black Diamond Songster.*

32. "Jenny Get the Hoe Cake Done," *The Black Diamond Songster.*

33. "Gumbo Chaff," *The United States Songster: A Choice Selection of about One Hundred and Seventy of the Most Popular Songs* (Cincinnati, 1837), 189–91 (American Antiquarian Society).

34. For slave deception and a recurring interest in their master's death in early Black vernacular culture, see Gilbert Osofsky, ed., *Puttin' On Ole Massa: Slave Narratives of Henry Bibb, William Wells Brown, and Solomon Northrup* (New York: Harper and Row, 1969), 9–48.

35. For trickster themes in Black vernacular traditions, see Lawrence Levine, *Black Culture and Black Consciousness: Afro-American Folk Thought from Slavery to Freedom* (New York: Oxford University Press, 1978), 102–33, and John Roberts, *From Trickster to Badman: The Black Folk Hero in Slavery and in Freedom* (Philadelphia: University of Pennsylvania Press, 1989).

36. The classic study that stresses how the politics of slavery made and unmade the two-party system is Michael Holt, *The Political Crisis of the 1850s* (New York: Wiley, 1978). For a look at the Democrats' commitment to slavery, see Joshua A. Lynn, *Preserving the White Man's Republic: Jacksonian Democracy, Race, and the Transformation of American Conservatism* (Charlottesville: University of Virginia Press, 2019).

37. The earliest appearance in songsters for "De Carolina Crew" is in *The United States Songster* (Cincinnati, 1837) and for "Old Wirginny" *Crockett's Free and Easy Song Book* (Philadelphia and Pittsburgh, 1839) (American Antiquarian Society for both).

38. The most detailed account of blackface minstrelsy after 1843 is Mahar, *Behind the Burnt Cork Mask*. See also Eric Lott, *Love and Theft: Blackface Minstrelsy and the*

American Working Class (New York: Oxford University Press, 1993), 136–233, and Roberts, *Blackface Nation*, 175–86, 234–45.

39. "Circus," *New York Herald*, September 13, 1843, 2; "Amusements," *New York Herald*, June 20, 1845, 4; "Theatrical and Musical," *New York Herald*, January 25, 1848, 3.

40. "Dark Prospects of the Darkies!," *Lantern* (New York), November 27, 1852, 215.

41. For the changing cultural landscape of the 1850s, including the role of *Uncle Tom's Cabin* and minstrelsy, see John L. Brooke, *"There Is a North": Fugitive Slaves, Political Crisis, and Cultural Transformation in the Coming of the Civil War* (Boston: University of Massachusetts Press, 2019), 89–201.

42. Isabelle Lehuu, *Carnival on the Page: Popular Print Media in Antebellum America* (Chapel Hill: University of North Carolina Press, 2000), 3–4.

43. Schmidt, *Consumer Rites*, 57–94. I would like to thank Erika Piola from the Library Company of Philadelphia for her assistance with information on valentines and rewards of merit sheets.

44. For comic almanacs as part of popular print culture, see Michael Joseph, "Old Comic Elton and the Age of Fun," *Children's Literature Association Quarterly* 28, no. 3 (Fall 2003): 158–70, and Michael Winship, "Pirates, Shipwrecks, and Comic Almanacs: Charles Ellms Packages Books in Nineteenth-Century America," *Printing History* 9 (January 2011): 3–16.

45. "Catalogue of Plays, Song Books, and Juvenile Works, Offered by Turner & Fisher: at Their Dramatic World and Song Repository, Almanack and Toy Book Warehouse, 52 Chatham Street, New York," n.d. (probably early 1840s) (American Antiquarian Society). This catalogue is likely from 1840 or 1841. The description of the Crockett almanacs matches the subtitles of the publications around 1840, and the songsters offered match songster titles by Turner & Fisher from the same period. Michael Lofaro, "The Hidden 'Hero' of the Nashville Crockett Almanacs," *Davy Crockett: The Man, the Legend, the Legacy*, ed. Michael Lofaro (Knoxville: University of Tennessee Press, 1985), 46–79. For numbers of comic almanacs in circulation, see Winship, "Pirates, Shipwrecks, and Comic Almanacs."

46. Lofaro, "The Hidden Hero of the Nashville Crockett Almanacs"; Paul Andrew Hutton, "'Going to Congress and Making Allmynacks Is My Trade': Davy Crockett, His Almanacs, and the Evolution of a Frontier Legend," *Journal of the West* 37, no. 2 (April 1998): 10–22.

47. *Davy Crockett's Almanack of Wild Sports in the West, Life in the Backwoods & Sketches of Texas, for 1837* (Nashville, TN [as part of the conceit, but probably printed in Boston by Charles Ellms], 1836), 3; *Davy Crockett's Almanack of Wild Sports in the West . . . for 1838* (Nashville, TN [as part of the conceit, but probably printed in Boston by Charles Ellms], 1837), 3. For a discussion of the origins of the so-called Nashville series, see John Seelye, "A Well-Wrought Crockett: Or How the Fakelorists Passed through the Credibility Gap and Discovered Kentucky," in Lofaro, *Davy Crockett: The Man, the Legend, the Legacy*, 21–45.

48. *The Crockett Almanac Containing Adventures, Exploits, Sprees & Scrapes in the West . . . for 1839* (Nashville, TN [as part of the conceit, but probably printed in Boston by Charles Ellms], 1838), 2; *The Crockett Almanac . . . for 1841* (Nashville, TN [as part of the conceit, but probably printed in Boston by Charles Ellms], 1840), 2.

49. *Crockett's Almanac for 1846: Scenes in River Life, Feats on the Lakes, Manners in the Back Woods, Adventures in Texas, &c, &c.* (Philadelphia: Turner & Fisher, 1845), 5, 9, 13; *Davy Crockett's Almanac for 1847: Daring Adventures in the Back Wood . . .* (Boston: James Fisher, 1846), 13, 16.

50. *Davy Crockett's Almanack of Wild Sports in the West and Life in the Backwoods, for 1836* (Nashville, TN [as part of the conceit, but probably printed in Boston by Charles Ellms], 1835), 3; *The Crockett Almanac for 1839*, 3; *The Crockett Almanac, Containing Adventures, Exploits, Sprees, & Scrapes in the West . . . for 1840* (Nashville, TN [as part of the conceit, but probably printed in Boston by Charles Ellms], 1839), 12–13.

51. "The Bull Nigger's Trap," *Ben Hardin's Crockett Almanac for 1842: Rows-Sprees and Scrapes in the West: Life and Manners in the Backwoods: and Terrible Adventures in the Ocean* (Boston: James Fisher, 1841), n.p., but with adjacent engraving. "The Indian and Crockett's Grandmother," *Davy Crockett's Almanac for 1844: Life and Manners in the Back Woods; Terrible Battles and Adventures of Border Life; with Rows, Sprees, and Scrapes in the West* (Philadelphia: Turner & Fisher, 1843), n.p.

52. *De Darkie's Comic All-Me-Nig* (Boston: James Fisher, 1845), Library Company of Philadelphia. *Crockett's Almanac for 1846: Scenes in River Life, Feats on the Lakes, Manners in the Back Woods, Adventures in Texas.*

53. *Davy Crockett's Almanac for 1845: I Leave This Rule for Others, When I'm Dead, "Be Always Sure Your Right, The Go A-Head"* (Boston: James Fisher, 1844); *Fisher's Crockett Almanac for 1843: With Rows, Sprees, and Scrapes in the West: Life and Manners in the Backwoods: Terrible Battles and Adventures on Sea and Land* (New York and Philadelphia, Turner & Fisher, 1842).

54. For a general overview of manhood in early America, see Eran Zelnik, "Masculinities in Early America," in *The Routledge Companion to Masculinity in American Literature and Culture*, ed. Lydia R. Cooper (New York: Routledge, 2022), 27–40. For some of the contradictions inherent to white manhood in the antebellum period, see Amy S. Greenberg, *Manifest Manhood and the Antebellum American Empire* (New York: Cambridge University Press 2005); Karl M. Kippola, *Acts of Manhood: The Performance of Masculinity on the American State, 1828–1865* (New York: Palgrave Macmillan, 2012); and most of the essays in Craig Thompson Friend and Lorri Glover, eds., *Southern Manhood: Perspectives on Masculinity in the Old South* (Athens: University of Georgia Press, 2004). For honor, see Wyatt Bertram Brown, *Southern Honor: Ethics and Behavior in the Old South* (New York: Oxford University Press, 1982); Joanne B. Freeman, *Affairs of Honor: National Politics in the New Republic* (New Haven, CT: Yale University Press, 2001); and Joanne B. Freeman, *The Field of Blood: Violence in Congress and the Road to Civil War* (New York: Macmillan Publishers, 2018).

55. For the relationship between white and Black manhood as a zero-sum calculus, see Edward E. Baptist, "The Absent Subject: African American Masculinity and Forced Migration to the Antebellum Plantation Frontier," in Thompson Friend and Glover, *Southern Manhood*, 136–73; Kathleen Brown, "'Strength of a Lion . . . Arms Like Polished Iron': Embodying Black Masculinity in an Age of Slavery and Propertied Manhood," in *New Men: Manliness in Early America*, ed. Thomas Foster (New York: New York University Press, 2011), 172–92.

56. Greenberg, *Manifest Manhood and the Antebellum American Empire*. This conceptualization is influenced by Pierre Bourdieu's concepts of field and capital: manhood is the *field* of struggle, and honor is a form of *capital* within that field.

57. The culture of restraint, contended the sociologists Pierre Bourdieu and Norbert Elias, was the end point of a long historical process of cultivating manners as an avenue to assert one's "distinction" and "civilization" over the lower classes of Western society, a process that went back to the medieval period. Norbert Elias, *The Civilizing Process*, vol 1, *The History of Manners*, trans. Edmund Jephcott (New York: Pantheon Books, 1982); Pierre Bourdieu, *Distinction: A Social Critique of the Judgement of Taste*, trans. Richard Nice (Cambridge, MA: Harvard University Press, 1979). For more scholarship that examines the reformation of manners and refinement in a similar vein, see Jorge Arditi, *A Genealogy of Manners: Transformations of Social Relations in France and England from the Fourteenth to the Eighteenth Century* (Chicago: University of Chicago Press, 1998); Philip Carter, *Men and the Emergence of Polite Society, Britain, 1660–1800* (London: Pearson Education, 2001); C. Dallett Hemphill, *Bowing to Necessities: A History of Manners in America, 1620–1860* (New York: Oxford University Press, 1999); Richard Bushman, *The Refinement of America: Persons, Houses, Cities* (New York: Vintage Books, 1993); Philip Mason, *The English Gentleman: The Rise and Fall of an Ideal* (London: William Morrow, 1982). For stadial views in the early United States surrounding the politics of gender and women, see Rosemarie Zagarri, *Revolutionary Backlash: Women and Politics in the Early American Republic* (Philadelphia: University of Pennsylvania Press, 2007), 115–47. For encounters between northern and southern men and considerations of honor, see Freeman, *The Field of Blood*.

58. "Literary Notices," *Portsmouth (NH) Journal of Literature and Politics*, June 9, 1838.

59. *Davy Crockett's Almanac for 1838; The Crockett Almanac for 1839; Crockett Almanac for 1846; Davy Crockett's Almanac for 1847: Daring Adventures in the Back Woods; Wonderful Scenes in River Life; Manners of Warfare in the West; Feats on the Prairies, in Texas and in Oregon* (Boston: James Fisher, 1846).

60. Carroll Smith-Rosenberg, "Davey Crockett as Trickster: Pornography, Liminality and Symbolic Inversion in Victorian America," *Journal of Contemporary History* 17, no. 2 (April 1982): 325–50; Daniel Herman, "The Other Daniel Boone: The Nascence of a Middle-Class Hunter Hero," *Journal of the Early Republic* 18, no. 3 (Fall 1998): 429–57.

61. David Brion Davis, *The Problem of Slavery in the Age of Emancipation* (New York: Vintage Books, 2014), 3–44; Brown, "Strength of a Lion," 173.

62. Brown, "Strength of a Lion"; Baptist, "The Absent Subject."

63. George M. Fredrickson, *The Black Image in the White Mind: The Debate on Afro-American Character and Destiny, 1817–1914* (New York: Harper & Row, 1971), 52. For Nat Turner's Rebellion and its influence on southerners, see Sinha, *The Counterrevolution of Slavery*, 9–62, and Freehling, *Drift toward Dissolution*.

64. On this anti-abolitionist riot and its influence on Douglass, see David Blight, *Fredrick Douglass: Prophet of Freedom* (New York: Simon & Schuster, 2018), 133–37.

65. For a biography that highlights how Douglass actively constructed his image and how his performance of manhood awed white audiences, see Blight, *Fredrick*

Douglass, 102–37. For a recent discussion of Douglass and gender, see A. Kristen Foster, "'We Are Men!': Fredrick Douglass and the Fault Lines of Gendered Citizenship," *Journal of the Civil War Era* 1, no. 2 (June 2011): 143–75.

66. For a discussion of the riots, see chapter six.

67. James Fenimore Cooper, *Notions of the Americans: Picked Up by a Traveling Bachelor*, 2 vols. (London, 1828), 2:264. For northern antebellum intellectual trends with regard to slavery, see Asaf Almog, "Revolutions and Insurrections: The North American Review and Haiti, 1821–1829," *New England Quarterly* 93, no. 2 (June 2020): 188–212.

68. Joanne Pope Melish, *Disowning Slavery: Gradual Emancipation and "Race" in New England, 1780–1860* (Ithaca, NY: Cornell University Press, 1998), 121. For the struggle against anti-Black sentiment and laws in the northern states, see Kate Masur, *Until Justice Be Done: America's First Civil Rights Movement from the Revolution to Reconstruction* (New York: Norton, 2021).

69. The classic account of how this tacit understanding came about is Edmund Morgan, *American Slavery, American Freedom: The Ordeal of Colonial Virginia* (New York: Norton, 1975). See also, Sally E. Hadden, *Slave Patrols: Law and Violence in Virginia and the Carolinas* (Cambridge, MA: Harvard University Press, 2001).

70. Melish, *Disowning Slavery*, 120–21. See also Fredrickson, *The Black Image in the White Mind*, 4–5. For a discussion of lynching as the most radical and violent expression of white constructions of freedom, see Jefferson Cowie, *Freedom's Dominion: A Saga of White Resistance to Federal Power* (New York: Basic Books, 2022), 232–49.

71. George Wilson Pierson, *Tocqueville and Beaumont in America* (New York: Oxford University Press, 1938), 237. For ideas and anxieties about the West, the classic study is Henry Nash Smith, *Virgin Land: The American West as Symbol and Myth* (Cambridge, MA: Harvard University Press, 1950).

72. April F. Matsen, "Challenge Dancing in Antebellum America: Sporting Men, Vulgar Women, and Blacked-Up Boys," *Journal of Social History* 48, no. 3 (Spring 2015): 605–34. For the urban origins of Black "break down" dancing in New York City, see Shane White, "The Death of James Johnson," *American Quarterly* 51, no. 4 (December 1999): 753–95.

73. Masten, "Challenge Dancing," 612. For cross-racial boxing matches as expressions of the tensions between manhood and civilization, see Gail Bederman, *Manliness and Civilization: A Cultural History of Gender and Race in the United States* (Chicago: University of Chicago Press, 1995), 1–44.

74. *The Black Diamond Songster.*

75. Mark Knowles, *Tap Roots: The Early History of Tap Dancing* (Jefferson, NC: McFarland and Co., 2002), esp. 86–96.

76. For the Virginia Minstrels, see Nathan, *Dan Emmett and the Rise of Early Negro Minstrelsy*, 113–42.

77. As with many other components of this book, this is influenced by John William Ward, *Andrew Jackson, Symbol for an Age* (New York: Oxford University Press, 1955). See also David Waldstreicher, "The Nationalization and Racialization of American Politics: Before, beneath, and between Parties, 1790–1840," in *Contesting Democracy: Substance and Structure in American Political History, 1775–2000*, ed. Byron E. Shafer and Anthony J. Badger (Lawrence: University Press of Kansas, 2001), 37–63.

78. Robert G. Gunderson, *The Log-Cabin Campaign* (Lexington: University of Kentucky Press, 1957), 74.

79. For the number of songsters and songs in the campaign, see Billy Coleman, *Harnessing Harmony: Music, Power, and Politics in the United States* (Chapel Hill: University of North Carolina Press, 2020), 91–92; *The Harrison Almanac, 1841* (New York, 1840); *Montgomery's Tippecanoe Almanac for the Year 1841* (Philadelphia, 1840); *Hard Cider and Log Cabin Almanac for 1841* (New York: Turner & Fisher, 1840); *The National Whig Almanac* (Cincinnati, 1840); *Crockett's Harrison Almanac, 1841* (New York: Elton, 1840).

80. Gunderson, *The Log-Cabin Campaign*, 117–218.

81. "Old Tippecanoe," *The Harrison Medal Minstrel: Comprising a Collection of the Most Popular and Patriotic Songs* (Philadelphia, 1840), 102–4.

82. Gunderson, *The Log-Cabin Campaign*, 8, 151.

83. *The Harrison Medal Minstrel*, 50–51. For the association between the Democratic Party and blackface minstrelsy, see Jean H. Baker, *Affairs of Party: The Political Culture of Northern Democrats in the Mid Nineteenth Century* (Ithaca, NY: Cornell University Press 1983), 212–58.

84. For a more recent look at the political and electoral, as opposed to the cultural, side of the campaign, see Richard J. Ellis, *Old Tip vs. The Sly Fox: The 1840 Election and the Making of a Partisan Nation* (Lawrence: University Press of Kansas, 2020).

85. *Crockett's Harrison Almanac, 1841*, n.p.

Epilogue

1. Alexander H. Stephens, "Cornerstone Speech, March 21, 1861," *The Civil War and Reconstruction: A Documentary Reader*, ed. Stanley Harrold (Malden, MA: Blackwell, 2008), 61.

2. Elaine Frantz Parsons, *Ku-Klux: The Birth of the Klan during Reconstruction* (Chapel Hill: University of North Carolina Press, 2016), 27–72. This combination of semi-clandestine and carnivalesque practices was part of a culture of "countersubversion" that was widespread during Reconstruction and in American history more broadly according to Mitchell Snay, *Fenians, Freedmen, and Southern Whites: Race and Nationality in the Era of Reconstruction* (Baton Rouge: Louisiana State University Press, 2007), 50–80.

3. Parsons, *Ku-Klux*, 31–38. For white violence and Redemption as animated by militant white manhood and the memory of the revolution, see Carole Emberton, *Beyond Redemption: Race, Violence, and the American South after the Civil War* (Chicago: University of Chicago Press, 2013), 136–205.

4. Parsons, *Ku-Klux* 78–97.

5. Snay, *Fenians, Freedmen, and Southern Whites*, 41–43, 50–80.

6. Allen Trelease, *White Terror: The Ku Klux Klan Conspiracy and Southern Reconstruction* (Baton Rouge: Louisiana State University Press, 1971), 56–58.

7. Trelease, *White Terror*; Parsons, *Ku-Klux*, 74–75.

8. For the significance of Black voting and the elections of 1868, see Emberton, *Beyond Redemption*, 136–67; Parsons, *Ku-Klux*, 75.

9. Parsons, *Ku-Klux*, 144–79.

10. For the relationship between elites and western mythology, including the Rough Riders, see Christine Bold, *The Frontier Club: Popular Westerns and Cultural Power, 1880–1924* (New York: Oxford University Press, 2013). For a recent account of the 1920s Klan, see Linda Gordon, *The Second Coming of the KKK: The Ku Klux Klan of the 1920s and the American Political Tradition* (New York: Liveright, 2017). For the 1990s militia movement, see Robert H. Churchill, *To Shake their Guns in the Tyrant's Face: Libertarian Political Violence and the Origins of the Militia Movement* (Ann Arbor: University of Michigan Press, 2009), 185–227, and Kathleen Belew, *Bring the War Home: The White Power Movement and the Paramilitary America* (Cambridge, MA: Harvard University Press, 2018).

11. Estimates taken from Belew, *Bring the War Home*, 5.

12. See, for example, the discussion of hunting and social status in Stuart A. Marks, *Southern Hunting in Black and White: Nature, History, and Ritual in a Carolina Community* (Princeton, NJ: Princeton University Press, 1991).

13. Jefferson Cowie, *Freedom's Dominion: A Saga of White Resistance to Federal Power* (New York: Basic Books, 2022), 7 and 238.

14. Richard Slotkin, *Gunfighter Nation: The Myth of the Frontier in Twentieth Century America* (Norman: University of Oklahoma Press, 1992).

15. Churchill, *To Shake Their Guns in the Tyrant's Face*, 153–73; Peter H. Amann, "Vigilante Fascism: The Black Legion as an American Hybrid," *Comparative Studies in Society and History* 25, no. 3 (July 1983): 490–524.

16. Churchill, *To Shake Their Guns in the Tyrant's Face*, 185–227; Belew, *Bring the War Home*, 103–34, 187–239. While Churchill accounts for the 1990s militia movement by highlighting the changing social and demographic circumstances of the period, Belew emphasizes the legacy of the Vietnam War.

17. Patrick Wolfe, "Settler Colonialism and the Elimination of the Native, *Journal of Genocide Research* 8, no. 4 (December 2006): 387–409.

18. Simon Robinson, "On the Beach with David Chapelle," *Time*, May 15, 2005, https://content.time.com/time/arts/article/0,8599,1061415,00.html.

Page numbers in *italic* refer to figures.